A Directory of British
Film & Video Artists

CW01475837

Edited by David Curtis

ACKNOWLEDGEMENTS

Thanks are due to the following for permission to reprint previously published material:

ICA Publications and Jeremy Welsh *Kaleidoscope* (Mineo Aayamaguchi) 1988.

Matts Gallery and Jean Fisher *Susan Hiller: The Revenants of Time* 1990.

BFI Publications and Leslie Felperin *Women in Animation; A Compendium* 1992 (Vera Neubauer)

ICA Publications and Stuart Morgan *The Rigmarole of Photography* 1993 (Steven Pippin).

Photographs have been supplied by the artists, the London Film-makers Co-op and the BFI Production Board

Every attempt has been made to contact organisations and individuals for the purposes of copyright. Any inadvertent omissions will be corrected in future editions.

British Library Cataloguing in Publication Data

A catalogue record for this book is available from the British Library

ISBN: 1 86020 003 6

Published by
John Libbey Media,
Faculty of Humanities,
University of Luton,
75 Castle Street,
Luton, Bedfordshire LU1 3AJ
England

Designed by Andrew Barron and
Collis Clements Associates

Printed in Hong Kong by
Dah Hua Printing Press Co Ltd

Contents

4

Screening the
Moving Image

Artists have been involved in Cinema's history since its beginning, contributing their own innovative films, videos and computer-based works and supplying visual ideas to the feature film mainstream and the advertising industry. But as makers of individually crafted and small-scale works, their economic and institutional position has remained marginal in an industry that has always been aggressively biased towards the monopolistic and the large-scale. Only those artists who have been willing to wrestle with the feature film format – in Britain notably Sally Potter, Peter Greenaway and Derek Jarman – stand any chance of making a living from their work. Even senior figures – such as Margaret Tait and Jeff Keen – prolific and active since the 1950s and early 1960s, remain unknown to the public at large.

Buried within Cinema's broad history is the chronicle of an on-going search by artists for an appropriate way to bring their work to an audience. In the 1930s and 1940s, artists dreamed of alternative exhibition networks based on film clubs; in the 1970s and 1980s tape distribution seemed to extend the promise of real markets; in the 1980s, arts funders struck deals with television, (which delivered film and video art to millions of viewers – but at the margins of the TV schedule); and now, in the 1990s, hopes are focusing on CDRoms and the apparently egalitarian Internet. Even within the art gallery – which film and video artists first colonised in the 1960s, and which they are again invading in the 1990s – the infinitely-reproducible moving image confronts an alien value system based on the uniqueness (and collectability) of the art-object. Perhaps the fragmentation of the film and television industry which we are now witnessing, and particularly the multiplication of the number of ways in which moving images can be delivered to viewers, will open up new possibilities for artist-made works. In the meantime, this Directory will serve as a guide to those who wish to explore further this rich field of work.

Working at the margins has its compensations. It encourages inventiveness, and gives artists the freedom to explore the unconventional forms. Included in this Directory are very long films (Larcher's *Monkey's Birthday* runs at six hours) and very short works (the ACE/BBC2 One Minute Television series); there are imageless films (Jarman's *Blue)*, and silent abstract ones; multi-screen and site-specific works; interactive and even game-based works. And an array of astonishing images.

The 120 film and video artists described on these pages were selected on the basis that their work is in active circulation at this time, and is the subject of critical interest and debate. Included in this active list are Derek Jarman, Stuart Marshall and Anne Rees-Mogg, whose deaths have robbed the British scene of three of its most influential teachers and guides. For some senior artists this publication represents – surprisingly – a first summary of their work, for others a reappraisal, while for a new generation it offers a considered response to replace the ephemera of programme notes and listings sheets.

In addition to the short essay on each artist's work – almost all of which have been newly commissioned – the entries contain descriptions of a number of 'key works' as an aid to curators and programmers, and biographical information submitted by artists or their agents, distributors or production companies. A major exercise has been the compilation of a List of Works for each artist which we believe to be the most comprehensive published to date.

Our defintion of 'active' means that many key figures from the recent past who are no longer producing or exhibiting have been excluded from this volume. Similarly, in a rapidly changing field, our choice of rising stars is inevitably partial. Those who are interested in further information about British work past and present, and who are looking for a more representative historical overview, are referred to *Diverse Practices – A Critical Reader on British Video* (ed, Julia Knight) and *The British Avant-garde Film 1926–1990, an Anthology of Writings* (ed. Michael O'Pray) which are being published by John Libbey and the Arts Council simultaneously with this directory. The bibliography on pages 234–239 is a source of further information about individual artists and works.

The first crucial stage in the long process of the compiling and editing of this work was undertaken by Tony Warcus. Gary Thomas has been general facilitator and custodian of the enterprise; the compilation and checking of the List of Works was very largely the work of Jem Legh; the bibliography was compiled by Chris Darke. Our ever-patient designer was Andrew Barron. To all of them, and to all the artists and writers involved, and to our partners John Libbey & Co, our sincere thanks.

David Curtis – Senior Film & Video Officer, Arts Council of England

The
Directory

Mineo
Aayamaguchi

Mineo Aayamaguchi has lived and worked in Europe for over two decades, producing a body of work across performance, installation and video that has shown a remarkably consistent development. Founded upon an unmistakably oriental aesthetic, his work has absorbed western influences to develop a unique blend of cultures. In western art historical terms, Aayamaguchi is video art's equivalent of an Impressionist; the central concerns of his work are light, colour, and form – here combined with the added dimension of motion – as they are encountered in the landscape, both natural and man-made. Light is perhaps the single most important factor in Aayamaguchi's work as a whole. In video installations it fulfils the dual function of producing the image, usually on a bank of television screens, and of modulating our perception of space in the play of electro-pastel colours upon surfaces of walls, ceiling and floor, which have often been augmented by reflective surfaces such as a mirror, polished glass, or metals. Earlier installations used projected slides, whose images were often interrupted by physical objects – doors, window frames – and diverted by mirrors, to produce traces of light that took on a mathematical quality in their delineation of sculptural space. Reminiscent of Nan Hoover's light pieces, these installations have a quiet and meditative quality that contrasts sharply with the works of many of Aayamaguchi's contemporaries: video installations that revel in the babel of media overkill and technological virtuosity.

Aaymaguchi's approach to making video tapes is simple and direct. Using a small lightweight camera, always hand held, he roves through the landscape finding details here and there which form themselves into images before his gaze. Often using close-ups, turning the camera upside down, focusing upon 'unfamiliar' aspects of the familiar, he dissects the environment into a series of abstract, formal arrangements which are then rearranged in the editing process to isolate particular visual qualities, and to explore the inherent rhythms within the motion of the images.

It is in his use of multiple monitors that the special quality of Aayamaguchi's work becomes most apparent. There is nothing unusual about a video installation using a wall of monitors, but whereas most artists use the device for emphasis, for dramatic effect, to multiply the output of information or imagery or to create a sculptural field within which the image is only one aspect, Aayamaguchi treats a wall of monitors like a canvas, a clean sheet to work on. *Kaleidoscope* (1988) is conceived of as a whole within which the constituent parts are precisely arranged, carefully orchestrated so that the composite image becomes more than just an assemblage of segments. The whole grid is planned and animated as a series of constantly changing geometric forms within which the complementary nature of individual screens produces fascinating and unexpected configurations.

Jeremy Welsh *Kaleidoscope* catalogue

Beyond Colour
1986, installation, 30min cycle, colour, 9 monitors, 2 players

The installation uses nine monitors arranged as a single square bank and a mirrored floor. Images range from billboards and neon signs to bridges and wildlife to parts of the clothed human body. Sometimes the whole image is used, but more often the camera records in close-up, emphasising the unfamiliar parts of the familiar and concentrating on colour, texture and contrasts.

Kaleidoscope
1988, installation, 10min cycle, colour, 25 monitors, 3 players

Twenty-five monitors are arranged in five rows with metal sheets placed beneath them, reflecting the video images and creating a continuous field of broken-up colour, shape, movement and texture. In front of the monitors – in the centre of the floor – is a circular shape made up of flat pieces of brass; a triangular formation of brass sheets hangs on the opposite wall. Images of light reflected on water, landscape and flowers create a series of constantly changing forms and patterns.

Obelisk

1992, installation, 8min cycle, colour,
4 monitors, 1 player

Obelisk is a video installation that is also a
sculptural experience. The work consists of
four monitors set into a nine foot high
shiny brass column. The images – close ups
of flowers, plants and landscapes – are
distorted by the digital video effects, so
nature becomes abstract form. The structure
of the column bisects the images and
contributes its own reflective surfaces.

Primary Contrasting Elements

1993, video, 1min, colour

Primary Contrasting Elements centres around
the relationship between the symbolic
qualities of the square, the circle and the
triangle and their colours. The relationships
between colours are explored to their fullest
extent in the endless combinations possible
within 60 seconds.

Born 1953, Takasaki, Japan. Studied at
St Martins School of Art, London, 1974-78.
Guest Artist at ESBAP, Porto, Portugal in
1979 and Artist in Residence at the
Stadtische Galerie Wolfsburg, Germany,
1981. His work has been exhibited at the
Tate Gallery and Institute of Contemporary
Arts, London; the Franklin Furnace, New
York; Sagacho Exhibit Space, Tokyo and the
National Museum, Singapore.

TOP:
**TWO STILLS FROM
BEYOND COLOUR**
BOTTOM:
**TWO STILLS FROM
KALEIDOSCOPE**

John
Adams

"All that I have managed to find out about John Adams is that he is English, although the tape was made in Massachusetts. This leaves me free to invent a John Adams, especially since the tape itself is obsessed with the undecide-ability of authorship."

The quotation comes from an essay by Christine Tamblyn in the journal Framework, where she attempts to invent a John Adams in order to construct a reading of his video tape *Intellectual Properties* (1985). *Intellectual Properties* was first made as a multi channel installation which was subsequently edited down to a one hour video tape. And, as Tamblyn asserts, John Adams is an Englishman. These are the facts, the rest is invention. And Adams is a master of invention, which Tamblyn would have realised had she delved deeper into his video works from *Stories* (1981) through *Sensible Shoes* (1983) to the aforementioned *Intellectual Properties*. Not least, John Adams has invented and reinvented John Adams throughout his career, and this process of mediated construction as invention is most poignantly expressed in *Goldfish Memoirs* (1993). Documentary and fiction, memory and anecdote merge together in a work that is visually spare, formally austere and beguilingly simple on first encounter. Beneath the surface, however, we discover another intricate construction whose lattice work of references extends back through Adams' work of twelve years and outward through the media saturated culture of the late twentieth century. The game of literary (self) invention that underlies Adams' work has reference points in the films of Peter Greenaway, among others, especially the early Greenaway films like *Dear Phone* or *A Walk Through H*. And it is a strategy that has recently become the basis of an exploding cultural milieu, the global computer network which functions as the arena for an almost unlimited experiment in self invention and the manipulation of identity. The parallels between Adams' cryptic, anecdotal stories and the sociological studies of researchers such as Allucquerer Roseanne Stone, writing on identity in cyberspace, are edifying. In the light of the recent explosion of

Intellectual Properties

1985, video, 60min, b&w and colour

The real joy...is its script. Beautifully paced and developed, the plot gradually comes together out of a series of witty set-pieces and sly sardonic jokes. A transatlantic culture of charge-cards, celebrity holograms and the chatter and clutter of an intellectual commerce that has stopped making sense, is reflected back with incisiveness and irony. Steven Bode

Goldfish Memoirs & The Think Tank

1993, installation, colour, 2 monitors, 2 players, plexiglass tank, 1000 litres oil, air pump

These days, apart from the occasional true life drama, my view of the world is filtered through a TV screen. In my experience, one would have to be pretty foolish to believe that the camera never lies. JA

Born 1953. BA Fine Art Newcastle Polytechnic 1979. Works as a freelance writer/director/editor; winner of four Royal Television Society Awards. Visiting lecturer at Sheffield Polytechnic, Massachusetts College of Art, Museum School of Fine Art Boston, Chicago Art Institute; Associate Senior Lecturer, Fine Art, University of Northumbria 1981-84; Associate Senior Lecturer, Media Production, University of Northumbria 1985- ; Lecturer, Computer Graphics, Sunderland Polytechnic 1988-89; Fellow, Salzburg Seminar 1994. Currently working on interactive multimedia projects. *Sensible Shoes* Best Video, San Sebastian Film and Video Festival 1983; *Intellectual Properties* First Prize, Bonn Videonale 1986.

'virtual communities', the MUDs and MOOs of the Internet, Adams' earlier works could almost be re-appraised as science fiction.

It is not surprising to learn that Adams is now researching the possibilities of digital multi media to create non linear narratives: in a real sense his work has been waiting for the technological tools to catch up with his ideas. Although the notion of the hypertext has existed in computer circles since the 1960s, it is only now entering the broader cultural milieu, and it has only recently become feasible for artists to work with multimedia technologies. The questioning of authorship, the elaboration of web-like structures, the invitation to read actively rather than to consume passively, are fundaments of the hypertext and have been hallmarks of Adams' work since *Sensible Shoes*. After an absence of several years, Adams makes a welcome return with *Goldfish Memoirs*, a work which once again demonstrates his facility with both language and media, and which testifies to the will of John Adams, artist, to survive in order to reinvent himself all over again.

Jeremy Welsh

John
Akomfrah

John Akomfrah's work has developed in a context which, while historically determined, actively seeks an engagement with history which problematises determinations. The emergence of a Black art practice in the eighties in a climate where its invisibility was endemic, demanded intervention of a specific kind. The intervention made by the Black Audio Film Collective – beginning with *Handsworth Songs* (1986) – was to constitute history through a distance that is political, cultural and aesthetic. "Instead of 'nowness'", writes Kobena Mercer, "the film reaches for historical depth, creating a space for critical reverie which counteracts the active ideological forgetting of England's colonial past in media discourses on Handsworth to articulate an alternative 'archaeological' account."

From *Handsworth Songs* to *Seven Songs for Malcolm X* (1993), sound is central to all Akomfrah's work, though the recurring word 'song' is a deceptively simple sign. Rather than being songs, his soundtrack-montages of music, voice and text emit stranger, more complex messages, complicated further by the image track. Even in *Who Needs A Heart* (1991), which tells the story of the activist Michael X through citations of documentary footage and elaborate period reconstructions, the musical soundtrack is not made up of ska or reggae, the 'authentic' sound of the 1960s British West Indian experience, rather, it is a montage of work by American jazz artists including Albert Ayler and Ornette Coleman, thus foregrounding the intellectual demands of reconstructions of the past. The defamiliarisation and reframing of familiar images and sounds, through the soundtrack and through visual juxtapositions, characterises all of Akomfrah's work. *Handsworth Songs* takes the overused name of a landmark 'riot' and produces an alternative to the familiar frame in which riots are situated and 'explained'.

Seven Songs for Malcolm X
1993, 52min, colour, 16mm

Shot in New York at the time of the release of Spike Lee's *Malcolm X,* this is a documentary on the life and times of the man now universally labelled as the father of the Black revolution, El Hajj Malik Shabazz, aka Malcolm X. Interviews and stylised reconstructions combine to provide a complex portrait of this innovative Black leader.

Key works

Handsworth Songs
1986, 58min, colour, 16mm

An exploration of the contours of 'race' and 'civil disorder' in 1980s Britain which presents a diversity of responses to the 'riots' of 1985.

Testament
1988, 80min, colour, 16mm

African exile and dispossession are examined in a film which follows the return of Abena, a British-based journalist, to her home country Ghana which she had fled many years earlier following the collapse of the Nkrumah regime and her arrest by the military.

Born 1957. Studied at Portsmouth Polytechnic. Director of the Black Audio Film Collective since its inception in 1983. Screenings include: Sydney International Film Festival, Festival Del Popoli, Chicago International Film Festival, Ghent International Film Festival. *A Touch of the Tar Brush*: ICA Biennial: 'Arrows of Desire'. *Handsworth Songs*: Grierson Award for Best Documentary. *Testament*: Grand Prix Riminicinema International Film Festival, Special Mention for use of Archive FESPACO Burkina Faso 1989. *Seven Songs for Malcolm X*: Best Feature Length Non Fiction First Film Festival of Black Culture, National Black Programming Award 1994. A panel member at the Cultural Identities season at the Commonwealth Institute, March 1986 and the Black Film British Cinema conference at the Institute of Contemporary Arts, London, February 1988.

Testament (1988) is a narrative of the return to the once-familiar; a British-based journalist's return to the post-Nkrumah Ghana she had fled from years before. A dialogue between the history of Ghana and the central character's personal history makes the known past a site of new discoveries, new knowledge. In *Who Needs A Heart*, the story of Michael X as told through newsreel is exposed as a history in the service of the system that hanged him. The film questions the possibility of telling just one history; the hero, the traditional heart of a history film, is rejected: "Who needs a heart?."

A seemingly more straightforward project, *A Touch of the Tar Brush* (1991) revises J B Priestley's limited survey of England and Englishness but conforms to Akomfrah's critical agenda of retelling history, so that history as an idea is transformed. The most eloquent expression of this ambition is *Seven Songs for Malcolm X*, produced in the context of the euphoria surrounding the reborn image of Malcolm generated by Spike Lee's film. Akomfrah's study of the hero's discursive image is the reverse of hero-worship, without being an attack on Malcolm X. The film's concern is with historical evidence, with the way the past survives in the memory and its representations.

Akomfrah's work to date adds up to a consistent and eloquent contextualisation of the representational norms of traditional documentary, a corpus of national and international importance within what is still an emergent film culture.

Karen Alexander

RIGHT:
HANDSWORTH SONGS

David
Anderson

David Anderson, one of the most admired of British short-form animation directors, and a successful director of commercials, graduated from the National Film and Television School at the beginning of the Channel Four years and just before the eighties boom. His first film *Dreamland Express* (1982), made at the NFTS, introduced his unique style of using multi-layered techniques to evoke a mysterious and atmospheric landscape. *Dreamless Sleep* (1986) and *Door* (1990), two films about nuclear disaster made for Channel Four, explored similar environments through the combined use of xerography, cel, model animation and special effects. *Door*, in particular, struck a chord with advertising agencies, and led to commissions in which Anderson quoted extensively from his own work, as in the McEwans and Purdeys commercials.

Anderson's career, like that of many British animators, has been pegged to Channel Four and its policy of commissioning innovative animation for adults. Within the commercial sector his work interestingly straddles art and advertising – a typically British phenomenon, and one which keeps the studios buoyant while at the same time creating the economic space for animators to pursue personal projects. Television audiences will remember his work for the Bank of Scotland and Access even if they have never seen his short films. Alternative outlets for animation directors in the UK include children's series and animated television specials and features, neither of which are natural Anderson territory.

Anderson's work has a dark, almost gothic side, also present in the work of other model animators, especially Joan Ashworth (who worked with him on *Dreamless Sleep*), though his approach is obscure and understated when compared to The Quay Brothers and Jan Švankmajer who belong to a more surreal tradition. He cites as his influences René Magritte, Bertholde Bartosch (the 1930s animator) and Jean Cocteau, and his films owe something to this mix of avant-gardism and surrealism, underpinned by an ambiguous romanticism.

In his later work, including *Deadsy* (1989), the first collaboration with the novelist Russell Hoban, and the most recent Channel Four commission, *In The Time of Angels* (1994), Anderson has moved towards live action; it is the animation itself which is hidden in a retelling of the Beauty and the Beast story. Object animation and special effects have all but displaced the cel and the model and with its narrative structure and use of actors the film constitutes a break from his previous work. Special effects animation, achieved in post-production rather that in production, is now equally the preserve of live action feature film-making and, for Anderson, may be an opportunity to develop his directorial talents outside animation proper. Others, most famously Terry Gilliam, have trodden this route, and commercials directing has traditionally been a jumping off point into feature films, as for Ridley and Tony Scott. Currently lecturing in the theory and practice of animation at Harvard, Anderson continues to work on live action projects and animation.

Jill McGreal

Dreamland Express
1982, 14min, colour, 35mm

A young boy is led by his mentor, a mysterious train, on a spiritual journey of puzzles and revelations culminating in the boy overcoming fear and, through his own inner strength, becoming the master of wild animals found in a strange circus at the edge of the world. Having completed his quest, the boy stands alone at the beginning of a new journey. Anderson's mixed animation techniques are matched by Dirk Campbell's music in their variety, and combine in layers of visual and aural richness.

Deadsy
1989, 5min, colour, 35mm

Writer Russell Hoban's disturbing narrative explores male fascination with weapons, and its links with sexual power and aggression. In this dark tale – a "Deadtime story for Big Folks" – a man's obsession with size leads logically but unexpectedly to a gender-bending conclusion. Anderson's inventive graphic interpretation combines live-action, Xerography, hand-rendering and model animation.

Door
1990, 5min, colour, 35mm

Door considers Man's relentless curiosity and the outcome of his actions when he takes one step too many. It examines the human race's ability to shut its eyes to exactly what those results are, or may yet be. Written and narrated by Russell Hoban, the film uses model animation, pixillation in outdoor locations, animation of photographic images.

In the Time of Angels

1994, 15min, colour, 35mm

"Have you ever wished you could reverse the passage of time, turn back the clock and unlock the frozen moments that contain our regrets?...The difference between fate and destiny is one of the keys to unlocking the riddles of this film" DA. An extra-ordinary gothic tale that uses the 'alchemy' of combined live-action and electronic post-production to transform the real and the unreal.

Biography

Born 1952. Trained as cameraman and director at the National Film and Television School, 1977-80, where he produced *Dreamland Express*: BAFTA 1982, Best Animation Award; Munich Film Festival Best Animation Award; Special Prize, Zagreb. *Deadsy*: Special Jury Prize, Edinburgh Film and Television Festival 1990; Best in Category, Golden Gate Awards, San Francisco 1992. *Door*: ICA Biennial: 'Arrows of Desire'; Post Office McLaren Award for Best New British Animation Film, Edinburgh Festival 1991. *Deadsy* and *Door* were premiered on Channel Four together with a documentary on Anderson's work.

Reece
Auguiste

Reece Auguiste can be identified, like John Akomfrah, with one of the most important British workshops of the last fifteen or so years, the Black Audio Film Collective. Though produced within the workshop-frame, Auguiste's work strikes a particular and personal tone, while preserving the specialised aesthetic that makes Black Audio's work unmistakable: contemplative long takes and calculated juxtapositions of form; constructions of the 'real' out of manipulated studio-bound conventions, lighting and stylised sets, and the re-construction of real locations so that they can be as easily manipulated; the visual characteristics of the Black Audio style are as much 'Auguistian' as 'Akomfran'.

Physical, factual and social realities are at the heart of Auguiste's work, but its genre cannot be easily reduced to the term 'documentary'. Events and experiences are documented, statistics itemised – eg, the 700 deaths in police custody that are invoked at the beginning of the *Mysteries of July* (1991) – but Auguiste's complex constructions of interpretation and response allow his films to be elegiac and emotional in their concreteness. *Mysteries of July*, in particular, mourns the loss of individual lives as it powerfully documents the responsibility of the police for those deaths. The evocation of the urban landscape in *Twilight City* (1989) is similarly elegiac.

Investigating the past through an overbearing sense of the present is, each in a different way, a preoccupation of both *Twilight City* and *Mysteries of July*. Both are concerned with the authority of voice, demonstrated by its displacement through narrators, interviewed subjects and recollected experiences. These concerns are inseparable from a discursive engagement with questions of representation, evident in published articles by Auguiste on other film-makers and on theoretical questions of Third Cinema.

In common with other Black British film-makers, the influences and inputs feeding Auguiste's work are eclectic, yet specific to a relationship with not just Britain, but Black America, the Caribbean, Africa and Europe. According to Auguiste, "European art cinema is literally where we are. Our models are different from films which affect Black Americans...we draw on many strands: English, Caribbean, African cultures." (*Vogue*, March 1991)

Through his theoretical work and practice, Auguiste has contributed to the formation of an identifiable aesthetic that is now central to Black film-making and analysis internationally. "The issue is that of producing new forms of aesthetics, of visual styles and experimentation with clear-cut political and social objectives that can contribute to the development of an art form so young as the cinema." (*Questions of Third Cinema*, ed Jim Pines and Paul Willemen BFI 1987)

Karen Alexander

Twilight City
1989, 52min, colour, 16mm

After 35 years of living in London, Olivia's mother returns to Dominica vowing never to return. They parted after a long and torturing silence. Ten years later a letter breaks the silence. Eugenia wants to come 'home' and she wants to be invited. Olivia is a journalist researching "the new London and the creation of wealth." She drives through London collecting interviews and watching the city of her childhood sink in the shadows of redevelopment. On her journey through the city she composes her reply. Using a hybrid of fictional biography, interviews and archive footage, *Twilight City* is a journey through contemporary London, a city in a state of transformation. The film looks at those sections of London's communities that stand to lose in this political reshaping; the homeless inhabitants of cardboard city, the lesbian and gay communities under Section 28, the vanished/vanishing communities of Lascar and Somalian seamen and the East End Chinese.

Mysteries Of July
1991, 52min, colour, 16mm

Centring on the mysterious death of Jamie Stewart by cocaine poisoning in July 1989, *Mysteries Of July* explores the themes of terror, death, and the private world of mourning, in its examination of the phenomena of deaths in police custody in mainland Britain, of which there have been over 700 in the last two decades.

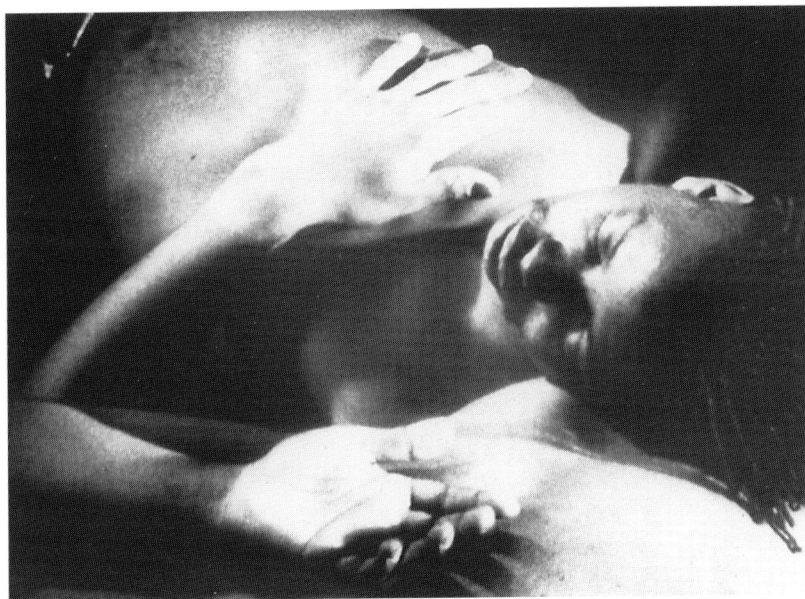

RIGHT:
TWILIGHT CITY

Biography

Born 1958, Dominica, West Indies. BSc in Sociology, Portsmouth Polytechnic 1982; MA in Comparative Literature and Cross-cultural Aesthetics, University of Essex 1985. *Twilight City*: awards include Grand Prize Melbourne International Film Festival; Best Film for the Promotion of Intercultural Dialogue, Mannheim Film Festival 1989; Gold Hugo for Documentary, Chicago International Film Festival; Special Mention, Diaspora section, FESPACO Film Festival, Ouagadougou, Burkina Faso 1991. *Mysteries of July* awarded Jury prize at Festival du Images Caraibes, Martinique 1992. Auguiste has taught at the University of Warwick, University of Geneva and the University of California, Los Angeles.

George
Barber

The footage may be 'found' but the wit is all his own. Though debased Hollywood footage forms the substantial core of George Barber's work, his transformation of it through editing is so complete, it becomes entirely his own. Initially, Barber carved out a niche for himself in 'Scratch Video' by making great use of colour and multi-layering fast-moving imagery. Then, with the compilation *The Greatest Hits of Scratch Video Vol 2* (1985), he moved on and incorporated into this mix the repetition of sounds and spoken phrases. By extracting isolated moments from Hollywood footage and cleverly inserting them into specially made music tracks, he short-circuited movie grammar, destroying the original meanings and offering them up anew, in the service of a much more abstract and painterly aesthetic. Who can watch *The Deep*, starring Brooke Shields, after the Barber treatment it got in *Yes Frank No Smoke* (1985)? Again, if ever there were a quintessential 'video art moment', it would be the repetition of Paul Newman shutting a car door intercut with a descending helicopter in *Absence of Satan* (1985).

Perhaps unexpectedly, Barber has always had an interest in writing, and this matured to good effect in *Taxi Driver II* (1987) a short starring Johnny Morris and featuring a memorable Robert De Niro evening class. More recently, he seems to have combined the two strands. In *Passing Ship* (1994) for example, he utilises a Warholian, *Chelsea Girls* split-screen format, setting one of his own monologues against footage from the famous disaster movie *Airport III*.

George Barber's work has an unusual breadth and is rarely less than alive and entertaining in its aims and effects.

Janet Lee

ABOVE:
**YES FRANK NO
SMOKE**

Biography

Born 1958, Georgetown, Guyana. BA St Martins School of Art 1980; MA Slade School of Art, London 1984. Screenings include Los Angeles Film and Video Festival; World Wide Video Festival, The Hague; Melbourne Video Festival; American Film Institute; Semaine International de Video, Geneva; Edinburgh Television Festival; Monte Carlo Film and Television Festival; European Media Art Festival, Osnabrück; Videonale, Bonn; ICA Biennial: 'Between Imagination and Reality'. DAAD Award 1986; Chicago Film Festival Gold for *Venetian Ghost* 1989; Ars Electronica, Austria, Prize for Computer Art, 1993. Founder member of *ZG Magazine*. Curator of video art display for Museum of the Moving Image. Director: BBC Late Show Special *A Happening History of Video Art* (1993). BBC Radio 4 writer and broadcaster. Journalist for *The Independent*.

Yes Frank No Smoke
1985, 5min, colour, video

Quick-fire scratch edit combining *Blue Lagoon* and *The Deep*. Repeated snatches of dialogue are orchestrated in a tape that cleverly reveals other more obscure aesthetic possibilities for Hollywood movies.

Taxi Driver II
1987, 9min, colour, video

Here, Barber's evident fascination with the glittering surface of Hollywood imagery moves away from an exploration of the play of surface-flow, from stripping images from their narrative significance and working on their purely formal qualities, towards articulating a new narrative structure. This revolves around Tim West, an advertising executive who is also developing a Channel Four programme on cooking for terrorists. Disillusioned by the hyper-reality of the media world, he joins a Robert de Niro evening class, but also falls under the pastoral influence of Johnny Morris. From the opening images of night-time, car-ridden streets accompanied by languorous sax on the soundtrack, through to the sub-Chandleresque voice-over narration, *Taxi Driver II* strikes you with its clever knowingness. But it's more than just a clever nod in the direction of contemporary *film noir*, just as it's more than an incestuous joke at the expense of the London-based media world: it's also a telling comment on the contemporary media culture of postmodernism.

Julian Petley *New Statesman*

"My commercial and corporate work heavily influences my own pieces which at their root are concerned with corporate propaganda, libertarian mythology and the processes of the invisible world of electronic capital." John Butler

Take a situationist with a talent for computer graphics, add a dose of 'bad attitude' and you'd arrive at somebody like John Butler. His work is incisive, amusing, and concise. Broadly speaking, the themes tend to be the contemporary interlinking of politics, big business, propaganda and technology, and how this affects us as a cultural formation.

The aesthetic involves spurious animated bar charts and spinning text. Catch phrases abound. In this respect, one can see a parallel with Jenny Holzer; both exhibit a paranoia about the power of corporate culture which is armed with so much capital and influence that anything it comes up with can be made to sound reasonable. Butler is the more direct. Using a clever combination of computer diagrams and ironic disco music, he pursues his enjoyable critique of consumerism and the multinationals, exaggerating and making fun of their claims and philosophies. For example, *World Peace Thru Free Trade* (1989) turns out to be the mission statement of an arms company called Globex; Joseph Heller would approve. Butler has colonised the corporate video, delightfully subverting the format's arrogance and extending it towards the realms of black comedy.

George Barber

World Peace Thru Free Trade
1989, 4min, colour, video

A satire on the dreams and slogans of free market libertarianism conveying a dystopian world of ever more outlandish consumer choices, executed through 3D graphics.

Leisure Society
1990, 5min, colour, video

State of the art graphics are used to evoke a future in which corporate ideology has totally dominated the media, and, by implication our collective imagination.

Born 1959, Dublin. Studied Painting and later Electronic Imaging at Dundee Art College. Works as a television graphic designer in Glasgow. *World Peace Thru Free Trade* won a Benson & Hedges Gold Award in 1989 and was broadcast on BBC2 and Channel Four. *Leisure Society* was broadcast on BBC2. *Leisure Society*: ICA Biennial: 'Arrows of Desire'. The installation *The Dream of Freedom* was toured as part of V-Topia to Tramway, Glasgow and Bluecoat, Liverpool. Works in collaboration with Paul Butler as Butler Brothers on interactive works.

ABOVE:
**SHOPPING SIMULATOR
FROM 'LEISURE
SOCIETY'**

Breda Beban
Hrvoje Horvatic

For many reasons, the work of Breda Beban and Hrvoje Horvatic stands apart from that made by others of their generation: perhaps the most unavoidable is that – being made by two people – it germinates and develops through an intense dialogue which began in 1986. Other intellectual, collaborative and indeed ideological considerations are inspirational but in the end are filtered through private experience. Since the overriding theme is that – as we are flooded by the world – we must love the world, it is no wonder that the content is about attachments and a definition of belonging.

The most relevant analogy to Beban and Horvatic's method of organisation is music. Before the artists begin filming they agree a strict concept, write it down, and decide how to frame the shots. The shots are of precise duration, frequently intimate, using Beban's face and body as the subject, and are built with deliberate colour and texture within the rectangular frame. They arrive and depart with the containment and the carry-over of passages in contemporary scores, for example, those of the German composer Thomas Koner who contributed the music for *The Left Hand Should Know* (1992). Although the structure is in sympathy with film as montage, especially recently, the results are not so orchestrated as, say, the work of Robert Bresson.

Even the relatively fast-paced *Absence* (1994) assembles its shots as if they were lines of poetry. They can be taken in sequence, but are also available when the attention wanders and the process becomes highly introspective, anticipating viewing on the home video monitor where one is allowed to replay and isolate passages. In that sense the later pieces can be treated something like the entries in Milorad Pavic's *Dictionary of the Khazars*, in which he advises his reader to "move through the book as through a forest, from one marker to the next, orienting himself by observing the stars, the moon, and the cross" or another time to alight on passages like a buzzard, remembering that "you cannot get more out of the truth than you put into it."

Key works

Taking on a Name
1987, 25min, colour, video

This performance based tape opens with a simple prelude of slow-motion waves unfurling in deep water; the image then dissolving to an ancient fresco painting, glimpsed beneath the surface of a rock pool. Beban faces us, standing on the shore of a lake, accompanied by the reverberant sound of bass notes. As the music proceeds through its processional spiral, she takes on a number of incarnations, finally ending as a vision of Venus bathing in the waters of the lake.

Geography
1989, 9min, colour, video

An elliptical poem of loss and displacement, shot at Ohrid, Macedonia, the location of *Taking on a Name*. An overall dreamlike structure and logic dominates, though captured through a very rigid use of image and sound. At the core of the tape is a man whose enigmatic gaze traces both a self-consciousness as well as a wistful melancholia of memories of places, events and people.

Michael O'Pray

The Left Hand Should Know
1992, 43min, colour, video

In many ways this tape is a stirring representation of Beban and Horvatic's theme throughout much of their work – the partly reviled quality of some kind of an unarticulated knowledge. The video traces a series of landscapes of often astonishing beauty. Set to the ethereal music of Thomas Koner, these haunting images somehow express the connectedness of things. On the other hand, feelings of isolation and disengagement are dispersed across numerous figures who blankly perform actions. They stare off-shot and sometimes into the camera thus accentuating the ambiguity of the actor/performer/real person.

Michael O'Pray

Before The Kiss
1993, installation, 3 projectors, 1 player, 2 cameras, transluscent screens

The subtle configuration of large scale video projections from closed-circuit cameras and pre-recorded performance footage, enhanced by exemplary use of light and ghostly insubstantiality of the much-magnified electronic image, creates a work into which the viewer is gently seduced. This intimate, contemplative setting – both mysterious and beguilingly enveloping – encourages numerous meanings in turn: some personal, some perceptual, invoking themes of presence and absence, real and imaginary, self and other, observer and observed.

Steven Bode

Beban born 1952, Novi Sad, Yugoslavia. Diploma in Painting at the Zagreb Academy for Fine arts 1976; DAAD grant to undertake postgraduate studies at the Hochschule der Kunste, Berlin 1984–85. Horvatic born 1958, Rijeka, Yugoslavia. Studied at the Academy for Theatre, Film & Television, Zagreb 1978-83. An independent film-maker since 1979. Beban and Horvatic's tape and installation collaborations began in 1986. Early work broadcast on Yugoslav television 1986–90; *The Left Hand Should Know* broadcast on Kunst Kanal, Amsterdam 1993. Many international screenings and numerous individual exhibitions include a retrospective of their single screen tapes at the Whitechapel Art Gallery, London in 1994. Guest professors at the Royal College of Art, Stockholm, 1992-93.

Beban and Horvatic also admire painters, especially those who exercise a similar discipline. The use of contour to recreate reality, the arcane geometrical relationship of object to frame and the luminosity found in Euan Uglow's pictures of single figures and fruit are models of observation matched with passion. For both, natural rhythms are respected so light breaks over a form, and stasis is subject to breathing and ripening. The duality of anticipation/instant memory, inherent in every time-based medium, extends the range, as with Tarkovsky, so that tranquillity and self-control may be paired with latent violence and the engulfing power of the city. Equally Beban and Horvatic's process relates to abstract imagery and the reliance on mark and gesture to bridge ideas. Ian Mckeever, analysing shots in the transitional piece *Geography* (1989) took the appearance of a fish-eye to refer to a time when a symbol was power, and what immediately follows, a polished metal street marker, as a modern sign. He saw here and elsewhere the transfer from "options of actions to the options of intellect", the common denominator being the function of 'gaze' as opposed to 'look'.

The installations by Beban and Horvatic come more from performance (which Beban practised while still principally a painter in the early eighties and was part of Horvatic's training in film and theatre). As the visitor enters the room in *Before the Kiss* (1993), they confront a huge screen image of themselves and then behind see a loop sequence of Beban and Horvatic circling around each other, eventually embracing and then periodically exiting. The demands are rigorous in a philosophical way, reminding us that part of the artists' education in central Europe took for granted the branch of knowledge defined as ontology – "the nature, essential properties and relations of being" – which assumes what these artists consistently maintain, "that everything is connected".

Catherine Lampert

RIGHT:
TAKING ON A NAME

Simon
Biggs

For many commentators, the crudity of the digital image has been a drawback; for Simon Biggs, it is one of its greatest assets. Not that Biggs' work is crude, or that the equipment he has made available for himself is inadequate. But the limitations of digital space have been the fruitful ground for more than a decade of exploration in the possibilities for a new spatial orientation. Most applications of computer-aided art and design aim for a hyper-real effect: Biggs uses the computer to explore the limitations of our spatial and temporal awareness. In installations like *Golem* (1988) and *Alchemy* (1990), these explorations are linked to the arcane sciences of the making of artificial beings, homunculi, both punning on the illumination of manuscripts and the illumination of the spirit in lost traditions of European hermeticism.

The interactive video projection *Heaven* (1992) moves these themes towards an intensive engagement with the Christian iconography of the Renaissance and the Baroque, continued in more recent single-channel pieces in which the spatial norms of classical painting and computer imaging are played against one another to reveal the organisations of vision particular to, and invisible in, each. The figure of the alembic, in the magician's almanac or cradled in the arms of the Mother of God, the vase in which the alchemist prepares the new life proposed so long ago by Dante and re-proposed in contemporary discourses of the cybernetic, evinces a continuing thread through the histories of European modernity. The demented clockwork of the artificer's making in *The Temptation of Saint Anthony* (1990) has little to do with the voluptuary Anthonys of Breughel and Ernst, everything to do with the mechanical sex that is their obverse. The baroque perspective of *Heaven* is reorganised in *The Rosenberg Variations: Mass Violin Suicide* (1991) and *Pandaemonium* (1992), the second of which in particular looks to the dissolution of the bonds between human and natural worlds as constitutive of the potentialities of our time.

Biography

Born 1957, Adelaide, Australia. Studied Electronic and Computer Music at the Elder Conservatorium, Adelaide University. Left Australia 1986. Screenings include Viper Film and Video Festival, Lucerne, Switzerland; Medienfest, Tubingen, Germany; International Video Art Festival, Locarno, Switzerland; Video Positive, Liverpool. *The Temptation of St Anthony*: First Prize Australian Video Festival, Sydney. *A New Life*: First Prize International Video Bienale, Medellin, Columbia. Installations include European Media Art Festival, Osnabrück, Germany; MUU Media Festival, Helsinki; Video Positive, Liverpool. Currently Head of the Digital Arts Department, Academyminerva, Rijkshogeschool Groningen, The Netherlands.

Key works

A New Life

1989, 4min, colour, video (music by Jon Rose)

Biggs animates elements of Mantegna paintings around themes from Dante. At one moment, the Christ of Mantegna's *Pieta*, with its notoriously impossible perspective, glides out of frame on the axis of its own vanishing point, incompatible with what the eye has presumed to be its relation to the figure. Other figures and groups move into frame on their own axes but move within or out of it according to the axes of others. Meanwhile computer-generated hearts and alembics argue with the spiritualised perspectives of the Renaissance sources for a virtual space that will accommodate both the polar space of the computer graphics and the planar space of the found images. This is a virtual space marked by its internal contradictions. The tape works on disparate spatial logics, whose incompatibility and refusal of coherence becomes the work's *raison d'être*.

Sean Cubitt

Alchemy

1990, interactive installation, colour, silent, video

Using two video monitors turned on their sides, *Alchemy* is a digitally illuminated 'book of hours', the playback system being laser disc with interactive software, enabling the viewer to turn the pages with the wave of a hand over a photo electric switch placed in front of the display.

The Living Room

1994, interactive installation, multi-channel sound, video

A large space (20m x 20m x 5m), dark, with controllable lighting. Using computer-based multi-media technologies, it is enlivened with numerous constantly changing images on the walls and sounds that emerge from specific locations, activating and defining the space. Images and sounds are individually interactive, being 'aware' of individuals in the space and able to interact with them. A studio site which is different to the traditional studio environment in that it consists of an interactive (or 'virtual') space within which works are developed (a laboratory of sorts). Its various components (sounds, images and digital video) respond individually to the presence and activities of people in the space. The artworks are created from 'within' their fabric, ideas and phenomena being developed interactively, dissolving the usual distinction between the art making process and the finished artwork.

The recent single-channel piece *Voices* (1993) continues to derive inspiration from literary and artistic sources, extending Biggs' visual iconography and the range of his vitally important musical collaborators. The 1990s installations, configured around the live studio *The Living Room* 1994 extend *Voices'* shift in interest from natural and mechanical to human motifs, photographed bodies adding to the repertoire of Renaissance hermeticism. These large-scale, interactive sound/image projections derive much of their power from their scale, and from the inventiveness of Biggs' engagements with the fictive spaces of the body, as rebuilt by both edge technologies and the major arcana. *Mouths* and *Angels* (fragments of *The Living Room*) also bring from *Voices* an interest in the (recorded, amplified, interactive) spoken word, as both musical element (like clapping hands, the body as instrument), and as poetry, most ancient of the interactive arts. If a new kind of awe is emerging in the works, it is perhaps because the work of the digital artist is no longer simply to explore, but to temper the emergent power of the medium. Recent on-line and performance experiments keep Biggs in the front line of European media artists.

Sean Cubitt

ABOVE:
ALCHEMY

23

Ian
Bourn

With early video pieces like *Lenny's Documentary* (1978), Ian Bourn began to define a downbeat and highly personal style that relied on deadpan monologues and melancholic characterisation. At a time when video art tended toward hi-tech effects and fast paced editing, Bourn's tragi-comic observations on those at the margins of society and the quiet pace of his tapes went against the grain of vivid imagery and editing tricks.

The End of the World (1982) epitomised Bourn's interest in the minutiae of everyday life and humdrum human relationships while *Sick as a Dog* (1989) marked him as one of the few British tape makers to fully explore the narrative potential of the medium. In *Sick as a Dog* the viewer takes a journey into the low-life escapades and last ditch ambitions of a frayed dog track tipster, Terry Childs, portrayed by Bourn himself. The sly humour and understated mood of the piece, with its video-within-a-video conceit, underline the bleak and sometimes uncomfortable humour of his genre. The deceptively simple *Breathing Days* (1992) focuses on the threat of eviction and homelessness as seen through the eyes of a main character whose alienation from authority and power is portrayed in a quiet yet intense and spare study.

Bourn's sometimes unfashionable themes of quiet desperation, marginal lives and muddled relationships have a particularly English quality to them. His tapes are notable for their use of plot and finely drawn characters; beyond this, their poignancy and atmospheric mood – frequently a milieu of missing Giro cheques, back street pubs and petty criminality – is imbued with a double-edged humour. In the act of smiling at some ineptitude we feel uneasy, uncertain whether we should find amusement in someone else's misfortune. There is a queasy recognition of our own foibles in Bourn's characters and their worlds.

A member of the influential Housewatch group, who pioneered a brand of filmic spectacle, Bourn is none the less more a storyteller than an image maker. His talent lies in low-key drama that reflects its times. Rooted in the grubby reality of English society, his art has an uneasy place in contemporary moving image culture. Something of an outsider to current concerns, Bourn remains important and singular in his portraits of an under-class and culture largely ignored by high art.

Nik Houghton

Lenny's Documentary
1978, 45min, b&w, video

In this monologue, Lenny thinks aloud the script for a planned or imagined documentary about his life and environment. He is portrayed as someone obsessed by a bleak vision of his past and present circumstances. The narrative is presented as fragments of time in what seems an eternal evening of dark introspection. A glimmer of hope remains in the tape's visual metaphor of Leytonstone High Road as a release from the dark interior and a possible way out for Lenny.

The End of the World
1982, 10min, colour, video

The heaven and hell of suburban domesticity is put in the spotlight in this tape involving a video game, a cup of tea and a Sunday afternoon. "He is in the still undecorated back room. She is in the garden, soaking up the sun. a cup of tea is called for." Featuring Ian Bourn and Helen Chadwick.

Sick as a Dog

1989, 30min, colour, video

In his video and Super8 diaries, Terry Childs addresses the viewer and offers tips on gambling at greyhound races. As the tape progresses it becomes clear that Terry is anything but a successful gambler. Sometimes he wins but mostly he is on a downward slide. The making of this tape – with its catalogue of folly – is, for Terry, just one last attempt to make money. *Sick as a Dog* is the tragi-comic study of a man trying to cheat his way through life. At odds with the society in which he finds himself, he is also a product of that society's values.

Breathing Days

1992, 14min, colour, video

A video narrative about bureaucracy and alienation. Martin Worth, the main character, is threatened with eviction and homelessness. He appears as a reflection on the glass division between himself and authority. Glass acts as a barrier in each of the scenes, serving to emphasise both the exclusion of Martin from people and society, and also the exclusion of the viewer from the inner lives of those behind the video screen.

ABOVE:
SICK AS A DOG

Biography

Born 1953, London. Studied at Ealing School of Art 1972-75; Royal College of Art 1976-79. Screenings include Bracknell Video Festival; Hayward Gallery, London; The Kitchen, New York; Museum of Modern Art, New York; Stedelijk Museum, Amsterdam; National Film Theatre, London. Co-instigator with Chris White of the Housewatch group of artists (see separate entry) in 1985. Bourn was the narrator in John Smith's *Slow Glass* (1991). His short story *Blokes* was published in the anthology *Brought to Book* (Penguin Books, 1994)

Ian
Breakwell

The 1960s saw a radical change in attitudes and artists found ways of bringing their work to the public direct. In this spirit, Breakwell has published his writings in paperbacks, magazines and limited editions. He makes work that is specific to a captive audience watching a film or live performance, a television set burbling away in a corner, a painting that waits in silence. The expectations of the audience are frequently overturned: his film *Repertory* (1973) dwells on an exterior view of a theatre leaving the audience to create the events occurring inside for themselves. Other films, *The Journey* (1975) and *The Institution* (1978) challenge the orthodoxy of traditional documentary and drama. The established conventions of the television play, news and epilogue are exposed in his three videos: *In The Home* (1980), *The News* (1980) and *The Sermon* (1983), which paved the way for the three series commissioned by Channel Four.

Ian Breakwell's *Continuous Diary* (1984) and *Ian Breakwell's Xmas Diary* (1984) formed a substantial part of a project that aimed to bring artists' work to the television audience and to use the context and the medium. The work was not headlined as art and simply appeared alongside other programmes. The *Continuous Diary* comprised 21 programmes of varying duration: as writer, presenter and co-editor, Breakwell was given free reign to create a televisual treatment using montage, text on screen, the talking head and re-enactments to full effect. The *Diaries* celebrate the "side events of daily life" as observed by Breakwell. Several of the series were timed to coincide with national events and anniversaries: the London Marathon and the sinking of HMS Sheffield during the Falklands campaign. The bleak and dark moments were not mediated or made palatable and it is a tribute to Breakwell's compelling presence on screen that he was able to take his audience with him.

Key works

Repertory
1973, 10min, colour, 16mm

The visuals in *Repertory* consist of one continuous tracking shot, during which the camera completely circles the exterior of a locked and empty theatre, recording its walls, doors and blank hoardings and catching fleeting glimpses of passers-by. On the soundtrack a voice describes a three week cycle of imagined presentations inside the theatre...the form allows Breakwell to gleefully attack theatrical representation on film.

Tony Rayns

Ian Breakwell's Continuous Diary
1984, 21 x 3–11min, video

Commissioned by Channel Four and made in collaboration with independent producer Anna Ridley, this series of short pieces was broadcast over a six week period in April and May 1984. Combining re-enacted scenes from his diary entries with reflections on current events of the time, these programmes were acclaimed as innovative interventions in the broadcast medium.

Public Face, Private Eye
1988, 5 x 3–11min, video

A narrative in five acts on the interplay between the public world of surface appearance and social roles, and the private world of the imagination. The five acts portray formative events in Breakwell's life and provide insights into his concerns as an artist.

Auditorium
1993, 32min, colour, video

Breakwell and Ron Geesin initially studied audience reactions across the UK in a variety of theatrical settings, taking fly-on-the-wall photographs and video footage with sound recordings using parabolic microphones and 'bugged seats'. Their belief confirmed that in dynamic live theatre the audience becomes part of a two-way performance, radiating an equivalent range of emotional expression to that emanating from the stage, they went on to work with and eventually record a 50-strong 'performing audience' at the Hawth Theatre in 1993.

Born Derby, 1943. Paintings in public and private collections including Tate Gallery, Contemporary Art Society, Victoria and Albert Museum; Museum of Modern Art, New York; Art Gallery of New South Wales, Australia. Writings include: *Ian Breakwell's Diary* 1964-85 Pluto Press 1986; collected illustrated fiction *The Artist's Dream* Serpent's Tail 1988 and *Free Range* published by Victoria and Albert Museum 1993. Videos in collections of the Museum of Modern Art, New York; Imperial War Museum, London and Bluecoat Gallery, Liverpool. Screenings include: World Wide Video Festival, The Hague; Videonale, Bonn; National Video Festival, Los Angeles. *Auditorium* was screened at the Institute of Contemporary Arts, London; Ferens Art Gallery, Hull; National Review of Live Art, Glasgow in 1994. Fellowship at Kings College and Kettle's Yard, Cambridge 1980-81; John Brinkley Fellowship at the Norwich School of Art 1982-83; Artist in Residence, Tyne Tees Television 1985; Artist in Residence, Durham Cathedral, 1994-95.

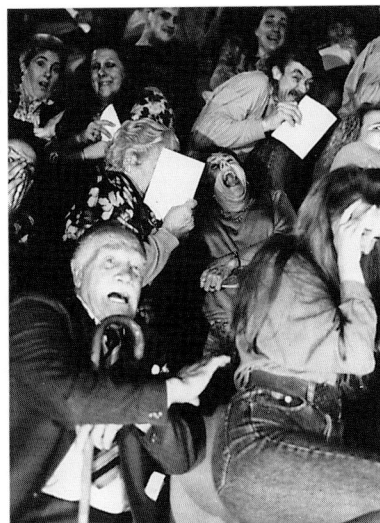

Ian Breakwell's Xmas Diary, an eight part series, gave the Breakwell version of Christmas. Devised and transmitted to link with Christmas week, it also marked his debut as TV chef and gourmet. *Public Face, Private Eye* (1988) being a specially written work, emerged as essentially autobiographical. The obsessions and pre-occupations in the *Diaries* are now revealed and documented. Magic, mystery and illusion underpin much of Breakwell's work – the inexplicable and the surreal which suddenly erupts out of the seemingly prosaic situations confirms for Breakwell the seething frustration that lurks beneath the surface.

Human emotions are wilfully exploited in *Auditorium* (1993) an installation/performance made in collaboration with composer and musician Ron Geesin and developed in various guises over five years. Here the tables are turned yet again and the audience are in the spotlight. Large screen or small, painted canvas or printed page – Breakwell, unlike some of his contemporaries, continues to widen his audience.

Anna Ridley

ABOVE:
AUDITORIUM

Paul
Bush

The films of Paul Bush have a clarity and precision which invoke the restraint of neo-classicism. It is, however, a neo-classicism firmly rooted in the coincidence of minimalism and conceptual art which dominated the art world of the late 1970s. What is so extraordinary about this body of work is the passionate clarity of the ideas which fuel it (cf. conceptualism) and the formal precision of the narrative and cinematographic structures which allow the viewer in (cf. minimalism). All the films engage with questions of history and narrative, in other words, with the question of time. It was a real liberation for the purists of the 1970s, struggling to find ways to represent philosophical notions of time, to re-discover narrative as the formal device developed over centuries precisely to perform this function.

Paul Bush's first film, *The Cow's Drama* (1984), is a contradiction in terms: the cow stands around in a field eating grass all day; in what sense can it be said to partake in a drama, to have a story or a history? The film takes us in, and we take part ourselves, becoming involved in the story which we cannot help but be aware we are making up. His second film, *O Quanta Qualia (So Many, So Magnificent)* (1987), uses sets derived from medieval illuminated manuscripts to tell the story of the great gothic cathedrals, exploring formal questions of how to represent another historical moment and how to connect that representation with our own time. *Forgetting* (1990) is the story of two lovers, one moving backwards in time, one moving relentlessly forwards. This double movement is a poignant metaphor conveying the way love's moment shifts, moves on, into something else. The floundering hypotheses of the character without a childhood, faced with the lover's expectations of an exchange of telling anecdotes, are painfully funny, and remind us how much love is about memory. *Lake of Dreams* (1991) parallels the landing of a human being on the moon in 1969 with the circling approach of falling in love: another historical drama, or drama of time.

Biography

Born 1956, London. Studied Fine Art at the Central School of Art and at Goldsmiths College, London. Established Clapham-Battersea Film Workshop in 1982 where he taught film until 1993. Films shown in over thirty international festivals including London, Edinburgh, Oberhausen, Hiroshima, Montreal, Paris and Bilbao. *Forgetting*: Gold Plaque for Short Film Drama, Chicago Film Festival 1991. *His Comedy* has won prizes at the 1994 Melbourne and Espino Festivals. Other films have been included in the British Art Show 1984/85, ICA Biennial: 'Arrows of Desire'. In 1992 he had a retrospective at Figueira da Foz Film Festival, Portugal.

Key works

Lost Images

1990, 1min, b&w and colour, video (2 versions)

At the end of the day's television a selection of images can be seen for a second time, removed from their context, simply assembled, one after another. It is a coda at the end of the day, a reprise, momentarily, for the image before oblivion, an index for a text which is irretrievable.

Lake Of Dreams

1991, 13min, b&w and colour, 16mm

Paul Bush updates the traditional association of love with the moon through a subtle and visually fascinating twin exploration of the physicality of the lunar object and a young couple's developing relationship in which their excitement, discovery, joy, consummation and inevitable separation is paralleled by the American moon programme's similar history.

Michael O'Pray

His Comedy

1994, 8min, colour, 35mm

The poet Dante is taken through the gates of the city of desolation and into the centre of hell. What he sees there is not simply an apocalyptic vision of the punishment that awaits sinners after death, but the very real horrors committed by human hands on earth. The film is based on Gustav Doré's nineteenth century woodblock engravings illustrating Dante's *The Divine Comedy* which are animated by engraving directly into the surface of the film stock.

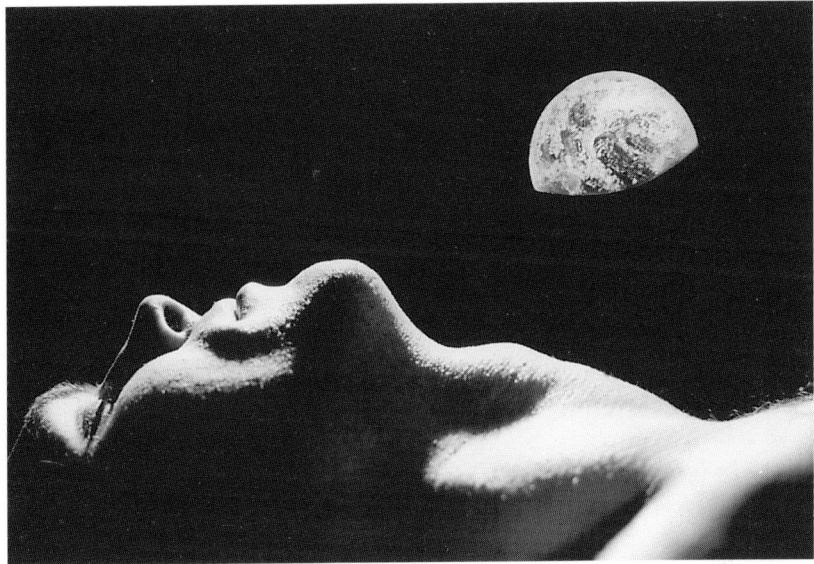

His Comedy (1994) is a departure: using a combination of live action, archive footage and images from the Doré illustrations of Dante's *The Divine Comedy*, all shot in black and white and printed on colour film, Bush (with the help of an assistant) set to work scratching onto the emulsion, repeating the labour of the professional engravers who painstakingly scraped out the wood in the spaces between Doré's drawn lines. The effects of this low-tech intervention are stupendous: the Doré figures are animated by the frame by frame movement of the scratched lines, while the colours released from the film stock flood the screen and the mind. The question of human violence and the potential end of history is invoked through the visual archetype of the mushroom cloud, while, as in *O Quanta Qualia*, Bush investigates the relationship of still and moving images, and how to bring pre-photographic still images and cinematic moving images together in the same space.

The secret preoccupation of these films, finally, is beauty. It may be the case that the film-maker, in focusing so relentlessly on issues of time, narrative, history, the intersection of the graphic and the cinematic, and the question of clarity of presentation, doesn't himself see it – but the viewer does. As if beauty were a necessary by-product of these investigations, beyond the intention of the artist, yet an inevitable result of his rigorous control and passionate pursuit of meaning.

Leslie Dick

Nick
Collins

Key works

All of Nick Collins' films since 1984 are concerned with the texture of subjective experience. Although documentary in their use of locations, they evoke an emotional response to places rather than being about them in a dispassionately observed way. This is often achieved through the replication of subjectivity by various devices: swinging or snatching camera movements, jittery focus and an interpolative manner of construction.

Consciousness finds a particular visual corollary in *Looking In and Out (A Winter Diary)* (1986). Here images of waves breaking are projected onto a steamed-up window, whilst the projector beam simultaneously throws shadows of flowers onto the window/screen. Water projected onto water, with stray rays of light passing directly through the porous screen and striking the film. Plates fall and smash in slow motion, contrastingly solid and yet weightless in their gradual descent.

Sanday (1988) was shot on the island in the Orkneys. Superficially it recalls the photographic work of Hamish Fulton in the choice of a remote and empty landscape, with the stillness that that implies. In fact, *Sanday* is the most heavily worked of Collins' films. The original footage has been reshaped in an optical printer in order to stress the rhythms inherent in scudding clouds and the repetitive motion of hand held walking shots. Time is concomitantly manipulated: frozen, reversed, repeated. This repetition seems to simulate the mental remembering of experience that we repeatedly enact even as we stand in the place of that experience. Through the use of intertitles we learn that Sanday has been inhabited since 3500 BC. It is this knowledge, combined with the evident inhospitability of the place that produces a strong sense of melancholy, infusing one's perception of the empty landscape with thoughts about how people could possibly have lived here. This process – in which a single thought irrevocably inflects the way a place is perceived – is at the heart of the film, and is in turn underpinned by the realisation that, even in an empty landscape, the very act of filming is a form of inhabitation that is as irreversible, for the viewer, as the building of a settlement.

In *Views From A City* (1992), Collins locates his interests in two places; Tel Lakhish, an ancient city south-west of Jerusalem, and contemporary London. Even so the work is still concerned with wider ideas about the city as palimpsest and our experience of it as such. There is considerable play on the contrasts between the durability of brick and stone and the ephemeral nature of events and experiences. We see the massive walls of Lakhish reflected in the twitching fleshiness of an eye, and a nine thousand year old human skull with shells for eyes. Stone reliefs in the British Museum represent the Assyrian siege of Hamanu: flames carved in stone, modelled in light, recorded on celluloid. Collins' films reconnect the viewer with the physicality of experience, a physicality which is relatively absent in the cinema situation, where bodily immobility is accompanied by a visual concentration which is focused elsewhere.

Nicky Hamlyn

After the Music by François Couperin: Les Baricades Mystérieuses
1979, 7min, b&w, 16mm

A film about a house, and about some things which might or might not have happened there. Fragments of a story act as a catalyst turning the stillness of the place to sudden movement. Music by François Couperin.

Looking In and Out (A Winter Diary)
1986, 9min, b&w, 16mm

Images are projected onto a misted window; an abstract drama takes place: a process of perception achieved by stages, a transformation and a reconciliation.

RIGHT TOP:
**TWO STILLS FROM
LOOKING IN AND OUT
(A WINTER DIARY)**
BOTTOM:
**TWO STILLS FROM
SANDAY**

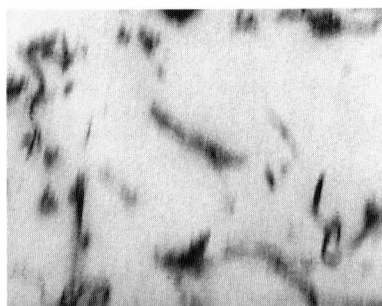

Sanday

1988, 16min, colour, 16mm

Shot on Sanday, one of the Orkney islands, the film is in four sections, each representing (and transforming) the film-maker's actions in and experience of a place at a particular time. Drawing on the qualities of these places and the long history of human habitation of the landscape (evidence for which goes back to 3500 BC), Nick Collins' intention was to make possible the experience of a series of linked mental/emotional states, seen through a landscape and movement within it.

Views From A City

1992, 19min, colour, 16mm

A film which examines the city as a temporal phenomenon, our direct, instantaneous visual experience of it, in relation to memory and to history, and in relation to how the camera sees and can see. The film is in three sections each using different objects and places – a decorated skull from Jericho, 7000 BC; images of cities from the British Museum; the dead city of Lakhish (in Israel); London filmed in 1898 and 1991; a wall reflected in an eye.

Born 1953, Walton-on-Thames. BA in History at Fitzwilliam College, Cambridge 1975; studied at the Slade School of Fine Art. Part time lecturer Falmouth School of Art, Maidstone College of Art and Design and Glasgow School of Art. Screenings include: European Media Art Festival, Osnabrück; Viper Festival, Lucerne; Image Forum, Tokyo; Oberhausen; Film + Arc 1, Graz.

Susan **Collins**

Made as a response to a given site or situation, the interactive installation pieces – usually audio and video – aim to engage viewers in an inquiry or reinterpretation of their role within specific and often everyday contexts. They are an attempt to make the audience recognise and question accepted behaviour in public situations while also showing, through ironic juxtaposition of images, sounds and site, the oddity of 'mundane' social interactions. For instance, in the publicly sited *Introductory Exchanges* (1993), passers-by walking in the Woolwich Foot Tunnel underneath the Thames were forced to step over video projected 'puddles' while triggering a series of strategically placed sound effects including sheep and running water. *Pedestrian Gestures* (1994) made for Hull Manchester and Nottingham Train stations, interacted with commuters through the projection of animated *trompe l'oeil* images of hands, mouths and eyes, which when approached, triggered a sensor-driven set of audio and computer-animated responses – including a dog howling and a voice saying indignantly "A-hem" and "Excuse me." The sites are central to the works and the viewer becomes active as collaborator and (often unwitting) participant, constructing individual and often independent narratives, depending on the pathway chosen through the space.

The viewer's fundamental role in the interpretation and realisation of the work is not confined to the publicly sited installations. *Handle With Care* (1993) at the Museum of Science and Industry in Manchester and *AudioZone* (1994) part of V-Topia at Tramway Glasgow, also worked with the concept of viewer-as-choreographer, but in the more controlled confines of the museum/gallery context. Whilst *Handle With Care* was a direct evocative response to the museum's previous function as a railway warehouse and engaged its audience with the site's history, *AudioZone* played on the expectations of visitors to a 'major show of interactive art' by constructing a parallel 3D audio world (only heard through headsets), which stroked, seduced and ultimately manipulated the viewer, irreverently encouraging participants to question just who is in command.

All this work is of a hybrid, cross-disciplinary nature, and threads together hitherto unexamined and unconnected issues surrounding interactivity, art and technology, public art and intervention. New technologies in particular throw up as many questions as they do opportunities. There is much to be researched, documented and investigated. If one accepts that communication is the goal of interactive and public artwork, it becomes clear that the questions to be asked concern not merely what these technologies can do for the artist, but in what contexts they can be used; and how, if used effectively, they may serve to bridge the gap between artist and viewer, providing a forum for mutually participatory forms of creativity, questioning and communication, and a re-examination of the role of author.

Susan Collins

Pedestrian Gestures
1994, installation, 3 computers, 3 video projectors, speakers, infra-red sensors

Evolved from ideas developed while working on the Woolwich Foot Tunnel piece, *Pedestrian Gestures* is also based on interpersonal communications in public spaces (and lack of it), with the images and sounds seeking to question and explore aspects of our often unconscious daily exchanges with both strangers and our surroundings. The piece is made up of a number of encounters, intimate in both nature and scale. Animated eyes, mouths, hands and verbal utterances examine the gesture as a form of communication. Viewers encounter short photographic and audio snippets as unexpected moments in their day, inadvertently choreographing their own experience of the work, with the sensors triggering a variety of audio and animated responses. Surveillance in reverse.

AudioZone
1994, 3D (virtual) audio and video installation, 3 computers, 3 video projectors, 3 infra-red sensors, 5 CD players, 8 infra-red transmitter/headphones

Throughout the gallery, various audio zones lie in wait for the visitor, who – via his/her headset – can tune in to a number of possible narrative pathways through a shifting maze of sound. Cajoling instructions, sounds and ephemeral video projections combine to seduce the viewer in a captivating experience where the listener is both hunter and hunted, and can never quite gain control. *AudioZone* fills the gallery with a rich, reverberant installation work for the inside of your head.

Biography

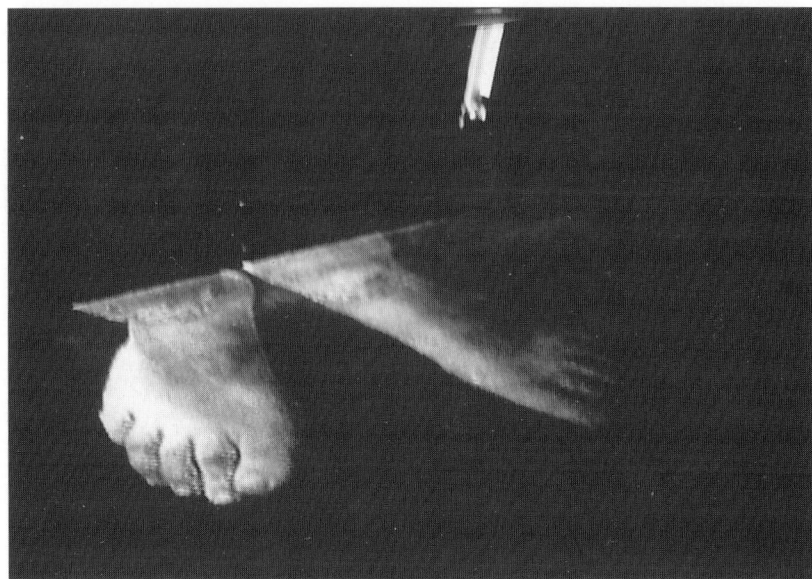

Born 1964, London. Studied Fine Art at the
Slade School of Art; Art and Technology at
the Art Institute of Chicago; Research
Fellow in Interactive Media and West Surrey
College of Art and Design; Fine Art PhD in
progress at University of Reading; American
Association of University Women
International Fellowship 1990: Fulbright
Travel and Professional Enhancement
Awards 1990-91. Screenings include:
Siggraph 92, London Film Festival, Museum
of Modern Art Rio de Janeiro, Institute of
Contemporary Arts London, Japan Graphic
Design Association Tokyo, Berlin VideoFest.
Site specific commissions in Glasgow, Hull,
Liverpool, London and Manchester.

ABOVE:
**PEDESTRIAN
GESTURES**

Lei
Cox

Lei Cox's work exists on the cusp between video art and the new, undefined and fledgling forms being thrown up by the collision of new technologies within the field of electronic imaging. His work does not sit neatly within the framework of traditional video art, even though it frequently exists in the form of video installation; it can be equally considered as an electronic painting, or a photograph – indeed, electronically generated photographs are frequently part of any presentation of his work.

Cox uses the tools provided by video and computer technologies to create images of the impossible and improbable. Fantasies of the inner mind are made tangible. Movement is subjugated to an organic principle rather than used to unfold a passage of time through sequential events; traditional narrative is a form that Cox eschews. Instead, he creates worlds and microcosms, new creatures that are hybrids of the imagination, but which also reflect the hybridisation of the technology he uses. Many of his ideas are rooted within our common mythologies such as that of Adam and Eve, clearly exemplified in *The Sufferance* (1993). However, his use of these concepts goes beyond past and present, hinting at the potential evolutionary paths of our future.

Jane Rigby

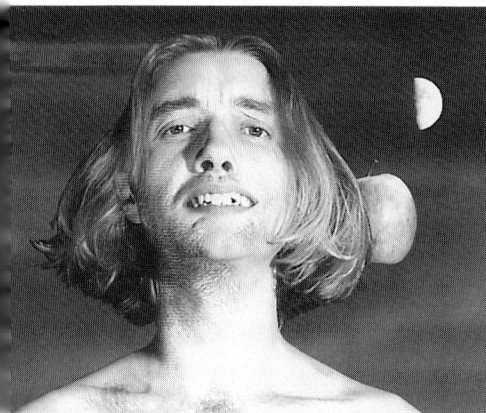

ABOVE:
THE SUFFERANCE

Biography

Born 1965, Kettering, Northamptonshire. Currently Lecturer at the School of Film and Television, Duncan of Jordanstone College of Art, Dundee, Scotland. Exhibition of installations include Video Positive, Liverpool; European Media Art Festival, Osnabrück; Clermont Ferrand; The Third Eye Centre, Glasgow. Single screen tapes have been exhibited internationally since 1986 and broadcast in France, Germany, Finland, The Netherlands, Japan and by the BBC. Also a photographer and music composer, including compositions for television documentaries and arts programmes.

Key works

The Sufferance
1993, installation, 3min cycle, 7 monitors, 7 players

The Sufferance is based around a form of self-inflicted crucifixion. It is not necessarily the crucifixion of Christ but a form of enjoyment, a punishment and warning for contemporary man and woman. There are however, overtones of a zen-like optimism of continual growth with hints of rebirth. The piece directly follows on from my video portrait work and in some ways is a full, life size video painting. It is partly an autobiographical and partly a universal statement.

LC

Magnification Maximus
1991, installation, 6min cycle, 4–16 monitors, 4 players

A multi monitor installation with quadraphonic sound, a hard-hitting ecological message and grotesque imagery of mutant sheep and screaming humans.

34

Key works

Disclaimer

1993, 5min, colour, video

The face of a woman is set in a smaller frame within the monitor frame. She repeats the familiar copyright law phrase "The characters and events portrayed in this videotape are entirely fictional. Any resemblance etc..." with increasing emotion, almost to the point of hysteria until cautioned by an offscreen voice that she is over-emoting. Minimal, effective and compulsively repetitious, this work indicates Curran's fascination with the duplicity of language and emotion-as-performance.

Amami Se Vuoi

1994, 4min, video

A young man is stretched out across the screen, naked; another approaches, bends over the first and begins to spit into his lover's open mouth. The naked boy strains to receive these liquid gifts in an agony of desire. His willingness to submit to what might be interpreted as a form of abuse reflects on the narrow definitions of eroticism the heterosexual norm dictates and the brutal frontality of the performance contrasts with the rose-tinted, soft focus depictions of romantic love in the media mainstream.

Catherine Elwes

Over a five year period, and while at Duncan of Jordanstone College of Art, Dundee and the Jan Van Eyck Akadamie in Maastricht, Michael Curran has fashioned a highly individual approach to video that combines elements of performance with an acute sense of stucture, diced with a resolute exploraton of sexual identities. Early tapes such as *Double* (1993) and *Disclaimer* (1993) are almost sister-pieces in that both share a to-camera frontality of performance staged in chroma-keyed frames set deep within the monitor frame. Calling on familiar registers of the image somewhere between pixelvision camera quality and the intimate otherness of the passport photo-booth, these pieces announce Curran's thematic and structural predelictions for the obsessive and repitious. Repetition in the videos ranges from a simple, increasingly insistent and emotive recitation of the copyright control phrase in *Disclaimer*, in which the logical absurdity of the legal provision "The characters and events portrayed in this videotape are entirely fictional. Any resemblance etc..." that traditionally accompanies fiction film becomes in itself a piece full of emotive possibilities for the actress giving it her best gulp-and-weep routine, to the use of classic romantic pop in *Larynx* (1993) and *L'Heure Autosexuelle* (1994) as both backround and pop-culture catalysts for silent, perversely ritualised performance pieces.

Works such as *Echo, Mutter* and *Translation* (all 1993), treat sound, and more particularly the human voice as a disembodied, double echo (with narcissism as an underlying component) caught in circuits of solipsism that the works suggest are inseperable from other constituent psychic elements of selfhood. In his most recent works, *L'Heure Autosexuelle* and *Amami Se Vuoi* (1994), in which sexuality is treated as alternately a bleakly humorous and dangerously confrontational ritual, the element of physical performance is reprised and developed, with the artist himself fairly, squarely and full-frontally a participant. These works promise further engaging austerity to come.

Chris Darke

Biography

Born 1963, Dalmuir, Scotland. Studied Foundation at CAT Newcastle 1982, Sculpture and Video Camden Institute 1988, BA Fine Art Goldsmiths College 1991, Post Graduate Diploma in Electronic Imaging Duncan of Jordanstone College of Art. Since 1993 at Jan Van Eyck Akademie, Maastricht. Exhibitions include: No Please Don't Stop Now (with Monika Oeschler, Whitechapel Open Studios); This Side of the Channel and Fresh (Film and Video Umbrella); European Media Art Festival, Osnabrück; Points de Vue, Centre Georges Pompidou.

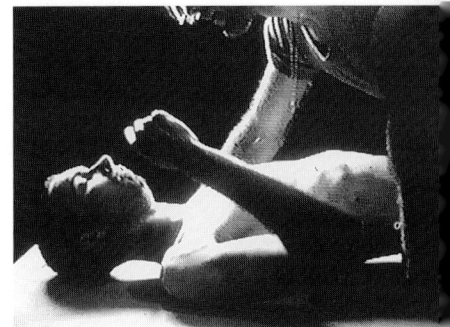

ABOVE:
AMAMI SE VUOI

Nina
Danino

There is a sense in which all of Nina Danino's films represent journeys of one sort or another, most literally in *Close To Home* (1985). This film is also the most specific in terms of place: place as home, place as refuge, place as exile. The main section, filmed from a car travelling through the streets of West Berlin, is contained within two sequences of footage of Gibraltar – where the film-maker grew up – shot from a departing ferry. Both locations were at the time of filming – though no longer – under blockade. The real site under surveillance, however, is internal: the expeditions of these films seem to be undertaken primarily as a gendered subject and the points on the map are through time, fixing on displacement, loss, the entry into the territory of the feminine, and on the connections between (matriarchal) generations.

Danino's soundtracks give prominence to a narrative voice, and it is her own voice that she uses, deliberately, measuring each intonation. Her narratives offer up fragments of what is said, but equally important are the pauses and intakes of breath that lie in between. They have their visual equivalents in terms of pace, rhythm and pitch. *First Memory* (1981), originally a two-screen, tape-slide piece, is characterised by its lack of image, its blank spaces. It reveals confined and confining space, glimpses of decor picked out of the darkness as if by torchlight while, at similar intervals, the slightly hesitant narrator releases discrete memories.

Biography

Born 1955, Gibraltar. Studied Painting at St Martin's School of Art 1973–77, Environmental Media at the Royal College of Art 1978-81. Co-editor of Undercut, the journal for experimental film and video. Visiting lecturer at Sheffield Hallam University and currently at Camberwell College of Art, London. Screenings include Tate Gallery, London; National Film Theatre, London; Whitechapel Gallery, London; Arsenal Cinema, Berlin; Pacific Film Archives, University of California at Berkeley; The Pleasure Dome, Toronto; L'Entrepot, Paris; Channel Four Television; Kunst Kanaal, The Netherlands; SBS-TV, Australia. British Council travel bursaries 1982 and 1994.

Close To Home
1985, 28min, b&w, 16mm

Filmed in a still divided (West) Berlin, *Close To Home* registers the most famous sights of the city. Rather than mapping out the geography of the city, it is a seamless, non-stop, disorientating journey, cordoning off an already walled-in place. The second half of the film is a sequence of shots of Gibraltar from a departing ferry. The time/place disconnections between the voice and the image set up a narrative of displacement which unfolds as the slow-paced measure of distance marked by the circulation of the car journey and the track of the ship's wake. The film builds up a melancholia of loss for home as an unlocatable place and for a lost identity.

Stabat Mater
1990, 8min, colour, 16mm

A re-reading of the eternal feminine of Chapter 16 of James Joyce's *Ulysses*. A short oracion, in the form of a triptych – iconographic space for the religious representation of the maternal in Western art – a main panel containing fluid light-camera skipping which bursts out of the frame, shattering the perspective of vision, framed by the blue and the white spacing of the Madonna and opened and closed by two songs, laments sung during holy week to the Mater Dolorosa. The frenetic hand held images define the movement of the body, the slipping cadences of the song enunciate the upper body and throat, the breathlessness of unpunctuated speech evokes the eroticism of the body – a maternal, homoerotic body. It attempts to locate a lost territory, unrecouperable mother – site of plenitude and loss.

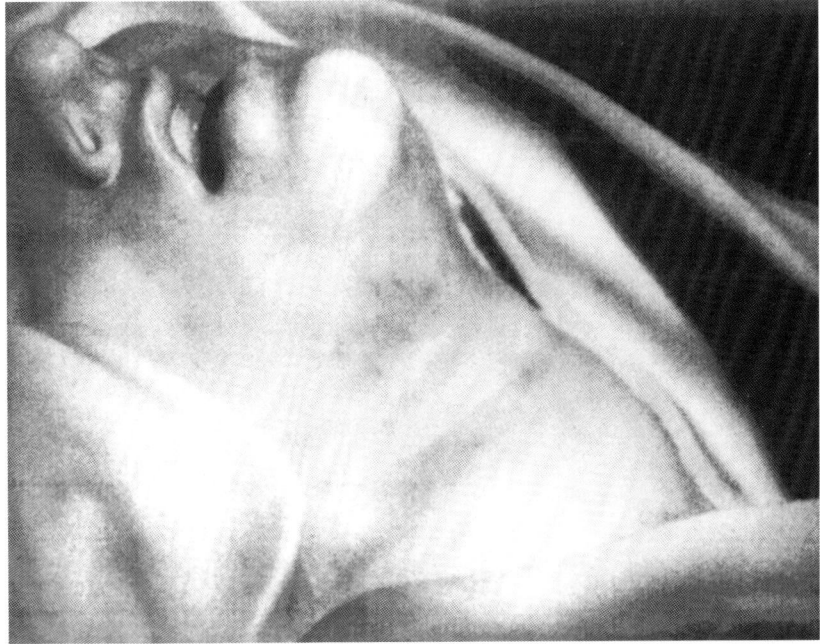

"Now I am yours"

1993, 30min, colour, 16mm

Using images of the Mass, intertitles, a garden of fragments of Xeroxed photographs, close-ups of flowers and epitaphs, and with central images of the famous Bernini sculpture *The Ecstasy of St Teresa* in Rome, the film constructs a narrative in sequences which is like a passage or event which struggles with language, identity, separation of death, loss and mourning. In the rich gilt and marble of the Baroque, the colour saturation of the Super8 Mediterranean flowers and the reach of impossible vocal pitch, it cross-fertilises themes of uncontainable excess. This garden is a place of opposites – the drive to death and pull to life – a push and pull – a borderlines territory. Teresa is petrified in stone, but the film attempts to 'resurrect' her to life. The corpse is also the beloved for whom the film and its soundtrack is a mourning cry of lament.

In *Close To Home*, the most methodical of her films, a woman's voice intones, one by one, the chronological stages of Berlin's division using correct official phraseology. Meanwhile the camera, from its fixed position in the moving car, picks out its landmarks without revealing the city's layout. The effect is disorientating, alienating with connotations of leaving, missing home. Danino's more recent work is much looser in character, integrating on the one hand, vivid, saturated colour and highly fluid, gestural camera-work and, on the other, a breakdown of grammatical speech patterns. *Stabat Mater* (1990) opens and closes with two sung laments, then launches into a breathless torrent of words and phrases, a re-reading of the eternal feminine of Joyce's *Ulysses*, which echoes the exultant/feverish swoop of the camera through a Mediterranean landscape.

It is important to note that sound and image do not exactly match or reinforce one another in Danino's films; rather they alternate, one taking over where the other leaves off. The emphasis on language and its borders and limitations, on what cannot be said, ties in with her theoretical base, her preoccupation with the nature of subject and identity. In her recent work, *"Now I am yours"* (1993), her choice of Bernini's statue in Rome – *The Ecstasy of St Teresa* – as a site for struggle, a resuscitation attempt on the inanimate via speech and camera, ties in precisely with these concerns.

Jo Comino

Tacita
Dean

Tacita Dean's major work to date, *The Martyrdom of Saint Agatha (in several parts)* (1994), is a speculative, inquiring and shyly humourous examination of the cult of sainthood. Le Cas Agatha, as one might imagine the French calling the history of this unfortunate saint, is a very particular case and fascinates Dean as much for its traces as for its facts. Or, rather, fascinates her because of the facts of those traces – in Agatha's case, her "three known pairs of breasts...recorded in the Book of Relics." The reading of the story that Dean proffers is one made rich by a willingness to take the associative path, signalling – but not always exploring – the resonances it has for religious iconography, the Western tradition of high art and the contemporary psychoanalytic and socio-historical interpretations thereof. Combining documentary location footage of Catania in Sicily with dramatised scenes of nuns packaging plaster reproductions of the breasts, Dean's voice-over acts with the image-track to question the techniques of representation of Sainthood, looking for the uncanny and the repressed denied by the religious ethos sanctioned by such art. With the combination of high-angle shots, circling camera movements and framings Dean employs in shooting the packaging sequence, allied to the voice-over disquisition on the art of the altar-piece that suggests that Sainthood might be "the ultimate vanity", there is a vital suggestion of humility in her approach that recognises the interrogative and therefore indefinite nature of her own venture in film.

Chris Darke

The Martyrdom of Saint Agatha
1994, colour, 14min, 16mm

Through a combination of drama and documentary this film investigates the cult of the Third Century Sicilian Martyr, Saint Agatha and the relics of her martyrdom, her breasts. Employing a quizzical, investigative voice-over and an image-track that alternates between straightforward location footage of the region of Sicily in which Agatha was martyred, suggestive shots of an iron foundry and staged shots of nuns packaging the breasts as icons of sainthood, the film ruminates on the relationship between art and religion, gender and representation.

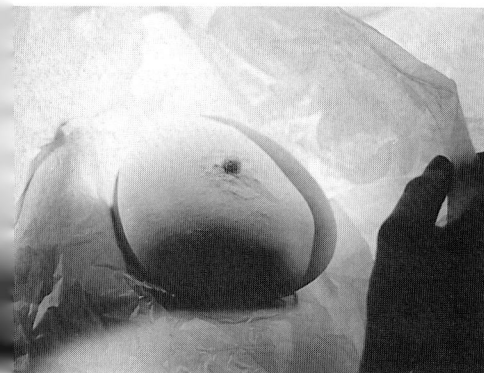

Born 1965. BA Falmouth School of Art & Design 1988, Greek Government Scholarship 1988-89, MA Slade School of Fine Art 1992. Barclays Young Artist Award 1993. Exhibitions include: BT New Contemporaries 1992 (Award); 'Watt' Witte de With/Kunsthall Rotterdam; Galerija Skuc, Ljubljana; 'Mise En Scene', ICA Gallery 1994. Part time lecturer in photography, University of Wolverhampton 1993–4; Artist in Residence, Ecole Nationale les Beaux Arts, Bourges, France 1995.

LEFT:
THE MARTYRDOM OF SAINT AGATHA (IN SEVERAL PARTS)

Mike
Dunford

Key works

Still Life With Pear

1974, 12min, b&w, 16mm

A strict method for the filming was used as a basis, or a model, for the real event. The actuality inevitably did not follow the model and thus the model and the actuality could be seen to reveal one another, and the filming process, in all its implications, to be exposed through the errors and adaptations. The film being viewed as much more encompassing than the physical entity of the film itself. The use of a still life, the archetypal subject of classical art, formed a focus around which to visually discuss the divergencies of a time-based art.

MD

Nohi Abassi

1989, 15min, colour, video

The intellectual core of *Nohi Abassi* is an oral text by Levi-Strauss documenting a myth of creation from the rain forests of Guinea-Bissau. The reading of this story by an African woman is one subtext, another being the somewhat baleful nature of capitalism's high-technology and its ideology of determinism. The exploitation of video technology, and a layering process creates a counterpoint between the two subtexts, one subverting the other, potentially pointing to the similarity in philosophical end-point of the two world views. Other levels include notions of storytelling, affective space, naturalism, video-space and abstract structuring.

The politics of structuralist film lay within the relationship of film-as-process to viewer, and the politicising and critiquing of that relationship, resulting in the attempt to create a film construct that would not replicate the ideological patterns of expectation, re-presentation and reception of industrial cinema. Films of mine that fall into this mode most clearly are *In the Dark* (1975), *Arbitrary Limits* (1974), *Still Life with Pear* (1974).

The early part of my video work began at a point where I had become active politically and so took the form of a kind of elliptical propaganda, but more recent work has returned to earlier themes, with the difference that in the intervening period, the video or film-work as a virtual construct has been more widely accepted within the commercial field, and the disjunctions of an earlier period are now the grammar of modern entertainment. One of the features of some English structuralist film work was the necessity of the active involvement of the viewer; a conventionally passive viewing produced only frustrated incomprehension. In my video work I try to maintain this stance, and I am also interested in working on several different levels in the work that do not reinforce one another, but allow combinations of meaning to emerge. I have been trying to work in a manner in which the various elements of a videotape are put into play rather than being ordered to one particular narrative end. Work best representing this would be *Nohi Abassi* (1989) and *Windless Closure* (1993).

Mike Dunford

Biography

Born 1946. Studied Sculpture at Goldsmith's College, London 1964–68; studied Film at the Royal College of Art, London 1974–76. Lived in San Francisco 1977–82; video artist since 1981. Screenings include Knokke Festival, Belgium; Serpentine Gallery, London; London Film Festival; touring programmes in The Netherlands, Germany and USA.

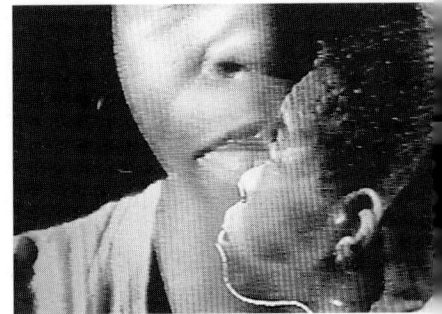

ABOVE:
NOHI ABASSI

Alnoor
Dewshi

Alnoor Dewshi's films are a celebration of hybridity, the cultural collisions and collusions of the dis-United Kingdom at the end of the twentieth century. "Where I come form we don't worry about where we come from." A quick and reflexive irony is secreted to lubricate the contradictions and complexities of an ambiguous reality: "Knocking back the cappuccinos and talking about post-colonial depression." "Post-coital depression more like..."

There is a striking tableau-like construction in some of the shots of *Latifah and Himli's Nomadic Uncle* (1992); an elaborate style and design to each sequence, combining the loose camera movements which follow Latifah and Himli through the streets with beautiful static shots of ethereal tents – which perhaps has its origins in Dewshi's exquisitely drawn storyboard. The implications of the nomadic are placed incongruously in the static, vertical modern city: "Solivitur ambulando. It is solved by walking." (Bruce Chatwin *The Songlines*)

Whilst in *Latifah and Himli's Nomadic Uncle*, irony moves through the entirely non-sync dialogue of the two young women and their ambivalent critique of "the way things are", in *The Airwave Spectrum Has Some Defections* (1989), a sharp sarcasm is created through a voice over of witty and alliterative assonance. The intentional double entendre in the title signals his earlier film's sharp response to the deluge of insistent implacable triviality that is broadcast across the airwaves. The use of the term 'defect' also connects with a counter-aesthetic of roughness – the scratches and high contrast of refilmed black and white demonstrate a strategy which directly challenges the spurious notions of 'professional quality' that surround the original television material. The claustrophobic airwave spectrum is in drastic need of cultural and political diversification. "Why, oh why, do they fill the sky with recurrent beams which pierce our dreams?" There is an even sharper irony that, like many other independent film-makers before him, several years after making *The Airwave Spectrum* at the London Film-makers' Co-op, Dewshi found himself working for the television industry, as an assistant producer for BBC's Tomorrow's World.

Coming form the cultural interstices of a disorientated Britain at the end of the millennium, Alnoor Dewshi represents a new generation of independent film-makers. The three films completed at this early stage of his short filmography indicate an exceptionally adept deployment of irony and an elegance of mind offering much promise.

Rod Stoneman

The Airwave Spectrum Has Some Defections
1989, 4min, b&w, 16mm

The Airwave Spectrum constructs a critique of the power and influence that television exerts, with specific reference to its representation of racial minorities. Shot in grainy black and white in a mix of film and video, the film intercuts hand-held shots of a broken television set with animated sequences of Action Man dolls and 'scratch' extracts of television footage and sound. [...] *The Airwave Spectrum* deconstructs the power of the medium by offering an oppositional view to the mainstream images of racial stereotyping that the medium pumps out.

Tim Highstead

Latifah and Himli's Nomadic Uncle
1992, 15min, b&w, 16mm

This is not a road movie but a pavement movie following the wanderings and wonderings of two South Asian women. The casually witty metaphor of nomads illustrates an emerging British identity. Nomads live in the industrialised world but do not belong to it: they adapt to it. Long ago they learned the skill of synthesising culture as a strategy for survival. Latifah and Himli echo the nomads' dilemma: should they retain their freedom or settle in the City? Shot in London, but set in a mythological and cinematically ambiguous time and place, the film is 'nomadic' in shape: it wanders from inconsequential anecdote to ironic insight – a journey through images of nomadic impulses and sensibilities.

Alnoor Dewshi

Biography

Born 1964, London. Studied Mathematics and Philosophy at Bristol University. Screenings include London Film Festival; Edinburgh Film Festival; Birmingham Film Festival; Innovation '93 – The Manchester International Film Forum; British Short Film Festival. *The Airwave Spectrum Has Some Defections*: ICA Biennial: 'Between Imagination and Reality'; *Latifah and Himli's Nomadic Uncle*: DICK Award Winner 1992; broadcast by Channel Four in 1993 as part of the Midnight Underground season.

TOP:
THE AIRWAVE SPECTRUM
BOTTOM:
LATIFAH AND HIMLI'S NOMADIC UNCLE

Vivienne
Dick

Vivienne Dick's Super8 films, dating from the mid 1970s in New York, through *London Suite* (1989) to the recent *A Skinny Little Man Attacked Daddy* (1994), are points on the itinerary of an Irish film-maker, born in rural Donegal, who has worked in two of the world's largest metropolises. In these different places she explores the cultural dislocations of individuals oscillating in unstable identities, creating a kind of urban ethnography of different groups living at the edge of the city. She has been enshrined in the (largely American) textbooks as 'post-feminist punk New York underground' and there are interesting shifts between the Super8 American films, produced on no budget, and those produced in England, in terms of the different contexts of production (more consistent funding and 16mm) and reception (college screenings and television transmission).

The construction of *London Suite* and *New York Conversations* (1991), gives rise to an underlying oxymoron: exact looseness. Despite its often digressive movement, there is a real precision in the films' underlying structure and editing. Like the unattached narratives of German film-maker Alexander Kluge, stories slide into stories, seemingly unfocused dialogue dissolves into interview, anecdote and parable. There is also a continuity between the work made in America and in England – uninhibited performances for the camera, whether highlighting New York underground stars or the motley bunch of friends assembled in *London Suite*. Their exhibitionist self-exposure calls to mind Ken Jacobs' seminal *Little Stabs at Happiness* and Andy Warhol's early work. This confessional psychodrama is a marvellous exploration of the weird and the strange which refuses a simple division between the factual and the fictional.

A Skinny Little Man Attacked Daddy represents a return, a settling of psychic accounts with her family and place of origin. The rural social landscape in Donegal contrasts with textures of 'big city' life in this gentle investigation into inherited identity and the route to mortality. The boundaries between the home movie and television social documentary are dissolved in an exploration of everyday life, as the film performs devastatingly honest open-heart surgery and tries to understand an individual experience, a personal version of the 'family system' from the inside.

Rod Stoneman

She Had Her Gun All Ready
1978, 30min, Super8

With Lydia Lunch and Pat Place, and set in the Lower East Side, NYC, this is a film about unequal power between two people (of any gender), or the repressive side of a person in conflict with the sexual powerful side. Karyn Kay calls it "..the contemporary unspeakable: women's anger and hatred of women at the crucial moment of overpowering identification and obsessional thralldom." Jim Hoberman of *Village Voice* listed it as one of the ten best films of 1979.

Beauty Becomes the Beast
1979, 45min, colour, Super8

Lydia Lunch plays both a rebellious teenager and a five year old in a film which looks at gender roles, sexual repression and violence. "To the intermittent screaming on the sound-track, Lunch journeys from ocean front to East Village tenement flat with a rubber baby doll, fights in front of her televsion set, and is besieged by grimacing, freakout monsters. The film, a complex, fragmentary assemblage of female images, plotlessly switches scenes and moods like a bored TV-watcher flipping the dial. It's horrifying, funny, poignant, enraged."

Jim Hoberman

London Suite

1989, 28min, colour, 16mm

London's cultural diversity unfolds as Vivienne Dick portrays her friends, their lifestyles, what they talk about and how they talk. In this kaleidoscopic arrangement of encounters and re-enactments, equal weight is given to the passionate and the banal. The camera's sudden hops from one reality to another and the disjointed conversations are drawn together by the musical score and the film's internal rhythm.

A Skinny Little Man Attacked Daddy

1994, 23min, colour, video

A look at the family and place where I grew up. So much of what is 'me' comes from attitudes, expectations, fears, habits, beliefs that I inherited from my parents (and they in turn from theirs). My work is to try to know myself because that is the only way I can let go of and accept my past.

VD

Biography

Born 1950, Ireland. BA in French and Archaeology, University College, Dublin. Lived in New York 1977-82 and began making films in 1977 taking courses at the Millennium Film Workshop and The Downtown Community TV Centre. Taught film-making at Rathmines College Dublin, 1982-85. Based in London since 1985. Distributed by Film-makers' Co-op NYC and Abao A Kou Paris. Screenings include Walker Arts Centre; Anthology Film Archives; Cal Arts; Whitney Biennial; Galway Film Fleadth; Cork Film Festival; Sydney Festival of Irish Film-makers 1991. *3am*: ICA Biennial: 'Arrows of Desire'.

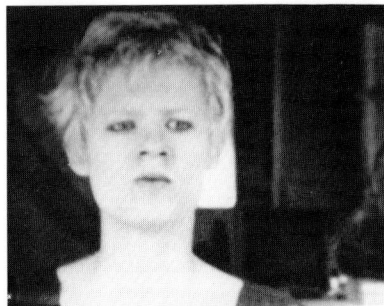

FROM TOP:
LYDIA LUNCH,
PAT PLACE IN
SHE HAD HER GUN
ALREADY
TWO STILLS FROM
A SKINNY LITTLE MAN
ATTACKED DADDY

Willie
Doherty

As in all his photo/text works since the late 1980s, and in the tape/slide projection installations since *Same Difference* in 1990, Doherty's source material refers directly to the conflict in Northern Ireland and in particular to the border zone in and around Derry where he lives. But what he is reflecting on is true of all war zones, of many border areas where limits between the Self and Other are felt to break down, where the role of victim and assassin become fluid and often interchangeable, where fear and paranoia take over, where tribal struggle and clichéd views of binary opposition (good/evil; same/different; coloniser/ colonised) supplant recognition of human complexity and critical awareness of the structures of language. Laying bare and opening up the restricted nature of the language of conflict, a language which has been constructed to control and simplify people's experience to encompass and restrict the possibilities of solution, lies at the core of Doherty's research as an artist. Within the attempt to create works which make the viewer aware of the stereotypes by which experience in Northern Ireland is determined, his work has had to deal with the language of the news media (newspapers, billboards, posters); with the nature of colonialist discourse in connection with paranoia, fear of the wilderness and loss of identity; with the subsequent development of mechanisms of surveillance and control; with the characteristics of community-bonding and of identification – both individual and collective; with borderline situations where psychological, physical and cultural limits blur.

But such topics are not dealt with from the outside. Doherty allows no external, detached modernist viewer into his world. His works use, instead, rhetorical devices from photography and cinema, able to prompt the viewer into identification and projection. He recreates conditions where stereotypical reactions such as fear, aggressiveness, desire for revenge, condemnation, victimisation, romantic heroism, political and religious fanaticism are felt, at times even embarrassingly, by the viewer. The eye of the camera becomes our own eye, hidden behind bushes on a hill, peering surreptitiously through the branches down at a town below, as in *Protecting/Invading* (1987). We are in hiding, or perhaps we are about to attack. We do not know if we are being watched. We cannot see the Other.

Carolyn Christov-Bakargiev *At the End of the Day*
(British School at Rome, 1994).

The Only Good One is a Dead One
1993, installation, 30min cycle,
2 video projectors, 2 players

Belying the long arm of its impact, *The Only Good One is a Dead One* is a simple project: a darkened room, empty but for two videos projected on adjacent walls accompanied by a voice-over. A rambling tape-loop speech, the soundtrack documents the interior monologue of a man vacillating between being the hunter and the hunted, between a vivid fear of becoming the victim of assassination and a violent fantasy of carrying out a murder himself. Although like all Doherty's work, the piece is clearly a meditation on the murky malevolence of the political troubles in his native Northern Ireland, *The Only Good One is a Dead One* works on less specific and more widely engaging levels as well, activating deep-seated universal emotions by playing off the paranoia, anger and desperation that lurks inside all of us at one time or another.

Jeffrey Kastner *Willie Doherty*

At the End of the Day

1994, installation, 30min cycle,
1 video projector, 1 player

The main reference is to the peace process underway since late August 1994 when the IRA, through Sinn Fein and the Social Catholic and Labour Party, unilaterally declared a cease-fire, strongly supported by the Irish and British governments in search of what the media describe as a 'permanent' peace settlement. Doherty more specifically addresses the problems of a visual language which has not been allowed to evolve out of the stereotypes of conflict in tandem with the political evolution. A one-minute view of driving along a road and coming to an abrupt stop at a road-block near the border, is incessantly repeated – a metaphor of frustration, of wanting to make progress but not being able to, a reference to a level of conflict that will continue to exist and that cannot be 'permanently' eradicated – even through a new mediated language of a 'permanent' peace is being constructed through a philosophical notion improperly appropriated by the political sphere.

Carolyn Christov-Bakargiev *At the End of the Day* (British School at Rome, 1994).

Biography

Born 1959, Derry, Northern Ireland. BA Sculpture, Ulster Polytechnic. Works in photography, installation and video. Installations include: *Siren*, A.R.E. Belfast 1982; *Stone Upon Stone*, Redemption Gallery Derry 1986; *The Town of Derry*, ARE Belfast 1987; *Unknown Depths*, Ffotogallery Cardiff 1990; *Imagined Truths*, Oliver Dowling Gallery Dublin 1990; *Same Difference*, Matt's Gallery, London 1990; *They're All The Same*, Centre for Contemporary Art, Warsaw. Solo shows in Paris, New York, Rome, Zurich etc. *The Only Good One is a Dead One*: Turner Prize shortlist 1994, Tate Gallery. Shortlisted for IMMA/Glen Dimplex Award 1994.

Steven
Dwoskin

Steven Dwoskin, though American, is a founding father of today's English avant-garde, as both an early organiser of the London Film-makers' Co-op, and a creative presence through 30 years, despite being disabled by polio in childhood, and directing/photographing from crutches or, latterly, a wheelchair. His films often centre on poise and pretence breaking down under frustrations, boredoms, ignominies – a woman's drift into masturbation in *Alone* (1964), the fantasticated self-images and seething resentments of *Central Bazaar* (1976), the humiliations, wryly borne, of the handicapped in *Behindert* (1974). His work falls into three phases. 1961–71 saw the short, formally 'tight' films, *Alone* and *Chinese Checkers* (1964) being, to my mind, his masterpieces. 1971–81 brought the longer, dramatic films pulsed by calligraphic camera-rovings over stories somewhere between 'happenings' and fringe theatre: *Dyn Amo* (1972) from Chris Wilkinson's play, *Death and the Devil* (1973) from Wedekind, with Carola Regnier, Wedekind's grand-daughter. Since 1983 his films have started from more objective, 'public' subjects – other artists, campaigns by the disabled – while remaining essays in sensibility.

Dwoskin's disability tightens the spring of a deeper inspiration. Often his films comprise a strictly limited situation within which uneasily controlled behaviour is intensively scrutinised; faces in close-up become psycho-physiological landscapes. If, in the early films, the exchange of looks between camera and player, and a certain temps-mortism, generate a 'fixity', inspiring comparisons with Andy Warhol, their aesthetic was never minimalist nor derisive, but highly elaborated, and by an inquisitorial curiosity, about fleeting, involuntary, spontaneous, detail: the camera transcribing, not just eye-movements, but subtler shiftings and rovings of attention. Thus a lateral panning might rove through the uneasy flicker of an eye, the space between faces, background colour-blurs, the hang of a hand in mid-air, and a succession of such responses, to become, not a simple montage of surprises, but a musical structure, with elements human, plastic or abstract unfolding like themes in music (Mahler and Ives were influences). If his 'microdetail' interest can leave non-modernist spectators floundering, its intensification of peripheral perceptions achieves a wide-open-eye counterpart to Stan Brakhage's 'closed-eye vision', and are overdue for phenomenological/cognitive analysis.

Key works

Alone
1964, 13min, colour and b&w, 16mm

Alone is a major departure into projecting feelings and senses loneliness, timelessness and the sensual self. The film presents moments that are passing tones in any life, yet far from registering a passive despair, protests against a traditional culture which unable to confront such moments passes them by as both trivial and obscene.

Dyn Amo
1972, 120min, colour, 16mm

Dyn Amo is a 'drama' exploring the distinction a person's self and his/her projection of that self to others; and it is a 'horror movie' tragically suggesting how a projection can become more substantial than the self behind it. Its subjects are role-playing (especially sexual role-playing) and the masochism of playing a role that conforms to others exploitative interests.

Behindert (Hindered)
1974, 96min, colour, 16mm

The main intention of *Behindert* is to express (as far as possible) some of the subjective perspectives within the social/private confinements of a personal relationship as seen essentially from the point of view of the physically disabled person. The film is composed of personal events and the total film is an accumulation of these events into one tangible statement.

Outside In (Das Innere Bloss)
1981, 105min, colour, 16mm

Outside In is a combination of memories from the visual diary of a disabled person seen from his point of view: the visual impression left during the process of integration into the so called able-bodied society over twenty odd years of adulthood, transformed into visual metaphors.

SD

RIGHT:
DYN AMO

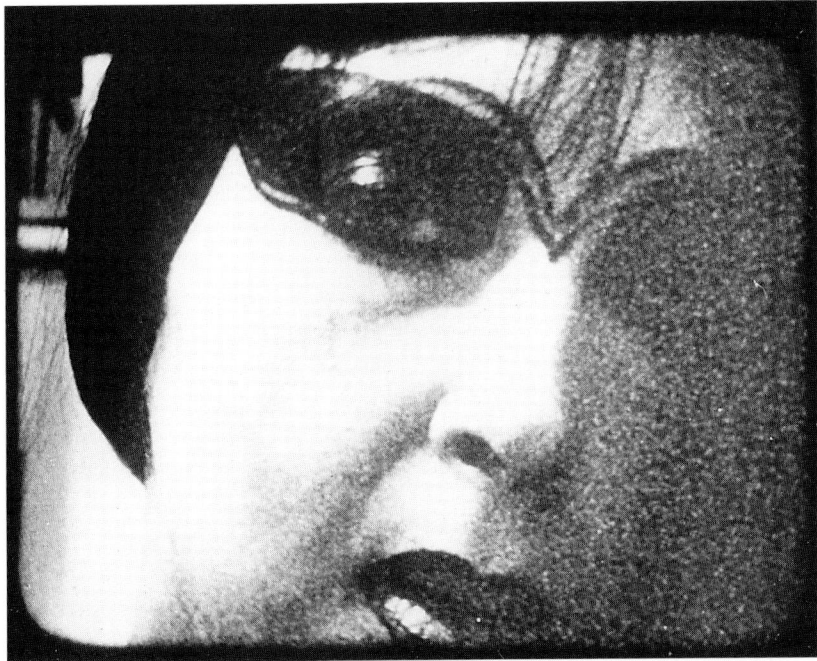

Born 1939, New York City. Studied at the Parsons School of Design and New York University. Freelance designer, photographer, film director and producer since 1959. Screenings include Cannes, Berlin, Rotterdam, Toronto, Lucarno, Pesaro, Mannheim, Oberhausen, Sydney, Melbourne, Hamburg, San Francisco, Turino, Riga. Films have been broadcast on Channel Four; ZDF-TV, Germany; INA, France; Radio-Television Suisse Romande, Switzerland; ARTE & La Sept, France. His collected works were awarded The Solvey Prize at the 4th International Experimental Film Festival, Knokke, Belgium in 1968 and Premiero Speciale for Cinema 'Noi, Glialtri' Italy. *Outside In* awarded L'Age d'Or prize Brussels Film Festival 1982. Has lectured at the London College of Printing; Royal College of Art, London; San Francisco Art Institute; San Francisco State University; University of Geneva; L'Ecole Superieure d'Art Visuel, Switzerland. A member of the Societé de Realisateurs de Film, France and the British Film Institute's Disability Committee.

His early films, with their bleak settings, forlorn faces, and studiedly harsh lighting, evoke the Beat phase of underground culture. His second phase fuses 'happenings', and their exploration of embarrassment, with spiritual influences from Georges Bataille. The recent documentaries are more accessible to a wider public.

Throughout his work, Dwoskin's formal patterns, now 'fixed', now restless, gratify partisans of 'concrete' and structural film. The interactions of camera-eye and players' looks-into-camera stimulate theorists of the male gaze, voyeurism, and related Lacanian notions; though Dwoskin relates his optical gluttony to a consideration of light as material substance (eg, colour bands like layers in a cake). The documentaries inaugurate 'block construction', with 'masses of duration' tensed against each other. *In Shadows from Light* (1983), Bill Brandt's still photographs, of nudes made monstrous by wide-angled lenses, are laid out beside each other like incompatible 'blocks' which Dwoskin's weaving camera re-relates. The film achieves a profound synthesis of another photographer's vision and its own, of past fixities and questing movement like an inconsolable present, of bleak expressionism, hard-edge (de)formalism and physical misproportion, seen, or rather felt, through tender and unsparing eyes.

Raymond Durgnat

Catherine Elwes

In women's art the address to a female viewer can be highly focused, often to the extent of speaking directly to specific groups – young women, old women, lesbians, mothers and daughters. For a long time this was considered to be structurally impossible. But in the context of a 30 year feminist history, the viewer can no longer be ascribed a fixed masculine identity any more than the canvas or the camera automatically represents a masculine point of view. Women can speak to one another one-to-one in art as they have always done in life.

Not only does the address of women's art speak one-to-one, but the content of the work often describes an individual experience of another human being – a mother, a son, a lover, even a specific oppressor. The political and economic forces of our society are still experienced by women through their individual relationships both inside and outside the home. The exploration of the personal, of one-to-one within a work of art, remains a potent expression of the feminist enterprise.

This conviction was central to the videos I made around my son Bruno Muellbauer. In the course of a seven-year collaboration, the narrative of the spoken word gradually gave way to a more poetic exploration of visual language and its ambiguities. The multiple narratives of sound, image, tempo, representation and abstraction interact and combine to create the meaning(s) of a tape.

My current work attempts to re-introduce the word – the word of the father, and in this case of a dead father who cannot speak for himself. Three 'surrogates' tell the stories of wartime exploits which each shared with him. The works examine masculinity, heroism, nostalgia and the father-daughter relationship which these profoundly influence.

There is a sense in which creativity is experienced as an act of defiance, which risks making us ugly, angry and treacherous – speaking what has been kept hidden. I am aware of courting beauty and the poetry of the visual image as a palliative to the dangerous woman I become in my guise as an artist.

Catherine Elwes

With Child
1984, 18min, colour, video

With Child is a highly controlled and precisely paced tape which manages to express a whole set of feelings, thoughts and desires: the nostalgia for the mother's own childhood through old toys and their simple mechanisms (clocks, music box, battered piano); the embodying of the future in the animated infant's clothes; fears of the doll/child as attacker, as threat, with flashing lights turning the doll into an uncanny object. Throughout, love and desire and the sexual act which initiated the pregnancy are represented by two cheeky soft-toy monkeys, who make love in a scene of wicked humour mixed with tenderness. *With Child* express a keen visual intelligence, a wit and realism born of working through fantasies not often acknowledged in women's visual work on the phenomenon of birth.

Michael O'Pray *Monthly Film Bulletin*

There Is a Myth
1984, 10min, colour, video

The conventional image of a mother suckling her child is deliberately frustrated, the breast is seen in close-up and the baby does not actually feed. There is no possibility of sentimentalising this scene, but the reality of the physical bond is established. The breast image is echoed in a passage where a woman sucks her thumb, intercut with a woman's mouth opening and shutting against a soundtrack of teeth snapping shut, perhaps an ironic metaphor for the castration fear expressed in the myth...this work contains a strong critique of conventional notions of mother-child relations. Elwes identifies an active physical love or desire quite unlike conventional notions of the mother's self-abnegation in her relationship with her child. Pleasure, Elwes suggests, may be the seat of women's power and men's traditional fear of it.

Catherine Kinley, *The Elusive Sign*

Autumn

1991, 18min, colour, video

This tape is the last in the *Three Seasons* series for Channel Four's Eleventh Hour programme. *Autumn* is a psychological landscape in which different facets of a woman's personality and experience are played out and resolved – if temporarily. Different elements in the landscape are at times malevolent or benign, symbols of creativity and fecundity or missiles of self-destruction. The real and the imagined are interchangeable, internal and external events fuse. The landscape is a canvas on which images are continually worked and reworked. They become analogous to the strength and resilience of the autumnal woman portrayed by the artist's sister Rosamund Elwes.

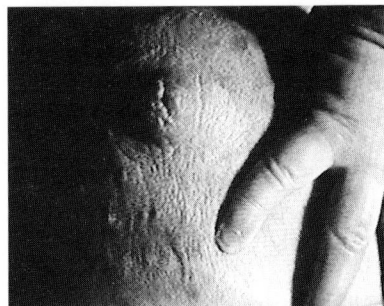

(Wishing) Well

1991, video installation

(Wishing) Well is a garden well built of natural stone in a darkened space, which the observer can look down into. From the depths of the well a video picture floats up accompanied by the voice of a child. The atmosphere is imploring, intimate and bewildering. It draws the observer into a maelstrom of thoughts and questions about interpersonal relationships, about unfamiliar forms of communication, even about one's own childhood, when, instead of a mirror image, the picture of a child is reflected up by the water.

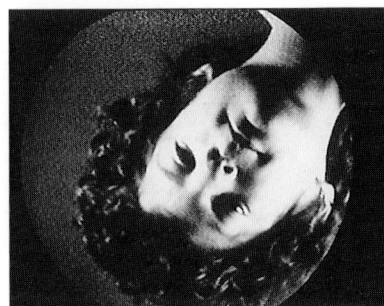

Petra Unnetzer

Biography

Born 1952, St Maixent, France. BA in Fine Art, Slade School of Art, London 1979; MA in Environmental Media, Royal College of Art, London 1982. Screenings include Berlin Film Festival; Video Biennale, Vienna; Video Positive, Liverpool; Trondheim Video Festival, Norway; Time-Based Arts, Amsterdam; Institute of Contemporary Arts, Boston; Museum for Contemporary Art, Basle; the Women's Research Centre, Bologna; the American Film Institute, Los Angeles. Tapes are in the collection of the National Gallery, Ottawa; Phoenix Video, Torino, Italy; Grey Suit, Cardiff. A member of the Women Artists' Collective 1976–81; co-organiser of the exhibitions 'Women's Images of Men' 1980 and 'About Time' 1980, Institute of Contemporary Arts, London. British Council travel grants 1979 and 1983. Reviews and essays in *Art Monthly*, *Feminist Art News* and *Performance*. Currently Head of Fine Art at Camberwell College of Art.

FROM TOP:
WITH CHILD
THERE IS A MYTH
WISHING WELL

Steve
Farrer

The Machine is simply a rotating camera. The shutter mechanism has been removed. Therefore it records everything. There is no stop/start, and a minimal play to the illusion achieved by the phenomenon of the persistence of vision. In its theatricality, it is reminiscent of the rotating platforms and projections of Piscator, and as with Warhol, Jack Smith, or whoever else is queer, what it records is as important and as 'different', as it is integral to the device. It will all be there, any movement, any thing, for the duration of the length the film runs.

Steve Farrer is a sculptor with film. *Ten Drawings* (1976) are drawn directly onto clear strips of celluloid. Spitting, crackling and shushing sounds make up the optical track. Farrer is happily locked into the structuralist/materialist mode. But with the increasingly punitive sense of 'denial' in mainstream formalism, he turns to the resource of diary films to express more earthly concerns. In *Real as a Dream* (1985) he fuses Ginsberg with flowing footage of Morocco. In 8mm or 35mm, *My First Gay Film!* (1984) or *Past Possessed* (1986), process, time-lapse and multiple exposure allow his sexuality to filter through. This becomes implicit in the cine-gauge material for The Machine. Between whirling images of landscapes and boats, Adam with flat top reclines, shirt half-opened, exuding maleness. In *Machine Tests* (1978–88), larger than life cartoon drawings of giant cocks whizz aggressively on and off. As the audience gathered eagerly round, blind as bats to the content, and thirsty only for the mechanism, The Machine vehicle stumbled to a halt, and the eponymous Mollies project began.

Anna Thew

Biography

Born 1952, Manchester. BA North East London Polytechnic 1976; MA Royal College of Art, Environmental Media 1978. London Film-makers' Co-op Workshop Organiser 1976-78 and Cinema Programmer 1980–81. Lecturer Wimbledon School of Art 1985–88. Camera operator and collaborator on works by Derek Jarman, Anna Thew, Isaac Julien and many others. Screenings include A Perspective on English Avant-Garde Film (international tour) 1978; Festival of Expanded Cinema, ICA 1976; Toulon XII Festival Jeune Cinema 1976. Exhibitions/Installations at the Diorama, London; Museum of Modern Art, Oxford; Middelburg, The Netherlands; Technologies et Imaginaires, Paris.

ABOVE:
MACHINE TESTS

Ten Drawings
1976, 20min, b&w, 16mm

This is a collection of ten short films. For each film, 50 x 18" strips of clear film were laid side by side to make a rectangle 18" x 36". A geometric shape was drawn on each rectangle and the strips of celluloid were joined to make a film. The sound is created by the image carried over into the soundtrack.

Machine Tests
1978-88, various lengths, colour and b&w, 35mm

Steve Farrer's Machine can be seen as a part of a return to the reinvention of cinema – its mechanisms of image transport, its projected possibilities and its spectator relations. This exploratory return extends to remaking the actual mechanisms of cinema – literally the frameline, gate and shutter – and to challenging its normative construction of movement in depth, the intermittent existence of narrative space. [...] Perhaps his *Machine Tests* also invoke the idea of 'the machine'; a constant focus of the externalised unconscious with its repetitive motor actions and drives (a fetishised displacement of sexuality/power?) from Kafka's *The Penal Colony* to Duchamp's *Bachelor Machines* and Claire Devers' *Blanc et Noir*. The grace of machinery that throws a relation between notion and motion onto a wall and thus makes a frieze move.

Rod Stoneman

Sera **Furneaux**

Lessness – Parts I, II & III
1986, 42min, colour, video

Lessness is shot in three separate sections with the camera remaining absolutely static throughout. A small naked child – the only protagonist in the tape – runs around an anonymous space. In *Part II* the space reveals white walls while in *Part III*, the child discovers herself in a round mirror placed on the ground. Inspired by Samuel Beckett's *Lessness*, this tape has the quality of a meditative dream.

Anxiety, Rest
1991, 12min, colour, video

The tape *Anxiety, Rest* is about putting pictures and words to sounds. It is organised around the definitions of anxiety and rest, taken from *The Penguin Medical Dictionary*, layman's dictionary. Sounds include Portuguese advertisements, Mazzy Star, Mozart, crashing glass, dripping faucets, rain and thunder, and Brahms' *Lullaby*. Images include: fish, a butterfly and flower, a souvenir snow scene, a honey bear, a medical eye dropper, an angry sheep, a dried puffer fish, and Rodin's *The Kiss*.

Simon Field

Sera Furneaux's videos alternate between a painterly concern with the image and a montage/collage aesthetic that plays image, sound and text off against each other. The painterly aspect of her work is manifest in tapes such as *Portrait* (1982) and *Portrayal* (1984), companion pieces that call upon classical conventions of portraiture which are extended and investigated through subtle editing and slow-motion effects. *Canvas* (1987) goes further in the same direction, moving from single sitter portraits to fully-fledged video tableaux vivants, where the elements of compositional precision, strong primary colours and the models' sculptural poses are enhanced by the effect of movement-in-stillness generated through a technical repertoire of slow-motion, wind-machines and camera reframings.

If Furneaux's attention to the painterly possibilities inherent in video includes a fascination with duration, this is given its most applied treatment in *Lessness – Parts I, II and III* (1986). At 42 minutes long, and with a three part structure punctuated by recurring fades-to-black, *Lessness* calls upon Beckett for its title and the post-apocalyptic connotations of its indoor lunar-landscape – a room, lit by ultramarine blue, with a floor of baked earth. A young child at loose in this otherworldy environment is examined – again, with slow-motion as the tape's principle motion-trope – as the principle of life itself, a combination of unselfconsciousness and, when presented with a mirror embedded in the earth, as an emergent consciousness of self. *Anxiety, Rest* (1991), Furneaux's most recent tape, appears to have relinquished the ravishing aestheticism of her earlier works, attending instead to an expressive, multi-layered and often humorous collage of image, sound and written text that seeks to give other symbolic and sensory dimensions to the workaday definitions of anxiety and rest offered by a medical dictionary.

Chris Darke

Born 1958, London. Studied at St Martin's School of Art, London, Maidstone College of Art and the Royal College of Art, London. Received a Fulbright Award in 1989 leading to the MFA at the School of the Art Institute, Chicago and in 1991 received a Regional Fellowship from the National Endowment for the Arts. *Lessness Parts I,II & III*: Outstanding Film Award, Hong Kong Film Festival 1987. Screenings include: Image Forum, Japan; London Film Festival; American Film Institute, Los Angeles and the São Paolo Festival, Brazil. *Anxiety/Rest*: ICA Biennial: 'Arrows of Desire'.

ABOVE:
LESSNESS – PARTS I, II & III

David
Finch

Born in Leicester, David Finch studied literature at Cambridge and film at the Polytechnic of Central London; this background reflects clearly on the preoccupation of his work – history, memory and identity. His early works, in particular *Troilus and Cressida* (1982) and *The Fall of the House of Usher* (1981) are literary interpretations with Brechtian concerns and a Godardian sense of mise-en-scène. It is not until *The Fog* (1982) that Finch's distinctive lyrical style comes into being with its poetic clarity and visual strength, created by a blend of Super8 and video editing.

Working at the London Film-makers' Co-op in the early to mid 1980s, Finch was exposed to a plurality of genres, post structuralist, new narrative, romantic and decadent, yet developed a highly personal practice. *The Fog* was followed by *Heart of Gold* (1985), *Forgotten Fictions* (1986) and *The Flying Trunk* (1987) which all used the lyrical technique of Super8 slow motion onto video, voice-over and music. These pieces wove together personal memory, myth and fiction into extremely evocative yet fragmented journeys. In all these works, there is a yearning for the past, for the forgotten, for the eroded images of an old country, for childhood's irretrievable moments, yet the work never falls into nostalgia, but rather remains on that delicate border between reflection and intimacy.

A key work which brings together many of the best elements is *Man of Stones* (1989), a tentative yet accomplished piece which explores the complex web of identifications of masculine iconography and the figure of the imaginary father, the Man of Stones. The strength of the work lies in the delicate melange of atmospheric visual imagery, a sensual pace and the diaristic camerawork emphasising a constantly shifting subjectivity. *Man of Stones* reveals a mature film language, complex yet accessible, personal yet readable, weaving together images of many origins (landscape, urban, archive...) into a fluid impression of the masculine unconscious.

Stone Steps (1992) is a return to a more direct approach to film-making, somewhat reminiscent of his *1983* (1983), where the camera questions people head on without the lyrical and metaphorical elements of his poetic works. *Stone Steps* uses interviews of his family and photographs of his childhood in an attempt to develop a cinema of intimacy mapping out the bonds between people. Through this highly personal work, the film-maker is documenting his identity, letting the viewer take part in the unveiling of the emotional layers which have created him. This latest strand in Finch's work has dispensed with the poetic exterior and these sparse and direct images draw us into the complex and often painful realities of our emotional ties.

Michael Maziere

The Flying Trunk
1987, 15min, b&w and colour, video

The *Flying Trunk* is a story of children by Hans Andersen, in which a young man loses his parents and inherits a flying trunk. I read this story as a child and was sent to boarding school when young, with a large trunk, which appears in the video. Shot on Super8, a video about separation and independence.

DF

Man Of Stones
1989, 32min, colour, video

Man of Stones begins with a dialogue I had as a child with my mother, in which I asked her "who made everything ?" and other questions. Her orthodox Christian replies contributed to a childish cosmology in which the universe was the body of a man, God the father, made of stones; like the constellation Orion, but so big that you couldn't see it.

DF

Man of Stones traces a young boy's subordination to the image of male hardness and strength, creating a dense web of images in a lyrical, diaristic form – the hard granite buildings, yards and monuments of an Edinburgh childhood, the phallic Cerne Abbas giant, clips from *Sink The Bismark*, football, parachute troops, tomb carvings – everywhere stones, landscapes of stones, bodies covered with stones – metaphoric traces of the patriarchal father, the Calvinist God, William Blake's grim Nobodaddy.

Peter Wollen

Stone Steps

1992, 21min, colour, 16mm

Stone Steps returns to the house, now derelict, where an old family photograph was taken in 1963. The film is a series of portraits of the people in the photograph. My family respond to my questions with caution, revealing something of their characters, and our relationships. Trying to describe a 'family', the film maps people, places and time, searching for an image as an aid to navigation, like the Plough and the Pole star, which my father always said I should know about.

DF

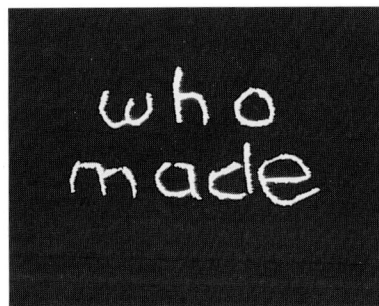

ABOVE:
MAN OF STONES

Biography

Born 1956, Leicester. BA in English Literature and Social & Political Sciences, St Catharine's College Cambridge 1978; PGDiploma in Film Studies, Polytechnic of Central London 1981; PG Diploma in Visual Communications, Goldsmiths' College, London 1982. *Forgotten Fictions*: Special Jury Prize International Festival of Super8 Film and Video, Brussels 1987. *Man of Stones*: Grand Prix, Locarno Video Festival 1990; Special Prix Video Essay prize, Festival International du Jeune Cinema, Montreal 1990; ICA Biennial: 'Between Imagination and Reality'. *Stone Steps*: ICA Biennial: 'Arrow of Desire'. Retrospective at the National Museum of Art, Osaka 1994. Distribution Organiser at the London Film-makers' Co-op 1982–85. Has taught in Finland and Germany; currently teaches film and video at Portsmouth College of Art.

Rose
Finn-Kelcey

Rose Finn-Kelcey's high reputation is based on a series of extremely diverse works, each with a distinct identity. In every case she has used material means suitable to the idea, which becomes inseparably associated with that particular work. Her use of media, therefore, is hard to divide up into categories. Film and video have been used occasionally, in ways which add further dimensions to her underlying concepts, rather than cultivated as media for their own sake.

One of her earliest uses of film was to elaborate the kinetic nature of her 'wind blown objects' made in 1970. These were large, hand-made flags whose verbal messages ('Here is a gale warning', for example) referred back ambiguously to the element in which they flew, or the forces which activated them. *Variable, Light To Moderate* (1971) was the name of the film she made to record the movement of her flags in different conditions of wind and weather, and the viewer's movement past at different speeds, to produce a complex of interacting forces.

In the early 1980s Finn-Kelcey was exploring her fascinating notion of the 'absent' or 'surrogate' performer, in relation to the problems of identity and authenticity posed by the development of live art. In *Glory* (1983) she, as live performer, acted as animator for over 100 white cut-out figures of historical heroes, politicians, film stars and images associated with war, "locked in a kind of Blitzkrieg on a large table in a small room." The subsequent video based on the event was not a simple documentary record but played suggestively with the film medium. The irony of the live performer working with 'cardboard' characters extracted from a two-dimensional filmic world was doubled, so to speak, in the video by returning the cut-outs to an artificial world where their exaggerated posturings out-performed the shadowy controller.

A film of *Bureau de Change* (1988) would certainly have been valuable for those who never saw this brilliant installation, but the film made (in 1992) is, again, more than a simple record. *Bureau de Change* is 'the-Van-Gogh's-Sunflowers-made-of-coins'. At least, this remarkable sleight of hand is the centrepiece of an installation which is also a performance since it includes a uniformed guard on the interposed wooden floor where the glinting transmutation of Van Gogh's famous picture is laid out. *Bureau de Change* may be seen as a polemic against the commercialisation of art, but is also a complex meditation on creativity. The film simulates the spectator's entry to the 'vault',

Glory

1983, 20min, colour, video
(with Steve Hawley and Harry Walton)

The raw material for this tape originated in a performance I gave at the Serpentine Gallery in May 1983. During that event I acted as both animator and controller of 100 surrogate performers who were locked in a kind of Blitzkrieg on a large table in a small room. The cut-out images were drawn from past and present historical moments, famous politicians, heroes, heroines and a multitude of images associated with war and the representation of conflict. The tape is not merely a documentation of the event but more essentially an extension of the performance and therefore a work in its own right, structured deliberately to emphasise the filmic references and an implicit eroticism.

RF-K

Bureau de Change

1992, 11min, colour, 16mm
(with Nick Collins)

Bureau de Change is about an art installation conceived at the time of the notorious Van Gogh *Sunflowers* sale in 1987 when £24.5 million was the highest price ever paid for an artwork. The installation, at Matt's Gallery, London included a reconstruction of the *Sunflowers* from a thousand pounds worth of coins, a false floor, a surveillance camera and monitor, a viewing platform and a security guard.

RF-K

Born Northampton. Educated Ravensbourne College of Art, London and Chelsea School of Art, London. Installation and live works since 1970. Screenings include the World-Wide Video Festival, The Hague; San Sebastian Film and Video Festival, Locarno; Montreal Video Festival; The Kitchen, New York; International Exhibition of Women's Art, Vienna; The British Art Show; Tate Gallery; ICA Videotheque.

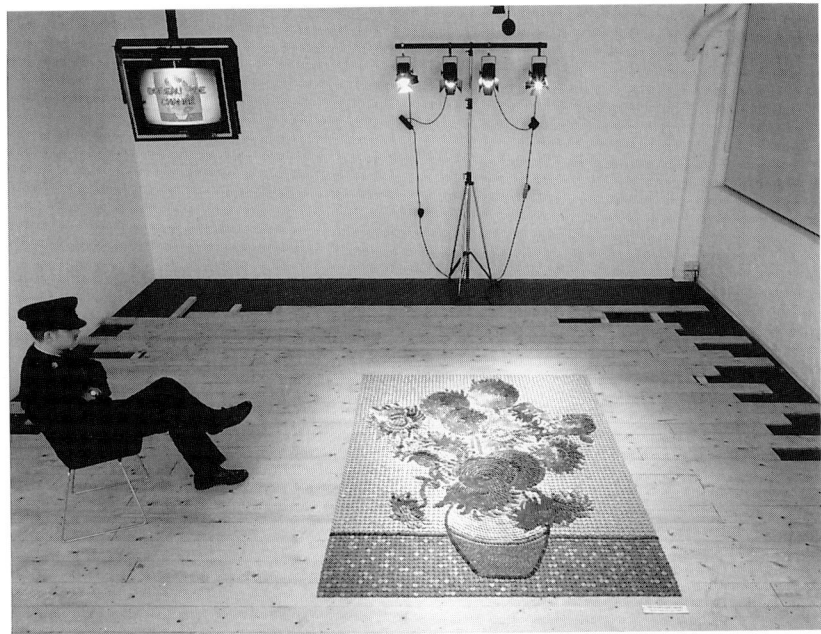

and gradual revelation of the piece, but, more important, is able to show the process whereby £1,000 of loose change (less than 1/2000th of the price paid for the original in 1987), an enormously heavy mass, was brought in small bags, meticulously laid out by the artist, and after the show taken away and put back again into ordinary circulation.

Steam Installation (1993) is suffused with the enjoyment and challenge of 'filming the filmy'. It consists of distant and close-up shots of Finn-Kelcey's 1992 piece, a huge apparatus, devised with engineering assistance, which draws air from outdoors into an enclosed room and evaporates it continuously in a cubic area, creating a room within the room of pure atmosphere. Made with broadcast-standard equipment and high-resolution lenses, the film gives the viewer time to appreciate all the nuances of vapour and droplets set against the suave steel of the meshes and ducts that make up the piece.

It will be clear from these descriptions that video and film, for Finn-Kelcey, have keyed in closely with an exploration of the ephemeral. They have added a new dimension to a series of works which have poetically and paradoxically questioned the relationship between material and spiritual values. They are used as another of her 'surrogates', and their images are no less real, or no more false, than any of the others.

Guy Brett

Terry **Flaxton**

Terry Flaxton has been an impassioned, indefatigable presence in British independent video for almost two decades. During this time he has assembled an impressive body of work encompassing powerful, polemical documentary (produced as a member of ground-breaking outfits Vida and Triplevision) and highly personal, poetic video art.

What unites these separate strands of Flaxton's video-making is a strongly held belief in the medium's ability to change our image of the world – or at least that restricted view of it obtained through the television screen. In Flaxton's eyes, a faith in video's transforming potential burns undiminished. More to the point, in Flaxton's hands, much of the medium's radical promise goes some way towards being fulfilled.

A gifted lighting cameraman, whose skills are extensively sought both inside and outside the industry, Flaxton brings a consummate polish to everything he shoots, exemplified equally by the verité *Prisoners* (1985) and the visionary *The World Within Us* (1988). A similar finely-honed sensibility distinguishes later pieces, like *The Colour Myths* (1990-95), which draw heavily from an up-to-the-minute palette of digital effects. Attempting the kind of rhapsodic fusion of image and language that few of his contemporaries could contemplate, let alone execute, Flaxton's later works have tended to divide opinion; but there is no doubting their vigour, integrity and sheer visual panache.

Steven Bode

Key works

Prisoners
1985, 16min, colour, video

Bringing a myriad resonance to the story of Ridley Scott's celebrated commercial for Apple Computers, the tape, in both its structure and its context, raises and embodies a number of particularly post-modern questions as to the way in which media representation, consumer capitalism and postmodernism are intimately interlinked.

Steven Bode *Picture This*

The World Within Us
1988, 16min, colour, video

In the literary voice over, the nameless character invokes finally "my severe right, my inviolable right, to be released from this fascination with the surface of things" as the introit to the last release. The weight and poetry of this particular tape is that it is so deeply fascinated with the surfaces, not even of things, but of their replication in the craft of video. The fascination with surface, expressed through 3D computer effects, lighting and props and meticulous set design, has to lay open again, in the context of a meditative tape on the death of an author, the question of the core vacuum in video's presence to itself.

Sean Cubitt *Timeshift*

The Inevitability of Colour
1990, 16min, colour, video

Using a high-tech array of digital effects, Flaxton uses the myth of Echo and Narcissus to explore the relationship between sound and image and its bearing on how ideas are received by the viewer within audio-visual media.

Echo's Revenge
1991, 5min, colour, video

Pursuing the concerns explored in *The Inevitability of Colour*, this tape deploys images referring to earlier moments in art (Magritte's Pipe, Duchamp's Dada, Craig-Martin's Oak Tree).

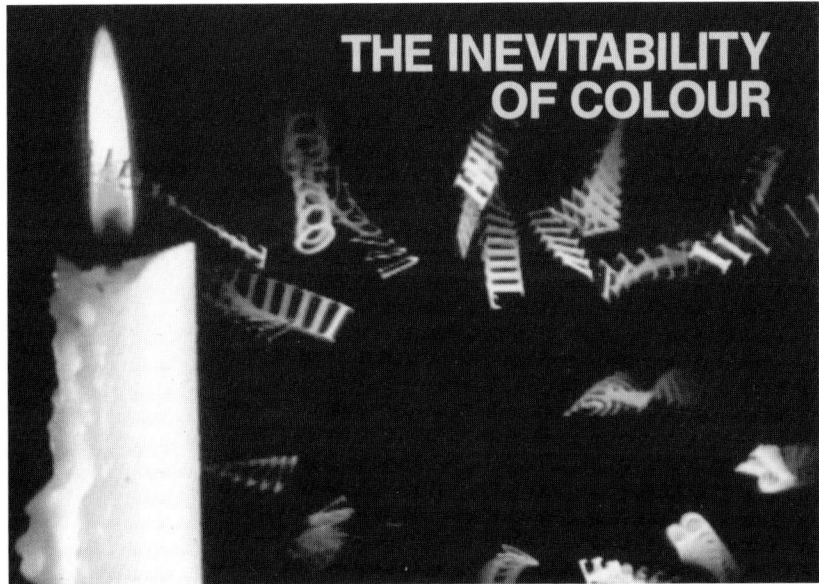

THE INEVITABILITY
OF COLOUR

ABOVE:
**THE INEVITABILITY OF
COLOUR**

Born 1953. BA in Communication Design,
North East London Polytechnic. Has
worked as lighting director on television
documentaries, pop promos, fashion videos
and for theatre. Advised the BBC on video
aesthetics for a series on architecture,
Building Sights and contributed to the series;
commissioned by Granada Television to
make a programme on video art, *In the
Belly of the Beast*. Screenings include Medien
Werkstatt, Vienna; Riga Film Festival;
American Film Institute, Los Angeles;
Fukui Biennial, Tokyo. Retrospectives
include X Works, Paris 1993; Bonn Biennial
1992; National Film Theatre, London 1992.

Forkbeard
Productions

The conjunction of film and live performance is frequently the occasion for works engaged in a dialogue of contrasting, often conflicting narratives. In the work of Forkbeard Fantasy, the discrepancies between then and now, there and here, fixed and uncertain, are breached in a manner that is both comic and provocative. The diverse activities of Forkbeard, spanning street and outdoor performance, stage works, film, animation and installations, are characterised by an acquisitiveness that owes no allegiance to its source but instead harnesses "the activities, inventiveness and gadgetry of specialists and experts" to the expression of a world view that flits between the surreal and the absurd. Film is used to extend the possibilities of their work, spawning the sartorially challenged Brittonioni Brothers.

Created for a showing of Forkbeard's films in 1985, the Brittonionis have since entered into the films so completely that formal distinctions between the optical space of the screen and that allotted to the performers in the theatre become blurred. The theatrical illusion of events unfolding in the present is undermined by the realisation that even the seemingly haphazard application of Brylcream owes its placement to that recorded on the film with which the performers synchronise their actions. Similarly, the autonomy of the film is challenged by its dependence on a narrative that delights in crossing the 'celluloid divide'. Forkbeard, however, are not primarily concerned with the disruption of form. Choosing to term their current work 'experimental theatre', they do not take the rigour of the laboratory and apply it to performance work but, instead, have the air of impoverished yet resourceful boffins going about their work on stage: that such figures are berated for producing nothing of real use is, in this instance, an empty charge. Forkbeard reject the assigned use-value of objects, ideas and technologies and determine them anew, producing performances as audacious in their conceits as they are humorous in their means.

Tim White

A Serious Leak
1989, 80min, colour, performance with film

An mixed media performance involving leaking taps, gurgling pipes, jets of steam and anarchic effects with sets and objects. A comic spectacle and 'eco-nightmare'.

Invasion of the Bloopies
1991, 80min, colour, performance with film

Commissioned by the Third Eye Centre, Glasgow, set in an advertising agency that sells everything from toilet brushes to 'bloopies', this is a fast-paced comedy on the horrors of consumerism. The stage – designed by Penny Saunders – takes an active role in the proceedings, with furniture exploding and apparently talking back to performers Tim and Chris Britton.

Biography

Chris Britton born 1950, Oxford. Tim Britton born 1953, Oxford. Forkbeard Productions was formed in 1974 and consists of Tim and Chris (who as performers take on the persona of the Brittonioni Brothers) as well as Ed Jobling, responsible for sound and film projection and Penny Saunders, in charge of sets, models and lighting. Performances include North Devon Film Festival; Brighton Festival; Institute of Contemporary Arts, London; Theatre Festival, Bogota; British Arts Festival, Rome; Centre for Contemporary Art, Warsaw. *The Birdwatcher* was commissioned for Channel Four. Forkbeard Productions have featured on arts programmes on Scottish Television.

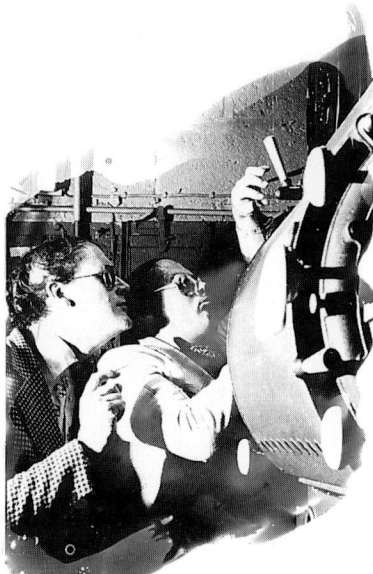

TOP AND ABOVE:
**THE INDIA RUBBER
ZOOM LENS**

Charles Garrad

Charles Garrad's background in sculpture, his extensive travels and a burgeoning interest in notions of time, cinematic illusion and perception of meaning, inform a wide range of practice from installation art to semi-documentary film making.

While his installation *Cinema* (Serpentine Gallery, 1983) played with the idea of a shared cinematic mythology and our capacity to create narrative around key objects – in this instance, a film noir-ish room that might well have been lifted from an Edward Hopper painting – *Monsoon* (Ikon Gallery, 1986) was more dramatic. Designed to recall a far-Eastern restaurant, this installation featured a television monitor constantly replaying the arrival of sinister figures by limousine, electrical flashes signifying lightening and a crash of thunder to underline the mood of threat. Recalling a moment from a film, yet designed to reveal artifice, *Monsoon* might well be seen as part of a groundswell of film related art practice that, in the 1980s, sought to flesh out the bare bones of structuralist and deconstructive theory evident throughout the late 1970s.

Reintroducing elements of tension and engagement, Garrad's installation work led him toward a large scale archival project, *TV Times* (1991), which was realised in collaboration with the curators of the new Museum of Contemporary Art in Sydney, Australia. Created as a centrepiece at the opening of the MCA, this accessible installation celebrated popular culture and 35 years of Australian television in a style which simultaneously sought to ask questions about the role of television in shaping memory and offered up a nostalgic platform for the medium. (Garrad had undertaken a similar, though smaller scale project for the Museum of the Moving Image in London, with an exhibit which 'recreated' the London Film-makers' Co-op as a context in which clips from avant-garde classics were screened.) The desire to engage with a larger audience beyond the art gallery coterie was explicit in *TV Times* and in his decision to work as a set designer and director in the film industry.

Latterly Garrad has directed a series of six ten-minute films which were screened on BBC2 in 1992 under the title *Time Passing*. Quirky and distinctive, these films explored the experience of time from a variety of perspectives in an often impressionistic and inventive manner. Marrying semi-experimental techniques to documentary scenarios, the films underlined his move towards an art that would find a broad audience. *Inside Out* (1993), a one minute film for the Arts Council/BBC2 The Late Show, expertly and concisely encapsulated the artist's ongoing concern with perception and illusion.

Consistent in his interests, Garrad's desire to move beyond the limited boundaries of a purely avant-garde practice and his work in a variety of film and television based media, locate him in a handful of unrelated artists who, by the late 1980s, were looking to blur the boundaries between 'pure' art and popular culture.

Nik Houghton

Time Passing
1992, 6 x 10min, colour, 16mm

A series of short, atmospheric sideways glances at how we experience the way time passes. Visually rich and inventive, these films explore the nature of time in an impressionistic rather than academic way. *One Year* is an anecdotal study of the miracle of growth and the extraordinary developments that take place in the first twelve months of a child's life. *The Tide* compares geological, architectural and human time scales as a replica of an elderly lady's bungalow is built by children on a sandcastle on the beach below it, and then swept away by the sea. *Wedding Day* explores two seemingly opposed temporal events; the repetitive process and the life-changing moment, in a light-hearted study of a day at a Registry Office. *Nine O'Clock* reminds us that things we regard as constant are really in a constant state of flux, as we follow a man through seasonal and other changes in his surroundings on his daily walk to work. *Eight Minutes* highlights the subjective nature of the way we perceive time – in eight one minute films shot in very different situations. *The Past* considers memory by drawing a parallel between the making of a film and the living of a life, as an old man relives his life via his own movies.

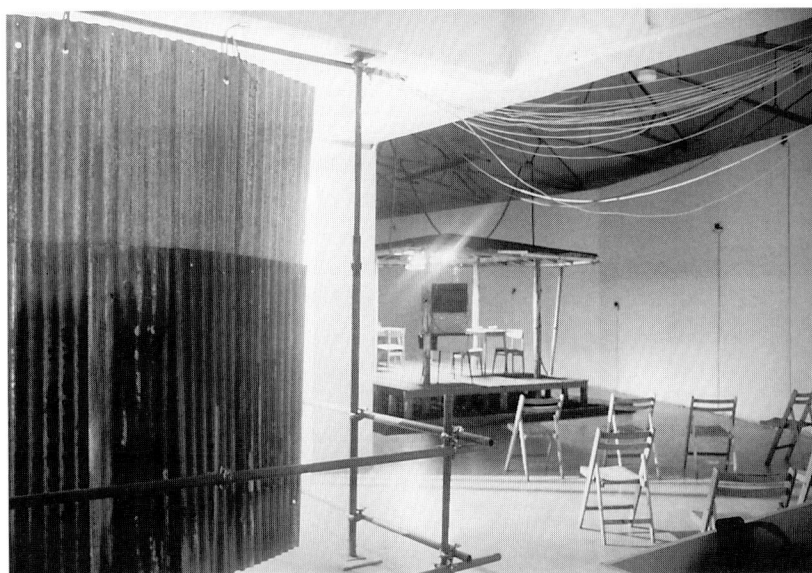

Cinema

1983, installation

A tribute to the atmospheres of film noir. The spectator approaches along a long corridor hung with a puzzling sequence of photographic clues: a telephone, an ashtray with a smoking cigarette, a light under a door. Suddenly, what seems to be the last of the photographs turns to be an opening in the wall, and spectators find themselves looking into the room itself. Through a partly opened bathroom door they see a pacing woman reflected in the mirror. Beyond a half-opened window is a brick wall, bathed in the thick yellow of sodium lighting. The air is heavy with a sense of urban crime. In the mirror of the wardrobe a flickering neon sign, reflected from outside, flashes on and off...'Cinema'. Moving on down the corridor the spectator turns a corner, and walks abruptly into the room itself. In plain view now are the various devices used to create the room's effects, the film loop of the woman in the bathroom, the light under the door, the neon cinema sign. But instead of solving the mystery the facts in the case of the room seem to deepen it.

Waldemar Januszczak

Biography

Born 1952, Somerset. Studied at Cardiff College of Art 1970-73, and Chelsea School of Art 1973-74. Works as a freelance director and production designer including *The Englishman Who Went Up a Hill But Came Down a Mountain* (as designer) 1995. Teaches on the MA Sculpture course at Chelsea School of Art. Artist in Residence at the Institute of Contemporary Arts, Brisbane 1979. His installations have been exhibited at the Serpentine Gallery, London; Ikon Gallery, Birmingham; National Museum of Wales; Whitechapel Art Gallery, London. The *TV Times* installation was exhibited at the MCA, Sydney, Performing Arts Museum, Melbourne; Woolongong City Gallery and Townsville Art Gallery. *Inside Out*: ICA Biennial: 'What You See is What You Get'.

Rob
Gawthrop

Principally concerned with art, manifested in the forms of film, music/sound and performance – where the context or site of the work is of increasing importance.

Generally, the work deals with the borders of the real, its representation and the process and materiality of its realisation. The conditions of: recognisable depiction, the abstract/conceptual, and the physical or material – are set into flux through various strategies including chance, predetermined systems and improvisation – placing the viewer/listener in an active position, free to deal with what they are experiencing. Sound is as fundamental as image, where the relationship between them is made explicit. The boundaries between music, noise, natural sound and silence and the association of one sound with another are constantly put into question. The material used is not neutral but is derived from places, things and activities. These bring with them their political or ecological implications (albeit on a conceptual level), but they also represent a simpler concern with the way things look and sound. People are only present, either physically, as in performance, as the audience or by implication within the work itself. It is the engagement between the viewer/listener and the work that is important.

Rob Gawthrop

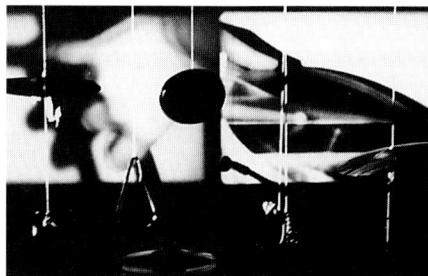

Biography

Born 1953, London. BA in Fine Art, Maidstone College of Art 1976; MA Royal College of Art in Film and Television 1979. Senior Lecturer, Fine Art/Time-Based Media, Humberside Polytechnic 1982–92; currently Course Leader, Fine Art, University of Humberside. Screenings include: Museum of Modern Art, Edinburgh; Tate Gallery, London; Arnolfini Gallery, Bristol; Experimental Filme Kultureveinigung, Linz, Austria. Founder member and Chair of Hull Time-Based Arts; founder member of the University of Humberside Band – an experimental music performance ensemble. Programmer of special seasons of experimental film and video art at the Hull Film Theatre 1988-93.

Key works

Projections for Percussion and Improvisation

1985-90, film/performance, 16mm and other formats

A series of films and performances which are concerned with improvised music, its depiction/recording and the listening experience – the actual moment of its perception. Technology is used as a substitute for live performers, so that a sort of simulated improvising band is formed using projectors, speakers etc, sometimes including a real performer.

What The Eye Doesn't See, Post Industrial Studies No 1 – Coal & Transport

1993, 12min, b&w, 16mm
(with Mike Stubbs)

A film that uses imagery of wet coal, pit-head winding gear and modern coal trains that is partially abstracted through overlays of positive and negative, repeated fades and white-outs set against fading and repeating archive sounds of steam trains shunting. The historical and political potency of the twin industries of Coal and Rail informs the film conceptually. The film sets out to deal with the shifting relations between the visual aesthetics, the content of the sound and the conceptual knowledge of the viewer. *Post-Industrial Studies* are an on-going series of films and events for specific sites and contexts.

ABOVE:
PROJECTIONS FOR PERCUSSION AND IMPROVISATION

Losing

1991, installation, 11 monitors, 1 video projector, 4 players, computer, slide projector

The form and ritual of football are used as the basis of a multiple monitor installation in which the viewer is presented with an integrated combination of computer-generated graphics and live-action footage unfold as a repeated narrative across the gallery space. The sculptural dimension of video installation is exploited in this complex commentary on mass entertainment.

NLV7

1990, 4min, colour, video

An exercise in geometry testing the viewer's observation of all that is Euclidian. The world of shapes is concealed within the sounds and colours of the playground.

Clive Gillman's work was born out of the sophisticated 'scratch' school of the early eighties in Sheffield, and has moved through a series of transformations which reflect many of the shifts within video art culture. His early works, such as *WAR (Warning Attack Recovery)* (1983), revealed a technical flair and aesthetic sensitivity which was to have a major influence on the development of the group, Nine Attrition Magnetic (9AM), (their name mythically taken from a Japanese brand of video tape) which consisted of Gillman and fellow artists St John Walker, Pam Smith and Sven Harding. 9AM created a number of pieces which delved into the post-modern pop pastiche of the late 1980s, with a specific inclination towards Japanese comic and futuristic cartoon culture. This blend of myth-meets-media in a soup of hi and low tech images reached its apocalypse in *Saboten Boi* (1988), a 46 minute foray into Japanese culture – seen through the eyes of a child.

During this period, Gillman reappraised his work and developed an interest in non linear forms which materialised as the *NLV (Non Linear Video)* series of tapes. These works had a repetitive, cyclical structure, were short and heavily layered with videographics. *NLV1 (Strange Attractor)* (1989), *NLV6 (Sublime)* (1990) and *NLV7* (1990) represent a shift from the single monitor linear construction to a more open, random system of creation and interaction, and led to the interactive installations which he is producing and developing now.

In *Losing* (1991), a multi-monitor piece, Gillman recreates a football team on monitors where individual footballers and commentators speak of their intense and emotional relationships to the game, the ball, and the act of losing. The viewers weaving a way through this imaginary field are faced with monologues and critical discourse on the game as they approach each monitor, concluding with an ode to the ball and the wishes invested in it. These touching confessions and intimate revelations lay bare the contradictions in the dominant image of football, while the multi-screen technology contrasts with the reality of the mud of the playing field. In this new approach Gillman opposes the mass televisual experience with an individual and personal relationship with the screen, its images and the pain of losing.

Michael Maziere

Biography

Born 1960, London. BA Fine Art Sheffield City Polytechnic 1983, MA Time-based Fine Art North East London Polytechnic 1987. Screenings include: Bonn Videonale; Festival de la Creation Video, Clermont-Ferrand; International Video Festival, Sydney; Video Brasil, Sao Paolo; Ars Electronica, Linz; Bluecoat Gallery, Liverpool. Facilities and Training Manager at LVA 1988–90. Developed MITES (the Moving Image Touring & Exhibition Service). Currently establishing access for artists to multimedia technology.

RIGHT:
LOSING

Constantine
Giannaris

Of all independently made and minded films produced in Britain in recent years, those by Constantine Giannaris may be the hardest to define and classify. Born in Greece, trained as an economist and historian, Giannaris came to film-making through involvement with the Lesbian and Gay Youth Project, which was formed to make the documentary tape *Framed Youth* (1984) and consolidated his new line of work by making music videos for the bands Bronski Beat and The Communards. To some degree, his subsequent films reflect these beginnings: their imagistic approach to questions of gay desire, their carefully crafted visuals and their tendency to narrative abstraction all have roots in the activist/avant-garde traditions of the 1980s, as seen in community-action tapes and non-mainstream music videos.

But Giannaris' work ranges far beyond these roots. *Trojans* (1989) is ostensibly a biographical documentary about the poet Constantine Cavafy, but it's also an attempt to construct the filmic equivalent of a Cavafy poem, not to mention a commentary on Greek-Alexandrian homosexual culture as it survives today. *North of Vortex* (1991) is founded on a Wenders-like infatuation with Americana – cityscapes, landscapes, the tawdriness of small towns – but frames its minimal road-movie narrative as a collage of subjective realities, memories and fantasies with scant regard for orthodox narrative logic. *Caught Looking* (1991), made for Channel Four, could be thought of as a semiotic investigation into the codes of gay erotica of various vintages, except that it is conceived as a sci-fi narrative about a solitary man and his on-line virtual reality terminal, which makes the film as much a wry anatomy of voyeurism as anything else. And *A Place in the Sun* (1994), is a conventional narrative movie, anchored in specific social realities, that is continuously subverted by inserts of non-narrative material: racing clouds, fast-motion flashbacks, abstract vignettes of places, atmospheres and landscapes.

All of this is to say that Giannaris has eclectic interests and a remarkable range. The overall timbre of his work is more European than narrowly British; it comes as naturally to him to quote Genet's writings (in the voice-over of *North of Vortex*) as to quote images from Pasolini (in the physique photographer in *Caught Looking* who buries himself like the maid Emilia in *Theorem*). As these references suggest, Giannaris stands well apart from the politically correct

Key works

Jean Genet is Dead
1987, 40min, colour, 16mm

Shot on a combination of Super8 film and video and dedicated to the memory of Mark Ashton, a gay political activist who died of AIDS in 1987, this work explores homo-erotic imagery in sumptuously layered sequences that are accompanied by a child's reading of a text by Genet that speaks of sainthood, imprisonment, love and friendship.

North of Vortex
1991, 58min, b&w, 16mm

North of Vortex unfolds against the visually sumptuous backdrop of the American landscape, from dark hotel rooms in New York City to desert wastelands in the West. Meeting by chance, the film's three main protagonists use each other to play out their erotic and sexual fantasies in a timeless world of desire and passion.

Caught Looking
1991, 35min, colour, 16mm

Using a virtual reality computer, the film charts the experiences of one man's odyssey into his own voyeuristic sexual fantasies. The virtual reality becomes a focus for the player's thoughts about sexual experience's in the past – boys he wanted, boys he met and boys he lost – and at the same time reveals the implicit unfulfillment and thus endless repetition of desire.

Michael O'Pray

A Place In The Sun
1994, 50min, b&w and colour, 16mm

Set in Athens, the film deals with a fleeting relationship between Ilias, a successful Greek man and Panayiotis, an Albanian refugee. Against the backdrop of the cacophony of voices and peoples that characterises Athens as the gateway to the West, they meet and part in a way that evokes the wider social traumas of the late twentieth century.

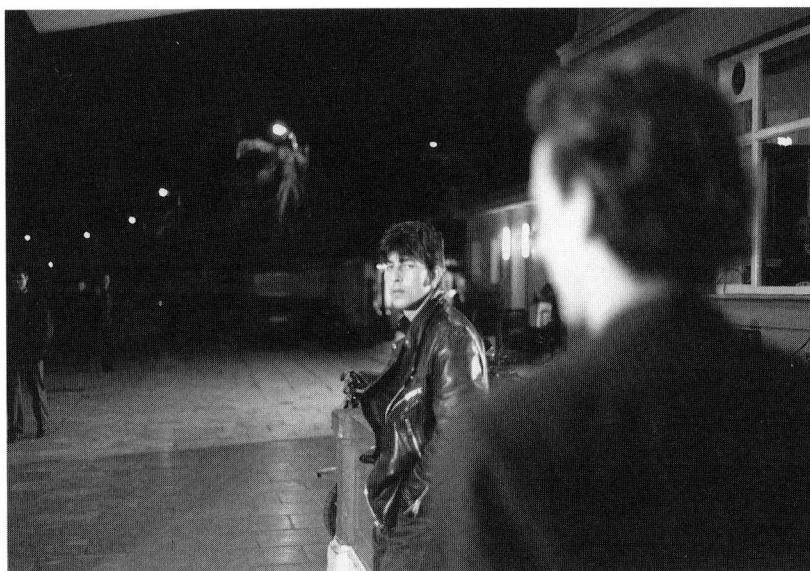

Born 1959, Greece. Studied economics before starting to make films. Worked as a pop promo director for London Records 1984-86, making videos for Bronski Beat and The Communards. Prizes include: *Trojans* – Gay Teddy Bear Award for Best Short Film, Berlin Film Festival 1990; *North of Vortex* – Best Black and White Short, Cork International Film Festival 1990, Silver Plaque for Best Short Drama, Chicago International Film Festival 1992; *Caught Looking* – Jury Prize, Cinema et Homosexualité, Brussels 1992. *Caught Looking*: ICA Biennial: 'Arrows of Desire'.

current in gay culture. He has no time for 'positive images'; his films get down into the dark crevices of desire, where passions are impure and often rooted in self-delusion and where violence is often only a kiss away. In short, Giannaris is as likely to offend the worthies of the gay movement as he is to alienate purists in avant-garde film circles.

Idiosyncratically balanced between narrative codes and non-narrative poetry, Giannaris' work points a possible new way forward for European film-making. It builds on the foundations laid by Europe's art movie masters, but adds formal and visual ideas more in tune with the avant-garde. All of his films have been made on low budgets, but none feels constrained by financial limitations. Giannaris shows just what is within reach of any film-maker with a grasp of present-day European financial and creative realities.

Tony Rayns

ABOVE:
A PLACE IN THE SUN

Peter Gidal

Peter Gidal remains the most important and most influential film-maker from the English avant-garde of the 1960s and 1970s. During this period his films and theoretical writings had an enormous impact, stimulating debate and providing young film-makers with a political and aesthetic framework that would distinguish them from their American, and to a large extent, from their European counterparts. His structural-materialist theory, published in 1975, was one of this country's most provocative art manifestos of the post-war period, and fused an aesthetic programme with a political critique in the Vertovian tradition of anti-narrative experiment. Yet his own reference points came as much, if not more, from painting, music and theatre, as from film.

Influenced equally by Soviet constructivism, Andy Warhol's early films and Samuel Beckett's writings, Gidal originally defined his theoretical and artistic position against the progressive moments of Abstract Expressionism and Minimalism. For him, film-making involves essentially the problem of the viewer and "the relation between the represented object(s) and the illusion of those objects." Vehemently anti-narrative, he is nevertheless equally vigorous in his refusal of formalism and abstraction; maintaining a stubborn resistance of representation as precisely the Kampfplatz of any rigorous film practice. The 'radical pessimism' of his position does not exclude its own horizon of cinematic possibility, and he has mined a seam of film-making of increasing power and imagination.

In his early films, eg, *Heads* (1969), *Clouds* (1969), Warholian issues of real-time duration and repetition dominated. The 1970s heralded a prolific period of film-making, producing about twenty films, characterised by an almost complete eschewal of the human figure, in which he developed a more complex aesthetic using hand-held camera, black leader, intense and ambiguous close-up and film-grain texture. *Upside Down Feature* (1972) with its Beckett-on-Proust text, double radio sound, and use of negative and leader has rich visuals as well as strong experimental strategies. Photographs were introduced as objects in *Film Print* (1974) and *Kopenhagen/1930* (1977), further complicating issues of

watches with fascination the representation of the objective world through the agency of light and its absence. An important enlargement of the historical conception of modernism, Gidal also poses the problem of the dialectic of representation, through representation (Rembrandt, Giacometti etc).

Malcolm Le Grice

Condition of Illusion
1975, 30min, colour, silent, 16mm

In *Condition of Illusion* what is not achieved is the stabilisation of reproduction in terms of a representation: effectively, the materials of reproduction that are engaged by the film are not stabilised into a representation (the photograph given precisely as holdable moment, why else a photograph if not for that?). The distinction between reproduction and representation is important though difficult...Duration and narrative thus come apart, narrative being exactly fixing, stabilisation...In *Condition of Illusion* nothing is held into a representation.

Stephen Heath *Cambridge Tapes on Narrative*

Guilt
1988, 40min, colour, silent, 16mm

Objects in the world given luminousness, light, are here less apprehendable to knowledge than that which has less light. What is there in never not the real. No recognition. Absence of the subjectivity of the body's scale. The simultaneity of abstract and real is not constant, it wavers, although the attempt is to make it constant.

PG

Key works

Clouds
1969, 10min, b&w, 16mm

Frantic frame edge defining nothingness. The anti-illusionist project engaged by *Clouds* is that of dialectical materialism. There is virtually nothing ON screen, in the sense of IN screen. Obsessive repetition as materialist practice not psychoanalytical indulgence.

PG

Room Film
1973, 55min, colour, silent, 16mm

[...] there is no describable content, but one

Born 1946. Studied at Brandeis University, Massachussets, USA 1964–68; University of Munich, Germany 1966–67; Royal College of Art, London 1968–71. Taught at The Royal College of Art 1971–83. Seminars given at Universities of Sussex, London, Cambridge, as well as Yale, Harvard and L'Ecole des Etudes, Paris. Co-founder of the Independent Film-makers' Association 1975 and member of the British Film Institute's Production Board 1978–81. Writer and theorist (see bibliography). Screenings include: Tate Gallery, London; Hayward Gallery, London; Royal Belgian Film Archive and Cinematheque; Centre Georges Pompidou, Paris; International Avant-Garde Film Festival, Riga; Museum of Modern Art, New York; Salzburg International Festival. A retrospective of his films was held at the Institute of Contemporary Arts, London in 1983. Guilt: ICA Biennial: 'Between Imagination and Reality'.

representation. In *Room Film 1973* (1973), one of Gidal's finest films, the difficulty of reading the film is central as the camera moves across the surface of a room and its often unrecognisable contents. Movement and focus are erratic, and darkness is broken only intermittently by light, so that the film image is constantly fluctuating between object-representation and screen-surface texture. Consistent repetition, sequence-for-sequence does not bring clarity nor is it meant to. No attempt is made to deny either the subjectivity of film (as hand-held in domestic space), or its representational mode; rather, the viewer works through and against the film with the film-maker, so to speak.

In the 1980s and early 1990s Gidal's output included three exceptional films – *Denials* (1985), *Guilt* (1988) and *Flare Out* (1992). These see the use of series' of exterior images, although their subject matter is no more easy to determine than before – space and scale often being ambivalent, matching the emotional tenor of the films. Texture is still rendered rich through lighting, printing and close-up, and there is perhaps a more emotional resonance in the works; one that speaks of anxiety in the face of the impossibility of fully-fledged meaning. Ambiguous landscapes in *Flare Out*, and what seems a monolithic stone glimpsed in *Denials*, bring their own disturbing qualities. In these recent films of the last decade, Gidal has established an unequalled authority and maturity.

Michael O'Pray

ABOVE:
CLOSE UP

Judith
Goddard

For a large part of the 1980s and up to the eight-monitor installation *Descry* (1992), Judith Goddard has been engaged in a passionate research into the video palette. To say that her work is about colour is a misnomer. What makes the range of electronic colours interesting is not their luminescence, though that is a part of it: it is the fact that they exist in time. This alters profoundly the relations of perception, and brings into play not just colour and its afterimages, but the colours of memory and anticipation. Works like *Time Spent* (1982), *Go Into Your Fridge (Stilted Life)* (1982) and *You May Break...* (1983) do more than investigate the capabilities of the medium: they unearth philosophical positions made available by video research that illuminate new avenues of perception and feeling.

Of her mid 1980s works, perhaps *Under the Rose* (1983) is the most successful, investigating, as so often in her work, the sensuality of flowers and the subtlety of their spectra in the context of a quiet but devastating act of self-reflection. *Lyrical Doubt* (1984) develops this theme in an elegant use of chromakey to map internal processes in terms of the circulation of flowers as both symbols and commodities, germinating the elements of a narrative marked otherwise only as the advancing hands of public clocks.

It was in 1985 that Goddard first experimented with Paintbox techniques that became something of a hallmark. *Celestial Light and Monstrous Races* (1985) traced internal visions of masculinity to the early accounts of explorers concerning one-eyed races, or tribes whose faces were in their chests. Later works like *Luminous Portrait* (1990) and the three-monitor installation *The Garden of Earthly Delights* (1991) continued this historical sense of the capabilities of digital manipulation, quoting from medieval arts to alert us to both the archetypal continuities between Western epochs and the fundamental changes that have come over them. In *The Garden of Earthly Delights*, in particular, some of the earlier concerns of Goddard's feminism return in a complex temporal montage of marriage, childbirth and adolescence against the background of suburbia and the city, seen as site of both struggle and spectacle.

The installation *Television Circle/Electron* (1987) represents another strand in

Biography

Born 1956, Shropshire. BA in Fine Art, University of Reading; MA in Environmental Media, Royal College of Art. Has taught at the Slade and the Reichs Academy. *Luminous Portrait*: ICA Biennial: *Between Imagination and Reality*. Exhibitions of installations include: Tate Gallery, Liverpool; Museum of Modern Art, Oxford; Leeds City Art Gallery; Bluecoat Gallery, Liverpool; Kettle's Yard, Cambridge; Berlin Video Festival; John Hansard Gallery, Southampton; Centro Cultural de Belem, Lisbon; Centre George Pompidou, Paris.

The Garden of Earthly Delights
1991, installation, 9min cycle, colour, 3 monitors, 3 players

Goddard's video version of Bosch's painting turns the 1990s into a surreal, nightmarish narrative of monstrous creatures, urban horrors and visual overload. Created using hi-tech computer animation effects and visual trickery in conjunction with live footage this triptych installation takes the viewer on a bizarre switchback ride through a cityscape of the imagination.

Descry
1992, installation, 5min cycle, colour, 8 monitors, 8 players

The title of the installation is germane to its visual play. To descry means to catch sight of, to dimly discern; etymologically it has less in common with scientific observation than with scrying, that is, crystal ball gazing. A dialectic between the scientific gaze and mystical vision, between vision and visionaries, is intelligently exploited.

Marina Benjamin

Reservoir
1993, installation, colour, Wimshurst machine, video projector, 3 monitors, 4 players, camera, water

This is a binary installation, consisting of two opposite yet complementary parts. In a white space, a Wimhurst machine enthroned in a perspex case faces a projection of a waterfall whose deep roar fills the air. The Wimhurst's majestic stillness is broken only when the beam-breaking viewer crosses an invisible threshold. Then it comes to life, with a smart industrial snap, producing electric

sparks, that are instantly magnified and projected in place of the water from the Villa d'Este. In a black space a trio of ceiling-mounted water drips release droplets one by one onto a metal tray passing time. When the beam-breaking viewer triggers a strobe, the light transforms the water drops into iridescent jewels that appear by turn to be suspended in space and to travel upwards in defiance of gravity. To one side of the space a trio of 3" LCD monitors broadcast the familiar trace of an ECG, the human equivalent of the disembodied spark, and every so often the transient, flickering image of a gender reassignment operation wipes over the three screens.

Marina Benjamin

Goddard's work, engaged in a pursuit of the metaphorical power of electronic imaging. Here video mediates not vision but electricity, from amber (the original Greek 'electron', source of static electricity and tomb of ancient insects) to generators, hotplates, pylons: and the webs of power emanating from government buildings along the Embankment in London. After *Urban Turner/First Light* (1989), an experimental video wall juxtaposing a Turneresque estuary sunset with architectural details, *Descry* picks up on motifs and themes from both *Electron* and *The Garden of Earthly Delights* to investigate the powers of vision. Seven monitors form a parabola whose focus is a smaller screen on which details of an operation on a retina are shown. Across the seven, intense colours move in swathes that illuminate the room, and over them images tumble from screen to screen as fine as stardust. One of the most professionally-produced installation pieces in British video art, its apparent simplicity the product of advanced technological skills as well as a remarkable conception, *Descry* forms part of a series in which *Reservoir* (1993) also takes its place.

Reservoir places vision between fire and water, creating an architectural space which mirrors the biophysics of the eye writ large, introducing a sense of awe, even terror, by the matching of tumbling water with a Wimhurst generator, which sends sudden sparks and the smell of ozone through the gallery space. In these recent installations in particular, the experimentation of the 1980s bears fruit in the creation of environments in which to be human becomes itself a mystery, its fragile and momentary wholeness in the face of vast physical processes exposed to a sense of sublimity that reframes the more jaded, though pressing politics of sexuality.

Sean Cubitt

Peter Greenaway

O ver the last few years, Peter Greenaway has repeatedly mooted the possibility of remaking in some other form his encyclopaedic set of fictional case-histories *The Falls* (1980). In 1994 it finally appeared refashioned in a literary form in English, French and Italian, and was made available for detailed re-perusal on commercial video. An illustrated German translation will be available by the end of 1995. But if the work is to be refashioned in a strictly visual medium, it seems plausible to imagine it will happen in the form to which his work seems naturally to be tending – CD-Rom. Of all the forms Greenaway has chosen to work in, this seems the most suited to his inclinations – to eschew linear narrative; to segment the image and make it as cornucopian as possible; and to maintain what can be best described as a pedagogic strand. Recently, in fact, Greenaway's work has centred as much on curating exhibitions and mounting installations (at the Venice Biennale and in Geneva) as it has on film-making *per se*.

Greenaway's work may only display some of the visual and narrative tropes of interactive video, rather than being interactive with the viewer as such (arguably, much of it implies a passive viewer, a willing pupil of the work's lessons). But the oeuvre has never ceased to interact with itself, each work offering itself as a set of comments or variations on the others. Thus, *Prospero's Books* (1991), with its elaborate use of high-definition television, is at once a commentary on filmed Shakespeare, and an amplification of Greenaway's earlier video 'annotation' of a classic text, *A TV Dante* (1989) (in collaboration with artist Tom Phillips). *Drowning by Numbers* (1988) is accompanied by its own television 'user's manual', *Fear of Drowning* (1988); and the historical 'staged documentary' *Death in the Seine* (1988) – a film about documents, recording a series of drownings during the French Revolution – is at once a precursor of the visual technique of *Prospero's Books*, and a variation on the encyclopaedic themes of *The Falls* and *Act of God* (1981), which both deal with sudden disasters.

Biography

Born 1942, Newport, Wales. Studied painting at Walthamstow College of Art. Exhibited paintings at Young Contemporaries, London Group, Lords Gallery. Worked for eight months at BFI Distribution then joined the Central Office of Information where he worked as an editor 1965-76. Continues to produce paintings, novels and illustrated books (see bibilography). *M is for Man, Music, Mozart*: ICA Biennial: 'Arrows of Desire'. Has recently begun to curate highly personal exhibitions: The Physical Self, Boymans Van Beuningen Gallery Rotterdam 1991, 100 Objects to Represent the World, Hoffburg Palace, Vienna 1991, Flying out of This World, Louvre 1992, Some Organising Principles Glynn Vivian Art Gallery, Swansea 1993. His films have been screened and broadcast world wide.

Key works

The Early Films of Peter Greenaway
1969–78, 92min, b&w and colour, 16mm

Six shorts currently available as a package from the British Film Institute: *Intervals* structures 13 images of small crowded Venetian butcher and barber shops – three times over, with an ever growing sophisticated soundtrack; *Windows*, humorous and macabre juxtapositions of shots of window-views with tales and statistics of suicides who had flying ambitions; *H is for House*, an irreverent alphabetical survey of domestic images tagged to the letter H; *Dear Phone*, a meditation on the gap between telling a story and illustrating it, using the uses and abuses of the red public phone box as content; *Water Wrackets*, a parody of natural history programmes; *Vertical Features Remake*, a fantasy on the disappearing rural landscape, at the same time as being a light parody on the behaviour of warring film academics, in which the works of the world environmentalist Tulse Luper are revisited.

A TV Dante (Cantos I-VIII)
1989, 8 x 10min, video, (with Tom Phillips)

An adaptation of the first eight cantos of Dante's *Inferno*, with John Gielgud as Dante and Bob Peck as Virgil. Multi-layered imagery and sound both draw on the cultural and historical contexts of Dante's work as well as explore contemporary resonances.

Prospero's Books

1991, 120min, 35mm

Sections of *The Tempest* are interlaced with elaborate depictions of 24 books – containing the sum of knowledge, ranging from bestiary, cosmology, pornography to Utopia – supposedly taken by the deposed Duke to his haunted kingdom.

M is for Man, Music, Mozart

1991, 29min, video

Part of the BBC's series of programmes to commemorate the bi-centenary of the composer's death, Greenaway's film uses a reproduction of Vesalius' 16th century anatomy theatre as a set in which half-naked on-lookers observe the body of a man come to life and acquire movement. The part of Man is played by Ben Craft, brought to life by two female dancers from The Ricochet Dance Company. The music is composed by Louis Andriessen.

Greenaway's status as a fabricator of densely-structured pageant-like narratives started in 1982 with *The Draughtsman's Contract*, and has continued with perhaps his best known film, *The Cook, The Thief, His Wife and Her Lover* (1989) and *The Baby of Macon* (1993), with its new emphasis on direct theatrical staging rather than the textural innovations of *Prospero's Books*. *Darwin* (1992) suggested a perfect marriage between Greenaway's operatic concern with staging and his anti-narrative concerns. A biography arranged in a series of tableaux, staged on a single set, this television piece attempted a new fusion of performed action with an emphasis on the presence of the camera.

This suggests that perhaps Greenaway's true forté – rather than the mathematically-plotted grand guignol spectacles he has become associated with – might in fact be a kind of descriptive cinema, one that rejects narrative in favour of an elaborate form of visual footnoting. His concern for dramatic symbolic music-associated spectacle, perhaps wisely, has been moved to the music-theatre where the conventions are better understood, with his first opera *Rosa* staged with music by the Dutch composer Louis Andriessen in Amsterdam, leaving his interest in cinema to be associated with the characteristics of his earlier fictions that lead up to *The Falls* – notably the 'commented' apocryphal film *Vertical Features Remake* (1978) and the meditation on map-making and fiction, *A Walk Through H* (1978). In works such as *Darwin* and the dance collaboration with Andriessen, *M is for Man, Music and Mozart* (1991), Greenaway's passion for segmentation and taxonomy merges with his flair for the baroque, and, acknowledging his belief that cinema took a wrong turn when it became obsessed with narrative, the most fruitful path for his future work could well lie in this direction – in evolving a flamboyant form of 'curatorial' cinema.

Jonathan Romney

David
Hall

David Hall's contribution to British video art is unparalleled. Not only are many of his video pieces classics – *TV Fighter (Cam Era Plane)* (1977) and the BBC commission *This is a Television Receiver* (1976) – but he has also made important and often brilliant contributions to experimental film, installation and sculpture. A successful sculptor in the 'new generation' school of the 1960s, Hall had accentuated the gallery space in his sculptures, especially the floor, creating large flat works hugging the floor surface, such as *Nine* (1967) in the Tate's collection. At the end of the 1960s he turned his attention to the less tangible media of photography, film and eventually video. A founding member of the video art movement in this country in the early 1970s, Hall was an influential activist on behalf of the infant art form. Tracing his work is to simultaneously survey the history of British video art before its fragmentation in the mid 1980s. Hall's practice emerged from the late 1960s art movement of conceptualism.

In his early film pieces Hall developed a sensibility and conceptual rigour that drew upon sculptural notions of form, representation and objecthood, only translated into filmic equivalents. *Vertical* (1970), *Timecheck* (1971) and *View* (1973), all dealt with illusion in relation to objects in space and time, and constructed filmic perspectives that distorted space, or rendered it ambiguous. His groundbreaking *TV Interruptions* (1971), later distributed as *7 TV Pieces* were made for Scottish Independent Television to coincide with the Edinburgh Festival. Shot on black and white film, the pieces were inserted unannounced into normal television transmission. Their imagery was intended to "redirect attention back to the box as object." Their imagery was often a single image using time-lapse, pixillation or the vagaries of the screen as a flat surface for three dimensional representation. Subsequently, he placed more emphasis upon the relationship between screen image and spatio-temporal illusion – as in *This Surface* (1973), with its witty use of text on image. The latter film anticipated the

Key works

This Is a Television Receiver
1976, 8min, colour, video

The image of a TV announcer talking about the machine we are sitting before and watching, is deconstructed through sound and electronic patterns, rendered problematic and revealed for what they are – an illusion.

Michael O'Pray

TV Fighter (Cam Era Plane)
1977, 11min, b&w, video

Hall takes the point-of-view shot in its most dramatic form, by using archive war footage of a fighter plane strafing a railway train and a ship at sea. The camera is obviously strapped to the plane. These shots are repeated and edited in slightly different

ways throughout the tape. One of the classics of British video art, it combines an exploration of the properties of video as a mechanical mode of representation and a confrontation with the illusionism of broadcast television.

Michael O'Pray

Stooky Bill TV
1990, 4min, colour video

This tape is a caustic glance backwards at the founder of television: John Logie Baird's legacy of 'dummy television'. But the tape is also a resounding formal success in so far as it presents an image equivalent to that one first produced in an attic in October 1925. All the trademarks of Hall's work are present here: dry wit, seriousness and the exploration of illusion; the awareness of material conditions and of cultural forms.

Michael O'Pray

The Situation Envisaged
1978, installation, colour, 8 television sets, 1 monitor, 1 player

Eight domestic television sets are supported side by side in a quarter circle, across the corner of a room. Each faces into the enclosure away from the viewer, and each is playing a different television channel. The viewer hears a cacophony of sound, and initially sees only the ever-changing glow above and beyond the line of sets. However, part of a monitor screen can be glimpsed through small gaps between them; its glass reflecting the television output layered over a tape of private ritual. The work confronts issues of power and the individual; the public and the private; the viewer and the viewed.

Born 1937, Leicester. Studied Architecture, Art and Design at Leicester College of Art 1954-60 and Sculpture at the Royal College of Art, London 1960-64. Founded the Time Based Arts department of Maidstone College of Art, Kent. Installation exhibitions include: Serpentine Gallery, London; Tate Gallery, London; Third Eye Centre, Glasgow; Museum of Modern Art, Oxford; La Ferme du Buisson Gallery, Paris. One man retrospectives at festivals and institutions including the ICA and Tate Gallery, London; ELAC, Lyon; Video Art Plastique, Herouville-St Clair, Caen; Photographers' Union, Warsaw. Works commissioned for broadcast by BBC, Channel Four, MTV Europe and Scottish Television.

video pieces, which stressed the materiality of the monitor in relationship to the image as representation, eg, *TV Fighter* and *This is a Television Receiver*.

Throughout the 1970s and 1980s, Hall developed video installation work that explored the relationship between gallery space and video in terms of light, mass and representation. In *The Situation Envisaged* (1978), sculptural qualities of object-mass and space interacted with a critique of television as one was confronted with a circle of television sets turned ominously in towards the wall, with only the light and sound emanating from its centre betraying its representational function. In a later version of this installation, *A Situation Envisaged: The Rite II (Cultural Eclipse)* (1988), the sets are arranged as a single block facing close to the wall except for one with a primitive, 30 lines panning image of the moon. With *Stooky Bill TV* (1990), made for Channel Four, Hall reworked the founding moment of television by producing an image with equipment identical to the original 1925 apparatus of John Logie Baird. Its biting critique of television reflects Hall's persistent engagement with its context as an institution and mode of communication. Over thirty years he has produced a body of work that has been intellectually rigorous without sacrificing the imaginative and aesthetic qualities of art.

Michael O'Pray

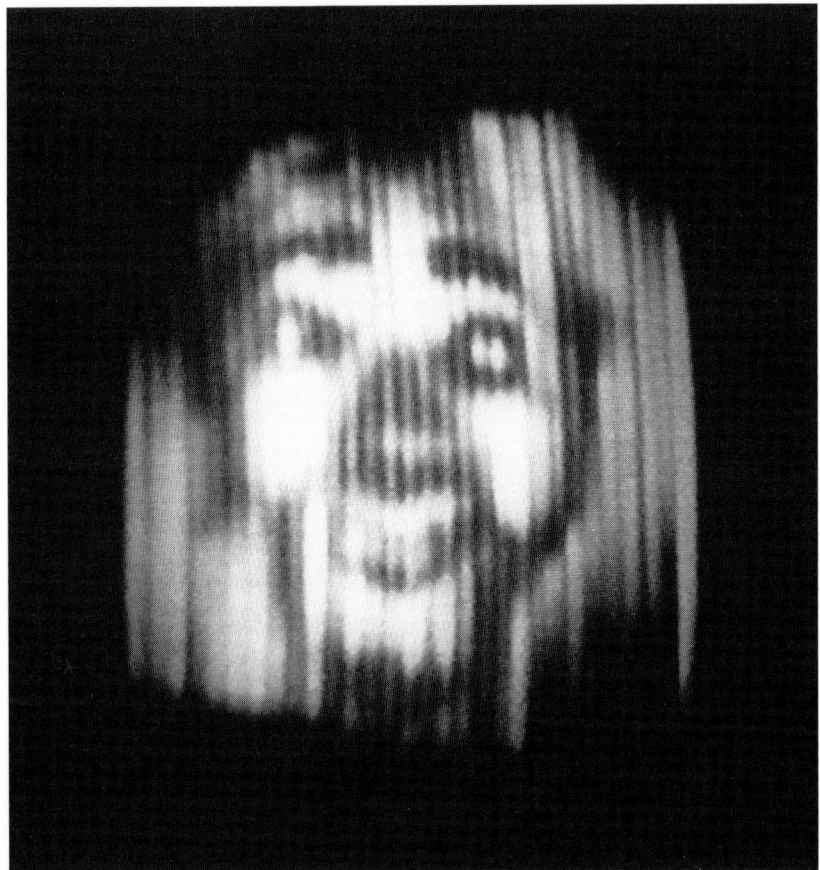

RIGHT:
STOOKY BILL TV

Nicky
Hamlyn

Almost all my work is set in interior, usually personal, spaces: even *Only at First* (1991), which is a landscape film, has been described by a friend as "an outdoor room-film." My films explore the paradoxical nature of light, the camera-eye, surface, structure, time and space. Light – ephemeral, ineffable – illuminates and models, but it also destabilises and can even obliterate solid objects.

The work is both documentary and constructed: 'documentary' in that I film existing spaces in available light – television studio lighting was used in *Minutiae* (1989) since the film's subject was a television studio; 'constructed' in that the primary nature of the work is its organisation according to formal imperatives. For example in *Anagram* (1982) a grid-like cycle of six repeating camera positions is imposed on an organic system of views, lightings and events. The resulting interaction produces the work. The foregoing could also be expressed as an interaction of the rational with the personal, the private space subjected to a disinterested, mechanical procedure. And this notion chimes with Bachelard's apothegm on the paradoxical quality of domestic space: "A house that has been experienced is not an inert box. Inhabited space transcends geometrical space." (Gaston Bachelard *The Poetics of Space*)

Recently I have become interested in the role of the body in negotiating space, because of how it contrasts with the implicit detachment of the monocular perspectival gaze, that is the camera's view. Seeing is a way of initially familiarising oneself with a space. But eventual familiarity with that space is to a significant degree physical and thus intimate in nature. If pure (ie detached) seeing subsequently returns to the scene it tends to distanciate since, in looking anew and re-apprehending that space differently, it disturbs the closeness of the tactile rapport.

I am interested in exploring the nature of this rapport and its relationship to the visual. The paradox implied in the use of a distancing device – the camera – to get close necessarily becomes central to the project. This recent train of thought was partly inspired by the case of 'SB', a blind patient of the psychologist Richard Gregory, whose sight was restored when he was 52: "we showed him a simple lathe...he was quite unable to say anything about it, but when he was allowed to touch it, he closed his eyes...and ran his hands eagerly over the lathe...then he stood back a little, and opening his eyes and staring at it he said: 'Now that I've felt it I can see.' "

I am also thinking about the film viewing situation in relation to seeing and feeling. By trying to reconnect the perceptual with the bodily I am addressing the disconnectedness of mind and body in the cinema environment, where the body is held relatively immobile while sight is concentrated elsewhere.

Nicky Hamlyn

Guesswork

1979, 11min, colour, 16mm

The film begins with a vibrant blood-red colour field that swamps the screen, reminiscent of such minimalist painters as Barnett Newman. Gradually the film reveals what we guess (hence the title) to be the source of this abstract image – a door. Different objects are presented to us through close-up so that their identity is indiscernible. Slight zooms and focus manipulation are also used to blur and render the image difficult to 'read'. At the same time, such formal devices create textures that pulsate, or swim with harsh grain effects. Hamlyn's ability to insinuate abstraction into images of 'real' objects produces a tension in his film, a visual edge whereby objects hover on the borderline between recognition and obscurity.

Michael O'Pray

Ghost Stories

1983, 30min, b&w, 16mm

Beginning with a quotation from Roland Barthes, the body of the film consists of fragmentary views of the interior of a house, in which desultory activity occasionally takes place, sometimes in front of the camera, sometimes not. A demonstration of the limits to our perception and knowledge of objects and people.

RIGHT:
INSIDE OUT

Minutiae

1989, 1min, colour, 16mm

By centring on one of the black plastic and chrome chairs normally occupied by interviewees, the film reverses the usual priorities whereby the television studio provides an unobtrusive setting within which interviews or discussions may take place. The chair is transformed through the use of an array of processes, all of which were deployed in-camera; single-frame animation, lap-dissolves, superimpositions, focus-pulls and extreme close-ups. The chair is contextualised at the beginning and end with wide shots of the Late Show studio. Commissioned by BBC2 and the Arts Council, *Minutiae* was shot in a single four hour session and edited entirely in-camera.

There Again

1991, 16min, colour, 16mm

Using multiple dissolves, superimpositions and extreme close-ups, architectural, poetic and personal conceptions of space are counterposed in a film which revisits the same location – a room in the film-maker's house – as his earlier work *Ghost Stories*.

Biography

Born 1954, London. BA Fine Art, University of Reading 1976. Screenings include Collective for Living Cinema, New York; Film and Architecture Festival, Graz; Tate Gallery, London; Institute of Contemporary Arts, London; AnnArbour. USA, London Film-makers' Co-op Workshop Organiser 1979-81; sessional lecturer at Kent Institute of Art & Design. Frequent critical writings for *Undercut*, *Art Monthly*, *Performance*.

Mona **Hatoum**

The work of Mona Hatoum – that of a Palestinian woman artist living and working in London since 1975 – appears to fulfill all the necessary multicultural criteria of a postmodern artistic practice driven by the concerns of identity politics. Yet, as much as video pieces such as *So Much I Want to Say* (1983), *Changing Parts* (1984) and *Measures of Distance* (1988) call upon the themes of sexual identity, geographical displacement and political dissidence that were almost de rigeur as touchstones in 1980s contemporary art, the formal structures of such tapes resist their being reduced to solely these concerns.

Hatoum's videos frequently employ material from her work in other media to strike new, unsettling layers of juxtapositions. Such material may derive from previous performance/installation pieces, as with the handheld black and white Super8 documentation footage of the performance piece *Under Seige* (seven hours naked and enclosed in a mud-filled perpsex container at the London Film-makers' Co-op in 1982). Incorporated in *Changing Parts*, these images intrude into and overwhelm the atmosphere of formal beauty and nostalgic remembrance of the first part of the tape. Equally, *So Much I Want to Say* was conceived as a live work made specifically for a Sloscan transmission between Vancouver and Vienna. The piece therefore exists as documentation and single screen text, with both elements contributing to the suggestion that, behind the global, electronic ether, in which talk is cheap, plentiful and deafeningly profuse, is a basic, unbreachable incommunicability. But the hands around Hatoum's mouth are male; incommunicability is seen to reside as much in processes of

transparent screen struggling to survive. The sound of the short-wave radio signals the exterior world of Beirut today, of the so-called Third World countries...the work is shot in black and white and has a supreme austerity, which controls the underlying violence.

Tamara Krikorian

Measures of Distances

1988, 15min, colour, video

This tape explores the artist's separation from her Palestinian family and in particular, her relationship with her mother whose letters from Beirut are read aloud as the soundtrack to the tape. The struggles of identity and sexuality are shown as inseparable from historical and political issues of exile and displacement.

Corps Étranger

1994, video installation, 10min cycle, video projector, player, amplifier, 4 speakers, wooden cylinder structure.

An installation commissioned by the Centre Georges Pompidou, Paris, consisting of a circular cell-like enclosure which one can penetrate through two narrow doors facing each other. A circular video image projected on the floor occupies the central area, leaving a narrow band all around, giving the viewer the option of either circulating around the image and viewing it from close quarters, or walking across the 'screen'. Both the video image (an extreme close-up shot of the body) and sound have been recorded using specialist medical equipment in this evocation of the body made vulnerable beneath the medical gaze.

Key works

So Much I Want to Say

1983, 5min, b&w, video

A series of still images unfold (one every eight seconds), revealing the face of a woman in close-up filling the screen. Two male hands repeatedly gag the woman and obscure parts of her face sometimes covering it completely. On the soundtrack repeated over and over again are the words "so much I want to say." First performed live in 1983 as a live sound and image exchange between Vancouver and Vienna using Sloscan and Telephone Music.

Changing Parts

1984, 24min, b&w, video

Changing Parts starts with a series of stills of the interior of a bathroom probably in Beirut and a soundtrack overlaid with Bach's *Suite No 4* for unaccompanied cello. This is a very private world. The details of the taps and the tiling remind us of our desperate need for familiarity. An abrupt change in action shows Hatoum trapped behind a

Born 1952, Beirut. Studied at Beirut University College 1970–72, Byam Shaw School of Art, London 1975–79, Slade School of Art 1979–1981. Lecturer at Jan Van Eyck Akademie, Maastricht and Central St Martins, London. Screenings of tapes include: Hayward Gallery, London; Museum of Modern Art, New York; National Gallery of Canada, Ottawa. Exhibitions of installation work includes: Chapter, Cardiff; Arnolfini, Bristol; Museum of Modern Art, New York; Serpentine Gallery, London; Reina Sofia, Madrid; Kröller Müller, Otterlo; Museum of Contemporary Art, Helsinki. Solo exhibitions include Centre Georges Pompidou 1994.

coercion and structures of power as it does in the Beckettian injunction to "Proceed by aporia" implied by the mantra "So much I want to say."

This layering which characterises Hatoum's video aesthetic is at its most refined and evocative in *Measures of Distance*. Here, the slow-dissolves and marginally unfocused still photographs of Hatoum's mother are visible behind the beautiful, intricately barbed mesh of Arabic calligraphy while, on the soundtrack, the voices of Hatoum *mère et fille* overlap in the reading of an exchange of letters. The distance between mother-at-home and daughter-in-exile is measured out as existing both between the tape's layered spaces of image, sound and text, as well as being the sum of these spaces.

Hatoum's most recent installation piece, *Corps Étranger* (1994) is both a consolidation of and departure from the features characterising her earlier installations. Carrying over the element of menace and entrapment present in a work such as *Light Sentence* (1992), *Corps Étranger* includes both video imagery of the body and medical imagery of its internal details which are staged and projected within a space that itself plays with the spectator's experience of this inside/outside duality. It is a piece that usefully sumarises that recurring feature of Hatoum's work – the body as abused and incarcerated physical entity as well as the site where issues of sex and politics, desire and identity converge.

Chris Darke

ABOVE:
MEASURES OF DISTANCE

Steve
Hawley

Steve Hawley's work recalls the idea of homo ludens; the delight in games and play, ingenuity and wit. The movement of irony is found and relished in the changes wrought through language and image.

Created on Paintbox, utilising advanced electronic technology, *Trout Descending a Staircase* (1987 and 1990) is a succinct video reference to the painting by Marcel Duchamp, *Nude Descending a Staircase No 2*. The video slips effortlessly between seriousness and play, movement and stillness; that tension between staccato movement and the held image echoes Duchamp's original. The enjoyment of electronic video effects (freeze framing, decay patterns and chromakey) recalls the photographs by E J Marey which had influenced Duchamp and the Futurists originally. *The Chemistry Set* (1987) also makes decorative play with a dazzling array of computer video effects.

A Proposition is a Picture (1992) invokes the soldiers who discuss postcard images in Godard's *Les Carabiniers*, or the use of domestic photographs in early Greenaway films such as *The Falls*. Hawley allows language to flow around the succession of ambiguous images, enjoying coincidences, spinning digressions, telling tales. Shadows fall on passing water or a snowscape while the first person voice elaborates a family history and investigates the 'specific gravity of meaning' with a deft irony: " 'You should never judge by appearances' – a particularly fatuous proverb for a doctor to use because, of course, everything is appearances."

Language instruction is playfully subverted in *We Have Fun Drawing Conclusions* (1982). Pictures of Peter and Jane from a children's primer are accompanied by the cosy clichès of a middle class English family where Peter washes the car with Daddy while Jane helps Mummy get the tea. The acquisition of language is bound into the acquisition of personal and social

Biography

Born 1952, Wakefield, England. Studied Fine Art at Brighton Polytechnic 1979–82. Screenings include: Geneva Video Festival; Australian Video Festival; Museum of Modern Art, New York; Stedelijk Museum, Amsterdam. *Trout Descending a Staircase*: ICA Biennial: 'Between Imagination and Reality'; *A Proposition is a Picture*: ICA Biennial: 'What You See is What You Get'. Work broadcast on Channel Four, Canal Plus, France, WGBH Boston TV. Tapes in the permanent collections of the Art Gallery of New South Wales, Australia. Currently Senior Lecturer in Fine Art, Video and Sound at Sheffield Hallam University.

Trout Descending A Staircase
1990, 1min, colour, video

Using effects generated by Paintbox, Hawley slides a variety of objects (a paintbrush; a banana; a flaming torch; a diving helmet; a trout) in front of a gilt edged frame, and the textures of the object's movements are repeated within the painting's frame. For each different object there is a different musical tune. The video gently teases the effort an artist has to expend whilst painting, by using the 'fast' technology of video to make a one-minute tactile work of art.

Tim Highstead

A Proposition is a Picture
1992, 22min, colour, video

Drawing on a range of visual material – including snapshots, postcards and Super8 home movies – the male narrator in this piece attempts to make sense of his relationship with his father, a neurologist with an interest in artificial languages.

Language Lessons
1994, 40min, colour, video
(with Tony Steyger)

There have been over two thousand invented languages, of which only a handful are still spoken in Britain. Using interviews with speakers of Ido, Esperanto and Volapuk, and rare archive material, the film examines the history and present state of the artificial language movement.

The Man from Porlock

1995, 30min, colour, video

Based around the story of the unknown 'person from Porlock' who interrupted Coleridge when he was writing *Kubla Khan*, causing him to forget the rest of the poem. A meditation on water and creativity.

relations, gendered roles. Gradually a number of logical syllogisms intrude on their complacent and well-ordered world: "No categorical sentences are false" – as in all reasoned argument the truth of the conclusion depends on the truth of the premises.

Continuing the preoccupation with language in previous work, the beautifully shot *Language Lessons* (1994), made with Tony Steyger, maintains a delicate equilibrium between a number of 'serious questions', such as power and language, internationalism and communication and a lighter delight in the diversity and eccentricity of some of the denizens of a very British demimonde of organisations competing to create an international language. One of the interviewees asserts, "English ties you to the world-view of dominant American culture", but the noble aspirations of artificial language are undercut by a babel of sectarianism.

Rod Stoneman

Tony
Hill

Trained as an architect and later as a sculptor, Tony Hill has consistently applied his interest in space, place and viewpoint to his practice as a filmmaker and installation artist. His early works in the 1970s were primarily experiments with space; *Steps* (1969), *Doors* (1973) and the floor installations *1st Floor Film* (1971) *2nd Floor Film* (1972) revealed his interest in the nature of filmic representation and his desire to question its construction. These works transformed the viewer's relationship with the screen and the illusionist deep space within it, by reconsidering the very cinematic apparatus of camera, projector and screen, and the position of the viewer in that equation. In the *Floor Films* for example, the image is projected via an overhead mirror onto a screen which forms the floor of a room-like space, and the audience can watch either by standing on the screen or by viewing it through the mirror – in which case those inside the room are viewed as part of the film. This architectural change in the cinematic apparatus emphasises the audiences' participation in both the physical and optical construct of the film image.

As his work developed in the 1980s, Hill used both specially constructed camera carrying devices and lenses to explore the body's relationship to space and gravity. In *Downside Up* (1985), *Water Work* (1987) and *Expanded Movie* (1990), Hill's seductive architectural and sculptural approaches blend powerfully with the subjects of everyday life, providing a visual counterpoint to what could be banal domestic scenes. The continually rotating camera in *Downside Up* places the viewer in impossible positions by rotating through 180 degrees over a series of genre scenes of the family home and landscape, with an apparent ease which skillfully underplays the complexity and visual dexterity of its production. This discarding of an anthropomorphic view of the world is the uniting element in Hill's work, as he creates a new and surprising visual interpretation of our daily lives.

While the images he creates are often playful and seem born of a simple view of the world, their bizarre and often humorous vantage points make us rethink our assumptions about perspective, gravity, size, scale and movement. The mechanical wizardry involved contrasts with the childlike vision we encounter; a series of visual miracles which surprise, engage and entertain us. It is worth noting that Hill has adapted some of his installations and films for children, as in the workshop *Sens Dessus Dessous* (1986) held at the Centre Pompidou, emphasising his closeness to the child's imagination, a space not yet colonised by optical laws of survival.

The recent award winning One Minute Television commissions *A Short History of the Wheel* (1992) and *Holding the Viewer* (1993), combine spontaneity and sophistication in works of unique visual pleasure, and have gained Hill a larger audience than exists for most experimental work.

Michael Maziere

Downside Up
1985, 17min, colour, 16mm

A film which, by the use of a simple camera movement, explores and re-views some relationships to the ground. The viewpoint continuously orbits places, objects, people and events. The observations, made slowly at first dwelling within the subject, gradually speed up to reveal a double sided ground flipping like a tossed coin, then slow again to oscillate about the earth's edge.

Water Work
1987, 11min, colour, 16mm

A sculptural film which explores the space on and just below the surface of a swimming pool. The film plays with orientation, weightlessness and particularly the surface itself, that peculiar boundary between worlds that is both window and mirror, both visible and invisible.

Expanded Movie
1990, 13min, colour, 16mm

An experimental anamorphic film with optically squashed and squeezed images which raises some questions about the perception of shapes. From the longest cow to the shortest car, the film contains bizarre, extraordinary and sometimes hilarious images. It weaves a path between home, street and playground, finally meeting with its own musical ending.

Biography

Born 1946, London. Studied architecture and sculpture. Currently Reader in Film at the University of Derby. *Downside Up*: Best Experimental Film, Melbourne International Film Festival; Stepping Out Prize, No-Budget Festival, Hamburg; *Water Work*: Best Experimental Film Prize, Melbourne International Film Festival; *A Short History of the Wheel*: Deutscher Videokunstpreis. *A Short History of the Wheel* and *Holding the Viewer*: Audience Prize, Chateauroux Festival 1993. *Holding the Viewer*: ICA Biennial: 'What You See is What You Get'. Broadcast screenings include Channel Four; Canal Plus, France; BBC2; La Sept, France; Kanal 4, Germany; VPRO, The Netherlands; WDR Television, Germany.

TOP:
WATER WORK
BOTTOM:
EXPANDED MOVIE

Susan
Hiller

Susan Hiller's video installations represent only a small part of her total oeuvre and yet they show an impressive understanding of the medium and its capacity to tap into our unconscious processes, evoking those strangely familiar moments which Freud called the 'uncanny': "something that ought to have remained secret or hidden but has come to light."

Belshazzar's Feast/The Writing on Your Wall (1984) draws on the experience of reverie – a trance-like state when the mind's censors relax their vigilance and imagination strays across time and space into fantasy. The original installation (in the Tate Gallery collection) uses wallpaper and photographs to simulate a domestic setting, one which became actualised when the work was screened as a Channel Four independent programme. In a version at the ICA, a cluster of four video monitors were arranged on the floor to suggest a campfire around which, at night, an audience would once have gathered to hear a storyteller relate collective identities. Here, we too become mesmerised by the image's transformation from sparkling lights into dancing tongues of flame, as the artist's voice begins to spin a tale: "What the fire says, Take One…" Yet the fire tells us nothing; rather we become engulfed in an indecipherable echolalia, punctuated by whispered accounts of newspaper reports of aliens transmitting messages on television after close-down. Hiller draws parallels between these mysterious apparitions and the phantasms of fire-gazing which, like the receiver describing the alien message as one of unspeakable horror, were often taken to be premonitions of disaster. How are we to account for these images except as projections of our own imaginings, marks of the limitations of rationalised language to restrain the figurations of repressed desires?

Biography

Born USA, 1942. BA Smith College 1961; MA Tulane University 1965. Conducted anthropological fieldwork in Central America; moved to Europe at the end of the 1960s, From the early 1970s, produced mixed-media works involving painting, sculpture, sound, printed texts and drawing. *Belshazzar's Feast* is in the collection of the Tate Gallery, London and a version was broadcast by Channel Four (1985) other works are in the collections of the Imperial War Museum, London; Leeds City Art Museum; Victoria and Albert Museum, London; Arts Council Collection. See bibliography for works as author.

Belshazzar's Feast/The Writing on your Wall
1984, video installation

The rehabilitation of the communal imagination, its reawakening from the restless, potentially lethal sleep imposed by corporate culture, is a major aspect of Hiller's work. In *Belshazzar's Feast*, she uses the TV set as a metaphor for the communal hearth, but on the screen, flames leap and flow with subliminal energy, like uncontrollable nature threatening to burst its cultural bonds...but also, at times, like the mesmerising autonomy of the airwaves. Domesticity is evoked by wallpaper in the installation: it too has its dark side, its own agenda, in the ideological message its pattern carries. On the tape, a 'preconscious' singing alternates with recollections of the Rembrandt painting and Bible story of Belshazzar's Feast enunciated by Hiller's son Gabriel, and with news stories about the appearance of alien faces on local TV screens announcing some doomful fate for the planet.

Lucy Lippard, *Out of Bounds*

An Entertainment
1990, 20min, 4 channel video installation

Excerpts from Punch and Judy shows are repeated over and over in fast-paced edits; some of the imagery in slow motion, phrases from the puppets are rendered unintelligible or uttered in uncanny isolation. Four sets of images are projected onto opposite sides of the room, leaving the viewer an unwitting participant in the Punch and Judy allegories.

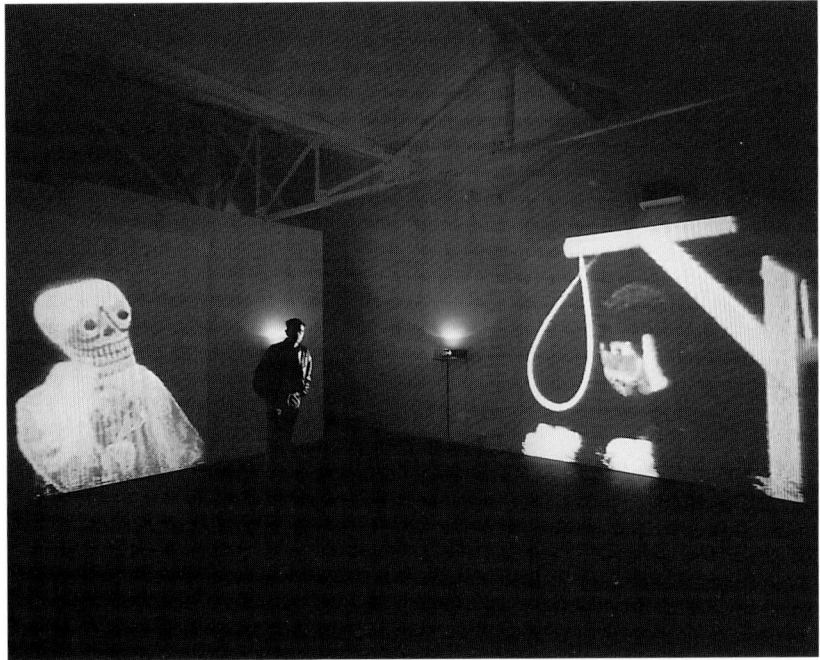

Magic and terror return in *An Entertainment* (1990), a mural-sized projection of four interlocking tapes and four speakers. Here, the shadow of death and violence gradually comes to haunt the affectionate domesticity and seemingly burlesque scene of Punch and Judy. The glove puppets, once perceived from a child's perspective on a high miniature stage, now dwarf us. The images unsettle us; their predominant chromatic range (black, white, red, pink, yellow) is that of the body itself – hair, bone, blood, flesh and skin. They assail us from all sides, sometimes flowing sequentially round the walls, sometimes arrested in freeze-frame, appearing in pairs in front and behind or to left and right. But, in any case, our field of vision cannot take them all in at once; the fourth place, the supplementary 'behind sight', always remains visually beyond our control however much we turn in the space.

An Entertainment presents us with a space we cannot occupy. Rather, it possesses us; it lures us, through its opening blood-red curtains, with art's promise of a sublime transcendence. But as the final curtain falls, we find ourselves once again brought to earth and gripped by doubt; we see that we have been artfully seduced by a sleight of hand, and drawn towards the revelation that art, representation, is the veil behind which there is [only] desire.

Jean Fisher *Susan Hiller: The Revenants of Time*

Stuart
Hilton

Although Stuart Hilton's work is uncompromisingly experimental – and breaks all the rules about sound reinforcing image – it remains more approachable than some animation in which sound and image are combined in conventional narrative form. His work bursts onto the screen in patches of colour and snatches of sound, yet despite (or perhaps because of) its challenging abstractness, it is both personal and passionate.

Hilton draws upon the tradition of experimental animation represented by Oskar Fischinger, Len Lye and Norman McLaren. His early piece, *Starting* (1988), a symphonic visual poem, explores the musical shape of line and the relationship between splashes of colour on an otherwise empty canvas. *Pendulum* (1991), with its bold primary colours owes something to Lye, and *Wrong* (1991), both made at the Royal College of Art, began his exploration of the fragmenting, multi-layered technique which he developed in *Argument in a Superstore* (1992) and *Save Me* (1994). In this later work, in which his main concerns are to disrupt the unity of sound and image and to express meanings through multi-layered non-linear forms, Hilton looks more towards other experimental filmmakers like Stan Brakhage and Harry Smith. And appearing somewhere in this mix are the visually witty, animated films of Robert Breer with their rough, hand drawn conjuring.

Hilton comes from a generation of animators produced by British art colleges which benefited from a teaching environment concerned with producing artists, and not exclusively preoccupied with training professionals. Hilton's post-college development has been supported by public funding, but like many animators, he also directs television commercials, continuing that other tradition in which art and commerce can be mutually and beneficially exploitative.

Jill McGreal

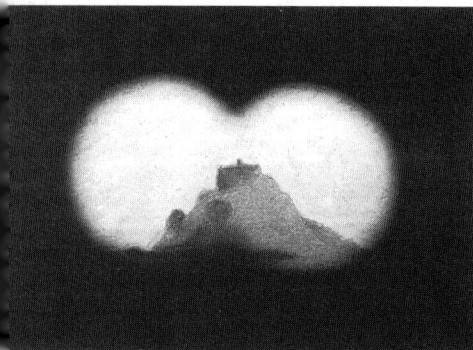

Born 1965, Preston. BA Graphic Design, Liverpool Polytechnic 1988; MA Animation, Royal College of Art, London 1991. Screenings include: London Film Festival; AVE, Arnhem; Annecy Animation Festival; Edinburgh Film Festival; European Media Art Festival, Osnabrück; Cardiff International Animation Festival. *Save Me*: ICA Biennial: 'What You See is What You Get'.

Pendulum
1991, 2min, colour, 16mm

Made at the Royal College of Art, *Pendulum* is constructed through repetition – of four abstract shapes and a few bars of music – which build to a co-ordinated climax of cut and pace and finishes in the minimal credits on the filmmaker's name. The canvas is fuller than in Hilton's previous *Starting*, but there is the same use of bold primary colours and a similar tight structure, described by Hilton as "an hypnotic mantra." *Pendulum* is the last film that Hilton made in which sound and picture are treated as a unity.

Save Me
1994, 6min, colour, 35 mm

In *Save Me*, Hilton's main concern was to further develop an approach to animated film-making in which sound and image, in direct contrast to most other animation, were not cut together to create either structure or meaning. The disjointed snippets of found images, drawings, texts and music tracks defy narrative thread and any conventional assembly of meanings. Nevertheless there are clear references in what Hilton calls the "splinters of representation" to the ideas and objects which signify in our daily lives.

ABOVE LEFT:
SAVE ME

Imaginary Opera

1992, film and video projection and performance with orchestra

What is particularly poignant for this body of work is not so much the content of each individually made film or video tape, but the constant search for an appropriate method of projection which will bring these film-makers into a new and direct relationship with their audience. *Imaginary Opera* was commissioned as a collaboration between Housewatch and the composer Steve Martland for the Fourth Contemporary Music Festival in Kyoto. The public were welcomed to the outside of a building onto which the film was projected but from where the orchestra could not be seen. The cyclists on film and in performance offered many musical associations. The spacing, the repetition, the sequences (sometimes single images, sometimes collective) hinted at visual analogies with a musical score. More pertinent still was the invitation (rarely taken up) for spectators to move behind the screen, to view the orchestra and finally to produce (by silhouette on screen) an image in the artwork itself.

Jeni Walwin

Little Big Horn

1992, film projections in motor vehicles

This mixed media installation consisting of six pieces using Super-8mm projection in real vehicles was organised for the Queen Elizabeth Hall Undercroft on the Southbank, in London. The pieces included: *Universal Power Drive* by Stanford Steele, in which a timber-tractor activated by passing spectators, flashed the message "Recovery",

Housewatch was formed in 1985, and is a collective showcase of individual works by artists Ian Bourn, Lulu Quinn, George Saxon, Tony Sinden, Stanford Steele and Alison Winckle. Their aim is to transcend the traditional framework of cinema, performance and gallery exhibition space. As individual practitioners, they have backgrounds in the production of experimental film, video, sculpture, live work and site-specific installation. As a collaborative group, they have used light, film, video, sound and performance to develop new and challenging venues in a variety of public spaces and ordinary urban situations, at locations in the UK and more recently, Japan.

Housewatch began by using the front windows and door of a house as a site for projection. The result was *Cinematic Architecture for Pedestrians* (1985), a programme of six, multi-projected pieces specifically for the context of the street. Since the formation of the collective, they have embraced a wide range of media and perceptual issues that explore a new interactive relationship between the work, audience and exhibition context.

The essential idea of a Housewatch event is about a transformation of the site; expanding the threshold – exploring a broader definition of art, cinema and cultural language. To begin with, the six artists agree a common framework that allows them to produce a work independently of each other. The final programme is structured to reflect their individual ideas and responses to the site; setting-up a situation of flux and change, as a means of challenging audience expectations and of keeping alive the collective spirit of debate – of Housewatch.

and emitted music from Monteverdi's *Orfeo*; Lulu Quinn's *Fatal Instincts*, which evoked the predatory nature of cars: the Hunter – a crouched, shiny black Morris Minor saloon, the sound of its engines combined with the menacing purr of a cat – and the Hunted – an ageing rusty Morris Minor. Oblivious of their impending doom, two chickens could be seen staking their newly acquired territory: the female settled down to feed and rest, while the male shrieked out his claim to territory with persistent vigour; and Tony Sinden's *Acceleration/Arrest* and *Deceleration/Desire* combined two static cars (a Volvo 66 and a Rover 67) with film, projection and sound, developing a sculptural-cinematic concept that momentarily arrested the viewer's perception of the car as cult object, and the desire to be mobile.

ABOVE:
PAPER HOUSE

Isaac
Julien

As someone who has expressed an interest in difference but a profound antipathy to essentialism, Isaac Julien cannot easily be discussed as either a 'gay film-maker' or a 'black film-maker', and still less a 'gay, black film-maker'. Rather, his work has displayed a series of shifting positions and styles, testifying to its fundamentally analytic, inquisitive project. Julien began film-making as a member of the Sankofa collective, which took its name, as publicity statements pointed out, from a mythical bird "which signifies the act of looking into the past to prepare for the future." His work accordingly involves a sifting-through of past images (media images, social documents, cultural memories), not so much to dispense with them, but to amplify them, and so move on to new arguments.

Julien's short *The Attendant* (1992), therefore, does not seek to erase certain High Art myths about power and sexuality, so much as to explore hitherto overlooked conjunctions between them, revolving around images of racial difference, social and sexual bondage, uniform and ritual, representation and slavery. While it may not be easy, finally, to say what the film is 'about' ostensibly, it is about the homoerotic fantasies of a black middle-aged museum attendant – its stylish elegance at least leaves behind a residue of images and suggestive connections.

The Attendant, with its video-generated dream apparatus, certainly confirms the suggestion that Julien, drawing away from Sankofa's rougher, low-budget aesthetic, has yet to fully reach a compromise with the seductions of style. *Looking for Langston* (1989) is very much about embracing style – a 'meditation' on the poet Langston Hughes and the Harlem Renaissance, it sets out to reappraise a certain social scene, a certain discourse, a certain manner of elegance. The film does not simply present archaeological explication, complete with archive footage, of a forgotten history of black gay culture. Rather, it strives to enter into the textures of its imagination; the film's most effective moment, poised ballroom scenes notwithstanding, is precisely its dream sequence. This is

Biography

Born 1960. BA in Fine Art Film, St Martins School of Art 1984. Founded Sankofa Film and Video Collective 1983. *Young Soul Rebels*: Best Feature, International Critics Week Cannes; *The Attendant*: Best Short Film, Chicago Gay and Lesbian Film Festival 1993; ICA Biennial: 'What You See is What You Get'. *Black and White in Colour*: New York Film Festival; *The Darker Side of Black*: 1994 Berlin Film Festival and many others. Member of *Screen* editorial board 1986-89; John Mcknight International Fellow, Minneapolis 1992; Senior Producer at Testing The Limits, New York for the ITVS series *The Question of Equality*. Writer and editor (see bibliography).

Key works

Territories
1984, 30min, colour, 16mm

Footage of the Notting Hill Carnival is radically interrogated in this experimental documentary which evokes the creativity of black street culture in the context of the contested space of the inner city.

This Is Not an AIDS Ad
1987, 14min, colour, video

An unashamedly erotic and stylish video which reclaims some of the territory seized by the new puritans of the 1980s. The first part contains lyrical images of death and loss, while the second half is assertive and celebratory, accompanied by a funk-heavy soundtrack.

Looking for Langston
1989, 45min, b&w, 16mm

The private world of the black artists and writers such as Langston Hughes who formed the Harlem Renaissance of the 1920s is recreated in a mythic dimension. The film switches from archive footage to a stylised version of the jazz and blues inflected Harlem to explore white society's barriers against black homosexuality as well as self-imposed 'discretion'.

The Attendant
1992, 8min, colour, 35mm

A history painting, *Scene on the Coast of Africa*, is brought to life as a tableau vivant, playing out the pleasures and dangers of a secret world. Memory mixes with desire as a museum attendant is caught up in sado-masochistic fantasies.

perhaps why the feature *Young Soul Rebels* (1991) fails so signally. It begins from the intriguing premise that the year 1977 in Britain can be reclaimed for soul culture – flying in the face of the orthodoxy that earmarks it for punk. But the culture of 1977 is evoked almost nostalgically, through the signposted minutiae of heritage-park re-creation; a less naturalistic evocation might have allowed the year to be dreamt.

The themes of *Young Soul Rebels*, nevertheless, mark the bridge between Julien's earlier Sankofa work, with its specific links with British black communities, and what has been seen as a move into the new terrain offered by Queer Cinema – a movement already begun in *This Is Not an AIDS Ad* (1987) with its implicit nod to the school of Jarman and Maybury. Certainly, Julien seems least likely of all directors to make solipsistic work (the home-movie aspects of *This Is Not an AIDS Ad* are as close as he's so far come). Rather, his films seem likely always to centre on the concerns of particular communities, or micro-communities – those marginalised by their hybridity, such as the gay Harlem of the 1920s. In *Territories* (1984), a film not so much about the Notting Hill Carnival as about the media stereotypes riding on it, the voice-over remarks that "colonial fantasy requires a fixed notion of black identity." Such fixedness is undermined throughout Julien's shifting oeuvre; the process certainly seems to have come full circle in *The Attendant*, in which colonialism itself seems no longer to have a fixed identity.

Jonathan Romney

Sebastiane (1976), a homoerotic account of the narcissistic saint and his martyrdom, was Jarman's first feature-film. Largely privately funded, and with Latin dialogue, it promptly became a controversial – if somewhat formally conservative – gay classic. *Jubilee*, which quickly followed, bore all Jarman's hallmarks: a bleak, apocalyptic view of contemporary England; a fascination with Renaissance England; a provocative collaging of 'personalities'; and a robust, irreverent and shocking sense of humour exemplified by Jordan's infamous *Rule Britannia*.

If *Jubilee* became the filmic model for Jarman's socio-political spleen and black humour, *The Tempest*, with its off-beat casting of punk-singer Toyah Wilcox as Miranda and poet Heathcote Williams as Prospero, established his ability to conjure a magical quality of time and place using the simplest of means. Aided by a chiaroscuro-lit set of startling conviction, the film was brought to a rapturous, camp climax by a sailors' dance and Elizabeth Welch's rendition of *Stormy Weather*.

The Elizabethan world of John Dee, Shakespeare and alchemical magic found in *Jubilee* and *The Tempest* was given a more personal and intensive poetic form in the shifting colours and erotic ritualism of the Super8 (blown-up to 35mm) film *The Angelic Conversation*, set to Shakespeare's sonnets. This was completed shortly after the unique *Imagining October*, in which he first merged private and personal concerns – the role of the artist in contemporary society, the processes of art and representation, the sexual and political repression of society by government, an ambivalent homoeroticism and remarkable documentary images of the peoples and buildings of Moscow and Baku.

Caravaggio, *War Requiem* (1989) and *Wittgenstein* (1993) explored the iconography of gay historical heroes with authority, wit and visual flair. *Edward II* (1991) was an angry gay interpretation of Marlow's play, and signalled a personal disillusionment with the Elizabethan arcadia. During the same period, he directed three experimental features of harsh beauty, savage polemics and apocalyptic vision – *The Last of England* (1987), *The Garden* (1990) and his final film *Blue* (1993). (*Glitterbug*, 1994 is a compilation of early home movies). Fierce visions, beautifully shot on Super8, they powerfully and inextricably intermixed the public and intensely private in dark, pessimistic anti-narratives of the near-future. In these later films, Jarman often appeared on-screen as their shaping consciousness, together with Tilda Swinton's vulnerable Madonna-like figure. In *Blue*, Jarman pushed his experiments to the final reduction of an unchanging blue screen accompanied by an intricate sound composition and voice-over; a diary of his observations as a person with AIDS dealing with encroaching blindness.

Michael O'Pray

Born 1942, died 1994. Read English, History and Art History at King's College, London. Studied Painting at the Slade School of Art 1963–67. Exhibited paintings at Young Contemporaries 1967, Lisson Gallery 1969, Edward Totah Gallery 1982, ICA retrospective 1984, Richard Salmon Ltd 1992. Designed sets for Sir Frederick Ashton's *Jazz Calendar* at Covent Garden; costumes and sets for London Festival Ballet and London Contemporary Dance Company; sets for Ken Russell's *The Devils* (1971) and *Savage Messiah* (1972). Appeared as Pier Paolo Pasolini in Julian Coles' *Ostia* (1987); as Patrick Proctor in Stephen Frears' *Prick Up Your Ears* (1987); roles in Ron Peck's *Nighthawks* (1978) and *Strip Jack Naked* (1991). Made music videos after 1973 for Marc Almond, Bryan Ferry, The Smiths, Bob Geldof, Pet Shops Boys. Author of several books (see bibliography). *Blue*: Michael Powell Prize, 1993 Edinburgh Film Festival; ICA Biennial: 'What You See is What You Get'.

Demolition/Escape

1983, installation, 7 monitors, 1 player, neon,
toy train set

A large model steam train moves back and
forth across the floor, [...] on the right of
the track is a vertical column of six
monitors placed alternatively upside down
so that the column resembles a steep
staircase. The monitors show a sequence of
the artist crawling with difficulty along the
floor and then ascending a ladder. On the
wall behind is a diagonally ascending line of
blue neon numbers. [...] *Demolition/Escape*
speaks of a childhood heavily infused with
fantasy. The emotional struggle of the artist
'imprisoned' in the monitors.. is taunted by
the old rational 'stare' of the train in its
pointless movement back and forth, and by
the equally empty rise of the numbers –
rationality to no purpose except as an
illusion of knowledge, and to that end a
prison of sorts.

Michael O'Pray

Faded Wallpaper

1986, installation, 11 monitors, 2 players

Based loosely on a short story by Charlotte
Parkins Gilmour, *Faded Wallpaper* is
concerned with visual perception, madness
and the search for identity. A woman,
isolated within a room, becomes obsessed
with the wallpaper surrounding her, seeing
within its faded patterns strange images – at
times pleasurable and seductive, at times
threatening and dangerous. As these images
become more insistent, she begins to strip
the wallpaper away in an attempt either to
banish the images or get to their source.
Words and sounds run through her head as
she peels away the layers, questioning her

Due to their technical inventiveness and levels of meaning, Tina Keane's works
do not fit easily within a narrow classification such as 'Film and Video Art'.
The use of new media by artists in the 1970s and 1980s, in often surprising
combinations, was an attempt to escape such institutionalising tendencies in
fixing the artist's identity. Indeed, Keane's work has shown a struggle from the
start to make visible and surpass restrictive classifications, beginning with those
imposed on women. It is in this spirit that she has pursued an undeniable
fascination with electronic media. She has combined video and film with
elements of performance, light, sculpture and drawing/writing.

In normal life, the electronic energy of television contrasts almost ludicrously
with the television set's domestic role as furniture, and its social role as an agent
of control and order. A transformation of this contradiction lies at the heart of
Keane's work. She has discovered new forms of beauty in the charged particles
of the television image (echoed in other favourite imagery of hers: the ripples of
water, the fleeting play of shadows, the aura of neon and even the patterns of a
snake's skin). With this has gone a wry and optimistic attitude to the video
monitor. For Keane, the television set is not an hypnotic monster transfixing the
spectator, nor a passive 'support' for the images showing on it, but a sculptural
element of metaphorical structures. Almost always these have stressed a
continuum, or process of linking: the ladder, the garland, spiral, bouquet,
escalator and other configurations. By means of these imaginative connections
she has returned again to an examination of social constraints and possibilities
of freedom.

After training as a painter, and working on light shows for Pink Floyd in the
1960s, Keane discovered her own voice. On a boat trip from Skye to Harris she
was fascinated by the shadows of passengers at the rail cast on the waves below
and intuitively took out her camera to film them. "I looked down and saw time
moving amongst the shadows." This film was later used, together with a
woman's voice narrating the consequences of the Clearances in the Western Isles
(a memory handed down through generations), in *Shadow of a Journey* (1980);
and it was used also in *Shadow Woman* (1977), a performance Keane gave with
her young daughter Emily, one of many collaborations between them.

The 'shadow' is both the linking and the restricting presence cast between
mother and daughter. There followed a long sequence of works using children's'
songs and games – *The Swing* (1978), *Playpen* (1979), *Clapping Songs* (1981),
Bedtime Story (1982), *Hopscotch* (1986). These explored, at several levels, a fine
line between freedom and entrapment. Children's uninhibited play, a metaphor
for artistic creation, is part of a continuum linking children throughout history,
yet the individual cannot return to childhood. The adult takes pleasure in
rediscovering her own childhood through her daughter, yet fears she will pass on
to her daughter the constricting social view of women imposed on her. Multiple
chains, comforting bonds and necessary breaks.

If much of Keane's work of the late 1970s and early 1980s was concerned
with exploring personal and collective identity, afterwards she passed to a more

'objective' treatment of the issues of freedom. The structure of her works however, has always retained the openness and accessibility of games. In *Media Snake* (1985) at the ICA, a huge spiral of monitors contrasted an insipid diet of TV soap with the sensuous presence of a snake shot in close-up sliding across the chain of screens. *Escalator* (1988) a similarly vast stepped structure of monitors at Riverside Studios, juxtaposed in ascending and descending lines the glitz of city boom architecture with the underground world of the homeless and destitute. *In Our Hands, Greenham* (1984) her tribute to the women's peace camp, presented the main visual narrative through the outline of continuously moving linked hands. Many recent works have played upon the ambivalent relationship between forms of patterning/order and the aspirations of human freedom and expressivity: *The Diver* (1987), *Circus Troupe* (1990), *Caution: Thin Ice* (1993) for example.

As Carlyle Reedy has perceptively pointed out, Keane's work is a search for equilibrium between "fleshy solid or sculptural qualities and ephemeral poetic qualities." These could be taken as an analogy for our uncertainties about the relationship between the 'real' body and the seductive electronic image. In her notes for *Caution: Thin Ice*, Keane compares the diamond-like brilliance of the ice skater's movements with the "dark liquid" which "moves stealthily below to an unknown destiny out of control." This aptly describes the dualities and contradictions she has pursued throughout her important body of work. Her words also suggest that this search is intermingled with her continuing love of the luminescent glow of the TV screen and neon tube against the surrounding darkness.

Guy Brett

own self-image, her imagination and her sanity. No solutions are given, only more questions.

Tina Keane

Escalator

1988, installation, 22 monitors, 2 players, 6 light boxes, scaffolding, lighting

Two tape sources show the steps of a London Underground escalator, giving the piece an immediate and striking visual impact as the spatial/sculptural arrangement of monitors gives the illusion of an ascending and descending moving staircase. ..[Superimposed] on the up and up, images of plaza-bound Big City whizz-kids, the high finance district hi-life, the perfectly reflected beauty of the skyscraper architecture of power – and on the down and out, weary commuters, faces drawn with fatigue and indifference, as homeward-bound feet pass by inches from the cardboard and carrier bag poverty of those men and women with nowhere to go or stay. Texts appear, sparingly used – "a city haunted by broken spirits" (going underground); "how many of Fortnum's customers are aware that some of their fellow citizens have taken up residence more or less permanently in cardboard boxes?" (on the upline).

Mike Jones

Neon Diver

1991, 16min, colour, 16mm and video

Neon Diver's skilful weave of ritual and frolic; its alternating moods of menace and playfulness; its images of female power, grace and beauty, produces a representation that is both fluid and disciplined. It provides pleasure while at the same time exploring the mechanisms of that pleasure. With the final exhilarating leap of the film-maker into the water, there is a real sense of breaking free from the traditional constraints of female subjectivity for film-maker and spectator alike. There is a rush that comes with the release of the repressed desire embedded in cinematic fantasy, and it is this feeling that *Neon Diver* expresses and celebrates.

Bev Zalcock

Biography

Born 1948. Educated at Hammersmith College of Art, London 1967–70 and Sir John Cass School of Art, London. Founder member of Circles – Women in Distribution. Member of the Arts Council's Artists' Film and Video Committee and the Art Angel Trust Advisory Committee. Screenings include: Tate Gallery, London; Institute of Contemporary Arts, London; Berlin Video Festival; Museum of Modern Art, New York; Montreal Film Festival, Jungen Forum, Berlin Film Festival. Installation exhibitions: Riverside Studios Gallery, London; Serpentine Gallery, London; Air Gallery, London; Institute of Contempoary Arts, London; Angel Row, Nottingham; A Space, Toronto; Studiogalerie Museum Morsbroich, Leverkusen; Artware Hamburg/Hannover, Germany; Sanart '92, Turkey; Museum Moderner Kunst Stiftung Ludwig, and Subway Station, Vienna; Vancouver Art Gallery, Canada. Currently a lecturer at Central St Martin's College of Art and Design, London.

TOP:
DEMOLITION/ESCAPE
BOTTOM:
HOPSCOTCH

Jeff
Keen

Born in 1923, Jeff Keen has been making films and expanded cinema since 1960, longer than any other English experimentalist still productive. His new work (now in video as well as 8mm and 16mm) is just as fresh and vigorous as the legendary rapid-fire collage of such early films as *Marvo Movie* (1967) or *Cine Blatz* (1968). Since the mid-1960s he has also combined live-action, tape, film and slides in mixed-media performance, in the person of his manic alter-ego, Dr Gaz. In the best sense, time has not tempered him. A true auto-didact, his single-frame art and prodigious output of drawings and sketchbooks are packed with a condensed, distilled and displaced iconography which originates in his cinematic 'primal scene'. In Keen's case, this goes back to his days as a bewildered teenager, a raw recruit for World War II, which he sardonically dubs "the greatest movie ever made." The passions and frustrations of youth burst through; young audiences are still among his best viewers, through the 1960s underground to punk and post-techno.

Many of Keen's films explore 'cut-ups' of mass culture imagery, using found footage and animation as well as icons culled from magazines. Others are pastiche dramas, as in *White Dust* (1972), where he evokes the arcane humour lurking in his source material – the 'cheap cinema' of fringe Hollywood genres and their imitators (like such favourites as *Godzilla Meets The Hulk*). At the same time, mass images – often the near-anonymous product of the commercial margins – are given his personal signature. In the early days, he used family and friends to make up an ad hoc cast for his films – the surreal characters Mottler, Silverhead, Vulvana, Baby Jelly. Alongside his 16mm fantastic and mock-action dramas (all climax and no story) he also made 8mm diary films in which the magic is drawn from the accidents of daily life. These themes fuse in the sequences of cornucopia – peace and plenty – which punctuate the more frenetic aspects of his work, to celebrate childhood play and free fantasy.

The Cartoon Theatre of Doctor Gaz
1979, 12min, b&w and colour, 16mm

Animation, cut-ups, found footage and a vibrant humour combine with the anti-establishment spirit of Dada.

Artwar
1993, (5 x 30sec, 1 x 2min), video

Commissioned by the Arts Council and Channel Four, *Artwar* is a short video consisting of five, thirty second pieces and a final two minute 'epic'. Artwork and warlike metaphors are deployed combining Super8 film, performance and animation.

Key works

Marvo Movie
1967, 5min, colour, 16mm

Combining both graphic and live-action sequences, *Marvo Movie* evokes Keen's fascination with Hollywood B movies and comic strip collage. Keen and family dress up and perform for the camera in a riotous appropriation of the surrealist tradition.

White Dust
1972, 35min, colour, 16mm

A collage narrative formulated as a homage to vintage movie serials and their idiosyncratic conventions. Parodic tableaux and chance happenings make this a subversive re-working of a despised form of 'low-brow' cinema.

Born 1923, Trowbridge, Wiltshire. Started making films in 1960; has worked with expanded cinema using a mixture of live action, film, slides and tape since the mid 1960s. Makes artists' bookworks and paintings. Subject of the Arts Council/Channel 4 film *Jeff Keen Films* (1983). Screenings include: National Film Theatre London; Arsenal Kino, Berlin; Centre for Contemporary Art, Warsaw; Queen's Film Theatre, Belfast; Museum of the Moving Image, London; Brighton Festival. *Artwar*: ICA Biennial: 'What You See is What You Get'.

Keen is also associated with mind-numbing montage, a melt-down mix of cartoon capers, new photos, modern art movements, ads and logos, puns and jokes, old movies and visual anarchy. Rapid and multi-layered, it purposefully "cuts the power lines", social and aesthetic. By contrast, *Mad Love* (1978) offers a more measured series of narrative and comic tableaux which still draw on Surrealism and its popular roots in 'low art'. Surrealism, filtered through the air of Brighton (where he has lived and worked for many years), is perhaps his strongest single influence.

Keen's new films and videos keep pace with the times, signalled in the ambition, theme and title of his *Artwar – The Last Frontier* (1993) – ie, the self-portrait of the artist as rebellious sorcerer of rapid-eye vision. Many of the titles of his latest films are defiant dada shouts, more sounds than sense (although he remains a classicist in his control of the medium); *Gazwrx* (1986), *Omozap* (1991), *B-B-B-BOM* (1990), *Platzmatic Blatz* (1991). As Jeff Keen said years ago, "When words fail – use your teeth."

A L Rees

ABOVE LEFT:
NADINE AS THE CAT WOMAN IN WHITE DUST
RIGHT:
ARTWAR

Patrick
Keiller

All Patrick Keiller's films to date adopt the same basic formula: images of townscape and landscape seen by a subjective camera are strung together into a fictional journey by a disembodied first-person narrator. Locations and trajectories vary: from the two travelling shots over footbridges in the vicinity of the North Circular Road in *Stonebridge Park* (1981) to the voyage over the Channel and across the Alps to Rome in *The End* (1986). What remains constant is the juxtaposition of mute images with non-synchronous sound. The disjunction or lacuna which results has resonances beyond Keiller's working method (picture-assembly first, voice-over second). Although actual delivery – a dry, fluent but quizzical male voice – tends to be highly restrained, the story-telling is portentous, discursive, outrageous, even lurid. *Stonebridge Park* incorporates the contemplations of a second-hand car salesman who has run off to Nice with his employer's money, and in a sequel, *Norwood* (1983), undergoes a new career as a property speculator, a tempestuous marriage, brutal murder and life after death.

Keiller's imagery, on the other hand, is formal (until recently always black and white), public (shots are usually exterior or in shopping malls, railway stations etc) yet particular, ordinary and extraordinary (a pre-requisite for surrealism) at the same time. With the exception of *London* (1994), human figures, other than in extreme long shot, are rare. Framing is precise; shots are set up in order to draw attention to movement or detail within them; for example in *London*, a procession of dairy cows – a model on the Swiss Centre building – dominates the shot in which the Queen is walking in Leicester Square. In *London*, Keiller's first film in 35mm and colour, camera movement is all but eliminated so that shots function like still images, animated postcards. Keiller's work seems to harness spatial and temporal contradictions, declaring "this has been" (Barthes on the photograph) at the same time as "there it is" (Metz on film).

Biography

Born 1950, Blackpool, UK. BSc, Dip Arch from University College, London; registered as architect 1976. MA in Fine Art, Department of Environmental Media, Royal College of Art, London 1981. Exhibited at Tate Gallery London, Serpentine Gallery, London and in the British Art Show 1990. Visiting lecturer in schools of fine art and architecture. Films broadcast by Channel Four (*The End, Valtos, The Clouds*) and exhibited widely in the UK and abroad at festivals and other venues including Edinburgh (1986, 1989), Turin (1989), Bombay (1990), Berlin (1990, 1994), San Paulo (1990, 1994), the Festival dei Popoli, Florence (1990, 1994), Vancouver (1994). *London*: cinema distribution in UK and USA; ICA Biennial: 'What You See is What You Get'.

The End
1986, 18min, b&w, 16mm

On one level, this is an account, narrated in the first person, of a wandering down-and-out, day-dreaming through contemporary Europe – a man who the film-maker suggests is "carrying the burden of European culture". The work is "a document of the last stand of its narrator – a poor creature, burdened by neo-classical conceits – against the disgusts and nostalgias which have crippled his existence". Ordinary scenes, factories, roads, German house-building, channel ports, railway stations set off a chain of reflexive and subjective rumination, delivered in the rich tones of a boulevardier, and bringing in Laurence Sterne and JMW Turner. Throughout, Keiller sustains an atmosphere of nostalgic pessimism, reinforced by the final section where Kathleen Ferrier sings part of Brahms' setting of Goethe's *Harzreise im Winter* against a blurred photograph of tourists in the Piazza Navona in Rome.

Catherine Kinley

Valtos

1987, 11min, b&w, 16mm

Romanticism is also an aspect of *Valtos*, a journey northwards from London through 1980s Britain, which has become transfigured, where the variable light of an unpredictable summer, given to overcast skies and sudden flashes of startling brightness, is translated into the curious luminosity of black and white film, and where the camera wanders about vagrantly, upsetting any predetermined conceptions about where the landscape ends and the imagination begins.

Caroline Collier

The Clouds

1989, 20min, b&w, 16mm

Black and white shots of the landscape in the North of England. Landscape and architecture blend in Keiller's precise cinematography. At the same time, the film-maker's voice provides a powerful narration with excerpts from Lucretius' *De rerum natura*, and creation myths from all over the world coming together in a monologue in which Keiller attempts to piece together the history of his life, and searches for his roots.

London

1994, 85min, colour, 35mm

London is a film about a city in decline, and about the roots of that decline in its culture and politics, in the form of a fictional journal of the year 1992. The journal is that of the film's unseen, un-named narrator: the companion, chronicler (and ex-lover) of the reclusive and unseen Robinson, who has summoned him from a long and unspecified exile to assist in the study of the 'problem' of London that is his life's work: "Robinson lives in the way that people were said to live in the cities of the Soviet Union. His income is small, but he saves most of it. He isn't poor because he lacks money, but because everything he wants is unavailable . . ."

Analogies abound between the personae of Keiller's narrators, his subjective camera and the figure of the *flâneur*, the idler who wanders through the city, drinking its pleasures. Literary associations with the romantic tradition of Baudelaire, Poe and Rimbaud reinforce this connection while references to Sterne and Defoe have a counterpart in the eighteenth century notion of bathos, the headlong plunge from the sublime to the ridiculous which seems crucial to the ironic juxtapositions within Keiller's work. In *London*, Keiller's most ambitious and sustained film, the project to explore the nature of the city spawns a chronological journey through the political events of 1992 – IRA bombings, the general election, pit closures – which disrupt and refuel the ruminations of the reclusive Robinson and his companion, the film's narrator. The view of recent history is resolutely unofficial, fluttering police tape sealing off bomb sites, ubiquitous film crews in the middle distance, a standpoint on Tory celebrations and Royal ceremonials from the edge of the crowd. The past is there too, retraced through an archaeology of vistas, pub signs, posters, statues and anniversaries. The filming process cleans up the image, just as it does the filth, pollution and noise of London, but the ingredient of 'affectivity' (as Buñuel calls it) transforms the way we see.

Jo Comino

ABOVE:
VALTOS

Andrew
Kötting

t would be short-changing Andrew Kötting considerably to dismiss him as an English Absurdist, but one of his achievements has certainly been to re-energise what had become a wearied trope over the previous decade – the parodic depiction of English suburban grotesquerie. Depictions of net-curtain banality had so much become the province of condescending social satire that it seemed there was little left to say on the matter. But Kötting's genuinely anarchic conception of British life seems to spring more from the tradition of the Goons or N F Simpson than from that of Mike Leigh or David Leland. His imaginary England is a sometimes cruel, always discordant universe in which nothing appears to make sense – least of all for the disoriented French tourists of *Là Bas* (1994), or the ill fated day trippers of *Smart Alek* (1993).

Smart Alek may have suggested that Kötting was reining in the abstract, disjointed tendencies of his earlier work in favour of the sardonic vignette (here reminiscent of Joe Orton with a taste of Jane Campion's *Sweetie*). *Là Bas*, however, shows his gamesmanship – and cavalier disregard for genre – operating at full tilt. Here the provincial, Play for Today comedy is brought into confrontation with the French New Wave, parodied in absurdly gymnastic sex scenes and wildly inconsistent subtitling.

Kötting's early films have a high proportion of performance art in them – they seem to document staged events which themselves have no apparent rationale. There is a consistent disparity between what takes place in the films and their implied origin – *Hub-Bub in the Baobabs* (1989), for example, looks like a scratchy ethnographic document, but images of African children blur into obscure enactments of what might be English Morris-style folk rituals, while the soundtrack shifts disconcertingly between Mali and Cecil Sharp House. *Self Heal* (1987), a fairy tale narrative played in exotic disguise, has a voice-over in mock-French accent and a soundtrack of Bulgarian chants, while the action

Biography

Born 1959. BA in Fine Art, Ravensbourne College of Art and Design, London, 1984; MA in Mixed Media, Slade School of Art, London 1988. Set up BadBLoOd&siBYL studios in the French Pyrenees. *Hoi Polloi* (10min version): ICA Biennial: 'Between Imagination and Reality'; joint Best Film, No Budget Festival, Hamburg 1990; *Acumen*: Best Film prize Turkish Film Festival 1993; *Smart Alek*: Silver Plaque Chicago Film Festival; Special Mention, Cork Film Festival; Special Mention, Edinburgh Film Festival; Best Drama/Script British Short Film Festival 1993; Silver Cup, Montecatini International Film Festival 1994; Best Film, Oberhausen Film Festival 1994 -Youth Jury; ICA Biennial: 'What You See is What You Get'.

Key works

Klipperty Klopp

1984, 12min, b&w, 16mm

Described by the film-maker as a post punk piece of pagan sensibility complete with bestiality, buggery and boundless energy, the film combines frenetic performance in a field with a tuneless song.

Hoi Polloi

1990, 1min and 10min, colour and b&w, Super8/video

Commissioned by the Arts Council and BBC2's The Late Show for their One Minute Television collection, *Hoi Polloi* demonstrates the enigmatic potential of the appearance of a brief, fragmentary avant-garde film in the context of a general arts programme. The modern day equivalent of the dadaist film *Entr'acte* (also made to be shown between performances), Kötting manages to hint at epic themes and existential quandaries while refusing to impose any overall meaning to the work.

Simon Field

Acumen

1991, 20min, colour, 16mm

Various characters appear stranded on a beach buried under large piles of their own memorabilia. Meanwhile an old woman pushes her loaded pram down the white lines in the centre of a country lane past a middle-aged couple who are trying unsuccessfully to combine watching television with playing miniature golf. Though often humorous many of his films have a darker more disturbing quality.

Philip Sanderson

Là Bas (Down There)

1994, 19min, b&w, Super 16mm

When 'Le Tunnel' unexpectedly closes for a security check, a French couple, Angeline (who thinks life is a perfume advertisement) and her toy-boy Jean Luc (who is exhausted by her sexual demands) end up at a bed & breakfast in Bexhill-on-Sea run by three lesbians. They are thrown together with a seven foot Geordie, a social worker and his two charges: Jackie (a mouth fetishist who sees things in terms of animals – a sudden flight of exotic birds or galloping giraffes in an African savannah) and Keith (who sees himself as an Olympic sprinter). Angeline believes the English have no passion and hate children, food and sex. She is quickly fed up and wants to go home, but Jean Luc is enjoying himself, tucking into a huge fry-up. Then Jackie throws a fit, and Angeline and Geordie fall in love.

takes place in an unidentifiable lunar landscape. *Klipperty Klopp* (1984) is perhaps Kötting's most testing essay in mock-primitivism, a monotonous recital on dilapidated-looking stock, giving the impression of unimaginably old, disreputable found footage.

These films have the rare quality of at once looking manifestly fabricated and at the same time of seeming to have been 'found', of bearing no recognisable origin in space or time (and, by that token, of bearing no recognisable authorial stamp). This gives them the status of artefacts expressly forged to look fake. Kötting's more conventionally crafted work sustains the same ambivalence. *Acumen* (1991) appears to be set in a bleak imaginary world whose laws are entirely unfamiliar – and yet, in which *Hawaii Five-O* and *Flipper* exist. *Acumen* is perhaps Kötting's most extreme provocation of the viewer – a disjointed series of vignettes that stubbornly refuse to reveal either their meaning or their relation to each other (a girl in a bath served fish by unseen hands, figures lying asleep in piles of detritus on a beach).

The glue for this disparity is an extremely vigorous editing style and attention to the disorienting possibilities of the soundtrack – as in *Smart Alek's* layered cacophony of voices. The only time that Kötting's aggression approaches the conventionally manic allure of pop-video speediness is *Gallivant* (1994), a seaside vox pop, and Kötting's twist on the British Mass Observation tradition.

Kötting's early, rougher work suggested an anarchic imagination entirely resistant to narrative. *Smart Alek* might have been taken as evidence that linear narrative would dilute Kötting's touch; *Là Bas* suggests that the tension between his style and narrative demands might make for a spectacular, highly comic battle. A *sui generis* stylist, Kötting is one of British cinema's brightest hopes, and definitely its wildest.

Jonathan Romney

Richard
Kwietniowski

Behind Richard Kwietniowski's elegant and witty short films lies the question: what can and should a gay cinema be in the 1990s? The question is not as simple as it seems, and Kwietniowski's answers are neither simplistic nor definitive. The most obvious characteristic of any gay cinema is that it is assertive: as in the pioneering days of Kenneth Anger's *Fireworks* and Jean Genet's *Un Chant d'amour*, there is a need to bring gay desires and passions into the light. But if achieving visibility is the first step, what is the next? Should the films be addressed mainly to gay audiences, straight audiences or both? Is gay cinema inherently erotic? Is it inherently political? Should it aim for a dialectic relationship with dominant 'straight' cinema, or should it stand apart? In Britain, these questions have been complicated by the overt hostility of certain sectors of government and the media to gay rights; in the 1980s, this unwelcoming and discriminatory climate pushed some apolitical gay artists like Derek Jarman into the role of activists. This is the context in which Kwietniowski makes his films.

Kwietniowski's stance is engaged without being confrontational, humorous without being evasive and exploratory without being obscure. His work, much of which has been screened on television in Britain and elsewhere, is addressed to general audiences but shot through with references and inferences that will mean most to gay viewers: the best of both worlds! Some of the films have a sharp political edge: *Ballad of Reading Gaol* (1988) was made in protest against Clause 28 of the Local Government Act, which bans the 'promotion' of homosexuality through public funds, but Kwietniowski would rather provoke a wry smile than a fit of rage. His method is to take some established norm – a structure from lexicography, literature, cinema, theatre or even psychoanalysis – and to give it an unblushing gay spin.

Alfalfa
1987, 9min, colour, 16mm

Subverting the Queen's English, *Alfalfa* takes us through the letters of the alphabet, and uses them to map out the pleasures and politics of contemporary gay subculture.

Ballad Of Reading Gaol
1988, 12min, colour, 16mm

A visual interpretation of Oscar Wilde's testimonial delivered from the Old Bailey in 1895 when on trial for gross indecency. Each word is skilfully used to make links between 1895 and 1988 and the threat posed by Clause 28. Voice-over by Quentin Crisp.

Flames Of Passion
1989, 18min, b&w, 16mm

A comic and subversive re-working of *Brief Encounter*, the film is a modern gay romance between two suburban commuters. Inspired by classic melodrama, *Flames of Passion* abounds in visual jokes and metaphors.

Proust's Favourite Fantasy
1991, 1min, b&w, 16mm (with Roger Clark)

A fragment on childhood, language and sexuality; featuring a hotel-room, gendarme and live chicken.

Biography

Born 1957, London. Studied Literature and Film at both the University of Kent and UC Berkeley. Worked in media education throughout the 1980s. His work has been broadcast in Britain, USA, Europe and Australia. *Flames of Passion*: ICA Biennial: 'Between Imagination and Reality'; Audience Award, Turino & San Francisco Lesbian & Gay Festivals 1990; Silver Plaque, Chicago Film Festival. British American Arts Association award for a US tour in 1989. Has directed for television since 1989; currently developing two low-budget features with British Screen, BFI and BBC.

Framed as a lexicon of gay slang, *Alfalfa* (1987) celebrates the gay appropriation of 'straight' language as a self-defence mechanism; it is founded on visual/verbal juxtapositions that quite literally play with denotations and connotations. It opens in a deliberately hesitant mode, but from the exact mid-point – "N is for Nancy" – is guided by its upbeat soundtrack to a cheering conclusion. *Ballad of Reading Gaol* takes the play with the space between words and images even further by proposing one image for every word in a passage from Oscar Wilde's courtroom testimony in his ruinous libel suit of 1895. Verbal logic meets visual logic in a bout whose only victor is gay pride.

Kwietniowski's more recent films are less rooted in formal experimentation, but equally skilled in their play with codes and conventions. *Flames of Passion* (1989) decorates its tale of a nervous gay courtship on a suburban railway station with images that evoke *Brief Encounter* (steam locomotives, anxious glances through train windows) and a text that evokes the heyday of Bette Davis; the result is an affectionate demolition of the principles of melodrama in the movies and, at the same time, a charmingly affirmative love story. *Proust's Favourite Fantasy* (1991) is a mysterious vignette of guilty sexuality that does for Freudian dream-sequences what *Flames of Passion* did for melodrama. And *The Cost of Love* (1991), a story told in stills and voice-over, gleefully attacks the moralistic convention of the 'twist ending' with a twist all of its own.

All of these films mark Kwietniowski as a child of the film culture of the 1980s. He has a post-semiotic interest in language in its widest sense, and a post-modern approach to the iconography of desire. But the central importance of his work lies in its contribution to the creation of a truly contemporary gay cinema.

Tony Rayns

RIGHT:
ALFALFA

Julie
Kuzminska

mage manipulation as a pathway to visual excitement – is the approach which dominates in Julie Kuzminska's work. Generally, the artist transforms her footage, converting even the ordinary into something inviting and unexpected.

In *Chaos* (1992), the fear of falling becomes the basis for a virtuoso display of image-mixing and colourisation. In sequences oddly reminiscent of Tarkovsky, layers of images are built up and overlaid with falling coloured shapes. Yet the work is by no means merely decorative, neither is it purely formal or painterly in intent; always a psychological power emerges, an ambience underneath. In *Chaos*, as if casting a spell, fragments of the artist's life metaphorically 'fall' in slow motion – sepia photos, memorable places, tokens of a personal history – inducing in the viewer trance-like thoughts on childhood, innocence, death. The effect is hypnotic and not without emotional resonance.

A similar quality arises in other works. In *Archaos I* (1990) and *Archaos II* (1991), the antics of the crazy French circus inspire a substantial foray into sound and image manipulation, but as ever, something ominous emerges alongside the apparently ornamental.

George Barber

ABOVE:
ARCHAOS I

Key works

Archaos I

1990, 11min, colour, video

Shot live at the performance of the circus Archaos, from Paris. It's about the spirit of Archaos, about wild mad people from the circus, the violence and beauty of the atmosphere. An emotional, very personal documentary.

JK

Chaos

1992, 3min, colour, video

A woman's fear of dropping dead is transformed into a tumbling and flickering sequence of fragmented images from childhood photographs; a glimpse of heaven, but more especially of the eternity of the cerebral chaos and the futile role of the individual in the eternity of time. A spiritual chaos – as enchanting as it is oppressive – is expressed in colourful flashes of light and other visual pulses.

World Wide Video Festival

Biography

Born 1963, Nottingham. BA in Photography, Film and Television from the London College of Printing 1985. Screenings include Australian International Video Festival; Nederlands Filmmuseum, Amsterdam; Medienoperative, Berlin; Video Positive, Liverpool; World Wide Video Festival, Den Haag.

102

Key works

Richard Land and his group 'i.e.' have been at the leading edge of developments in interactive video and multi-media installation since he and his former colleague Richard Brown first joined forces in 1986. Both graduates of the Royal College of Art, they quickly established themselves as major players in the emerging field of digital multi-media, specialising in the creation of what they call 'interactive environments'; sophisticated computer-controlled platforms in which the viewer/user has a pivotal role in triggering a constantly changing series of images and events. Although their original and eclectic techniques found numerous commercial applications (notably in the area of exhibition and interface design), other equally striking examples of their work began to appear in art galleries.

Installations like *The Tunnel* (1988) and *The Mirror* (1989) are among the early milestones in the field of interactive computer art in this country and abroad. Leaving behind conventional button-pressing notions of interactivity, these works favoured an open-ended, intuitive approach, in which a powerful, allusive image-play afforded a more resonant and intimate level of involvement. Devised at a time when computers were considerably less responsive than they are today, both pieces involved a technical ingenuity belied by the elegant simplicity of the finished work.

Mirror Images (1993), an interactive video link (completed after Brown's departure in 1990, and with Land increasingly assisted by designer/programmer Paul Lamb), offers further evidence of Land's ability to endow complex technology with an accessible, human face. An occasional series of single-screen pieces – including *Flux* (1990) and *Flight* (1991) -provides an interesting counterpoint to the interactive works, in which treated video-graphics are combined with computer-triggered sound to create a mesmeric, ambient flow.

Steven Bode

Mirror Images
1994, installation, monitor, camera, computer (with Paul Lamb)

Mirror Images is a mirror which reflects time as well as light. An observer at first sees their own reflection as in any other mirror. But as they continue to look, they begin to see the mirror's past. At first, they catch glimpses of themselves a few seconds ago, but then *Mirror Images* begins to delve back further and further into its own past, cutting to short sections of previous visitors. At the same time, of course, the present observer is becoming part of that past... The mere presence and interest of an observer is enough to trigger *Mirror Images* into action. Thereafter the piece depends on a feedback loop of stimulus and response to develop and grow. The observer gets more out of the piece by spending longer with it and posing more extremely. At the same time, the piece gets more out of the observer and can use the poses it remembers to encourage further antics from subsequent observers.

RL

The Tunnel
1988, installation, video projector, computer

As one moved through the space, light and sound seemed to alter, and the images on the projection screen changed. At first it seemed that this was a carefully orchestrated sequence of events,which somehow would take account of how an average person might negotiate the space, but after a while, it seemed that one's own movements and behaviour were influencing the course of events.

Jeremy Welsh

Biography

Born 1959. Studied at the Bartlett School of Architecture. Taught himself computer programming by designing a computer-aided design package for a textile designer. Studied AI and interactive video at the Royal College of Art from 1984. After graduation started IE with Richard Brown. Exhibitions at ICA London, V-Topia in Glasgow and Liverpool; *Mirror Images*, simultaneously in Derby and European Media Art Festival, Osnabrück 1993.

RIGHT:
MIRROR IMAGES

Sandra **Lahire**

An exhaustive line of enquiry runs through Sandra Lahire's films. Sparked off by personal preoccupations, they comprise a barrage of facts and statistics, images and sounds, loosely interwoven around a specific topic and branching off into wider issues. The earlier work, low key and unofficial in its tools – 16mm and Super8 film, some camcorder footage and Walkman sound – flouts so-called documentary objectivity. *Arrows* (1984), a disturbing treatise on anorexia, sets self-portraits against pecking, bird-like images while a confessional voice-over shifts discussion into the field of cultural representation. Four stays in Elliot Lake in North Ontario, Canada, where the multi-national Rio Tinto Zinc owns a huge uranium mining operation, instigated the films *Uranium Hex* (1988, a pilot), *Plutonium Blonde* (1987) and *Serpent River* (1989).

Serpent River is the most rigorously organised, both in the formal progression from ice and snow imagery to fire and brimstone and back again, and rhetorically, as an investigation into a latter-day body politic. Taking a multi-layered approach, it centres on medical, political and social issues, with the river as (contaminated) life-blood of the community. Testimonies and interviews (the staple of traditional documentary) are linked with performance which, featuring the film-maker herself, anchor the content of the film, inscribing it as personally perilous. The film is further removed from conventional investigative reporting by the way in which both sound (synthesised Geiger counter noises) and image (slow-motion, freeze-framing, repetition, solarisation and flicker effects) are extensively reworked.

Lahire's integration of sound, image and intent is often apposite; there are flashes of inspiration in the way, for example, the view of a bared back, with muscles painfully flexing under the skin, is succeeded by shots of drills pounding away at the rock face. Her manipulation of colour is excellent, conjuring up sulphurous yellows to match the description of yellow cake residues or, in *Uranium Hex*, causing a field of flowers to flare up like a Warhol screen-print. Occasionally the parallels, more often when stated as opposed to drawn, can seem over-laden; the way in which, for instance, the notion of vulnerability fixes on a group of schoolchildren.

Biography

Born 1950, London. BA in Philosophy from the University of Newcastle-on-Tyne; BA in Fine Art Film, St Martins School of Art 1984; MA in Film & Environmental Media from the Royal College of Art 1986. Writings include *Lesbians in Media Education* published in *Visibly Female* (ed Hilary Robinson, Camden Press, 1987) and articles for *Undercut*. Many international screenings include: Creteil Film Festival; Locarno; Sao Paolo Film Festival; Berlin Film Festival; Turin Film Festival; Jerusalem Film Festival; Feminale, Cologne.

Arrows
1984, 15min, colour, 16mm

Arrows combines live action and rostrum work to communicate the experience of anorexia and to analyse the cultural causes of the condition. The pressures placed upon women to be thin are articulated by an account of a new technique for the surgical removal of fat. The film ends with a poem by Sylvia Plath, *The Thin People*, which speaks of people who starve themselves – and people who are actually deprived – locating the condition of anorexia firmly in western culture.

Serpent River
1989, 30min, colour, 16mm

A complex interweaving of documentary strands evokes the hazardous existence of the Serpent River Community in Ontario, which lives in the shadow of the Rio Tinto Uranium mine. The landscape, people and natural resources bear the scars of their involvement with this industry. Diane, a woman miner, and Dr Rosalie Bertell, a radiation expert, describe the mining process and the far-reaching effects of contamination.

Lady Lazarus
1991, 25min, colour, 16mm

A visually woven response to Sylvia Plath's own readings of her poetry. These readings plus extracts from an interview given just before her death provide an anchor for a film which celebrates her macabre humour and cinematic vision. A carousel of images in windows, an atmosphere of constant metamorphosis; her poetry as cinema.

RIGHT:
NIGHT DANCES

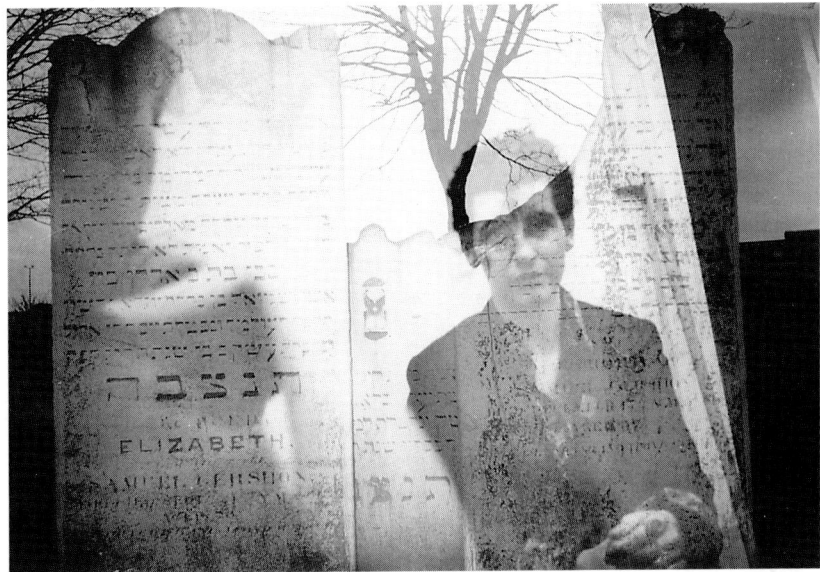

Night Dances

1995, 15min, colour, 16mm

Displaced on a boat sailing through the timeless twilight waterfront of the city, two ferrywomen talk and two Yom Kippur night-angels dance. One angel guides us through dark doorways past Hebrew inscriptions on worn gravestones, and drinks a toast to life amid threats of desecration. We are on the journey of my mother who died suddenly – bound in a lovers' discourse between the living and the dead. 'Night' dances – to the music of her speaking piano and to our fractured conversation, joined by Sylvia Plath in poems like *The Night Dances* and *A Birthday Present*.

SL

In *Lady Lazarus* (1991) which introduces itself in the opening titles as "a film spoken by Sylvia Plath, 27th October 1932 – 11th February 1963", the biographical structure, with its insistence on cinematic pilgrimage, has its limits. A woman (Sarah Turner, a film-maker herself) is captured on film responding to the Plath recordings, standing in for her in a sense, on the image track. While this can be interpreted by the viewer as period re-enactment, the narrative thread gives context and continuity to Lahire's visual similes for the obsessive rhyming patterns of the poems.

The one minute long *Eerie* (1992), commissioned by the Arts Council and BBC2's The Late Show, is of necessity, much tighter and more muted. It draws visual and aural analogies between the act of film projection and the operation of a cable-car carrying the loved object, framing her, much as the rectangle of the screen does. These few shots, intercut with a romantic interlude – an encounter, a dance, a kiss – are evocative but also focus our attention on the process of image-making, on the nature of cultural representation (crucially, as a lesbian film) and the potential for appropriating, as Lahire does, such images.

Jo Comino

David
Larcher

It is sad to report that David Larcher's early films have all but disappeared: he has a copy, too frail for screening, of *Mare's Tail* (1969), which Stephen Dwoskin described as "one of the best of its kind and size in the world". Of *Monkey's Birthday* (1975), which ran at six hours, the London Film-makers' Co-op holds only one reel, the section *Cart Tracks to Konya* in which Laurence Sterne's digression on digressions and the Silver Surfer act as guides into a luscious other world of flickering colour that, in 30 minutes, uses almost every technique then available, from printer effects and refilming to video feedback and single-frame editing. The lack of the rest of the film leaves this reel a monument to the loss of the whole, a metaphor of the forgetting and fading that were to haunt his later work.

EETC (1986) and *Granny's Is* (1989 and 1990) combine film with electronic media in an intensive investigation of the processes of memory and perception, grounded in portraits of women and the artist's relationships with them. Drawing on personal archives and manipulating them with an extraordinary range of invention and technique, these works share a sense of both the losses and gains implicit in thinking, image and sound recording, and perhaps perception itself, as always being already in the past. The personal dimension is the heart of the films' drama, though there are only hints of story, only the skeletal remains of familiar narrative structures. In touch with the great anarchist tradition of modernism, not least in cinema, *EETC* works from accident (migrating cranes forming a letter E in the sky) and its interface with design to argue, poetically, a utopian belief in the powers of film to renew perception and provoke liberation. Juxtaposing, for example, a detailed alchemical-sexual account of the physics of photography with images of laundry, babies and

ABOVE:
EETC

Born 1942, London. BA in Archaeology and Anthropology from the University of Cambridge; Postgraduate year in Film and Television at the Royal College of Art, London 1964. In the 1960s worked as a photographer. Gulbenkian Video Fellowship 1982; DAAD scholarship 1983. Has worked at the Centre International de Creation Video Montbeliard, Belfort since 1993. Screenings include: Pacific Cinematheque, Vancouver; Millennium, New York; Tate Gallery, London; Centre Georges Pompidou, Paris; Centre for Contemporary Art, Warsaw; Image Forum; Japan. *Granny's Is*: ICA Biennial: 'Between Imagination and Reality'; *videØvoid* : ICA Biennial: 'What You See is What You Get'; Best Video, Viper Festival, Switzerland; Best Experimental Film, Oberhausen. Tapes are in the permanent collections of the Centre Georges Pompidou and Image Forum, Japan.

Mare's Tail
1969, 150min, colour, 16mm

An epic flight into inner space...The moon, the flesh, the child, the room, the waves are part of our hieroglyphics making up the combinations of our trip.. What each of us sees is more than what we see.. let your eyes water in the colours, and follow the lines moving into orbits.

Steve Dwoskin *Film Is*

Monkey's Birthday
1975, 360min, colour, 16mm

An odyssey in which Larcher and his crew wander across Europe. A year of travelling and filming were edited into the six hours of footage which represents *Monkey's Birthday*. The film is at once a diary of that voyage, a romanticisation of the quest implicit in the conceit of the wandering protagonist, and a universalisation of that quest beyond the individual protagonist.

Hendrik Hendrikson

EETC
1986, 69min, colour, video

In *EETC* Larcher works with images, colour, speech and music to produce an imaginative and striking visual document. The film begins with a close-up of a painting of an alchemist looking into a transparent phial – it explodes into a cascade of vivid colours and images which gradually coalesce into fragments of the film-maker's past. The 'E' of the title is the first letter of Elizabeth, the name of Larcher's sister and of his partner. It forms the starting point for his extraordinary collection of audio-visual material –

fucking – women's work – the film both celebrates and mourns the artisanal mode of production as irreducibly grounded in the family. Anything but ideologically sound, Larcher's magnetic honesty in his account of the conditions of his own work and the aesthetic limits of perception ("our consciousness of the world is a consciousness of traces") recalls Roland Barthes, poet of the impossibility of representation, faced with the photograph of his mother that was all that remained of her. The personal, which is only possible outside the commercial realm of film production, is unstable, guilty, fading, but the only pledge we have against the dying of the light.

Granny's Is develops these themes in a bravura remastering of video footage of the director's grandmother in old age. Video feedback in particular becomes not so much a metaphor as an allegory of the process, the active and ongoing process, of forgetting. Another modernist tenet, of film as universal hieroglyph, a picture language that might heal the pain of Babel, is worked through, upside down: as if the true Utopia would be one that had forgotten all traces of why and how it had come into being. As the original footage is reworked, it appears at times cruel: as medical photography, as mockery, as surveillance. But at other moments there is an extraordinary tenderness, perhaps most of all in a shot of Granny's legs, unexpectedly erotically coded as if from an infant's point of view, as the artist traces the movement of perception from "Granny" to "a dejected old woman who I did not know." As the editing speeds up (as little as four frames per edit at one point), and the high-tech image mastering proliferates motion in every corner of the screen, Granny can be heard saying "David, stop it" and later "Get rid of the lights." The ensuing gloom gives way to another burst of images, marked by a powerful but somewhat occluded symmetry, as the film hurls the drama of perception in the face of death, and still finds space to understand that both the death of memory and the welter of the senses produce a similar result, a momentary bliss, a fleeting utopia.

Larcher's most recent work, *videØvoid* (1993), is a jokey but visually entrancing game with electronic imaging, and a particularly beautiful soundtrack. A skilful clown, Larcher plays upon the dead-end of the aesthetics of medium-specificity until it produces a Zen encounter with the void at the heart of the work and, by inference, the medium of electronic imaging itself. More serious humour would be hard to find: a gag worthy of the Zen masters. A more luxuriant mind or intellectual hedonist does not exist in British experimental media.

Sean Cubitt

reworked and refined – which is the trace of associations, memories and fantasies.

Granny's Is

version one: 1989, 47min, colour, 16mm;
version two: 1990, 78min, colour, video

A semiological portrait of a personal and often painful relationship. From Proustian remembrance to post-aesthetic fragmentation the tape presents a kaleidoscope challenge to the viewer. "The most interesting piece of work I have seen to date."

Jacques Derrida

videØvoid – The Trailer

1993, 33min, colour, video

The intention was to build on the parapraxes of machine error with image by-products produced through processes of fast spooling, desynchronising, derouting (la deroute du signal), bugging et al. The machine was to have been contextualised using video metaphors of the key, line and field blanking, black lift etc, with electromagnetic theories, juxtaposed with technical, philological, nonsensical notions of the vacuum, the void, non being.

DL

William
Latham

There are no mortals in computer space.

My work brings together artistic creativity, creativity from nature and the generative powers of computers, and deliberately blurs all three.

My role as an artist is to create and set in motion an 'alternative evolutionary system', and then see what is produced. I can steer the course of evolution by using such computer commands as 'breed', 'bud', 'kill' and 'marry', as well as using a customised form of genetic engineering.

My films are slightly sinister but always have a sense of fascination – as if one was witnessing some living microscopic event, or the birth of an entire universe. The viewer becomes a voyeur, not sure what they are looking at, their brains desperately trying to read meaning into what they see, but like the natural world, the event is uncompromising and as a human one, is insignificant.

I am fascinated by the creative potential that exists in multidimensional computer space where as an artist one can create entire universes. In the virtual world one can be God and the Gardener.

William Latham

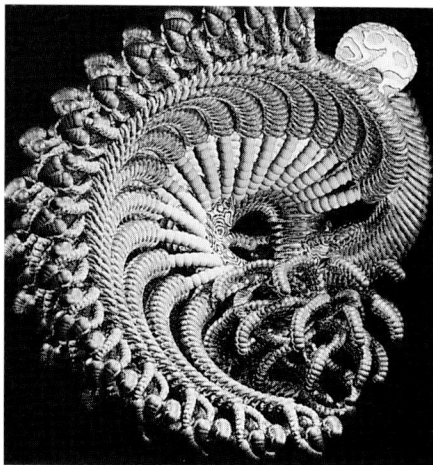

ABOVE:
MUTATIONS

Biography

Born 1961. Studied at Ruskin School of Drawing and Fine Art, Oxford 1979–82; Fine Art at the Royal College of Art, London 1982–83; Computer Graphics at City of London Polytechnic 1984–85. MA from the Royal College of Art, 1985; MA Oxford 1986. Research Fellow at IBM UK Scientific Centre, Winchester 1988–93. Currently runs his own company, Computer Artworks Ltd collaborating on projects with the IBM Scientific Centre and IBM New Markets Investment. Animation and design for the feature film *Hackers*. Screenings include: SIGGRAPH, Dallas; Ars Electronica, Linz; Videotheque de Paris; Biennial of the Moving Image, Madrid; Cardiff International Animation Festival.

Key works

The Garden of Unearthly Delights
1993, CD-Rom

In this multimedia culmination of Latham's 'Evolutionist Art', the user is able to navigate his way through an eerie 'garden' of alien forms and kaleidoscopic colours which are mutating and revolving in computer space. The full range of current CD-Rom technology is incorporated on disc, combining high quality colour graphics, animation sound and an element of interaction.

Biogenesis
1993, 5min, colour, video

Biogenesis shows the evolution of artificial life forms in a synthetic universe where 'survival of the fittest' is replaced by 'survival of the most aesthetic'. We see cellular evolution and the replication of mutations forming chain-like structures resembling coral. The artist is like a gardener – breeding and selecting, marrying and steering the course of evolution for creative ends. The film is a record of this evolutionary process. It can be viewed as a psychedelic experience or a more subtle parody of man's relationship with the natural world through modern technology.

WL

David **Leister**
Kino Club

Key works

Wind-Up

1985, 12min, b&w, 18fps, 16mm

A man obsessed by the sound of a record disc becomes unable to separate music from memory. He plays a series of records, each one tragically broken as it ends, until finally he closes the lid on his wind-up gramophone, and on his unhappy memories. Bordering on the pastiche with its melodramatic point of view and use of improvised music, *Wind-Up* refers to early cinema in its animated approach to movement and in its antiquated printing and processing techniques which make it resemble a 'rediscovered' silent classic of the 1920s. With music by Aleks Kolkowski, Alex Maguire and David Wilson.

Lacing Film

1993, 14min, b&w, 16mm

Described by the film-maker as a self parody of a personal obsession with film and film collecting, *Lacing Film* attempts to link the 'experimental' notion of film-making with the collective consciousness of a film jumble sale. The film takes its inspiration from the musings of valve amp aficionados, and from an actual 16mm instructional film on "How to Lace Your Projector." Hammond/Wurlitzer organ by the Fabulous Bates Brothers, and Alex Maguire.

RIGHT:
DAVID LEISTER

The Kino Club is a collaboration between film-maker David Leister and a number of improvising musicians. The presentation of images, multiple projections, and 'live' visual editing to film and music creates a highly charged dialogue in which each has immediate influence on the other. It is as much improvised film-making as it is improvised music.

A wealth of images stolen from archive films made for home, cinema and education conjure up strange and cryptic references and individual remembrances. Film-maker and musician challenge the spectator's preconceptions of the visual and aural relationship that has too often become cliché.

The musicians share the performance space with the blank canvas of a projection screen. Across the room the projectionist is hidden behind a battery of film projectors, tape decks, sound mixers and additional mysterious technical paraphernalia. Films illuminate the screen; some are especially devised for the occasion, others are based on found footage and stock shots. Images become intertwined and a visual depth is created by further distortion of the light-beams by the projectionist. Prisms, gels, lens adapters and variable apertures combine to give a layered effect of movement.

An influence has been the early cinematic history of magic lantern shows which relied on manipulation of simple images to achieve startling results. The improvising musicians add a contemporary quality to otherwise outdated imagery – giving it a secondary life. This mix of sound and image creates an ironic twist of vision that challenges an audience's imagination and sense of irony.

A personal collection/obsession with archive film material and equipment plays an obvious role in the creation of Leister's film works. Over 800 titles exist in the Kino Club collection which is used as a source for many self-funded productions.

David Leister

Biography

Born Milwaukee, Wisconsin. Postgraduate Diplomas in Photo-Printmaking, Central School of Art and Design 1982, Visual Communication (Film), Goldsmith's College, University of London 1984. Organiser and promoter of Kino Club since 1987, with performances at The Two Eagles pub in Elephant and Castle; at the Institute of Contemporary Arts; Comedy Store; Museum of the Moving Image; National Review of Live Art, Glasgow; South Bank Centre, London.International screenings include: Millennium, New York; Tate Gallery, London; Centre For Contemporary Art, Warsaw; Light Cone, Paris; European Media Art Festival, Osnabrück.

Malcolm
Le Grice

Malcolm Le Grice's cardinal and catalytic role in English experimental work has been sustained since the mid-1960s when he introduced a film course for painters at St Martin's School of Art, and was involved in the formative days of the London Film-makers' Co-op. His work was at the centre of English structural/material film in the early 1970s but has transformed and renewed itself several times since – to the point where it is currently pushing the boundaries of experiment with new electronic technologies.

Le Grice's early films were drawn into the vortex of super-rationalist discourse centring on *Screen*, the BFI and the London Film-makers' Co-op, and he contributed to these debates himself in his book *Abstract Film and Beyond*, written in 1974. While the discourse around structural film places his work in a specific theoretical and historical context, the actual films inevitably extend beyond the value systems which first validated and mediated them. Le Grice has been insistent in restating political and modernist terms when discussing his work, but the films also offer other rewards. They work for the desires of the senses as well as the self-conscious cognitive processes of the mind.

The project his films address has transformed itself several times. *Berlin Horse* (1970) is created through step printing, Brian Eno's music paralleling its visual loops. Combining 8mm footage shot in Berlin, (a small village near Hamburg,

Biography

Born 1940, Plymouth. DipFA, Slade School of Art 1965. Practised and exhibited as a painter until 1969 and as a film-maker since 1965. Chair of the London Film-makers' Co-op 1970–73; member of BFI Production Board 1971–75; Chair of the Arts Council's Artists' Film and Video Committee 1986–90. Currently Professor and Head of Harrow School of Design and Media, University of Westminster. Retrospective screenings include: Carnegie Institute, Pittsburgh; Pacific Film Archives; Museum of Modern Art, New York; International Arts Symposium, Lublin, Poland; Multi Media Centre, Zagreb; Institute of Contemporary Arts, London. Mixed media work exhibited at Documenta, Kassel; Hayward Gallery, London; Centre Georges Pompidou, Paris. Films in the collections of the Centre Georges Pompidou; Royal Belgian Film Archive, Brussels; National Film Library of Australia, Canberra; Friends of the German Cinematheque Archive, Berlin; National Film Archive of Taiwan and Archives du Film Experimental, Avignon. Writer and theorist (see bibliography). Subject of the Arts Council/Channel Four documentary *Normal Vision* (1983)

Key works

Berlin Horse
1970, 9min, colour, 16mm (one or two screens)

The film is in two parts joined by a central superimposition of the material from both parts. The first part is made from a small section of film shot by me in 8mm colour, and later refilmed in various ways from the screen in 16mm black and white. The black and white material was then printed in a negative-positive superimposition through colour filters creating a continually changing 'solarisation' image, which works in its own time abstractly from the image. The second part is made by treating very early b&w newsreel of a similar subject in the same way. As a two screen film the second screen has a b&w version of the whole film.

MLeG

After Lumière – L'Arroseur Arrosé
1974, 12min, colour, 16mm

After Lumière plays with the audience's speculation of the 'out of shot' state of affairs and the expected development of the work. Based loosely on the Lumiere Brothers' film *L'Arroseur Arrosé*, it adds a character not featured in the original. Like Le Grice's *After Manet*, this work is concerned with the procedures of cinematic production and the structuring of film material.

After Manet, After Giorgione, Le Dèjeuner sur l'Herbe, or Fête Champêtre
1975, 60min, 4 screen, colour, 16mm

A *dèjeuner sur l'herbe* is simultaneously perceived from four different camera positions in a work which engages with the pro-filmic in order to question documentation, illusion and the film viewing process.

Finnegan's Chin – Temporal Economy
1981, 80min, colour, 16mm

Le Grice depicts the Michael Finnegan of the children's song (though with Joycean overtones) as he gets up in the morning, shaves the eponymous chin, makes breakfast and prepares to go out. These events are multiply re-enacted, fragmented, rearranged by editing and counterpointed by an equivalent mosaic of mainly disjunctive, unsynchronised sounds, including a variety of monologues by Finnegan and an extensive musical accompaniment, sometimes featuring the 'theme' song.

Sketches for a Sensual Philosophy
1988, 60min, colour, video

A series of nine short video 'songs', conceived like a music album, some in collaboration with other artists or musicians, whilst three of them explore computer generated image and sound. Each begins from its own artistic proposition drawn from sensual responses to sound or picture. Though complete, the pieces are intentionally provisional – the base for future development or transformation.

MLeG

Chronos Fragmented
1995, 55min, colour, video

A video work based on video8 and hi8 material shot over six years. Chronos is the Titan – the time god who rules the universe – the flux in which events are born, mature and decay. The work explores video as a creative form of memory. it moves outwards from the particular and personal images of a diary – the fragmentary and inconsistent building blocks of memory – towards their transformation into more fundamental symbols in the cycles of days, seasons, birth and death. This transforming symbolic memory is all placed in the context of the social and political events of the world – particularly China and the Balkans – as they are encountered in the personal space.

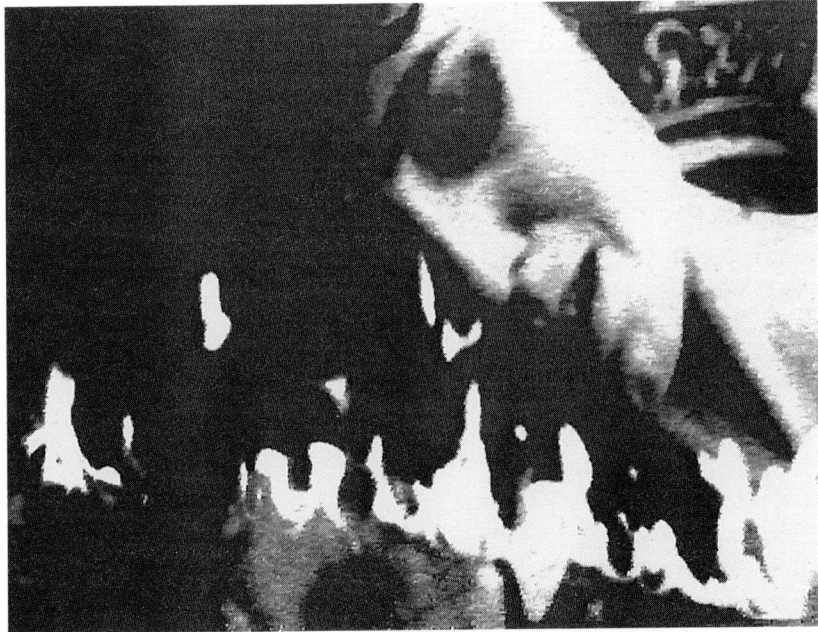

ABOVE:
CHRONOS FRAGMENTED

not the capital city), with 'found' footage from an English film from the beginning of the century, it constructs a fertile if unexpected relationship between the avant-garde and early film.. The film-maker's resultant "uncertainty about what it means and also about its decorative qualities" welcomes the polysemy and openness of a resonant text.

After Manet, After Giorgione, Le Dèjeuner sur l'Herbe, or Fête Champêtre (1975) – its cumbersome title pointing to a certain intertextual relation to painting and its particular history of spatial representation – involves four-screen projection which has to be 'performed' anew each time it is shown. The four quarters of the screen offer a relational perspective on the space of the restaged picnic, while simultaneously exploring cinema's 'palette' – positive and negative, black and white and colour, sound film and silent, and the grammar of editing. Taking the parameters of performance further, the shadows and shapes of *Horror Film 2* (1972) throw the physicality of both the film-maker/performer and the projection process into focus, as they interact in a unique and transient way.

The trilogy of feature length films made by Le Grice in the late 1970s, *Blackbird Descending – Tense Alignment* (1977), *Emily – Third Party Speculation* (1979) and *Finnegan's Chin – Temporal Economy* (1981), constitute an extensive exploration of perceptual structures. Following the acronym of Dr Who's time machine, one might say that they address Time And Relative Dimensions In Space in a sustained way. Working around the edge of small-scale narratives, they stimulate self-reflexive perceptual activity; the spectator comes to consider "how the eye works and how the mind builds up a perceptual rhythmic structure." They explore the political interstices of formal work: "How society produces stereotypes, ie, triumphs of artifice, which it then consumes as innate meanings, ie, triumphs of nature." Roland Barthes, 'Lecture', *Oxford Literary Review vol4 no1.*

After a number of years of almost complete silence (devoted to his work as a college principal) Le Grice's work entered a new electronic phase, and a renewal through an ensemble of shorter pieces collectively presented as *Sketches for a Sensual Philosophy* (1988). These extend the earlier structural materialist preoccupations into digital form. Despite the differences of means and format, continuity exists between these works and early pieces like *Whitchurch Down* (1972) – the percussive, permutative editing, semi-figurative images, a relation to Jazz extemporisation and improvisation.

Le Grice's work continues the search for significant form, often in the domain of the domestic -"stabs at the personal for fragments of experience". It is an exploration which takes place within the modernist notion of art as a terrain for rational and scientific enquiry as well as the pleasures of images and sounds.

Rod Stoneman

Steve
Littman

Littman's work came out of a unique moment of British Video Art (centred at the Royal College of Art), cross-breeding mid-1970s conceptual rigour with an avowed concern for social critique. Mass media themes – power, status, glamour – were undermined, ironically enough, by turning mass-culture's stylised language against itself, as in the fast-flowing colour of *The Winner* (1986) or in the mind-numbing repeat-edits of *In the Name of the Gun* (1987). These tapes explore the edge between public and private imagery, a theme pursued on the grand scale of montage in the video-wall installation *On a Clear Day You Can See Forever* (1989), and complemented by the cooler purview of domestic space and street scene in the television piece *Big Time – The House* (1990).

Littman's hallmarks have been the sheer energy of his image making and his strong sense of performance (he has documented many leading contemporary UK dance and drama groups, such as Impact Theatre). For a long time, his work has been linked to the high-tech end of experiment in video and electronic media. However, his recent multi-monitor work *The Enlightenment* (1993) is also his simplest or most elemental to date, a radically reductivist creation-myth in which flicker-edited lightening and the shadow of a walking man are stark and moving icons of personal vision and natural light.

A L Rees

On A Clear Day You Can See Forever

1989, installation, 8min cycle, colour,
3 video walls, 3 players

This work brought all my images I used in the 1980s together. I had been developing a meta-language within my single screen works which questioned the notion of the avant-garde in relation to broadcast television, and which explored and experimented with the flow of time and subject matter. This work used 3 channels of video – shown on three inward-facing video walls in a circular structure. It also extended the motif – first used in *The Name of the Gun* – of a man firing a gun at the viewer. This image was placed among three other key structural elements. On every channel was a rhythmic background of images collected over ten years, which emerged from and retracted into a green surface. On a second layer was the image of two men running back and forth; one white, the other black. The third image was of myself, as a self-portrait amongst my images, either walking back and forth or kneeling naked in a foetal position.

SL

Big Time – The House

1990, 4min, colour, video

Setting experiential reality against televisual reality, the home against structural planes, this tape confronts viewers with their activity of 'watching' commercial television. *Big Time – The House* starts with an image of the corner of a room and finishes with a monitor receding into the corner on a television set and, (one presumes) into the ether of electronic signals.

Born 1957, London. BA in Fine Art, Coventry Polytechnic 1980; MA in Environmental Media, Royal College of Art, London 1983. Has taught at the London College of Printing; Newcastle Polytechnic and Duncan of Jordanstone College of Art. Currently Lecturer in Communication Media at the Kent Institute of Art and Design. Screenings include: Centre for Contemporary Art, Warsaw; St Gervais Video Festival, Geneva; World Wide Video Festival, Den Haag, Herouville St Clair; Video Positive, Liverpool.

ABOVE:
**ON A CLEAR DAY YOU CAN
SEE FOREVER**

Loophole

Loophole Cinema is a collective of light, sound and shadow constructors and performers. The group currently consists of Bea Haut, Ben Hayman, Greg Pope, Ivan Pope and Paul Rodgers.

We specialise in large scale installations and performances usually of a site-specific nature, in which light, sound and other elements are manipulated together. Our aim is to create environments and events which harness the potential of multiple-projection in combination with constructed kinetic machinery, sampled, live and recorded sound, shadow play and bodily interventions. Our work deals with the deconstruction of traditional image/viewer relationships, breaking through theatrical conventions in order to explore unrealised possibilities within the 'two way shadow'. We create audio visual confrontations and collisions; a sequence of events continually shifting and searching through different ideas, formats and media. We draw on the influence of the pre-cinematic history of the projected image; Javanese shadow puppets, magic lanterns and the optical toys of the 19th century, combining these with post-cinematic digital and video technologies. Our events aim to juxtapose high-tech, low-tech and no-tech, setting these different elements against each other in a controlled cacophony.

Loophole Cinema

ABOVE:
CIRCUS OF THE SENSES

Circus of the Senses

1993, film, video, slide projectors, moving screen, crane, fire

Set in a disused steelworks, the audience moves through three different warehouse spaces. The performance builds from minimal acoustic sounds and slide projections to the staging of a large scale multiprojection shadow show and sound performance. The event utilised the full grandeur of the space with video/strobe installation, fire cabinets and a vast moving cinema screen suspended from a gantry crane.

The Fire Cabinets

1993, film, metal cabinets, strobe, extractor fan, fire distress signals

This event was constructed around nine metal lockers or cabinets, set along the edge of an outdoor swimming pool. Into the cabinets were built shadow screens, film projections, kinetic strobe installations and combustible materials. During the event the performers activated the cabinets, producing a cacophony of light, image, sound and smoke projections.

Biography

Bea Haut, film-maker and light manipulator; Ben Hayman, a film-maker and sound manipulator; Greg Pope, (founder), film-maker and projectionist; Ivan Pope, installation artist, sculptor and electronic imaging specialist; Paul Rodgers, film-maker and manipulator of surreal musical instruments.

Tim
Macmillan

Key works

Time-Lines Compilation

1993, 10min, colour, silent, video

Let us take an example – the Time-Slice Camera records a dog jumping through it. What the viewer sees when watching the film is the dog frozen in a single instant, something akin to a high-speed 'still'. However, the viewer is also moving around the dog, in the fashion of a circular tracking shot, and therefore experiences the dog in three-dimensions in the space in which both camera and dog are situated. This poses a paradox – how can one freeze time yet move through space? The paradox is so bizarre that it may take the viewer a while to realise what is 'wrong' with the image (in terms of what we accept as 'film'), and some may even think that the dog is 'dead' in some way. This is quite a natural response because we do not normally experience an animate object being inanimate other than when it is dead.

TM

Homage to Edgerton

1994, 4min, colour, silent, video

The Time Slice Camera explores a sequence of moments during the event of a droplet impacting on the surface of a bowl of milk. The subject is much enlarged as through a macro lens, but remains ambiguous in terms of scale because there is no other reference, ie, background by which to judge this. The film creates a visual bridge between notions of macrocosm and microcosm, order and chaos.

TM

These works are concerned with the exploration of new filmic and photographic descriptions of time and space. The first Time-Slice Camera was built in 1983 while undertaking post-graduate studies at the Slade School of Art and has since been developed in Japan and the UK by the artist as a film/video installation piece. The concept behind the films is influenced by several historical precedents and contemporary developments in our understanding of the time/space relationship. The development of early photographic experimentation from Fox Talbot through to Muybridge, Marey and the first film-makers give us the example of a period when it was difficult to distinguish technical and scientific advance from artistic development, because they were so inter-related. After some initial exploration and the acceptance of the phenomena as valid 'media', development became a matter of the refinement of production techniques, leading to the mass production of 'film' and 'photography'. Not until the work of Edgerton with high-speed still imagery and the first images of the Earth from space do we receive a fundamentally new view of the 'reality' we experience day to day.

The Time-Slice Camera can be made to any shape, and the purpose of the circular version is twofold. It allows the viewer to first focus on and absorb what is happening to a subject positioned at its centre; and then to conceptually tie together a singular moment in time with infinity. The film is a loop and therefore has no beginning or end other than that caused by the editorial necessity of turning the projector on or off.

Since its creation the Camera has been used to explore the kind of subject matter and imagery that best describe the effect: water, the human form, animals and objects in motion. Early films include references to the works of Muybridge, more recent films explore a more lyrical construction of the image and with inclusion of 'time' elements with the 'non-time' image.

Tim Macmillan

Biography

Born 1959, Portland, Oregon, USA. BA Fine Art Bath Academy of Art; HDip, Slade School of Art, London. Exhibitions include: Yamaguchi Gallery, Tokyo; Sagacho Gallery, Tokyo; F Stop Gallery, Bath; Solo shows: Montage Gallery, Derby; Untitled Gallery, Sheffield. Lived and worked in Japan 1985–89. Has organised photography and animation workshops for the Museum of the Moving Image, London. Works as a commercial photographer/photojournalist. *Homage to Egerton:* ICA Biennial: 'What You See is What You Get'.

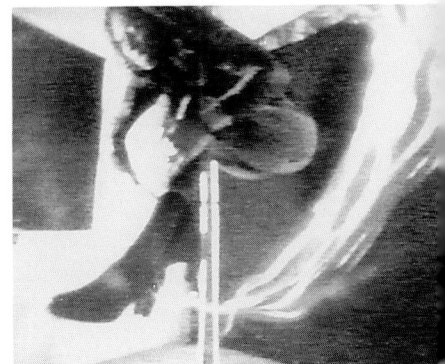

ABOVE:
**TIME SLICE CAMERA
A JOURNEY AT THE
SPEED OF LIGHT**

Juliet McKoen

My work centres around the creation of film symbolism. I use sound and image to express ideas, emotion and experience by indirect suggestion rather than direct expression. A central struggle is to make unambiguous symbols which communicate with the viewer. Most of the emotions expressed in my films are inspired by deeply felt personal experience. The process of making each film is always cathartic and sometimes painful.

At present I am particularly interested in using video footage obtained through medical processes such as keyhole surgery and body scanning to explore the many visual parallels between the interior landscape of the body and the exterior landscape of the planet.

John Ruskin coined the term 'pathetic fallacy' to describe the use of landscape to express human emotion. The landscapes of South Cumbria have a compelling spiritual and emotive power. Since living there I have become interested in using landscape to evoke human emotion and to convey meaning. It is my love for this landscape and concern for its inhabitants which has encouraged me to develop the political-ecological side of my work.

Sound plays an important role in my films. I prefer to shoot most film mute. The sound is separately recorded, often in a studio, and post-synched and track laid using computerised technology. The sound produced this way is very pure, with almost surreal definition, uncompromised by background noise. It has strong emotional connotations, which underpin and enhance the visual symbolism.

Juliet McKoen

Biography

Born 1955. Leamington Spa. BA English, University of York. Worked as a film editor 1981–86; Production Officer Greater London Arts 1986–88; Production Advisor to the Arts Council's Black Arts Video Project, One Minute Television (BBC2), Experimenta (C4) and Synchro (Carlton) schemes. *Blood Sisters*: Gold Award, Huston Film and Television Festival, 1992. Screenings include: Whitechapel Gallery, London; New Visions, Glasgow; Cinewomen – Norwich Festival of Women Film-makers; Oberhausen; ICA Biennial: 'Arrows of Desire'.

ABOVE:
BLOOD SISTERS

Key works

Blood Sisters
1991, 17min, b&w and colour, 16mm

Three blind, mute sisters pass an eye and tooth between them. A woman tenderly cradles a miscarried foetus. Two sisters struggle enmeshed in a net, then wheel their disabled mother through an avenue of trees. My film examines the iconography of sisterhood by showing how the relationship has been portrayed in myth and tale. The Graeae who, in sharing an eye and tooth, illustrate the potential for conflict and closeness in the relationship. Cinderella – a tale of rivalry and separation; the Furies, born from blood dropped from severed male genitals; the Fates, who spin the threads of life and death. The film intercuts images from these myths with sequences in which the film-maker and her sister use performance to explore the peculiar intimacies and paradoxes of sisterhood.

JMcK

Song of The Sands
1993, 12min, colour, 16mm, (with Peter Croskery)

The first of a proposed *Sands* series set in Morecambe Bay which will use the landscape of the Bay to explore themes of death, loss, desire and pollution. In this elegy for a dead lover, the body of a man dying of cancer is linked through texture, sound and image with the polluted body of the world. The insistent image of a train carrying nuclear waste, over the estuary sands to Sellafield, forms a chorus line to the film.

Possession

1991, 18min, b&w, 16mm

Based (very loosely) on the oedipal fairy-tale *Little Red Riding Hood*, Mulloy's *Possession* uses animation intercut with live-action footage to construct a Freudian tale of lewd perversity in which oral and anal regression reign supreme. The excretion and vomiting of objects places the film in the subversive tradition of the grotesque and manages to playfully engage with the psychoanalytical themes of the original story without succumbing to academicism.

Michael O'Pray

Cowboys

1991, 18min, colour, 35mm

A series of six three-minute films which comment on contemporary values through a reinterpretation of the myths of the old Wild West.

Ding Dong Bell

1992, 1min, colour, 16mm

An interpretation of the children's nursery rhyme *Ding Dong Dell* in the light of what the 'Old Bill' have been up to recently.

The Sound of Music

1993, 11min, colour, 35mm

Wolf cleans the windows by day and plays the saxophone by night, but things get out of hand when the food runs out at one of his gigs. The antidote to all that is kitsch and sentimental in animation.

PM

Phil Mulloy's film-making has involved a unique trajectory – from documentaries and half a dozen fiction films to experimental animation. He at first studied painting but then entered the Royal College of Art on the film course while the department was under the direction of Stuart Hood, and was associated with particularly brave and energetic experimentation. *A History and the City* (1977) which dates from this period, has a dominant formal structure; while a foreign voice narrates the history of Ireland the camera tracks through the imperial architecture of London's Square Mile, and a figure emerges from within ominous statuary. *In the Forest* (1979) offers an imaginative and picaresque sweep of English history from the 14th to the early 19th centuries; a voice asks "What is history, but a fable agreed upon?" *The Return* (1988) – in which a brother is absent in London while his mother is dying in Ireland – is an Oedipal drama trawling the psychic lake bed for more disturbing psychological material.

Inevitably the perspective and the sensibility that created these features carries through to the animation shorts – but the limited scale and more easily controllable means of production has led Mulloy to explore the imaginative leaps, disjunctions and combinations that are more possible in animation than live-action.

The strong black line of Mulloy's drawing connects with his acerbic, stark view of the human condition; an economy of means sharpens the astringent satirical ends. Inheriting Jonathan Swift's 'saeva indignatio' (savage indignation) about the human condition, Mulloy's 'adult cartoons' have included several subversive and acrid incursions into the cowboy genre. *That's Nothing* (one of the *Cowboys* series, 1991) is an acerbic indictment of feral masculinity. The visceral humour of *The Sound of Music* (1993) continues Mulloy's severe look at the most specious of species.

Rod Stoneman

Born 1948, Wallasey, Merseyside. Studied painting at Ravensbourne College of Art; film at the Royal College of Art. *Give Us This Day*: Grierson Award 1984; *Possession*: Kino Animation Prize, Melbourne Film Festival 1991; ICA Biennial: 'Arrows of Desire'; *The Sound of Music*: 1993 Dick Award; McLaren Award 1994; Zagreb Critics' Award 1994; Eulenspiegel Award 1994; ICA Biennial: 'What You See is What You Get'. Other screenings include: Clermont Ferrand Film Festival; Hong Kong Film Festival; Stuttgart; European Media Art Festival, Oberhausen; Tampere Film Festival.

ABOVE:
THE POSSESSION

Stuart Marshall

Stuart Marshall was an exceptionally gifted artist and teacher. His creativity was expressed through many forms: avant-garde music, video, performance and installation art as well as film. He was also a gay man with unstinting political commitment to supporting lesbian and gay lives through his work. His passionate desire was to reclaim a history which had been forcibly and violently suppressed and to lay it out in such a way that it resonated contemporary lesbian and gay experiences. Challenging the hegemony of the dominant ideology, especially in the media, Marshall helped to shape an emerging gay aesthetic. For just as AIDS has sanctioned expressions of homophobia and revised supposedly outmoded methods of controlling sexuality, the conflation of AIDS with homosexuality has clarified political positions for many lesbians and gay men. As Marshall himself said in *Bright Eyes* (1984), "Every image of a gay man is in danger of becoming two pictures of a homosexual. When his image is just a depiction of a man he remains an individual. When he is identified as a homosexual, then he becomes a member of an exotic species and a case history of a pathological sickness."

Bright Eyes is a direct attack on the mass media's representations of AIDS, and in Marshall's subsequent work the attack was continued with cunning variety. He worked to make forgotten or suppressed histories available and to change the agenda and form of work about and by lesbian and gay men. Marshall had embraced video in his early years, as a democratic and accessible medium, but turned to film to make *Desire* (1989) for Channel Four. In it he examines lesbian and gay history in Germany from 1910, through the rise of National Socialism and finally into violent suppression under the Nazis. He returned to the theme of history in *Comrades in Arms* (1990), a documentary on

Key works

Pedagogue
1988, 10min, colour, video

A short performance to camera by the artist Neil Bartlett, exploring in comic style the possible implications of Clause 28 for gay teachers and artists.

Comrades in Arms
1990, 50min, colour and b&w, 16mm

The Second World War is re-examined through the eyes of a group of gay servicemen and servicewomen, whose experiences range from ENSA-style entertainment to the River Kwai prison camp. Personal reminiscences, archive material and staged recreations of gay romances shot in the style of a 1940s black and white movie are combined in a humorous reclamation of a hitherto unrecorded history.

Robert Marshall
1991, 10min, video

Instigated by the discovery of 8mm footage of the artist's father in the possession of Canadian relatives, the tape is both a moving essay on the death of his father and Marshall's own struggle with being HIV positive.

A Journal of the Plague Year '84
1984, installation

Commissioned for the exhibition Video '84 and shown later that year in Galerie Optica in Montreal, Canada and the Royal College of Art, London, the installation was Marshall's response to the homophobic AIDS reporting in the English tabloid press. Since the 1970s the gay movement had constructed a complex support structure for its own new definitions of gay identity which both journalism and the medical establishment attempted to re-pathologise in the wake of AIDS. The work counterposed representations of gay identity from both the public and private sphere to demonstrate the struggle over the meanings of homosexuality.

Born 1949, died 31 May 1993. BA Fine Art 1971; MA in New Music Composition and Ethnomusicology, Wesleyan University, Middleton, Connecticut, USA 1972. Senior Lecturer in Media Studies, Newcastle Polytechnic 1973–77; Tutor, Environmental Media department, Royal College of Art, London 1977–86; Senior Lecturer, Alternative Media, Chelsea School of Art, London 1987–90. Prizes include: Audience Prize for Documentary Films, Turin Lesbian and Gay Festival 1991; Official Selection, Berlin Film Festival 1990. *Robert Marshall*: ICA Biennial: 'Arrows of Desire'. Works in the collections of the Museum of Modern Art, New York; California Institute of Arts and Ohio State University. Marshall was a founder member of London Video Access (now London Electronic Arts).

lesbians and gays in the Second World War. For lesbians and gay men no official archive exists, so in this film Marshall fashions beautifully poetic vignettes: gay couples embracing while sheltering from the Blitz, or two lesbians in uniform finding time alone together in their army car. For any group to have no history, is to be denied true understanding of the present. The historical mechanisms of oppression and repression shown in *Desire* and *Comrades in Arms* were resonated in the present treatment of lesbians and gay men shown in *Over Our Dead Bodies* (1991), a film documenting the rise of activist groups in the face of the failure of conventional politics to deal with the AIDS epidemic.

Marshall's last broadcast film, *Blue Boys* (1992), is a complex exposure of the UK's Obscene Publications Squad. Back to working on video after the space of some years, he was here at his most journalistic. At the time of his death from AIDS, Marshall was working on two projects which clearly reflected his personal and political drive. The first was a personal plea for patient choice and the expansion of medical options for people with AIDS. The second, *A Bit of Scarlet* aims to retrieve lesbian and gay images and iconography from the history of British television and cinema. This last film for cinema will be made by his collaborator Andrea Weiss and is due to be released in 1995.

Marshall was one of Britain's most important political film-makers and one of our best teachers. He was always in the vanguard, supporting lesbian and gay lives. His life and work gave young lesbian and gay film-makers a sense of their own history and a space in which to work.

Rebecca Dobbs

John
Maybury

John Maybury has developed a unique hi-tech blend of richly layered images which he culls from popular culture, especially the media, and from the exotica of sexual display and exhibition. He is that rare being, the 'cross-over' artist, who works with equal authority in popular culture and high art. He has enjoyed enormous success over the past decades as a music video director, with award winning work for Sinead O'Connor, Neneh Cherry, Boy George and others, but has also established a reputation within art circles for his recent pieces *Man to Man* (1992), *Premonition of Absurd Perversion in Sexual Personae Part One* (1993) and *Remembrance of Things Fast* (1993).

In the early 1980s, Maybury was a member of a loosely formed group of film-makers including Cerith Wyn Evans, Michael Kostiff and Holly Warburton, who worked mainly in Super8. Known as New Romantics, but not really a part of the wider sub-culture, they forged a style of visual excess, sexual 'performance' and cultural allusion. They also represented the first concerted attack on the modernist formalism of the traditional avant-garde. Maybury had worked as a set designer on Derek Jarman's *Jubilee* (1978), but his own films were distinctive, embracing performance, text, dance and the paraphernalia of sexual 'deviation'. They were also firmly embedded in the images and icons of a gay culture. His reference points were underground film, art cinema and a theatricality influenced by Andy Warhol, Kenneth Anger, Jean Cocteau, William S Burroughs and Jean-luc Godard. In his brilliant *Tortures that Laugh* (1983), shot on 16mm, Maybury uses rhythmic repetition, ritual and symbolism with an hypnotic and insistent soundtrack. Cultural narcissism, sex, drugs and a dark claustrophobic world are convincingly constructed out of borrowing from Surrealism and aesthetic devices hijacked from structural film-making, while he continued to reject the structuralist belief system.

Remembrance of Things Fast
1993, 60min, video

In a work which mocks the conventions of television and satellite broadcasting, a range of characters including Tilda Swinton, Rupert Everett and 'drag queens, devils/angels, men in suits etc' perform actions and rituals in a series of electronic tableaux vivants. Painterly landscapes (created with digital video techniques) and invented cities form the location for fictional and authentic stories of sexual encounters.

Premonition of Absurd Perversion In Sexual Personae Part 1
1993, 60min, video

Drawing on a decade's accumulation of personal images, with material from London's fashion and night-club worlds, this multi-layered work explores the polymorphous field of desire and sexuality.

Key works

Absurd
1990, 5min and 40min, video

Weaving a rich tapestry of decadent, erotic and personal imagery, *Absurd* combines a collage of earlier work with new footage. A frenzied evocation of the pleasures and traumas of the 1980s.

Man To Man
1992, 73min, 16mm

An adaptation of Manfred Karge's one woman play, *Man to Man* stars Tilda Swinton as Ella Gericke who surveys her life disguised as a man during and after the Second World War. Video imagery is used to express the fragmentation of Ella's identity.

Maybury confronts low-culture subject-matter – as Punk had a few years earlier – and rejects purist formalism for a quintessentially post-modern use of bricollage, deconstruction, a historicism and fragmentation. In the longform video *Circus Logic I–IV* (1984), he established his characteristic style of collage and spatial dislocation in which found-texts from newspapers and television flatten and disturb found-images of cultural icons, and combine with music to create an atmosphere of violence, sexual repression and cultural incoherence; Maybury's own bleak flow.

In *Big Love* (1984), he displayed a more Brechtian stance and a refusal to 'entertain', as mythical figures and camp personalities break the illusion of seamless imagery with the aid of pedagogic written texts. This frontality has been further developed in *Remembrance of Things Fast*, in which Tilda Swinton, Rupert Everett, and assorted drag queens speak to camera in a series of bizarre, fragmented, nightmare-like narratives, and different worlds (some surreal, some hi-tech, others almost realist) clash and merge in a provocative, pessimistic montage. The use of written text with its slogans and gnomic assertions subverts any easy narrative coherence.

Michael O'Pray

Born 1958, London. Studied Fine Art at North East London Polytechnic. Designed sets and costumes for Derek Jarman's *Jubilee*; worked on Jarman's *The Last of England* and *War Requiem*. One man retrospectives at the Institute of Contemporary Arts, London 1983 and Viper Festival, Lucerne, Switzerland 1991. Designed video projections for the Glyndebourne production of Harrison Birtwhistle's opera *The Second Mrs Kong* 1994. Has made music videos for Neneh Cherry, Boy George and Sinead O'Connor, winning MTV and Grammy awards for O'Connor's *Nothing Compares 2 U*. *Absurd*: ICA Biennial: 'Between Imagination and Reality'. *You Do Something to Me*: ICA Biennial: 'Arrows of Desire'. *Remembrance of Things Fast*: Special Jury Golden Teddy Bear Award Berlin Film Festival 1994; Best Experimental prize Viper Festival 1994; The Douglas Edwards Independent/Experimental Award, LA Critics' Circle Awards; ICA Biennial: 'What You See is What You Get'. Has exhibited his paintings in Britain and abroad.

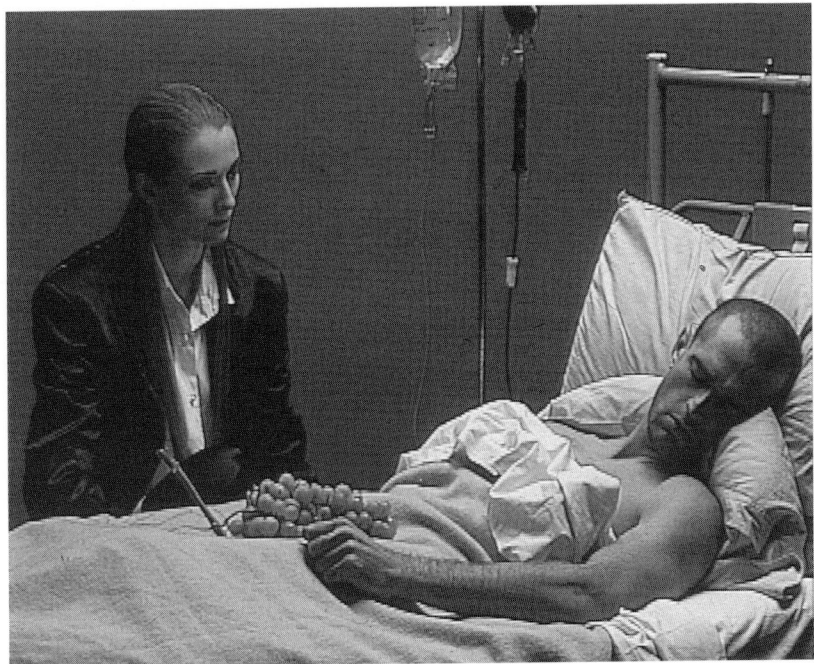

ABOVE:
REMEMBRANCE OF THINGS FAST

Michael **Maziere**

Michael Maziere's films, characterised by their intense vibrant colours and saturated imagery, are poetic reveries on memory, loss and sexuality, in which he finely balances "fear and pleasure." His early works, *Clear Cut* (1979), *Untitled* (1980), *Colour Work* (1981), *Silent Film* (1982) and *Skylight* (1983) were precociously brilliant in their camera work and formal effects. Vertiginous zooms, quick pans and fine editing characterised these films in which rhythm, repetition and a formal experimentalism were stressed in accordance with his then theoretical commitment to a materialist cinema. This stress on film as a process imprecating labour, materials and signifying systems created a tension with his strong aesthetic sensibility. If Maziere was a structural-materialist film-maker during these early years, his films were quite different to the muted, rough-grained work produced by others in that school. Rather, his work displayed an astonishing voluptuousness of colour and clarity of image that set his work apart in photographic terms.

This painterly sensibility went hand in hand with an urgent fast-cutting editing style and fluid camera movement. It also involved a strong sense of light. In his films of the mid-1980s, Maziere developed a more studied approach to subject-matter, eschewing the formalism of his earlier work. For example in *Les Baigneurs* (1986), part of *The Bathers Series*, he celebrated the body in motion in water. Light, movement, water and colour (brilliant light-reflecting whites and blues) coalesce through optical printing effects into a film that along with *Swimmer* (1987), marked his move to a more poetic form. Often filming in his native Aix en Provence, the lighting achieved in his films is Mediterranean in its warmth and clarity. Through this aspect of his work, Maziere has distanced himself from what he calls "Anglo-Saxon puritanism."

Biography

Born 1957, Grenoble, France. Diploma in Creative Photography, Film, History of Art at Trent Polytechnic, Nottingham 1979; MA in Film and Television, Royal College of Art, London 1982. Has worked as Film and Video Editor of *Independent Media* magazine; Cinema Programmer, London Film-makers' Co-op; Editor of *Undercut*; Distribution and Exhibition Manager, London Video Access. Currently Director, London Electronic Arts. Retrospectives/one person shows include: Museum of Modern Art, New York; Museum of Modern Art, Osaka, Japan; Pacific Film Archives, San Francisco; Universita Degli Studi Di Roma "La Sapienza"; Scratch Projection, Paris; Moderna Museat, Stockholm; Experimenta, Melbourne. *Swimmer*: ICA Biennial: 'Between Imagination and Reality'. Has published critical writings in *Independent Media*, *Undercut*, *Artist's Newsletter* and *Performance* magazine.

Key works

Les Baigneurs
1986, 6min, colour, 16mm

Shot in Italy, the film captures fragments of a summer's afternoon; recorded, degraded and fixed. A series of instances transformed.

MM

Swimmer
1987, 7min, colour, 16mm

The second film in a trilogy titled *The Bathers Series* inspired by the paintings of the same name by Paul Cezanne. The film is a celebration of the body in motion within a synthesis of water, light, colour and sound – through the use of intense editing, printing and saturated images a tension is created touching on pleasure, pain and desire.

MM

Cezanne's Eye II
1991, 20min, colour, 16mm

An experiential journey through the body of a unique landscape – that of Cezanne's Provence. Using intuitive and expressionist visual language and a striking specially composed soundtrack the film is a movement through land, sky, colour, sound and music that is both sensual and visually challenging.

MM

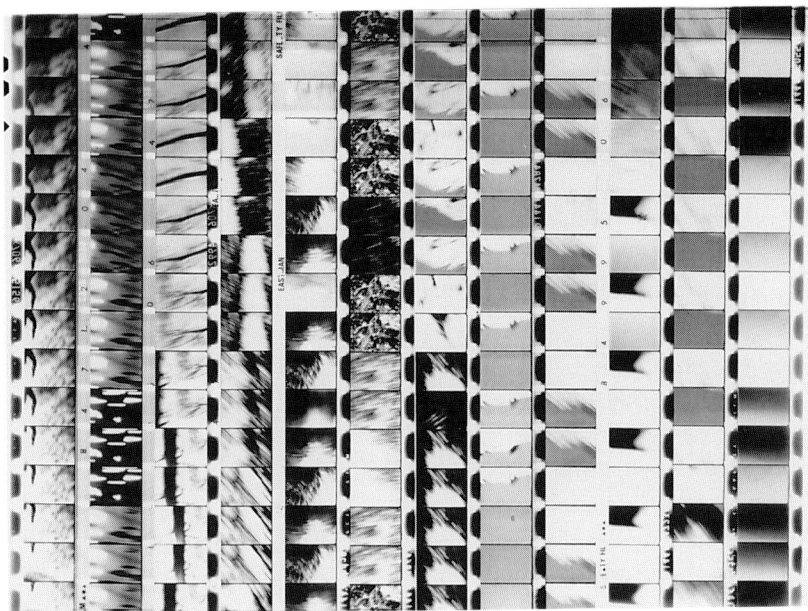

The Red Sea

1992, 20min, colour, 16mm

A journey through land, sea and the body – across territories of sensuality, pain and memory. This quest is a tragic journey of self-discovery, where disturbing images and the striking soundtrack are a testament to intense emotional territories which often remain unspoken or censored. *The Red Sea* is the bearer of lost images: beauty and terror reel past in a disturbing celebration, a ghost dance set in the depths of an imaginary world.

MM

In his most recent films, *Cezanne's Eye I* (1988), *Cezanne's Eye II* (1991) and *The Red Sea* (1992), Maziere has successfully consolidated a poetic and imagistic aesthetic which allows for the expression of personal feelings, if not narrative in any full-bodied sense. In *Cezanne's Eye II* – a collaboration with composer Stuart Jones – music plays an intrinsic part, transforming the formalistic and beautiful silent version into a moody portrayal, less of what Cezanne saw and more of what we are to understand he experienced emotionally. *The Red Sea* contains an exploration of memory, history and a muted sexuality, conveyed through images of newspaper titles, found-footage and home movies, and marks a distinct shift in direction. What was obliquely suggested in *The Bathers Series* – figures in the sea, voices on the beach, a radio overheard – is fleshed out with all the powerful resources of colour, light, camera movement and editing which Maziere has developed for more than a decade. *The Red Sea* fuses enormous technical facility with a "journey through land, sea and body – across territories of sensuality, pain and memory." Maziere's achievement is exceptional in its forging of an aesthetic of poetry, beauty and personal expression.

Michael O'Pray

Chris Meigh-Andrews

Few video artists have worked so determinedly within the conceptual problematic as Chris Meigh-Andrews. However, his commitment to the intelligence of art as a way of thinking has, in a career spanning sixteen years, been more than theoreticist. Early works share the neo-modernist aesthetic of his contemporaries, unpacking the dominance of television to unearth a mode of practice entirely appropriate to video. The works of the 1980s are language-based and semiotic in inspiration, but marked, especially in *Time Travelling/A True Story* (1982), by an attention to the making of the image which lifts it out of the run of *Screen*-derived work of the period. *Interlude (Homage to Bugs Bunny)* (1983), for example, loops a detail of an impossible chase from a Chuck Jones cartoon, while the soundtrack churns a detail of music into existential vertigo.

Mid-1980s single-channel works return to earlier autobiographical studies, but with a meticulous sense of the capacity of the video image to generate unreality as fast as it builds recognition. In *The Stream* (1987), elementary, even elemental aspects of an English landscape are slowed, mirrored and colourised to produce a statement on the transmutation of nature that balances between the philosophical and the alchemical. Other tapes explore the transformation of the personal in this most intimate of media, notably in *An Imaginary Landscape* (1986) in which a recognisable domesticity is reconfigured out of illegible but carefully equilibrated pixels, digitised into blocks of colour. As the image clarifies, the scale of abstraction rises, while the symmetry of the frame about its vertical axis intrudes further into consciousness: is this landscape imaginary because it is symmetrical? Like mud sedimenting out of river water, the raw footage emerges as the imaging of the imaginary, of self-image and imagination. In *Other Spaces* (1986), images of interior and exterior meet, compound and confound one another, marked in each instance as the trace of someone constantly passing out of vision, a figure (the artist?) running across the screen, This interplay of natural and artificial, of perception and image-making, underlies Meigh-Andrews' major work in installation since the beginning of the 1990s, notably in three sculptures, *Eau d'artifice* (1990), *Streamline* (1991) and *Perpetual Motion* (1994), each of which draw natural and artificial into complex interplays, The first reconstructs a rococo fountain, the second a stream from Monet's Givenchy garden, from monitors, playing on the flows of water and current, while the third uses the standard electricity supply to power in turn a fan, a wind-turbine, a computer and its images of the wind – a kite in the ceiling, blown grass on the floor. In all three, the complexities of drawing the natural world into the gallery provide the founding metaphor for the work. More recently, these researches have been enhanced by an adventure in interactive media, notably in CD-Roms drawing on a library of self-portraits amassed over years. Throughout a distinguished career, Meigh-Andrews' meticulous craft and intelligence mask a slow-burning, passionate commitment to the interface of technology and intimacy.

Sean Cubitt

The Stream
1987, 12min, colour, video

The constantly moving and ever changing surface of the stream is intended as a model for consciousness and an analogue for the video image itself. The movement of the actual water is compared with the illusory movement and representation of the televisual image. The images express the variety and complexity of the patterns flowing water and the surfaces and undercurrents which must necessarily co-exist.

Streamline
1991, installation, 9 monitors, 9 players

The installation simultaneously provides a representation of a 'natural' phenomenon whilst clearly remaining a constructed object made of separate elements. The bridge across the stream can be understood as both a platform from which the monitors can be viewed as individual objects and a device which underlines the idea of the line of monitors as a continuous 'stream' between the two concepts. Images of flowing water are visible through the wooden slats of the bridge, and from this vantage point it is possible to watch paper boats pass underneath: the images of boats, bridge and water drawing on a wealth of associations from literature, the cinema and television.

Biography

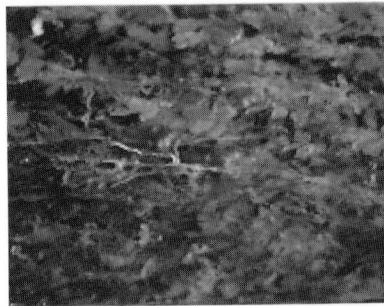

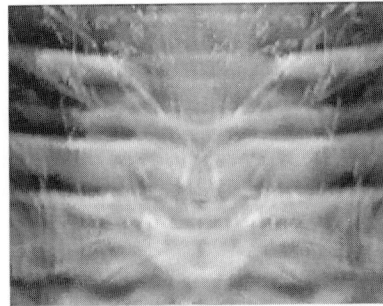

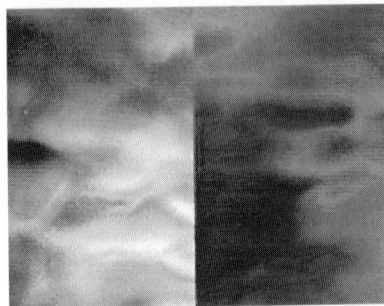

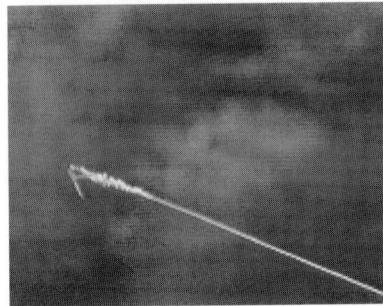

Born 1952, Essex. Higher Diploma in Photography, Film and Television, London College of Printing 1979; MA in Fine Art, Goldsmith's College, London 1983. Artist in Residence: Saw Gallery, Ottawa 1994; (Electronic Imaging) Oxford Brookes 1994. Currently Area Co-ordinator for Time-based Media, University of Central Lancashire. Exhibitions include: New British Video, Museum of Long Beach, California; Recent British Video, Madrid; Quick, South Bank, London; European Media Art Festival, Osnabrück. Installations have been commissioned by: Harris Museum, Preston; Bluecoat Gallery, Liverpool; Camerawork, London; Oxford Sculpture Project. Publications (see Bibliography).

Katharine
Meynell

Since the early 1980s Katharine Meynell has developed a refined and evocative vocabulary of female subjectivity in works that span performance, installation and single-screen video. Meynell sees this subjectivity as existing simultaneously on several levels – social, symbolic and mythological – but always as being possessed of the intrinsic faculty for transgression. In her work such a faculty becomes a talent, a way out of tight corners, particularly if those corners are the straitened cul-de-sacs of patriarchal symbolic exchanges. "My work is the direct result of the confusions and paradoxes of my beliefs as a feminist", Meynell has stated, describing her approach as one based in narrative, "...empirical fictions rather than theoretical certainties." Mythology is one repertoire of narratives whose empiricism is constantly available for re-reading and orienting anew, so it is that *Medusa* (1988), possibly Meynell's most acheived revisiting of myth, opts for a sideways take on the power of the ancient fables. Via an often humorous updating, and recast in a pungent modern vernacular, the myth of Medusa, with whom Poseidon is described as having "had his pleasure and pissed off", becomes a feminist celebration of the "monstrous-feminine", whose lightness of touch only just reigns in the ambivalence underlying the work's attitude to the experiences of birth and motherhood. Elsewhere, such intimate adventures appear to be more straightforwardly celebrated, as in *Hannah's Song* (1987), Meynell's excursion into a more recognizably "poetic" form of single screen video, in which a wordless collage of stills, close-ups and negatives, deliver a suitably pre-linguistic form by which to address what Meynell describes as "the slippage of roles in the post-partum period."

Meynell's single-screen works generally tend to confront the viewer less on the level of structure or material than on that of symbol and narrative, and offer a visual pleasure in keeping with the clarity necessary for her recurring

Biography

Born 1954. BSDip Byam Shaw School of Art, London 1976; MA Royal College of Art, London 1983. Founder member of the Women's Media Resource Project. Screenings/exhibitions include: Berlin Videofest; Film Museum, Amsterdam; Orchard Gallery, Derry; International Centre for Photography, New York; Kettle's Yard, Cambridge. Member of the Arts Council's steering group for the Live Art Archive. Freelance camera operator and director involved in the documentation of visual theatre, performance and installation work, including Rose English's *Walks On Water*; Station House Opera's *Bastille Dances*, Trevor Stuart's *Taboo*, Brian Catling at the Serpentine Gallery. Currently Senior Lecturer in Fine Art at Middlesex University and working on a PhD on time-based work in Britain since 1980 at the Royal College of Art.

Key works

Hannah's Song
1987, 8min, colour, video

A poetic work evoking the slippage of roles in the post-partum period. A cyclical cross-generational sense of loss and separation culminates in the image of the child passionately kissing her own image in the mirror.

KM

Medusa
1988, 20min, colour, video

Taking the form of a mother-daughter remembrance, the tape moves between age-old archetype and its arch updating in the present. Medusa, seduced and abandoned and pregnant with the bastard Pegasus, first seethes at her fate, then disdains to deliver her child, refusing to yield up her space to the man-made vocabularies of either medicine or madness.

Steven Bode

Eat
1992, installation, 5 monitors, 1 projector, 6 players

A large projection onto the plaster wall of the gallery creates an electronic fresco. The image is a still life, a table obliquely suggesting a last supper formally laid with five places, each an arrangement of food and objects. A child walks across the table, playing with the food. Five monitors are suspended with their backs visible, sound and light spilling out. A single part of a larger still life is placed within the frame of each monitor over which images are enmeshed and overlaid, to form footnotes and subtexts.

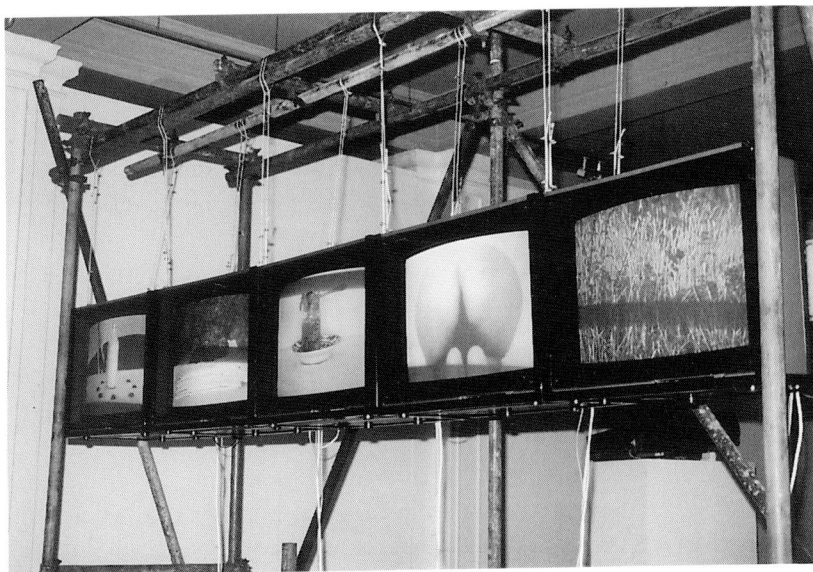

Vampire S Eat

1992, installation, LCD screen, chair,
1 player

Vampire S Eat comprises a single LCD
screen embedded into the cushion of a
chair, the image and sounds of a licking
tongue slurping against the glass conjuring
up numerous horrors. It benefits from
humour and simplicity, playing against
the functional intentions of the chair.

Chris Meigh-Andrews

engagement with primal and archetypal imagery. The most recent example
of this polished, "broadcast-friendly" aesthetic is her piece for BBC Scotland,
*As she opened her eyes she looked over her shoulder and saw someone passing the
other side of the doorway with a strange smile* (1990), in which the dances,
ritualised movements and exchange of symbolic objects between three women,
the Musician, the Reader and the Dancer, creates a dream space of metaphorical
and unspoken communication.

In her installations Meynell extends her preoccupation into more
confrontational realms, whilst maintaining the meditative characteristics of
her tapes. The twin pieces, *Eat* (1992) and *Vampire S Eat* (1992), confront the
spectacle of food and its socialised settings with more subterranean sexual and
illicit associations. In the former work, the little girl as a figure of an as-yet-
unschooled-curiosity, and therefore the agent of transgression, guides the
spectator through the installation's catalogue of the carnal contained by the
social. *Vampire S Eat* is more direct still, placing a monitor image of a hungry,
gorging mouth in the seat of a chair, the simplicity of the image and the
perverse accuracy of its placement trigger all manner of associations which
include those of a consummate orality and an inverted vagina dentata.

Chris Darke

Laura Mulvey
Peter Wollen

Laura Mulvey and Peter Wollen's filmmaking is very clearly marked by its cultural provenance – it emerges from the British independent film movement in the 1970s, a powerful set of intellectual, institutional and social contexts. The BFI (Wollen worked in the Educational Department) had become energetic in politicising film culture, the Independent Film-makers' Association provided a broad alliance for cultural producers, and also there was what Robin Wood described as the 'felt moment of *Screen*'...

Their first film, *Penthesilea* (1974) loosely connecting with Kleist's original play, has a brave and overt structure – an unswerving passage through the five sections, in the second of which Peter Wollen wanders in a sunny conservatory reflecting on the intellectual strata of the piece in a spectacularly wide-ranging discourse. Their attempt to "free up cinema for the poetics of theory" proposes uninhibited intelligence and evanescent glimpses of abstract thought in the diffuse but corrosive anti-intellectual climate in Britain.

The symmetrical structure of *Riddles of the Sphinx* (1977) provides a formal framework for the narrative elements which focus on motherhood as problem and possibility. The film relates issues of day care both to conscious political action and to desire and self-construction. *AMY!* (1980) offers a lively and

Biography

Laura Mulvey: born 1941, Oxford. BA History St Hilda's College, Oxford. Has lectured at London College of Printing, University of East Anglia. Currently Head of MA Programme at the British Film Institute. Writer and theorist (see Bibliography). Organised Women and Film event, Edinburgh 1992 (with Lynda Myles and Claire Johnston).

Peter Wollen: born 1938, London. Read English Literature at Oxford University. Worked at the British Film Institute 1967–69 where he edited the *Cinema One* series and wrote *Signs and Meanings in the Cinema* (1969, revised 1972). Has taught at Northwestern University, Illinois; Columbia University, New York; Brown University, Providence; Vassar College, Poughkeepsie. Currently Professor in the Film Department, University of California, Los Angeles. Wrote the script for Michelangelo Antonioni's *The Passenger*, (1974 – with Mark Peploe). Currently alternates between making television programmes in England and teaching in the United States. Writer (see Bibliography). Films have been screened and broadcast extensively. Joint curatorial work includes *Frida Kahlo and Tina Modotti* exhibition at the Whitechapel Gallery, London, 1982

Key works

Penthesilea
1974, 90min, colour, 16mm

Opening with a mime performance of Kleist's play about the Queen of the Amazons, Penthesilea is an extreme example of counter-cinema. Refusing the rhythms and conventions of editing, it uses a highly visible system of montage by juxtaposing five sections, each consisting of a twenty minute continuous take. Taking as its starting point Kleist's twist on the original story, the film reflects theoretically on the mythology and iconography of Penthesilea from the point of view of feminism and psychoanalysis.

Riddles of the Sphinx
1977, 99min, colour, 16mm

The role of the Sphinx in the Oedipus story is used to consider the mother/child relationship, again in the context of feminist interest in psychoanalytic theory. The central section of the film consists of thirteen 360 degree pans, which tell the story of a mother and her two year old child in selected, exemplary, moments. using London as its location, the film combines the chance elements of the long take with a highly formal pattern, including digressions into the material of film and theoretical reflection.

128

Crystal Gazing

1981, 90min, colour, 16mm

More than anything, *Crystal Gazing* resembles work from another Depression era – the satirical novels (*Antic Hay, Chrome Yellow*) of Aldous Huxley come to mind. Under the brittle surfaces (much credit to camerawoman Diane Tammes) and droll dialogue lurks personal despair and political impasse. Where Huxley's set were Hampstead and Home County, Wollen and Mulvey play off the Portobello Road. Sometimes the quilting wears a bit thin – on a shopping visit to Rough Trade, or during Laura Logic's several musical spots. There's even a certain annoying cheek in Wollen and Mulvey, long-term anti-narrative campaigners, making such a slick movie. But lets celebrate the Left dancing so wittily on the graveyards of past and present.

Chris Auty

The Bad Sister

1983, 90min, colour, video

[...] aspects of *The Bad Sister* emphasise the theme of the unconscious. The narrative structure continually focuses on Jane's mind through her tape diary – which the male video maker calls "a message written in code." Furthermore, within the dramatisations of her life, there is a continual shift between conscious and unconscious thought, between dream and waking states, between imagination and reality. Clare Johnston has stated that "a desire for change" in woman's art "can only come about by drawing on fantasy", and clearly, in *The Bad Sister*, this is what Mulvey and Wollen attempt to do.

Lucy Fischer *Shot Counter Shot*

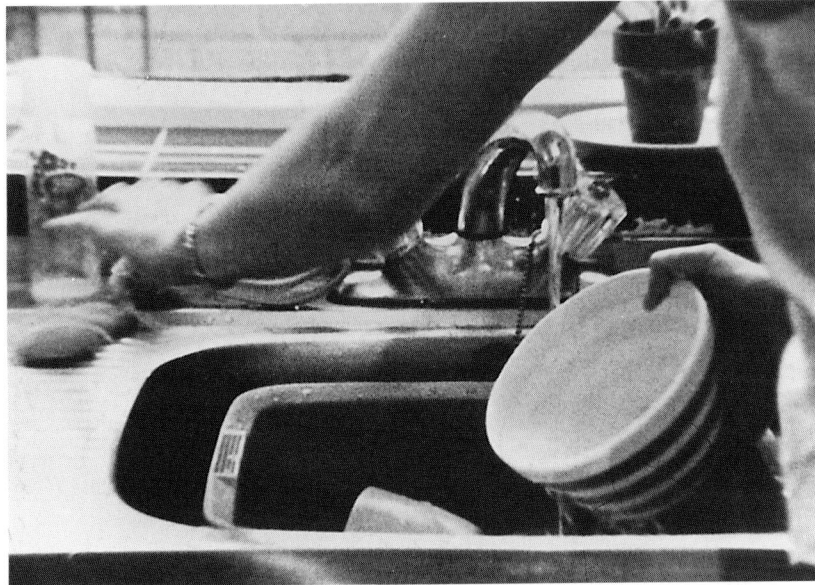

ABOVE:
RIDDLES OF THE SPHINX

inventive mixture of archive, live action and rostrum work. An archaeological moment of female heroism is carefully disinterred and swerves into vision in a fresh and contemporary context.

After their documentary feature *Frida Kahlo and Tina Modotti* (1982), their last two feature films reveal a considered response to the changing atmosphere of the 1980s. *Crystal Gazing* (1981) is an early response to the impact of Thatcherism and *The Bad Sister* (1983), commissioned by Channel Four, was shot on video as an experiment in fantasy effects for television.

Both Wollen and Mulvey are now possibly better known for their writing and teaching on cinema than for their film-making. As writers they are what Italians might describe as 'saggisti' (essayists): engaged intellectual analysts playing a catalytic role in a culture. Peter Wollen's seminal collection *Signs and Meaning in the Cinema* (1969) introduced semiology and a structural version of the auteur theory to a recalcitrant English-speaking audience. Laura Mulvey's essay *Visual Pleasure in Narrative Cinema*, reprinted in her collection, *Visual and Other Pleasures* (1989), is one of the most footnoted and photocopied essays in film studies.

Their writing and their film-making ranges across exceptionally eclectic cultural interests, from Allen Jones to Disney, from Sirk to Surrealism, from Situationism to Modotti and Kahlo. This refusal of pertinent boundaries embraces a diversity that predates the fashions of post-modernism by several decades. Their commitment to a politics of culture redefined by the events of 1968, particularly feminism and its persistent focus on the politics of the everyday, was manifest in their writing and film-making. Their film work was immediately seen, by *Screen* for instance, in a contemporary international context where a number of film-makers were exploring radical form: Godard, Straub/Huillet, Akerman, Snow, Rainer. Indeed it seemed to illustrate and extend the magazine's concerns with the interstices between psychoanalysis, semiology and radical politics; and the films were seen and discussed extensively in universities and colleges.

Since their working partnership dissolved they have continued individually to find softer ways of challenging orthodoxy. Laura Mulvey's intelligent documentary on Russian iconoclasm, *Disgraced Monuments* (1992) and Peter Wollen's contributions to The Bandung File – *Images of Atlantis* and *Full Cycle* (1992) are interventions at the edge of arts television. Wollen has also made an imaginative low-budget feature based on his own short story *Friendship's Death* (1987).

Rod Stoneman

Key works

Blowing The Whistle

1991, ½min cycle, football stadium lightboard (with Anna Douglas)

Electronic animation created for the scoreboards of Everton's Goodison Park and Oldham Athletic's Boundary Park. Displayed on November 16 1991, this is a humorous tribute to the women's participation in football both as players and supporters and features images produced by Amiga computers of gyrating washing machines, steaming irons and jostling team shirts.

Screen Deep

1992, 20min cycle, colour,

As artist-in-residence at the National Portrait Gallery, Myers examined two pairs of portraits: Andy Warhol's *Elizabeth Taylor* and *Mick Jagger* and older icons of beauty exemplified in *John Wilmot, 2nd Earl of Rochester, after Jacob Huysmans* (c.1665-70) and *Nell Gwyn*, studio of Sir Peter Lely (c.1675). Myers captured each portrait with a video camera, transferred the image to a Amiga desktop computer, then manipulated it on screen and altered and exaggerated their features.

Julie Myers' current involvement with computer graphics derives from her experimentation across a range of media, including traditional painting, film and video. Her animations are quirky and sketchy in style, whilst her multi-media projects combine computer originated drawing with complex electronic manipulations of iconographic images taken from media or fine art sources.

Whether producing single screen animations such as *Trim to Fit* (1993) – which explores changing fashions in female beauty, or large site-specific light-board animation for football pitches such as *Blowing the Whistle* (1991) – which celebrates the unsung heroines of football, or smaller, intimate interactive conversation pieces on CD-Rom, Myers raises issues of female identity, gender stereotyping, sexuality and equality. These prevailing themes are investigated through a combination of computer generated art, hand drawn images, photography and live video footage. By juxtaposing images of assumed reality with her own fantastical animations, she takes an ironic glance on the world to expose its more commonplace injustices.

Myers' light-hearted investigative approach results in work which is widely accessible. During recent residencies at the National Portrait Gallery and the Museum of the Moving Image, a broad range of people have been encouraged to bring to the galleries their own portraits of personalities and stars, and through learning basic computer manipulation techniques have come to question their assumptions of beauty and stardom. She is currently collaborating with poets and writers, developing computer manipulated text and performance works.

Anna Douglas

Biography

Born 1961, Bramhall, Cheshire. BA in Fine Art, Middlesex Polytechnic 1983; PG Diploma in Film and Television 1986; MA in Image Synthesis and Computer Animation, Middlesex University 1992. Consultancy work includes computer animation workshops with Jackdaw Productions for Video Positive, Liverpool; CD-I Graphic designer for Philips Multi-media, Paris. Screenings include: Cinewomen – Norwich Festival of Women Film-makers; Institute of Contemporary Arts, London; ISEA Festival, Helsinki; Hong Kong International Film Festival. Currently Associate Lecturer in Fine Art, Middlesex University and part-time Lecturer in Fine Art, Intermedia Department, Kingston University.

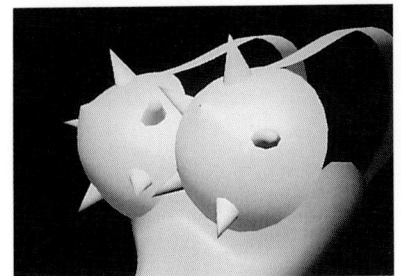

ABOVE:
KILLER CORSET

Vera Neubauer

Thematically and aesthetically, [Vera Neubauer's films] resonate with the tradition of female film-makers that starts with Maya Deren and leads to Yvonne Rainer, Cecilia Condit and Leslie Thornton; experimental film-makers whose employment of bricolage and Brechtian mannerisms, radical feminism and repetition, avant-garde montage techniques and Mother figures, makes them the darlings of feminist film theory [...]

Born in Czechoslovakia, Neubauer moved to Britain in 1968 and began studying print-making at the Royal College of Art, but then switched to film in which she graduated. She made short films using animation, which she perceived to be a medium not unlike printmaking – both techniques generating a limited series of images and requiring a high degree of repetitious work. She soon developed her unique style which uses seemingly crude, thick wobbly lines to create simply drawn characters that move through a sparse background, formally reminiscent of the work of Emile Cohl.

Neubauer's work strikes the viewer as *faux-naïf* with the accent on *faux*, for her simple drawing style belies the complexity and sophistication of her subject matter, which uses strong, even shocking images to illustrate her concerns. Thus, her films have a raw, spontaneous quality that enhances and underscores the sketchy narratives that they illustrate, often drawing on the imagery and elliptical qualities of fairy tales. The tension in Neubauer's draughtsmanship – which manages to appear fresh and direct rather than clumsy or badly drawn – is symptomatic of the tension she maintains throughout the body of her work on a thematic level. Like some of the women film-makers cited above, Neubauer tells stories through a montage of striking images and fragmentary scenes which refuse to pull the wool over the spectator's eyes. Instead, time in her narratives is fractured, the 'plots' are cut up and reassembled on the editing table, evoking the feeling of stories half-remembered, narrated by someone perhaps with the digressive tendencies of Tristram Shandy, or perhaps with an unreliable memory, or perhaps just someone trying to say not "this and then this" but everything at once [...]

By rejecting the glib perfectionism of mainstream animation and its fetishism of fluid movement and cleaned-up graphics, these films force the viewer to confront their own expectations about the animation, and indeed film.[...]

Neubauer's work insistently reminds the viewer of its own constructedness as art, and thus of the construction of the themes with which it deals, such as sexuality and power relations.

Leslie Felperin Sharman *Women in Animation; A Compendium*

Animation for Live Action
1978, 25min, colour, 16mm

A combination of animation and live action bringing dream and fantasy into ironic collusion with reality and actuality. In a series of encounters between animator and animated images, an alter-ego figure is taken through a variety of adventures, exploring and destroying stereotypical women's roles, in a dynamic demonstration of women's creativity.

The Decision
1981, 33min, colour, 35mm

Beginning and ending with a fairy story heard on the radio, the film evokes the problem faced by 'any princess' – is it a question of being decisive or having to choose? This leads to a series of explosive images which confront housework, psychoanalysis, film-making, women's oppression and sexual desire.

Mid Air
1986, 16min, colour 16mm

Women, like the witches of old, learn to fly and use their magical powers, and male authority is overthrown when the housewife turned witch produces a potion that makes men menstruate. The film uses a combination of stills, fabric cut-outs and puppetry, together with a mock operatic soundtrack.

Don't Be Afraid

1990, 28min, b&w, 16mm

In this musical we follow four rebellious Brixton youths of mixed race through part of their adolescence and an upheaval which results in the birth of a potential cabinet minister. Stereotype and prejudice are turned firmly upside down. The situation may be bleak, but the combination of local music, a circus of choreographed rebellion and irresistible performances from the sexually ambiguous foursome, create a fierce sense of optimism.

Born 1948, Prague; nationality, German. Studied art in Prague, Dusseldorf and the Akademie der Bildender Kunste, Stuttgart. Studied film-making at the Royal College of Art, London. Film-maker and teacher since 1972. Taught at Royal College of Art, St Martin's School of Art, and other colleges in Britain. Screenings include: Ottawa Film Festival; *Mid Air*: Best Fiction Film, Melbourne Film Festival 1987; *Don't Be Afraid*: First Prize, Youth Jury, Oberhausen Short Film Festival; Best Short, Melbourne International Film Festival: Best Short, Montreal Film Festival, 1991; Edinburgh Film Festival. One Person retrospectives include the International Animation Festival, Bristol 1987 and Unity Theatre, Liverpool 1987.

ABOVE:
**ANIMATION FOR LIVE
ACTION**

Chris Newby

With British cinema in the early 1990s increasingly dominated by calls for a ruthless transatlantic commercialism, this might seem the worst possible time for a director of unashamedly abstract proclivities to enter the narrative mainstream. Chris Newby's shorts, however, suggest a director fully qualified to take on the mainstream on his own terms. His first feature *Anchoress* (1993) lives up to a traditional conception of 'art cinema', being as rarefied in its subject matter (the religious and sexual travails of a woman in the Middle Ages) as in its visual sensibility. The film's real problem, however, is that the imagery is never allowed to dictate its own argument, reined in as it is by the demands of a fustian script. Consequently Newby's style looks not so much imagistic as picturesque.

Newby clearly needs a narrative space that can accommodate the profligate visual imagination that gives his shorts their considerable charge, *The Old Man of the Sea* (1990) is dense enough in its imagery to defy any attempts to read it as, for example, an allegory of the human body, its drives and its ageing process. At first glance, the film seems to operate along associative lines of classic surrealism, but in fact the visual metaphors it strings together are strictly motivated and quite traditional. The armature of a leaf leads to the vaults of a cathedral, the rigging of a ship, the bones of fish or of men. Although the connections may sometimes appear obvious, the film derives its fascination from the fact that no one term is given a dominant value – which means that the film at once invokes and evades narrative construction.

Newby's visual parallelism at times opts for the bathos of the simple pun, thereby providing welcome relief for the manifestly 'poetic' associations. In *The Old Man of the Sea*, the old man's fishing line catches a boy's bathing trunks, and the languorous erotic tenor of the imagery suddenly stops dead on this gag. The following close-up of an aged hand feverishly tugging the line becomes a masturbatory image, providing a humorous orgasmic discharge for the film's erotic parallels for the human body.

In *The Old Man of the Sea* and *Kiss* (1991), Newby uses elaborately staged single moments to purely associative effect. In *Kiss*, however, the staging is often so wilfully sensuous that it treads a thin line between dream-narrative and the aesthetics of advertising (the proximity is understandable – both address the libido). In *Relax* (1991), however, Newby's impulsively rhythmic visual and soundtrack editing makes a successful compromise with realism. The story is of a nervous young gay man's wait for the result of an HIV test (Newby provides both 'positive' and 'negative' endings); the film belies its title by never once allowing hero or viewer to relax. It begins with a close-up of a male crotch being furiously scrubbed, to the sound of an alarm clock; elsewhere, spurts of shaving foam and oil act to similar shock effect. Newby punctuates the film with footage

The Old Man of The Sea
1990, 20min, b&w, 35mm

The old man could never be caught. Now man, now eel, now the very salt of the sea – no fisherman ever snared this slippery customer.

CN

Relax
1991, 25min, colour and b&w, 16mm

A portrayal of the thoughts and feelings of one gay man who has just taken the HIV test and awaits the results – aware of the likelihood of being HIV positive and understandably worried about having his fears confirmed.

Anchoress

1993, 108min, b&w, 35 mm

In a remote village in the fourteenth century, an illiterate peasant girl, Christine Carpenter, becomes the focus of a power struggle between the Church and the Manor. She refuses to marry the Reeve (steward of the Manor) and appears obsessed by the wooden statue of the Virgin Mary in the village church. The ambitious Priest sees his chance to seize spiritual power from the Reeve and announces Christine as a holy Anchoress with spiritual powers to communicate with the Virgin Mary. Christine is duly enclosed in the walls of the Church, according to the Anchorite tradition and much to the distress of her sceptical mother. Gradually, Christine's enclosure begins to threaten the foundations of the church and the community as a whole. The priest whips the villagers into a frenzy of hatred which culminates in a brutal witch-hunt but the purity of Christine's spirit remains undefiled.

of blood coursing through veins, and throughout creates external correlatives for the workings of the body – a set of umbrellas seen from above performs a dance of red and white corpuscles.

Relax, visually the least extravagant of the shorts, nevertheless maps out a strategy for merging near-autonomous imagery with mainstream narrative. *Anchoress*, however, doesn't follow it – partly because its quite traditional metaphors (golden hair/corn) appear simply to be superimposed on the narrative. In future, perhaps, Newby's imagery will be allowed to generate its own narrative. Certainly, the imaginative compromise of *Relax* suggests more than one way to make a film which at once addresses the realities of contemporary Britain, fantasies about it, and physical responses to it. Newby could prove well qualified to give new British narrative cinema the erotic language it deserves.

Jonathan Romney

Biography

Studied at Leeds Polytechnic and Royal College of Art, London. *Relax*: Golden Teddy Bear for Best Gay Short Film, Berlin Film Festival 1991; ICA Biennial: 'Arrows of Desire'.

135

Jayne **Parker**

Jayne Parker studied sculpture before she made films, and you sometimes feel that a sculptor's eye is still sizing things up before a shot is exposed. This eye looks all round the space, sees how objects and bodies are integral to the frame, seeks the change of shape as the sight-lines move, traces connections. The result is pure cinema, but her characteristically clear image-making perhaps goes back to scrutinising static forms that remain ambiguous or 'other'. So does her confidence that the visual image (often silent or nearly so) can convey a precise idea which words evade. Apart from all that, art schools should teach you to follow your own nose (she went to Canterbury and the Slade.) For the handful of film-makers who – like Parker – began to make work in the very late 1970s, there was little choice but to find their own way; the structural movement was disintegrating, new options beckoned. In the brief cusp between the avant-garde of the 1970s and the retro-garde of the 1980s, Parker laid an independent path for herself to which she has kept. Nonetheless, the vision and freedom of her first films also declare the rigours of formal film just as they anticipate the waves of more personal, emotive and gendered film-making to come.

Parker's early films explore the hinterland between animation and performance art (her drawn films are stark, funny and 'creepy'; cats, fish, blood). In *RX Recipe* (1980) a woman bandages an eel, and then her own leg, to whispered instructions – body language, binding images. The breakthrough film is *I Dish* (1982), her first to fully explore narrative space. Here, a young man and woman enact rites of washing and cooking that are both informal and highly charged. Framing – and the viewer's imagination – links the protagonists in the same small room, even as the montage radically divides them by never showing them in the same shot. In a final sequence, the woman – now naked by the sea, sifting stones – moves to freedom as her gestures take her 'almost out', beyond the edge of the shot. In her later films, Parker refines film as metaphor, using recurrent images that avoid fixed symbolism but evoke transition (fish, water, guts, the naked body). The long video Almost *Out* (1984) is uniquely a candid confrontation between mother and daughter, camera and protagonist. The shock of raw imagery and frank talk is slowly mediated by the gradual revelation of the work's artifice. Video's intimate scale matches the key themes; family, fantasy, dreamwork, identity.

Biography

Born 1957, Nottingham. BA in Fine Art, Canterbury College of Art 1980; Higher Diploma in Fine Art, Experimental Media Department, Slade School of Fine Art, London 1982. Screenings include: National Film Theatre, London; Eiszeit Kino, Berlin; Tate Gallery, London; Light Cone, Paris; Whitechapel Gallery, London. *K*.: ICA Biennial: 'Between Imagination and Reality'; *The Pool*: ICA Biennial: 'Arrows of Desire'. Currently Lecturer at Goldsmiths' College and the Slade School of Fine Art, London.

RX Recipe
1980, 12min, colour, 16mm

A woman cares for an eel. She washes it, feeds it and wraps it. She administers the correct prescription for its comfort and then cares for herself.

JP

I Dish
1982, 16min, b&w, 16mm

I Dish is a fractured and achronological account of the catching, cooking and devouring of a fish which, edited with care and imagination, turns into a disturbing, violent metaphor for the animosity between a young woman and a man.

Sheila Johnston

Almost Out
1984, 105min, colour, video

I film my mother in a studio. She is naked. She can see her image in a monitor. I want to see my mother as she really is, but I don't know how to look at her. I want her to desire me. She says she doesn't. My mother allows me to film her because I am her daughter.

My mother is a symbol for power, authority, control. I want to please my mother. I feel that she is inside me. She is very heavy. I want to push her out, gently, because I care for her and don't want to hurt her.

JP

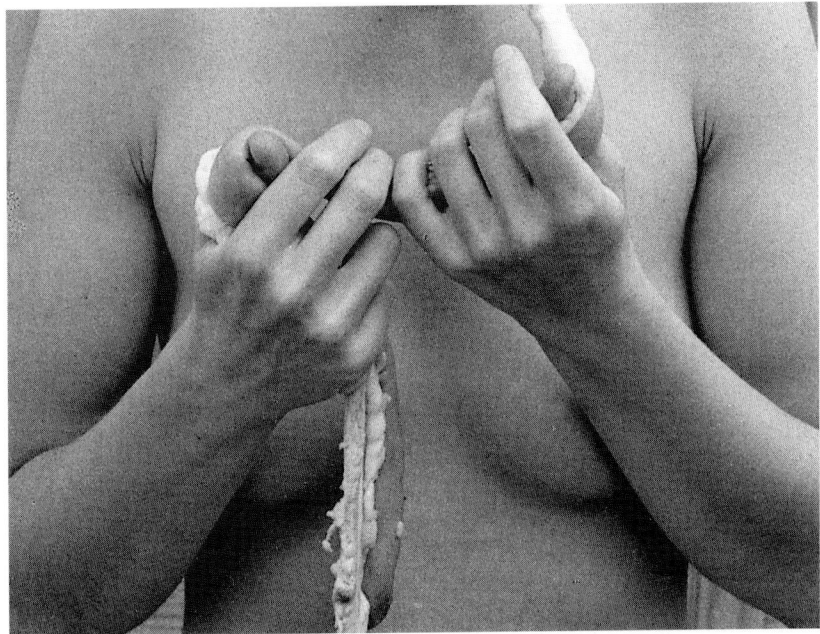

K.

1989, 13min, b&w, 16mm

I bring my intestine up out of my mouth.
It falls in a pile at my feet. I take the
intestine with my arms. I stand on the edge
of a pool. I make myself dive again and
again. I bring out into the open all the
things I have taken in that are not mine,
and thereby make room for something new.
I make an external order out of an internal
tangle.

JP "

K. is concerned with facing up to fears,
exerting control and gaining strength. Its
balanced structure and serene pacing reflect
the artist's ultimate imposition of internal
order."

Alexandra Sage

After this incursion into language, Parker's recent work is firmly pictorial.
Each is an 'artist's statement', finding images to imply the act of making and the
search for source. They have the direct, presentational immediacy of
performance art. K. (1989) knits a garment from extracted innards, while *The
Pool* (1991) explores the inner rhythms of dance and movement. *Cold Jazz* (1993)
is a crisis-poem to music; stark and luminous shots of an older woman playing
the saxophone are cut against a younger woman eating oysters, vividly making
ironic a major thread (concept-conception) in all three films. Parker's radical
modernism looks outwards to the viewer's contemporary space. Photogenic,
crisp and often surreal, her films are as lucidly gnomic and true as Bishop
Butler's famous utterance: "Everything is what it is, and not another thing."

A L Rees

Kayla **Parker**

As an artist I have chosen animation because of its unlimited possibilities. Animation is to me about movement and change, the potential for manipulation of image and sound at 24 frames a second. Animation combines all the things I do, writing, drawing, sound composition and so on. It's also a very physical medium, and has become an integral part of my life. Events that happen, the way I'm feeling, all quite naturally affect my work, so there is a strong autobiographical element. This is more apparent in my own films, but is also present in commissioned pieces – title sequences for instance – for television.

Animation-making is my way of finding meaning in – giving sense to – my life, and myself as a woman. The ingredients for my work come directly from my notebooks which are a creative record of ideas, images, dreams, memories. I've kept notebooks in one form or another since childhood, and they are the most constant, continuous element in my life. The techniques I use in film-making originate from my early work in performance, using notebook material as a basic source, automatic drawing and writing, improvisation, chance and found elements. The final form of the work evolves organically from the creative and technical process of its making.

Animation has become an increasingly popular form of film-making for women because it gives a high degree of independence and control over all aspects of the film-making process. It is possible to do everything yourself, in the way you want to; it's easier to fit in around day to day life than, say, making film-drama which can involve co-ordinating a number of actors, crew, and quantities of equipment. I am not particularly interested in making humorous, animated comic strips, and I have a fundamental abhorrence of authoritarian structures. I am much more concerned with developing methods of film-making which are individual, collaborative, spontaneous. The outreach work I do in the community is an important part of my work. As a film-maker, one of the most directly political acts I can undertake is to go into a school and to enable kids to devise and make their own film. I believe that art, ideas, and the means of production should be accessible to all.

Kayla Parker

Key works

Nuclear Family
1990, 5min, colour, 16mm

A mother recalls incidents from her daughter's childhood, and the three imaginary friends who 'came down from the stars' a quarter of a century before in a Somerset mining village. The film-maker draws images of childhood directly onto the surface of the film in the manner of the wax crayon and scratch pictures she made as a child.

Unknown Woman
1991, 9min, colour, 16mm

A woman's psychological journey which externalises an inner world filled with suspense and pursuit. Animated ink and wax drawings are inter-cut with pixillated sequences of a woman and a crow originating in dreams.

Cage Of Flame
1992, 10min, colour, 16mm

An alternative view of menstruation which celebrates the time of the month when dreams and the imaginary dominate. A counter to the sanitised, pastel-pretty version we are conditioned to accept. The creative period – what the TV ads missed out.

KP

Night Sounding
1993, 1min, colour, 16mm

The film is literally an aural and visual 'sounding' from the shoreline of an industrial, fishing and military port. It describes the experience of living where land, sea and air meet, of being on the edge of the world. Living close to the harbour, my consciousness has been infiltrated by the to and fro of tides, the movements of warships and trawlers; I am aware of the conflicts which exist between people, and the sea itself. The coast around here is treacherous, the sea floor littered with the bones of ships. *Night Sounding* evokes a sense of place and the resonance of association – the lights and siren which warn of danger, the wreckers and sirens who entice ships to their doom.

KP

Biography

Born 1955, Birmingham. Studied Design at
Norwich School of Art 1978 and Fine Art
at Gwent College of Higher Education 1985.
Attended a short introductory animation
course at Chapter Film Workshop, Cardiff.
Festival screenings include the London Film
Festival; Women in the Director's Chair,
Chicago; Feminale, Cologne; Viper,
Lucerne; European Media Art Festival,
Osnabrück; Hiroshima Animation Festival;
Stuttgart Animation Festival; Cardiff
International Animation Festival. *Unknown
Woman*: ICA Biennial: 'Arrows of Desire';
Night Sounding: ICA Biennial: 'What You
See is What You Get'. Other screenings
include: Tate Gallery St Ives; Tate Gallery,
London; Institute of Contemporary Arts,
London; Deuxièmes Rencontres
Internationales Art Cinèma/Vidèo/
Ordinateur (Mutations de L'Image), Paris;
National Film Theatre, London

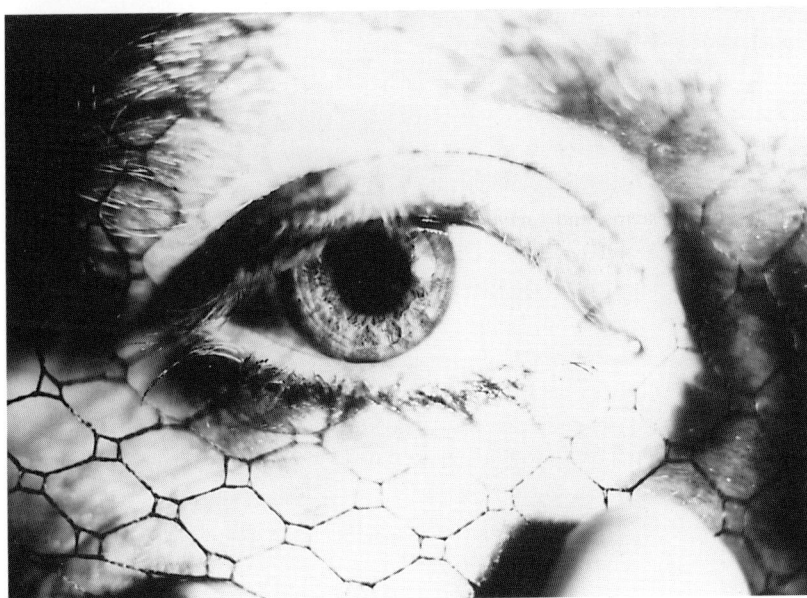

TOP:
UNKNOWN WOMAN
BELOW:
CAGE OF FLAME

Pratibha
Parmar

Throughout Pratibha Parmar's powerful documentary work run interconnecting threads: her profound awareness of global struggles against oppression – such as homophobia in *Khush* (1991), AIDS in *Reframing AIDS* (1987), female genital mutilation in *Warrior Marks* (1993); and her distinctive aesthetic – the product of weaving together an intertextual fabric of archive footage, interviews, inventive studio sets, world music and dramatic monologues, poetry and dance. Motivated by the need to address the silences and misrepresentations in white, heterosexual culture, her work is fired by an urgency and passion that manages to avoid didacticism, to carve out a unique place in televisual form.

The lyrically understated video poem *Sari Red* (1988) – dedicated to Kalbinder Kaur Hayre, a young Asian woman murdered by white youths – celebrates Indian culture in the face of British racism, and determines the territory and style of later work; the sensuous use of early Indian feature film in *Khush* and the hauntingly sensitive portrayal of young African women in *Warrior Marks*. In *Warrior Marks*, she can visualise the horror of female genital mutilation – unexplicit, yet overwhelmingly charged – through the simple and direct use of a choreographed dance. She guides the narrator, Alice Walker, through her own experience of 'patriarchal wounding' to the wider suffering of women now in Africa and in the Diaspora, delicately combining revelation with respect, discretion with exposure of pain, to present a complex argument against the practice.

Khush, taken from the Urdu word meaning 'ecstatic pleasure' and now reclaimed by some Asian lesbians and gays, gives space to communities in both Britain and in India to articulate for the first time their definitions of desire. Exquisitely erotic performances brought British television some of its first sexual images of Asian women together. The work celebrates a vibrant Asian gay and lesbian culture, both contemporary and historical, as well as negotiating the difficult interstices of family traditions, race, sexuality and exoticised 'otherness'.

Parmar's dynamic and witty *Double the Trouble, Twice the Fun* (1992) dramatically explores a disabled gay man's active sexuality. Tender and gripping, it contains none of the disempowering worthiness of many earlier representations of disability and sexuality. Her portrait of three African-American artists and activists – June Jordan, Alice Walker and Angela Davies – in *A Place of Rage* (1991), is a salient and punchy homage to black women's political agency, both in the Civil Rights movement and in America today.

Parmar is a key figure in the struggle to define what it means to be political, and to embrace and expand what it means to be a cultural activist. Her vision is unflinching as it persistently uncovers suppressed voices while broaching the awkward political contradictions around race, sexuality and gender. Her ability to draw out testimonies of self-knowledge and affirmation from her interviewees while in pursuit of a rigorous form, distinguishes her work.

Cherry Smyth

Key works

Sari Red
1988, 11min, colour, video

A video poem of remembrance of Kalbinder Kaur Hayre, a young Asian woman who was killed by three white racist youths who drove a van into her, crushing her against a wall. The tape both captures the ever-present reality of racist violence as well as celebrating red, the colour of the sari, as a symbol of sensuality and intimacy between Asian women.

Khush
1991, 24min, colour, 16mm

'Khush' means ecstatic pleasure in Urdu. The lives of South Asian Lesbians and Gay men in Britain and India are celebrated in a film that combines documentary style testimonies with sensually choreographed dance sequences.

Memsahib Rita
1994, 20min, colour and b&w, 16mm

Memsahib Rita is a story of a young woman, Shanti, living in the East End of London who is pursued by a racist thug. It is also the anniversary of her mother's death. At a crucial moment of confrontation, she is guided by a femme fatale who is a Rita Hayworth lookalike and an Asian movie star. A 'ghost' story with a difference, *Memsahib Rita* explores questions of mixed race identity, bereavement and racist violence, whilst borrowing imaginatively from the genres of magical realism, film noir and thrillers.

The Colour of Britain

1994, 50min, colour, 16mm

The Colour of Britain is about the work of artists who are redefining British Culture and the image of their nation. The internationally successful British Asian artists Anish Kapoor (sculptor), Jatinder Verma (theatre director) and Shobana Jeyasingh (choreographer), offer a new controversial idea of what it means to be British and by extension, what constitutes British Art. The challenge and excitement of breaking down boundaries is captured in the work and in interviews with visual artists Supta Biswas, Chila Burman and Zarina Bhimji. Bhungra music, which mixes Vivaldi, House and Hip-hop, provides more evidence that some of the most innovative artistic work in Britain is being produced by artists who reflect the shifting pattern of British cultural identity.

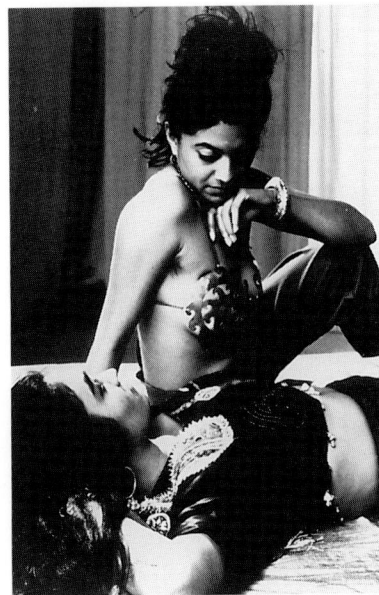

TOP:
SARI RED
BOTTOM
KHUSH

Born 1955, Nairobi, Kenya. One person shows include Museum of Modern Art, New York and the Walker Art Centre. *A Place of Rage:* Best Historical Documentary, National Black Programming Consortium 1992. Recipient of the Frameline Award for her contribution to lesbian and gay media 1993. *Sari Red* is in the collections of the Centre Pompidou, Paris and the Museum of Modern Art, New York. Writer and editor (see Bibliography.

141

Stephen **Partridge**

A s a young artist in the early 1970s, Stephen Partridge was amongst the first to take up video, a medium new to fine art, as a primary means of expression. The first available equipment was rudimentary compared to that used by video's glossy rival – television – but its comparative lack of attributes opened up the possibility for a new syntax and formal language to be developed. Partridge's work *Monitor* (1975) marks the start of his abiding fascination with the interplay and relationship between technique and visualisation.

At first, public galleries were quick to make space to show this dynamic and contemporary new medium, and Partridge was invited to exhibit nine installations between 1976 and 1979, mostly due to one or two far-sighted curators. He was one of the founding group of artists who set up London Video Arts (now LEA), seeing the potential of distributing single screen work to a wide audience.

The rapid development of electronics finally produced light weight equipment that was of an acceptable broadcast standard and facilities such as Quantel's Paintbox offered limitless potential for the creation of composite images. Partridge maintains that it is impossible to ignore the impact of television on the viewing public. Television is not simply a vehicle, a transparent

Biography

Born 1953, Leicester. Studied at Maidstone College of Art 1972–75 and the Royal College of Art 1975–76. Screenings include: Tate Gallery, London; Paris Biennale; The Kitchen, New York; ELAC, Lyons, France; Kijkhuis, Den Haag, Netherlands; Fukijoka Museum, Japan. A founder member of London Video Arts (now London Electronic Arts); director of Fields and Frames Productions Ltd, an art projects and television production company. Curator of Video Art 78, UK TV, National Review of Live Art 1988–90, 19:4:90 television interventions and touring video packages Made In Scotland I, II, III. Currently Head of the School of Television and Imaging, Duncan of Jordanstone College of Art, Dundee, Scotland. Work in the collections of the Museum of Modern Art, New York; FRAC Limousin, France

Key works

Dialogue For Two Players
1984, 18min, colour, video

Commissioned and broadcast by Channel Four, this work centres around the behavioural manipulation of two people placed in an environment in which they appear to have freedom to act as they will. This freedom, however, is an illusion; they may make only the limited moves prescribed by the rules of the game. Split screen techniques reveal the relationship between the participants and the structural manipulations which occur, both as part of the original recording and in the post production process.

Vide Voce (The Three's in the Four)
1986, 10min, colour, video, (with David Cunningham and Mary Phillips)

The idea for this work is founded in the experience of the Scottish landscape which is often threatening but always powerful. The threat to this seemingly unchangeable presence was tragically underlined by the Chernobyl disaster. Partridge invited David Cunningham, composer and music producer, together with Mary Phillips, singer and performer to collaborate with him on this project. The sound was created solely from the voice of Mary Phillips, where the acoustic perspective mirrors that of the landscape. The composition of the images parallels the sound structure weaving the parts together to complete the marriage.

Interrun

1989, 3 channel, 34 monitor videowall, colour, (sound by Lei Cox)

An abstract, quick-flowing work which explores the dynamics of the camera's 'window on the world'. A number of scenes containing movement are covered by the camera – using different camera movements (tracking shots, panning etc), a high shutter speed and a slow-motion machine – to develop the dynamics of the work. These scenes are then programmed into a videowall to create a complex play of flow and counterflow.

The Sounds of These Words

1990, 4min, colour, video

Visual and philosophical games are played with and on language in this tape, which was commissioned for the 19:4:90 television interventions on Channel Four. Text and spoken words are fragmented, the written word is contrasted with the spoken, and utterances are repeated at different speeds till they lose their meaning.

medium; therefore programme-makers' techniques should come under scrutiny – a rare occurrence in broadcasting. *Dialogue for Two Players* (1984) a seminal work – aligns content with method and makes visible and available information normally edited-out, demonstrating exactly how material can be transformed. Commissioned by Channel Four as part of a series of artists' works for television, it was broadcast as an autonomous piece within the regular programme schedule. Similar concerns were developed in *The Sounds of These Words* (1990), which, by contrast, intervened in the television schedule.

Partridge's commitment to this area of artistic practice extends to assisting other artists. He set up The Television Workshop at Duncan of Jordanstone College of Art which gives access to expensive and sophisticated equipment, runs summer schools and provides a forum where artists may come together with their counterparts from other countries. With his partner Jane Rigby and Fields and Frames, he continues to create opportunities for artists' work to be funded, screened and exhibited.

Anna Ridley

ABOVE:
**DIALOGUE FOR
TWO PLAYERS**

Jo
Pearson

I n Jo Pearson's work simple physical actions form the basis for heavily textured, rhythmic films. *Do What You Like* (1992) begins with a regular flash of orange accompanied by a crashing beat. The orange blur is gradually revealed as a ball which is being bounced by a woman. *Edge* (1992), which shows a woman shaving, and *Closed Circuit* (1992), which uses looped shots of a woman weight-training, follow a similar pattern. All three begin with images and sounds abstracted from live events which are subsequently revealed and resolved.

Much of Pearson's imagery is stroboscopic: the bouncing ball, brightly lit fingers moving through dark space and passing railings silhouetted against the sky, generate spontaneous flashes which disturb the vision. In *All in Your Head* (1991), such patterns pervade the footage in an autobiographical work about epilepsy. In two contrasting monologues, one by a doctor and one by the patient, various symptomatic disturbances of vision and changing sensations are recounted.

In *Extract* (1993), railings again appear, this time as one of a number of barriers accompanying a monologue about a disastrous relationship. Iron bars, wire grilles and netting are the physical barriers which are echoed in the grid pattern of a paved floor, the panelled roof of an abandoned factory and a receding row of street lamps. Pearson's approach is striking for the way in which content is meticulously integrated within a strong formalist aesthetic. She is alive to the ephemeral rhythms unwittingly generated by quotidian human activity. This activity gives rise to diverse optical phenomena which disrupt the vision, making us question its certainty.

Nicky Hamlyn

Biography

Born 1963, Rotherham, South Yorkshire. BA in Art History and Spanish, Leeds University 1985; studied Fine Art, Central St Martins 1988-91; Post Graduate Diploma in Electronic Imaging, Duncan of Jordanstone College of Art 1992. Screenings include: Sheffield Media Show; Cinevideo, Karlsruhe; Norwich Festival of Women Film-makers; Video Positive, Liverpool; London Film Festival; Edinburgh Film Festival; New Visions, Glasgow; British Short Film Fest-ival; New Contemporaries; AVE, Arnheim.

ABOVE:
EXTRACT

Key works

All in Your Head
1991, 6min, b&w, video

All in Your Head raises the profile of epilepsy in an exciting and imaginative way, and aims to challenge stereotyped ideas about this 'invisible' disability – which affects at least 1 in 200 of the population. Moving away from the traditional documentary format, it explores sensations, vulnerability and emotional dimensions by drawing on personal experience: the patient takes control of her own representation and looks at epilepsy from the inside out.

Extract
1993, 7min, b&w, 16mm

A series of arresting northern landscapes provides the sensual backdrop to a haunting soundtrack; the voice of a female narrator reads extracts from a letter to her former lover. Together, these elements tell a story of physical and emotional dislocation and a sifting through fragments for a sense of identity.

Pictorial **Heroes**

The Cover Up

1986, 10min, colour and b&w, video

The Cover Up takes the form of an improvised diatribe by a member of this country's 'underlying trend' – covering several years of Conservative Party rule. In addressing a number of subjects and events which occurred during the period, the tape adopts two different styles; an uncoordinated rant by a man wandering King Lear-like through a desolate factory site, and an interjecting sophisticated 'voice of reason', which is distanced by media processing and never fully revealed. The concern which underpins the work is for the suppressed rage of those left out of the mainstream image of prosperity that has been attributed to this country throughout the 1980s. What action can be taken when your potential, pride and community history is derided, devalued and destroyed?

Pictorial Heroes

Work, Rest and Play Episodes 1–5

1991–5, 90min, colour and b&w, video

Available as separate episodes of roughly 20 minutes each or as a feature length *Special Edition*, this work centres around the commentary of the adolescent Boy Driver, a child of the computer game generation, and his journey/rite-of-passage. Bizarre encounters (including characters from the films he sees – Michael Caine, Cliff Richard) surreal observations, evoke the technologised state of dreams, fear and loathing that exists in the late twentieth century.

The work of Doug Aubrey and Alan Robertson is primarily image and icon led, being characterised by extensive processing and manipulation of the image through use of sophisticated post-production techniques. Text is frequently employed, but as a visual tool rather than as a point of initiation or route through which to decipher meaning. Works such as *Sniper* (1987) and *Reflections on the Art of the State* (1988) present a deliberately frenzied proliferation of images, whereas *George Squared (1919–1990)* (1990) and their series *Work, Rest and Play* (1991–95) are visually more meditative. However, despite their mastery of very different visual styles, frequent use of hybridised cinematic conventions and shifting perspectives, a deliberate discourse on the socio-political nature of our society is present throughout the works.

The Cover Up (1986) for instance, takes on the anger of the culturally dispossessed while *George Squared (1919–1990)* examines context and place through the distorting lens of history. Both works address the politics of control and surveillance, the loss of political radicalism (submerged and subverted by consumerism), and the political disillusionment of their generation – the post 1950s babies for whom the promises of socialism, though ever present, have never been delivered. *Work, Rest and Play* continues this theme but from a different and perhaps more considered perspective. Using the narrative tradition of the road movie, it questions and re-evaluates the core values of society in the face of rampant individualism; caused by loss of identity in the remote-controlled armchair world of consumerism and ad-breaks, where the experience of second-hand dreams substitutes for reality.

Jane Rigby

Doug Aubrey: born 1959, Singapore. Alan Roberston: born 1961, Wellingborough. Collaborative work as Pictorial Heroes began 1985. Exhibitions of video installations include: Royal Scottish Academy; Third Eye Centre, Glasgow; Riverside Studios, London; Glynn Vivian Art Gallery and Museum, Swansea. Screenings include: MIMA, Melbourne; Video Positive, Liverpool; World Wide Video Festival, The Hague; Berlin Interfilm Festival; Edinburgh Fringe Film and Video Festival.

ABOVE:
THE COVER UP

Keith
Piper

I n Keith Piper's video installations there is a consistent pre-occupation with displacing and re-working the notion of the black body within Western culture and history. His work references a range of Western and black Diaspora histories, theories and discourses, through their cultural objects – such as icons, signs, codes and signifiers. What is important about Piper's work is how his complex ideas are expressed and formulated through the medium of video art. Video has enabled Piper to select a range of found objects, sounds and images, and by use of digital technology, to duplicate and manipulate them to produce innovative video art installations within the museum and gallery sectors.

Piper's early tape *The Nation's Finest* (1990) re-examines the black body, sport, heroism, nation and nationality. The black athlete is often valorised as powerful and heroic, yet the idea of winning for the nation and national belonging are always poised as a question. At the same time, within this web, the black athlete is equated with ideas of 'sheer animal' physicality. Piper uses these ideas to explore the ambivalent relationships that the dominant white culture has to the black subject, and the difficulties faced by black people trying to negotiate this society. The track and stadium become a series of metaphors to suggest an arena of spectatorship and voyeurism in which to view the black body. This space is like the cage of a controlled territory that keeps black people in their place as physical objects of desire. This is expressed textually in the piece through the constant repetition of the phrases, "enclosure", "holding pen" and "the natural order of things." The Union Jack, war monuments and footage of Linford Christie and Ben Johnson appear and are disrupted. Centred in the frame a black male and a black female are poised at the starting position of a track event. They rotate and dissolve into a mosaic of imagery and sounds which unravel the complex relationships of the British empire and modern colonialism.

Biography

Born 1960, Malta. BA in Fine Art, Trent Polytechnic, Nottingham 1983; MA in Environmental Media, Royal College of Art, London 1986. Exhibitions include: Kijkhuis, Den Haag; Merseyside Maritime Museum, Liverpool; Camden Arts Centre, London; Black Art Gallery, London; Hayward Gallery, London; Whitechapel Gallery, London; Reina Sofia, Madrid. Writer and essayist (see Bibliography. Artist in Residence, Banff Centre for the Arts, Canada.

Key works

The Nation's Finest
1990, 7min, colour, video

Through a collage of images, text and voice-over, this is an examination of some of the issues raised when black athletes are called on to 'represent' nations historically perceived as white in the international sporting arena. Produced initially for the Manchester Olympic Video Festival, the tape juxtaposes nationalistic heraldry and the heroic imagery found in public monumental sculpture, with the bodies of two young black athletes.

Surveillances/Tagging the Other
1991, installation, 4 monitors, 4 players

This multi-screen installation, produced for the exhibition 'PhotoVideo' at the Impressions Gallery, York, uses computer montage animations, together with sound and slide projection, to examine the issues of race, classification and surveillance within the borders of what has been described as 'Fortress Europe'.

Trade Winds
1992, installation, 12 monitors in crates, 4 players

In *Trade Winds*, Piper explores some of the multiple legacies of empire and maritime trade, with special reference to the English ports of Liverpool and Bristol. This install-ation, produced as part of the 'Trophies of Empire' exhibition, held at the Merseyside Maritime Museum, Liverpool and the Arnolfini in Bristol combines twelve monitors which are encased in wooden crates with four video sources.

In *Cargo Cultures* (1992) and *Trade Winds* (1992), Piper returns to the black body, the empire and colonialism with a powerful narrative of vision and sounds. In these multi-track installations he weaves together the histories of slavery, anthropology, criminology, civil rights, citizenship and surveillance to expose the West's exploitation and obsession with the black subject. Repetitive dissolving archival imagery reminds the spectator of distant and past cultures that have been colonised and made extinct. Fragmented images and sounds serve as starting points from which to jump cut through to a set of narrative sequences. We have entered Piper's world in which he reworks the historical [and cultural] baggage that we all carry around. He re-articulates this experience to produce environments that are seductive and confrontational, where fact and fiction, fantasy and reality, history and memory, fear and desire are blurred – in order to enable the viewer and spectator to re-think these historic and cultural references, thereby overturning the conventions that have supported these racist ideologies.

With British video art we are witnessing a movement in which artists are exploring the relationship of digital information to the late twentieth century's technologies of representation and reproduction, and their impact on the identities of both makers and consumers. Piper's work is centrally positioned within this movement, but is also shining proof that video is one of the leading art forms of the late twentieth century.

David A Bailey

RIGHT:
**SURVEILLANCES:
TAGGING THE OTHER**

147

Steven
Pippin

For ten years Steven Pippin has considered the conditions of photography, a project as playful as it is forensic. Beginning with two conventional genres, the nude and the seaside snapshot, he embarked on the project of converting his bath into a camera and taking it out of doors. Standing still and naked for twenty minutes by his bath, now a pin-hole camera loaded with photographic paper, then lying on Brighton beach, again without clothes, to be photographed by a folding version of his bathtub camera, seemed a surrealist proposition. Yet the apparent lightness of the idea was deceptive. For Pippin had begun a full-scale investigation of photography – epistemological rather than social, practical rather than theoretical, developing according to the changes in himself as much as the questions to be answered; questions which altered very little as time elapsed. At the outset, the camera was compared to – or superimposed on – other closed spaces. In the enamelled bath form, the shapes of font and womb united, while the addition of a wooden covering made it resemble a coffin. This mixture of clowning and tragedy involved in Pippin's solitary vigil derives from the solipsism of a process which results in no more than a ghost, an inverted shadow, an absent presence. Lonely and in traditional terms uncreative, the process of the generation of the image is reminiscent of the attitude of Beckett's heroes, even of the cynical dandyism of Duchamp's Bachelor Machines. Instead of analysing the product, Pippin's viewers are drawn in to the preparation; on the one hand a hushed, deliberate process, like an exorcist waiting for a ghost, on the other, a balmy, seaside escapade, all sunbathing and snapshots.

Memories of student digs or seaside boarding houses might have inspired Pippin's Wardrobe/Camera Obscura, a disturbing object with the combined characteristics of a pissotier, an upright coffin and a boat, his Lavatory Camera and his Washing Machine Camera. Pippin's works posit a state of affairs of which the objects are merely parts. Items like wardrobes, cupboards, and cameras mimic daily life itself, with its manic emphasis on small, separate rooms where others cannot bother us, an untruth and an unjustifiable one. Whether we examine the apparatus, the finished photographs, the documentation of the entire conception is the main critical problem in dealing with Pippin's work. All claim one's attention, as indeed do written accounts of the making.

Stuart Morgan *The Rigmarole of Photography*

Biography

Born 1960, Redhill. BA, Brighton Polytechnic 1985; MA, Chelsea School of Art, London 1987. Screenings include: London Film Festival; Leicester Film Festival. One Person Introspective: Institute of Contemporary Arts, London 1993. Exhibitions include: Museum of Modern Art, New York 1993; 'Work from the Recession', Victoria Miro Gallery, London 1994; 'Addendum', Portikus, Frankfurt 1994; 'Interior', Regen Projects, Los Angeles 1994.

Key works

Launderama
1989, 9min, silent, b&w, 16mm

A film of a commercial washing machine going through its normal wash cycle. The 16mm black and white film was then loaded into the washing machine and processed within the same machine, adding chemicals through the soap-powder draw. Produced using an Ipso 16 Commercial washing machine.

Laundromat Pictures
1991, 15min, colour, video

A commercial washing machine inside a public laundromat is converted into a pin-hole camera. Produced during a residency at Sculpture Space, Utica, New York.

The Continued Saga of an Amateur Photographer
1993, 22min, colour, video

A toilet on board a British Rail train travelling between London and Brighton is converted to take photographs.

FAR LEFT:
SAGA OF AN AMATEUR PHOTOGRAPHER

You Be Mother

1990, 8min, colour, 16mm

Using domestic objects, photo-montaged in a self-portrait, the film looks at a woman's struggle to free herself from an imposed role in society that feeds psychical reality. The traditional role of the woman as provider, giver and container of milk and child, like a vessel emptying itself. The film is an expression of the complexities involved in the process of breaking free from sexual and familial stereotypical role and behaviour patterns. Portraits function to produce fixity of identity. The superimposition endeavours to cut through such clichés. The relationship between the different objects on the table – such as the cup and saucer – contributes to their identities, which become inextricably tied together by association.

Milk and Glass

1993, 10min, colour, 16mm

The instability of the boundaries of identity is played out in the film in the projection of body parts onto inanimate objects. Julia Kristeva's theory of abjection discusses how bodily fluids threaten the boundaries of subjectivity. They are a reminder of our relationship to the inanimate, to mortality, to our dependence and connectedness to the inanimate world, (including food). The film attempts to deal with this subject/object conflict from both a feminine and lesbian experience.

The projection of images of the body (sensory orifices) onto inanimate (domestic) objects has so far formed the basis of my work in film. My work has stayed within the range of focus of the close up, the magnification of which evokes either the psychology or the claustrophobia of the domestic scene. In my existing films the main ingredient has been the image. In later work I will explore live action in combination with the 'still life'.

The very fact that the nature of the imagery I have worked with is 'super-real', in other words photo-montaged, in some ways links it with Surrealism. Also, there are thematic links such as the relationship between the animate and the inanimate, the fragmentation and projection of the self (woman's body), and the abject. As a woman, the subject/object relationship that underpins these areas of concern is of particular pertinence, because for a woman, her body represents both the self and 'Other' within patriarchy.

Sarah Pucill

Born 1961. BA in Creative Arts, Manchester Metropolitan University 1987; MA, Slade School of Art, London 1990; MPhil in Theory and Practice of Fine Art, University of East London 1993-. Currently Lecturer in Fine Art at Staffordshire University, Stoke-on-Trent. Photographic work exhibited at Camerawork, London; Cornerhouse, Manchester; The Bottom Drawer, a nationally touring show of women's photography. Photographic works in the Charles Saatchi collection. Screenings include: New Contemporaries 1990; Oberhausen International Short Film Festival 1991; European Media Art Festival, Osnabrück 1993; London Film Festival 1994; Women in Profile Film Festival, Glasgow.

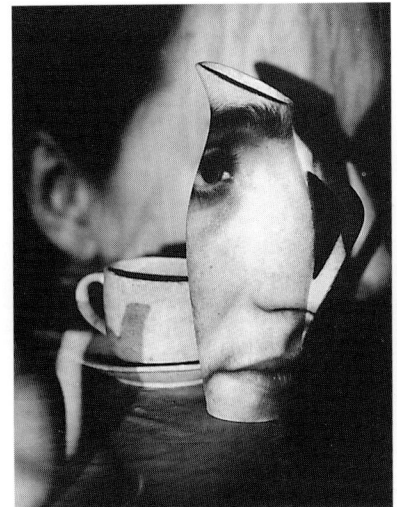

ABOVE:
YOU BE MOTHER

Sally **Potter**

eginning as an 8mm film-maker in the 1960s (she knew by the age of 14 she was going to be a film-maker: "I announced it to the world at school!"), Sally Potter explored a variety of experimental techniques, sometimes in collaboration with Mike Dunford.

The most accomplished of the early films is probably *Combines* (1972), a seven-part, multi-screen piece, made when Potter was a student of dance, as a collaboration with Richard Alston and the London Contemporary Dance Theatre. (Potter had already joined Alston's innovative dance company, Strider). Working with one, two and three images, with sound and silence, in colour and black and white, and with both the reality and the depiction of the performance space, Potter provided an introduction and a conclusion to the Dance Theatre's performance, and transitions between its six sections. In the years after finishing *Combines* and her dance training, Potter formed her own Limited Dance Company and later performed with several touring music bands, making no films of her own in this period.

Then came *Thriller* (1979), a substantial contribution to what Laura Mulvey would later call "scorched earth" feminist cinema: *Thriller* refuses virtually all the exploitative pleasures of commercial movies. Focusing on references to Puccini's *La Boheme* and Hitchcock's *Psycho*, Potter used a minimal budget and minimalist tactics to deconstruct the traditional sacrifice of women for the audience's pleasure in both high and pop art. The bare attic (of a squatted house) within which Colette Lafont and a small cast perform suggests both the moral bankruptcy of conventional film with regard to women and the thrill of starting from scratch to construct a new, progressive feminist cinema.

Potter's next project, the low-budget 35mm feature, *The Gold Diggers* (1983), was an attempt to fuse Marxist/feminist theory and film history. Using Julie Christie to represent cultural history's deification/exploitation of women, and Colette Lafont to represent those women (and aspects of women) traditionally marginalised, Potter attempts to engage viewers in a sustained meditation on the relationship between gold as the essence of economic power and female beauty

Biography

Born 1949, London. Trained at the London School of Contemporary Dance in the 1970s. Joined Strider as founder member and later formed the Limited Dance Company with Jacky Lansley. Choreography credits include *Aida*; *Who is Sylvia?*; *Hurricane*; *Combines*. Solo shows and collaborative theatrical performances include *Wheat* with Dennis Greenwood; *Mounting; Death and The Maiden*; Berlin, all with Rose English. A lyricist and singer since 1978, she has performed throughout Europe in Jazz and New Music Festivals. Her films have been shown at all major international film festivals and *Orlando* was released for commercial theatrical distribution in 1993.

Key works

Thriller
1979, 35min, b&w, 16mm

A critical and feminist re-working of Puccini's opera *La Bohème*, in which the tragic death of the heroine Mimi is investigated by the character called Mimi in the film. The mythologising of the role of the male artist as well as the victimised status of women in opera are unravelled in a number of retellings of the opera's narrative in a manner that parodies the conventions of film noir and exposes the social structures disguised by this art form.

The Gold Diggers
1983, 90min, b/w, 35mm

Colette, a black Frenchwoman working in the City of London as a computer operator at a bank, begins to investigate the significance of the figures she copies, and discovers gold to be the secret key to the circulation of money. Ruby, a beautiful blonde star is a cipher passed from man to man in a ballroom; Colette bursts in on horseback and rescues her. Through Colette's questioning, Ruby begins to understand her role as woman and as cinematic icon, pursuing her own memories and the history of movie heroines.

The London Story
1986, 15min, colour, 35mm

A 'Technicolor spy musical' in which a woman enlists the assistance of two civil servants to help Britain decide whether its political allegiance should lie with Europe or the United States.

Orlando

1992, 93min, colour, 35mm

Based on the novel by Virginia Woolf, (itself a spoof biography of Vita Sackville-West), *Orlando* is the story of a youth who starts off as a landed Elizabethan aristocrat, remains young over four centuries (but changes sex half way), winding up in the twentieth century, stripped of privilege and property but spiritually empowered.

as the essence of cinematic pleasure, especially as they have combined to propel the evolution of commercial film history – implicitly traced in Potter's allusions to Chaplin and Griffith, Busby Berkeley and George Cukor; and to the Western, the Musical, and film noir.

Despite Babette Mangote's stunning cinematography, *The Gold Diggers* was so critically controversial and economically unsuccessful, that it threatened to end Potter's career. She subsequently proved herself capable of engaging conventional audiences in a spoof of spy films *The London Story* (1986) and in two documentary projects for Channel Four: one, on women in Soviet cinema, *I am an Ox, I am a Horse, I am a Man, I am a Woman,* (1988), the other, a four-part series on emotions, *Tears, Laughter, Fears and Rage* (1986).

In retrospect, the considerable shifts in Potter's film-making career, including her 'sudden' re-emergence in 1992 as director of *Orlando* – a big-budget adaptation of a noteworthy novel – seem nicely psychodramatised by Orlando's sudden jumps through time and change of gender. During the late 1980s and early 1990s, Potter laboured (often in collaboration with Tilda Swinton) on a script for Woolf's novel, foregrounding its cinematic qualities and giving brilliant new energy to an under-evolved film technique for establishing connection between protagonist and audience: the on-screen character's look at the camera. By echoing our exchange of glances with loved ones, and with ourselves in mirrors, Orlando's looks 'at us' create and sustain an intimacy that suggests that we, and cinema, have the imaginative power to transcend biology and transform history.

Scott MacDonald

Simon
Pummell

Key works

Simon Pummell cites Cronenberg, Roeg and Hitchcock as his major cinematic influences, directors whose work is characterised by distinctive and recurrent themes and motifs. His own films are marked by an insistent return to particular images and related ideas; the skeletal shadows of *Secret Joy of Falling Angels* (1991) recur as self-quotation in *The Temptation of Sainthood* (1993); his curiously grotesque, misshapen drawn images appear in *Surface Tension* (1986) and *Secret Joy of Falling Angels*, and all his works abound in the language of intrigue and mystery.

Other more intellectual concerns are expressed through narrative as well as image, although Pummell's narrative, in structuralist fashion, often presents the movement through time as a series of interconnecting ideas rather than as a straightforward linear causal path of events. In this way the link, for example, between childhood and adulthood can be more analytically explored. In *The Temptation of Sainthood* Pummell unravels this theme discursively within a directly Freudian context, reconstructing and enacting the life of the paranoid and deluded Schreber, the transvestite Judge who believed himself to be in direct sexual communication with God. This device allows him to follow several personal strands: the complexities of sexual orientation, bondage and other types of sexual fetish, the inadequacies of orthodox psychoanalytic explanation and his own ambiguous notion of God. His interest in narrative culminates in the live action featurette *Rose Red* (1994), co-written with science-fiction novelist Simon Ings, in which the recurring themes of fetish, addiction and otherness are pulled together in a futuristic detective story. *The Temptation of Sainthood* is the turning point in Pummell's career after which the storyline becomes the axis around which the themes revolve, eclipsing the personal, multi-layered approach of his earlier work.

Stylistically, then, Pummell's work pulls in two directions – animation/ experiment on the one hand, live action/narrative on the other. Fans of the award-winning *Surface Tension* will have welcomed *Secret Joy of Falling Angels* as a development of early ideas but may have been astonished at the departure into live action and narrative in *The Temptation of Sainthood*. In *Rose Red* Pummell moves away from animation to test out complex cinematic ideas about narrative structure, using art directed sets, props and costumes in various land/cityscapes,

Biography

Surface Tension
1986, 26min, b&w, 16mm

Intercutting live action footage with animation, *Surface Tension* depicts the possible memories, repression and fears of the leading character. The animated sections consist of a series of monologues and obsessive gestures by a male figure drawn to highlight the tensions between rigid and fluid body structures, skeleton and flesh. The monologues are by turns vulgar, hysterical and lyrical.

Secret Joy of Falling Angels
1991, 12min, colour, 35mm

The film is inspired by 15th century depictions of The Annunciation, viewed through the prism of the visual grammar of early cartoons and drawing traditions from abstract expressionism to academic figure drawing. It depicts a confrontation full of ambiguous shadings (of attraction and mutual fear) between a woman and a winged figure.

The Temptation of Sainthood
1993, 14min, colour, video

Combining drama sequences and morphing, shadow animation, Harry composites and pixillation; the tape tells the story of Daniel Paul Schreber, one of Freud's most famous cases, who believed he had a direct relationship with God. His story – of a man who was misunderstood by the medical world in a way that mirrored his mistreatment as a child – ends in madness and despair.

Rose Red
1994, 19min, colour, 35mm

Combining the grotesque body imagery of Pummell's earlier, more abstract films with a fast paced narrative, the film is a science fiction thriller set in the very near future and investigates a Security Cop's violent and recurring sexual dream.

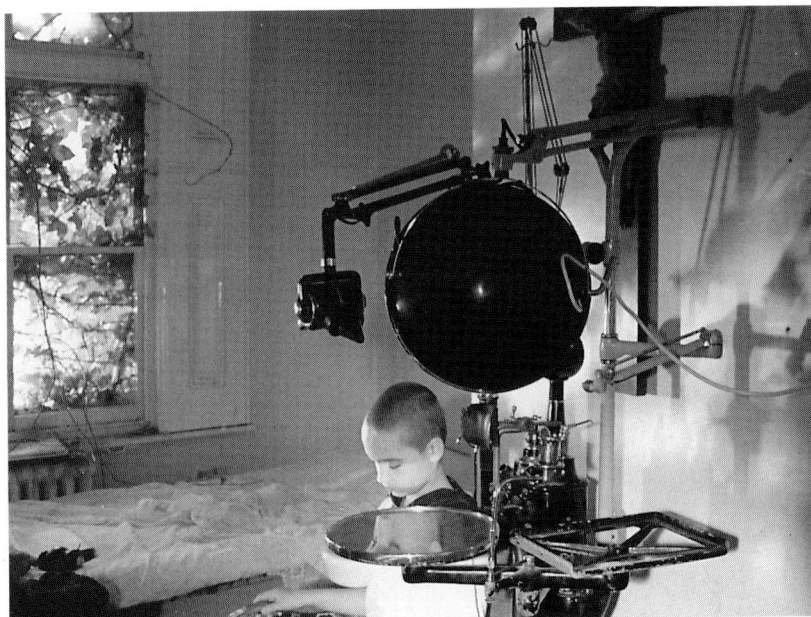

Born 1959. BA in English Language and Literature, Mansfield College, Oxford 1980; MA in Film, Television and Animation, Royal College of Art, London 1986. *Surface Tension*: Mari Kuttna Award for Most Original New Animated Film, London Film Festival 1986; *Secret Joy of Falling Angels*: Grand Prize, Oberhausen 1992; Best Experimental Film, Stuggart Film Festival 1992; *Temptation of Sainthood*: Main Prize, International Jury, Oberhausen Short Film Festival 1993; Fantasporto Best Short; Special Prize, Berlin Videonale; ICA Biennial: 'What You See is What You Get'. Has worked as a Digital Paintbox artist and designer and as line producer on over 40 commercials. Visiting Lecturer: Royal College of Art, National Film and Television School. Created film backdrops for English National Opera's production of Judith Weir's *Blond Eckbert* 1994.

the traditional stuff of feature film making. In his more obviously experimental work in animation he exploits the small screen medium, for which *Secret Joy of Falling Angels* and *Stain* (1992) were specifically commissioned, by keeping close to the images and using semi-abstract forms to explore intellectual themes. Pummell's output to date bears the characteristic mark of the Koninck studios which have nurtured the Quay Brothers, Jan Švankmajer and other directors whose work cannot be narrowly defined and categorised.

Pummell is currently working on two projects around which his various interests coincide and through which his dichotomous stylistic approach is reconfirmed: in the first place, a short animation for Channel Four, *Butcher's Hook* (1995), described as an experimental horror film and, by contrast, with writer Simon Ings, a live action science fiction feature film.

Jill McGreal

Brothers
Quay

I f animation is a ghetto, as the Brothers Quay have called it, then the Brothers Quay, with their methods and aesthetic, have wilfully created a ghetto within a ghetto – or rather, on the margins of one. They have turned their back on one of modern animation's dominant aims – the desire to evolve an expressive, gestural language usually considered alien to live action – and instead developed a rigorous style that, perversely, privileges the lifelessness of animation.

To bring their puppets to life, the Brothers work painstakingly through frame after frame of static postures, building them up into the semblance of motion – the paradox that underlies all cinema, but which live action tends to conceal. Paul Hammond has called their technique "nudged *nature morte*", and the ambivalence of *nature morte* and still life is always foremost in their work. The Quays do not so much animate dead matter as dramatise the deadness of matter. The figures in their films – dolls, predatory clowns, battered toys that have uncannily outlived their purpose as fetishes of affections – are things that have died and been recomposed, re-animated like miniature mummies. They are ghosts, inhabiting the phantom landscapes – cities, theatres, forests – that the Quays build in *trompe l'oeil* boxes (their constructions often suggest Joseph Cornell pieces taken to the highest elaboration).

Working in the literary wake of E T A Hoffmann, these most militantly anti-anthropomorphic of animators manipulate the preciosity conventionally identified with dolls. We might attribute human feelings – most commonly, fears and hungers – to the Quays' creatures (notably the hunted protagonist of *Street of Crocodiles* (1986), but we can never ignore their absolute difference from human and animal laws of motion, the way that they constantly assert the autonomy of the material from which they are made, and into which they constantly threaten to decompose.

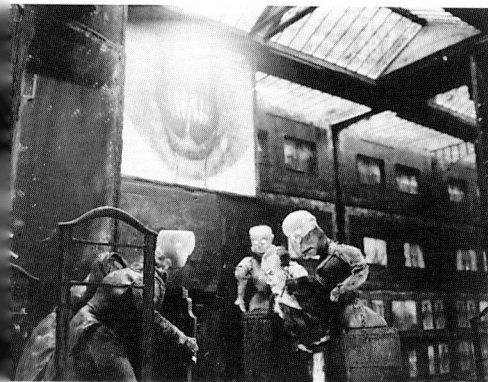

ABOVE:
THE STREET OF CROCODILES

Biography

Born Pennsylvania 1947. Studied at the Philadelphia College of Art and Royal College of Art, London. In 1980 they formed the production company Koninck, with Keith Griffiths. *Street of Crocodiles*: Fairytale Prize at Odense, Denmark, Science Fiction Prize Sitges, Spain 1986, 3 Prizes at Zagreb 1986. *Stille Nacht*: ICA Biennial: 'Between Imagination and Reality'; *Stille Nacht II*: ICA Biennial: 'Arrows of Desire', Best Music Video Utrecht 1992. *Stille Nacht IV*: prizewinner at Leipzig 1993. Their work was the subject of an exhibition at the Animation Festival, Bristol 1987. As well as music documentaries, music videos and television idents, they have designed for opera and theatre, including Richard Jones' productions of *Le Bourgeois Gentilhomme*, *A Flea in Her Ear*, *A Love for Three Oranges* and *Mazeppa*.

Key works

Street of Crocodiles
1986, 21min, colour, 35mm

A somewhat decrepit caretaker enters an equally decrepit museum and (by accident or design) lets a gobbet of his saliva fall into a Kinetoscope machine. Inside the machine, mechanisms begin to turn over, wires run around pulleys, and flaps and hatches open. The puppet figure of a man is conjured into motion. The man severs the wires from which he hangs and begins an exploration of the 'Street of Crocodiles', a suite of near derelict rooms in which screws turn of their own volition at his approach. He observes robotic figures in a strange workshop, is harassed by a mischievous boy (who may be his own younger self), and eventually finds himself dissected, remodelled and reclothed in the inner recesses of a dubious tailoring establishment.

Tony Rayns, *Monthly Film Bulletin*

Rehearsals for Extinct Anatomies
1987, 14min, b&w, 35mm

These stories for the eye have recently been refined to an extreme. *Rehearsals for Extinct Anatomies* is built entirely around avatars of the line – the lines that compose a Fragonard engraving; a computer bar code that drifts in and out of focus; the strings that cross the screen, twanging imperceptibly; even the strings on the soundtrack; above all the lines of sight.

Jonathan Romney *Sight and Sound*

Spinning parables of entrapment using puppet protagonists (mute shabby men with withered heads and suits of shabby cloth) and recalcitrant objects (whirling household screws, dancing sewing pins, tiny machine parts), the Quays concoct a tiny, miniaturised, locomotive universe full of inexplicable flickerings and disproportionate shadows.

Village Voice

Stille Nacht I

1988 1min, b&w, 35mm
Commissioned by MTV for one of their 'Art Breaks' – *Stille Nacht* was inspired by a typically arcane Quay source; the strange 'micrograms' of writer Robert Walser. 'Micrograms' being the tiny, folded pieces of paper on which Walser wrote complete stories in microscopically small words. The short format suits the Quays well, offering an obsessive 'fragment' of dream-like intensity which leaves the spectator's mind reverberating. [...] In a space of uncertain scale and location, a rectangular object quivers, iron-filings dance and drift like dust, whist a mildly astonished doll looks on as the minutiae of the world come alive.

Simon Field, *Between Imagination & Reality*

Stille Nacht II (Are We Still Married)

1991, 3min, b&w, 35mm
This dark claustrophobic film shot in shadowy black and white involves an Alice-in-Wonderland-like figure and a rabbit together with a rather horrific creature just glimpsed scraping on a window. Feet flutter in fast-motion, a white ball with a life of its own chases around the room and the little girl seems to grow taller, much to the amusement of the rabbit. The Quay's talent for hinting at darker and often strangely erotic things is at the forefront of this disturbing yet witty film, set to a casually delivered off-key lament. And in the final ambivalent shot, we are given our only glimpse of the girl's face in tight close-up – the face of a siren whose eyes sexually beckon from behind a black wall.

Michael O'Pray *Arrows of Desire*

Their short film *The Comb* (1990) is unusual in that the presence of a human sleeper makes explicit the dream-like nature of their rudimentary narratives, complete with the ambivalently erotic meanings that attach to objects (it is as if the object themselves were cruelly mocking human sexuality). In this sense, the Quays are among the few film-makers whose work genuinely merits the description 'surreal' – it draws on discarded, unlabelled bric-a-brac just as dream reworks and recontextualises scraps from waking life. The Brothers are also unique in their consistent reference to an oneiric tradition in writing (Kafka, Bruno Schulz, Robert Walser) and visual art (Arcimboldo, Max Ernst). They are often regarded simply as acolytes of a card-carrying Surrealist, the Czech animator to whom they paid tribute in *The Cabinet of Jan Švankmajer* (1984). But where Švankmajer's central trope is metamorphosis, the plasticity of objects, the Quays foreground the immutability of things. For them, objects can only be transformed through violent amputation – as in the meticulous brutal-ities of *This Un-nameable Little Broom* (1985) and *The Street of Crocodiles*. Instead, fluidity in their work has increasingly been located in perception itself – in the mechanics of the lens, and in types of motion that belie the solid nature of stop-motion animation. This is seen notably in the extraordinary flickering ball that is the key motif of *Stille Nacht II* (1991), a promo for the US band His Name Is Alive. The eye's attempt to locate and identify objects, to make the world briefly stable, becomes a narrative theme in itself.

If the increasingly hermetic world of the Quay's films suggests something of an impasse, a new departure is promised by their first live-action feature, *Institute Benjamenta* (1995) (based on a Robert Walser novel). However, the Quay's stated intention to instil their human players with "the power of the puppet" suggests that they may after all be not departing from, but further stretching the boundaries of their own familiar territory.

Jonathan Romney

William
Raban

Over the past twenty years William Raban's films have been marked by a fascination with landscape and seascape, often using formal devices to achieve ends that are firmly within the English Romantic tradition. At the same time, he has explored film as process in a way that has never eschewed a beauty of imagery. Raban's career spans an early commitment to a rigorous structural film aesthetic, a Romanticist landscape minimalism, a modernist-symbolist narrative and recently a radical documentary poetics. As a leading figure in experimental film-making in the early 1970s, Raban was associated with the formalist explorations taking place around the London Film-makers' Co-op. He was a leading proponent, notably with Chris Welsby, of the landscape film tendency, using the 'material' qualities of film stock to achieve colourist ambitions – as in *Colours of This Time* (1972), or time-lapse for painterly ends – as in *Moonshine* (1975). The structures and the material properties of film were coupled with arbitrary determinants, often of weather and natural light. These early works have a melancholia and austere beauty meshed with a process-art aesthetic.

River Yar (1972) is a classic of English avant-garde landscape in its merging of process and Romanticist imagery. A tidal estuary filmed in time-lapse over three weeks in Autumn and Spring is shown on two adjacent screens, each having a soundtrack that was recorded on a sampling basis. Colour 'temperature' and its interaction with colour film was explored in the beautiful *Colours of This Time*. Further, more rigorous experimentation followed with *Angles of Incidence* (1973) emphasising framing through camera position. A whole series of landscape films were made in the early 1970s continuing into the multi-screen expanded films of the late 1970s, including *Moonshine* and *Thames Barrier* (1977).

Raban's broader and more explicit later concerns were already apparent in *Time Stepping* (1974), *After Eight* (1975) and *Autumn Scenes* (1979) in which he

Biography

Born 1948, Fakenham. BA in Painting, Saint Martin's School of Art, London 1971; MFA in Painting, University of Reading 1974. Lecturer in film at St Martin's School of Art 1976–89, and Course Director of MA in Independent Film and Video. Published bi-monthly *Filmmakers Europe* (1977–1981). Represented in Documenta 6, Kassel and Arte Inglesi Oggi, Milan 1976. Screenings include: Tate Gallery London; National Film Theatre, London; Centre for Contemporary Art, Warsaw. Retrospectives: Museum of Modern Art, New York; Multimedia Centar, Zagreb; Anaemic Cinema Festival, Madrid. Television transmissions include: *Thames Film*, Channel Four 1987 and 1990; *From 60 Degrees North*, Channel Four 1992; *Sundial*, BBC2's The Late Show 1992 and Channel Four's Midnight Underground series 1993.

Key works

Angles of Incidence
1973, 10min, 2 screen, colour, 16mm

The film frame is modified by filming the view through a basement window. The window shape and the street outside is animated as the camera moves to viewpoints on an arc that is described within the interior space. Movements on the opposite side of the arc are complemented by balancing points on the opposite sector so that the window becomes both transparent and a reflective plane. The mirror quality is enhanced by the 2 screen format and plays on Newton's First Law of Mirrors: angles of incidence = angles of reflection.

Black and Silver
1981, 75min, colour and b&w, 16mm (with Marilyn Halford)

Based on Oscar Wilde's story of a dwarf's infatuation with the Infanta of Spain, inspired by his seeing Velazquez's painting of the Spanish court, *Las Meninas*, the film is in two parts, both enacted in mime and dance, accompanied by music, sound effects and voice-over, including snatches from Wilde's text. The first part deals with the meeting of the dwarf and Infanta (both played by Marilyn Halford) on a beach and an encounter with the cameraman (William Raban), further exploring the theme of mirrors and reflections. After the rejection and death of the dwarf, symbolic actions are staged involving dancers, musicians, the Infanta and the cameraman, in a dance-space reminiscent of Velazquez's painting.

Thames Film

1986, 66min, colour, 16mm

By filming from the freeboard of a small boat, the film attempts to capture the point of view of the river itself, tracing the 50 mile journey from the heart of London to the open sea. This contemporary view is set in an historical context through use of archive images and the words of the travel writer Thomas Pennant, who followed exactly the same route in 1787.

A 13

1994, 12min, colour, 16mm

Winter twilight on the A 13 and the dawn traffic moves slowly into London. An illuminated roadside display flashes the latest FTSE index to the residents of the high rise council flats in Glenkerry Towers. Through the plate glass walls of the *Financial Times* building, giant rolls of pink newsprint are lying amongst the printing machines. Ahead, the dark superstructure of the Canary Wharf complex looms over the western horizon. It is blacked out, save for the pulsing strobe of the air navigation lights, making it look like a ship adrift in the ocean.

incorporated urban scenes and contemporary elements like radio soundtrack (a news item on an IRA bombing in *After Eight*) and graffiti-covered walls and urban dereliction. In these films the potential 'drama' of the content (never realised but always latent) deflects the spectator's attention from what are tight formal structures. These are fascinating precursors of the recent political-poetics of his recent documents of London past and present.

Black and Silver (1981) made with Marilyn Halford, is an innovative, experimental narrative based on Oscar Wilde's tale *The Birthday of the Infanta*, in which Halford played the princess depicted in Velazquez's painting *Las Meninas*. Beautifully shot, using costume, dance and seascape, it incorporates a meditation on the nature of representation through a deconstruction of the original painting, with the camera replacing the painter's canvas.

The ambitious *From 60 Degrees North* (1991) made with Begonia Tamarit, turns to a form of 'documentary' to explore historical reconstruction of physical and geographic spaces through landscape and seascape filming, engaging with historical recovery and the haunting presence of the past. In *Thames Film* (1986), an analytical reverie on London's river, Raban initiates a socio-political critique of policies leading to the social neglect of the city. He develops this further in *A 13* (1994), with its comparisons between the post-industrial wasteland of the East End and the capitalist arrogance and aggression of the Canary Wharf tower. The latter is also the subject of the witty *Sundial* (1992) which with great economy reflects both the beauty and oppressive nature of the tower.

Michael O'Pray

Anne
Rees-Mogg

Anne Rees-Mogg's *Real Time* (1974) was a turning point in my life. To me, it was a perfect poem like no other. It did what paintings could never do. It used words.

Through a series of black and white photographs, re-filmed to a set number of frames, the process of Anne growing older is captured on celluloid. Her account of being close to death and "preparing to live or die with equal equanimity" remains one of the most poignant personal communications in film. "This connected shining perfect continuing consciousness, like a small bright bead of almost nothing, and to me this became a thing, and as a thing it existed and could not be destroyed." The language is simple, on occasions faltering and beautiful; as one of four 100 ft rolls of film records the motorway drive West and homewards. "I love that clock" is intercut with the drone of traffic sound. Bright red poppies tremble on the verge, as the reel is changed. Anne drives the length of film time in her Ford Cortina. "Film is a succession of still photographs." Film is a thing. Film is a 100 ft. roll of daylight reversal, with flare outs and clapperboards consciously included. The mistakes, "oh, shit!", or "have you got a watch?", are set on an equal footing with a reading of T S Eliot.

Anne's films are about time, memory, personal relationships and the discovery of film-making. Where others took up Super8 in the late 1970s (Jarman's Home Movies, et al), Anne preceded them using 16mm, collecting, capturing and tirelessly documenting the people, objects and spaces, that are one's life. With the use of crackly old thirties music, ivory letters, the inflatable Coca Cola bottle, the vast collection of enamel signs and mementoes, academy leaders and old Kodak spools, the round mirror-topped table heaped with cut-glass decanter tops – every room of Anne's house was like a living Joseph Cornell box. The collecting phenomena was the key to her films.

Anne was pioneer and great aunt of an alternative film practice to the dominant formalism of 1970s structuralist film; a camp and renegade eccentric, who gave over half her life to encouraging others to take up the camera, (for which we are truly thankful).

Anna Thew

She Draws her films out of her life, using friends and family almost as in a diary – *Sentimental Journey* (1977) or a memoir – *Real Time*, bringing to mind recent feminist re-evaluation of such 'home-movie'-like material. But the material drawn on is transformed and worked through, providing the films with their formal interest, and giving Rees-Mogg's concern with time a cinematic as well as personal dimension.

Laura Mulvey

Real Time
1974, 32min, colour and b&w, 16mm

A personalised 'narrative documentary' based on a visit to the film-maker's childhood home with conversations with her mother and incidents from their past re-enacted by the film-maker's niece. The first part of a trilogy containing *Sentimental Journey* and *Living Memory*.

Sentimental Journey
1977, 30min, colour and b&w, 16mm

The first part of the film is in colour and consists of an argument about how to make films and what films to make. The film then changes to black and white and the argument continues about houses and planning, with shots of the destruction of a house, and shots from other films of the house as it used to be. The arguments are not conclusive and the film is about doubts rather then certainties.

AR-M

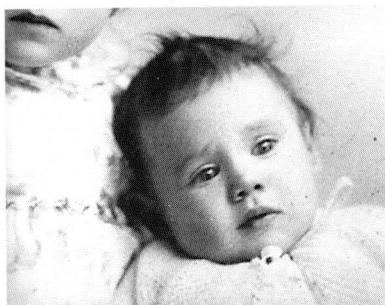

Biography

Grandfather's Footsteps

1983, 33min, b&w, 16mm

In *Grandfather's Footsteps* the film-maker re-evokes the presence of her great-grandfather, Henry Stiles Savory, a Victorian clergyman, photographer and scientist. It's not a costume drama; bringing in his writings, and his personal effects – books, machines, photographs – Anne Rees-Mogg emphasises her own links with him and his preoccupations. She achieves a real sense of timelessness.

Jo Comino

Born 1922, died 1984. Educated Bristol Art School; Central School of Arts and Crafts. Taught at Regent Street Polytechnic from 1951, Chelsea School of Art 1964-1984. Chairperson and a Director of London Film-makers' Co-op 1981–4. Retrospectives included screenings at the London Film-makers' Co-op; National Film Theatre, London; Avignon and Edinburgh Film Festivals 1978. Film London 1979. Complete retrospective London Film-makers' Co-op 1985.

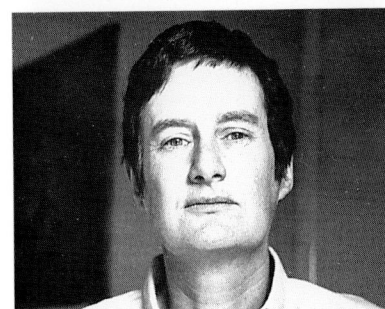

Daniel
Reeves

Working in both single tape video and installation art, Daniel Reeves has produced a wide range of work in both the UK and his homeland USA. Widely praised for bringing a sense of the mystical and poetic to video art, Reeves experiences as a marine in Vietnam and his interest in metaphysics has informed his tape making throughout a varied career.

Although he had made both tapes and music prior to 1981, it was *Smothering Dreams*, of that year, that brought him to the attention of the video community. With its themes of man's inhumanity and its images of toy soldiers and children's wargames, *Smothering Dreams* set the tone for his key work, *Ganapti/ A Spirit in the Bush* (1986). A mournful and moving testament to animal suffering, *Ganapti* used slow-motion techniques, archive footage and text in an impassioned and provocative exploration of man's reductionist thinking.

Continuing the artist's development of a style that matched technique to content, Reeves' experimental video poem *Sombra A Sombra* (1988) takes the viewer into a sunbleached landscape of ghosts, memory and visual poetry set to the words of Peruvian poet Cesar Vallejo. With careful use of slow-motion and image mixing techniques, Reeves' expert camerawork and the slow pace of his sweeping images brought a visionary quality to video art that bore comparison with America's figure-head tapemaker, Bill Viola.

In his most recent tape, *Obsessive Becoming* (1995), Reeves delves into his own troubled family history. Typically, this piece uses interview footage and a restrained and elegant use of state-of-the-art image processing to create an intimate and visually rich experience.

Alongside these pieces, Reeves' installation work includes *The Well of Patience* (1988), shown in both Glasgow and San Francisco in 1990. Described by one commentator as "like being at the still point of the turning world", this complex piece highlighted the layered meaning of Reeves' art.

Key works

Ganapati/A Spirit In The Bush
1986, 45min, colour, video

A song of mourning, praise and compassion for the sentient creatures with whom we share this planet. Focusing on the myth, history and natural life of the elephant and its relationship to man, the tape explores the gulf we have created between ourselves and animals by the devaluation and calculated exploitation of other forms of life.

Sombra A Sombra
1988, 17min, colour, video

Immersed in the evocative poetry of the Peruvian poet, Cesar Vallejo, the tape weaves images of scorched territory of empty houses, religious icons, flowing water and beautiful landscapes with musings on memory and death.

The Sleepers
1993, installation, 3 monitors and players, 7 architectural fragments, 3 crystal spheres

A video sculpture suggested by a poem of Walt Whitman's with the same title. Sculpted from ancient sandstone, features from a burned down house and crystal globes of moving imagery, a balance is created between the sleeping mineral world and the world of time, endless becoming and eternal activity.

Obsessive Becoming
1995, 60min, colour, video

A free-form and surreal autobiography concerned with childhood and adult rituals and the search for meaning and connection based on the often wildly absurd events of Reeves' family life. Exploring memory and the inner landscape of image as poetic form, the film looks into the roots of dysfunction, suffering and abuse in Reeves' family and the possibilities of healing as an adult.

Biography

Born 1948, USA. Enrolled in the Marines in 1965, was wounded in action in Vietnam in 1968, and subsequently worked for the anti-war movement. BS in Cinema Studies, AS Anthropology at Ithaca College New York 1976. Artist in Residence WNET TV Lab 1980; Guggenheim Fellow Video Art 1983. *Sombra A Sombra* was commissioned by WNET and Channel Four and won First Prize Video Biennial, Medelin Columbia, Golden Gate Award San Francisco Film Festival. *Ganapati*: Golden Gate Award; Grand Prize, Yugoslav Biennial; *Amida*: First Prize, Video Culture, Canada; *Smothering Dreams*: First Prize, Video Art, USA Film and Video Festival; winner of 3 Emmy awards. Works in the permanent collections of Musuem of Contemporary Art, California; Museum of Modern Art, New York; ICA, Boston.

Now resident in Scotland, Reeves might be tagged as something akin to a video philosopher, such is the depth of his highly personal tapes. In an area dominated by urban imagery – cities, alienation, information overload – Reeves has introduced a slower, deeper mood to video art. Although connections and influences are difficult to prove, Reeves might be seen as part of a renaissance in video installation and tape making, an integral component in a late 1980s/early 1990s move toward a moving image form that is often open ended and almost spiritual. Similarly, the lyrical, almost trance like sensibility at work in Reeves' best work now seems echoed in the work of other video artists.

Nik Houghton

Lis
Rhodes

"**S**he refused to be framed" *Light Reading*

The enduring importance of Lis Rhodes as artist and film-maker is attributable to her quiet and powerful radicalism. Rhodes' work juxtaposes an artistically and theoretically rigorous practice with passionate commitment. She has developed a mode of film-making inspired but not enslaved by feminism, which has sustained and grown regardless of fashionable trends in art and representation.

Grounded in the making of abstract experimental film, Rhodes in her classic films *Light Reading* (1978) and *Pictures on Pink Paper* (1982) was uniquely positioned not just to flout the conventions of mainstream cinema but also to challenge the predominantly male voice of the 'muscular' avant-garde. Amy Taubin in 1978 commented on how Rhodes' images were "mysterious, dangerous and highly personal, all qualities...absent from the very rational work of the English avant-garde in recent years."

Rhodes has always refuted the 'lone voice' of the isolated woman artist by publicly supporting and celebrating other women film-makers from the past, present and future. The work that she – and other women associated with the distributor Circles (now Cinenova) – devoted to excavating the work of women film-makers, transformed the landscape of film history. Rhodes has collaborated with other women artists, such as Jo Davis, Lindsay Cooper and Rose English, while retaining her singular voice. She is a pivotal figure in a history stretching from Dulac and Guy through Deren, and the feminist film-makers of the seventies to the generation of women who appear in these pages: although it is not really appropriate to be too linear; Rhodes herself said, "I prefer a crumpled heap, history at my feet, not stretched above my head."

Biography

Studied at the Royal College of Art, London. Cinema Curator, London Film-makers' Co-op 1975–76; Founder member of Circles Women's Film & Video Distribution 1979, member of Four Corners Film Workshop, Arts Adviser to the Greater London Council 1982–85. Part-time lecturer, Slade School of Art, London since 1978. Screenings include Anthology Film Archives, New York; Hayward Gallery, London; Tate Gallery, London; Cinémathèque Française, Paris; Pacific Cinematheque, Vancouver; Musée d'Art Moderne, Paris; Massachusetts Institute of Technology. *Pictures on Pink Paper* and *Hang on a Minute* were broadcast by Channel Four.

Key works

Light Reading
1978, 20min, b&w, 16mm

A voice speaks in the third person. A photograph of a seemingly bloodstained bed provides the film's central image into which the camera vertiginously and repeatedly zooms. Fragments of words, letters and text are perplexingly intercut into this image providing a strange lexicon of signs and language...The energy and violence of the film's techniques, rapid-editing and zoom, are set against the monotonous voice-over. Fragments of a narrative, of incidents outside the viewer's knowledge and vision are hinted at so that we are finally unsure about this dream which seems to be constantly tilting over into a nightmare. Are we witnessing the bloody scene of a murder? Is it a delusion of the part of the narrator, or on our part, a deception of the chiaroscuro? The enigmatic quality of *Light Reading* and its refusal to embrace a facile cinematic vocabulary of narrative or voice, makes its essential radicalism all the more insistent.

Michael O'Pray

Pictures On Pink Paper
1982, 35min, colour, 16mm

A closely-textured work in which pictures and meanings are experimented with, brought together or pared down to abstraction in order to challenge and re-create. Rhodes shows us how the apparent inevitability of 'the natural' and immutability of 'the normal are held neatly in place by those to whom such an order is an advantage. *Pictures on Pink Paper* is – women talking, thinking aloud and questioning this order.

Hang On A Minute

1985, 13 x 1min, colour, 16mm

Thirteen short films which grew out of a series of short poems written by Lis Rhodes, reflecting on the traditional patterns of oppression in women's lives (pornography, violence, nuclear weapons) and the many forms that resistance takes.

A Cold Draft

1988, 28min, colour, 16mm

A Cold Draft shows the surveillance of a woman by overseers who have judged her to be mad. What is most provocative about this film is that it proposes multiple credible points of view even as the woman is being certified insane by the 'Censors.' We voyage into the skull of a woman and peer out to a monumentally static cold waste with planetary slow motion. It is a bunker-eye view.

Sandra Lahire

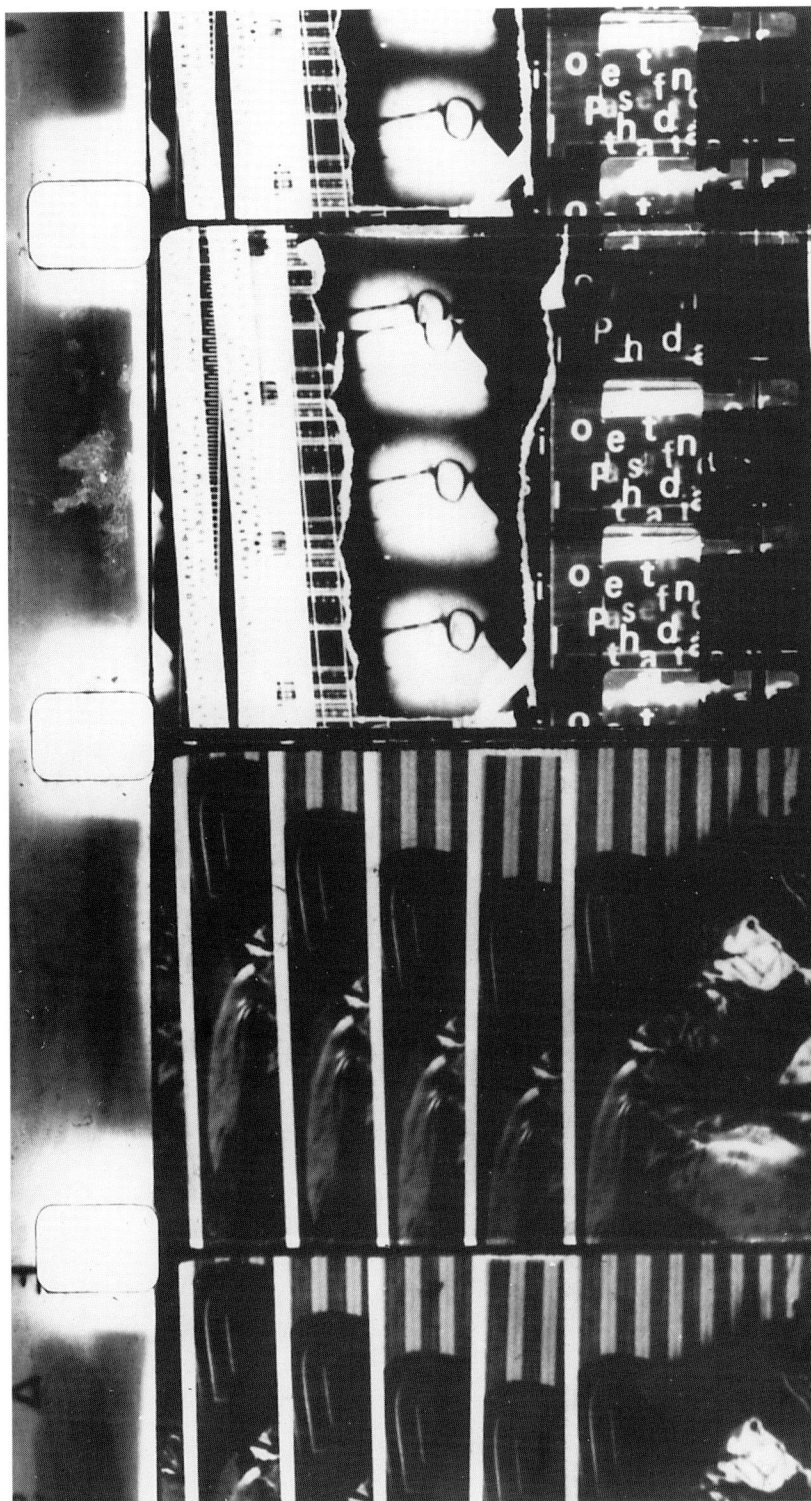

The work Rhodes has produced has consistently rejected political posturing in favour of a belief in the interdependence of politics and form. This has remained the bedrock of her work when other women artists have turned away from formal experimentation or rejected the perceived embarrassment of the label 'feminist'. Language has been and remains a primary concern, from the inadequacy of male 'sense' to the collision or interplay of spoken, visual and musical language. Voice overs, often dislocated from the image, combine the minutiae of the everyday with meditations on 'history' – a history which is not 'hers'.

"If believing wasn't seeing, saying might make sense" *Just About Now*

Rhodes' manipulation of, and dexterity with, cinematic technique is a constant throughout her work. *Light Reading* is, as Michael O'Pray states, "a technical and aesthetic tour de force" of rapid fire editing, myriad techniques, a compelling text which both manipulates and questions language. In her latest works, *A Cold Draft* (1988) and *Just About Now* (1993), drawn images, with the simple power of woodcuts, dissolve painfully into each other, images of imprisonment, repression, of forced conformity. The images conjure with a Nature, desecrated and corrupted and a bombed urban landscape where Lessing meets Orwell. It is fascinating to view her later pieces, creating abstract worlds of surveillance and policing from her multilayered graphics, calligraphy and simple, repetitive, manipulated footage and then look anew at *Light Reading* and *Pictures on Pink Paper*. The camera that makes you dizzy, the manipulation of the familiar into unknown territory, the virtual absence of the body, the constant themes of repression and the price of rebellion, all anchored around the hypnotic, elliptical voice; Rhodes has honed her chosen instruments to razor sharpness.

Gill Henderson

Kathleen
Rogers

The Art of Losing Memory

1991, 10min, b&w, video

An exploration of the analogy between computer memory and personal memory, Rogers shows a woman doing handiwork, following a certain pattern until it becomes a textile product of memory. In contrast to the performer's graceful movements, a computer asks simple questions to which only "yes/no" answers are possible. Using an Amiga 500 home computer and a low resolution intertext, the tape challenges the simplicity of the binary system and computers' lack of the rich texture of remembered experience.

The Still Room

1992, 60min, b7w, video installation

Made entirely on a home computer in black and white, *The Still Room* takes the form of an experimental drama documentary and develops a number of overlapping narratives using symbolic images, music and poetic rolling text. The tools and techniques of video and the computer are used to express the craft and social history of the 'bobbin' lace-workers of Devon.

Biography

Virtual Reality has the potential of providing us with a new perspective on the fantastical architecture of our bodies and minds. If you take the process of architecture as a metaphor for the expression of an individual life then the void that exists at the central core can be used by that person to write in their inner selves.

Using currently available VR headsets and sensor technologies, we can create in VR the sensations of floating, falling, flying and spinning that we all experience in our dreams. In a VR world, our proprioceptive sense is destabilised and somatic transformations of the body and its sensations can be synthesised or altered. The qualitative perceptual shifts that occur and the spatial and temporal abstractions that result, offer us a lucid dreaming space where altered states of consciousness can be explored.

The Surrealists ransacked the basement and attics of their dreaming unconscious minds applying automatic, unthinking modes of behaviour and hallucinatory states. They provided a fund of much needed symbols for the visually barren language of the new physics of their time by creating images in which paradoxes were not absurd. Their work helped break the rigid mould that previously limited the imagination by helping us to assimilate new ways to think by first offering new ways to see.

Art and science have a symbiotic relationship which reflects the spiritual condition of a culture. In order to learn something new we have to imagine it. We literally need to project an image of it or on to it. Scientific disciplines suffer from manifold concept problems, and the current recursive processes of surveillance, substitution and assimilation are lacking something as metaphors. They can nevertheless fundamentally help us remap and explore the morphic characteristics of what we perceive as inside and outside.

Kathleen Rogers *Sleepless Dreaming*

Born 1955, Feltham, Middlesex. BA in Fine Art, Wimbledon School of Art 1983; PG Diploma in Fine Art, Experimental Media, Slade School of Fine Art 1985. Panellist on the Delegation of the Arts Plastique, Paris; residency at the Banff Centre for the Arts, Canada. Screenings include: Ars Electronica, Linz; Video Positive, Liverpool; Femme Totalle, Dortmund. Currently Senior Lecturer, Duncan and Jordanstone College of Art, Dundee.

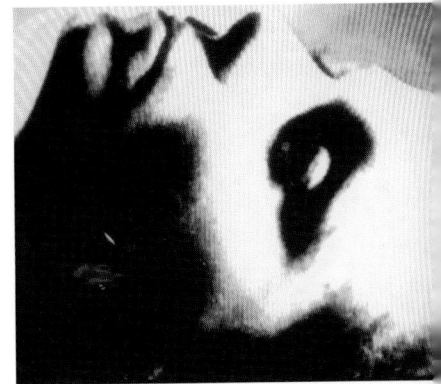

ABOVE:
THE STILL ROOM

165

Simon
Robertshaw

Simon Robertshaw's consistently compelling work in the field of video and multi-media installation has marked him out as one of the brightest stars on the British electronic art scene. He is also one of those rare artists whose flair for technical and formal invention is allied to an equally powerful political focus. Embodying the socially aware and analytical slant of mind that has long been a feature of British video-making, Robertshaw makes pieces in which an adroit use of up-to-the-minute technology is shadowed by a strong and acute sense of history, and difficult, elaborate concepts are located close to home, in the here and now.

Much of this orientation stems from Robertshaw's preoccupation with issues of representation – not solely in a formal and aesthetic sense, but out in a larger cultural and political arena. A long standing commitment to mental health questions (born of a working involvement with mentally disabled people and bolstered by practical and theoretical insights) has similarly extended to reflections around the wider themes of scientific classification, surveillance and social control, along lines inspired by the philosopher Michel Foucault. As Robertshaw's ideas have grown increasingly sophisticated, his methods of illustrating them have burgeoned accordingly. Moving from single-screen tape to installation after *Biometrika* (1987), his work has continued to push the boundaries of the form, often incorporating an interactive dimension as the central dynamic component of an impressive and reverberant multi-media environment.

Three installations – *From Generation to Generation* (1989), *Bio Optic* (1990) and *The Observatory* (1993) – chart Robertshaw's recent development. The stark Orwellian register of *From Generation to Generation* (with its direct reference to Nazi eugenic experiments and its allusions to Foucault's writings on Bentham's Panopticon), although undeniably potent in its own right, gives way to the more wide ranging perspective opened up by *Bio Optic*, whose choice of visual material (moving from satellite pictures of the heavens to fibre optic cameras probing the inside of the human body) startlingly evokes the penetrative scope of today's image technologies.

The follow up *The Observatory* gives an even clearer indication of the direction in which Robertshaw is heading, and confirms that his imaginative use of interactive techniques has clarified rather than complicated his ideas. Arranging a number of industrially embossed glass screens in a tight sculptural circle, and making use of the properties of the glass to reveal or reflect a wealth of contemporary and historical imagery, he presents the viewer with the experience of seeing and simultaneously being observed. The implications are immediately clear, and Robertshaw's recurring obsession with social control and surveillance is resolved with a new found elegance and authority.

Steven Bode

Biometrika
1987, 11min, colour, video

Drawing upon historical documentation and archive film and television material, the tape draws parallels between the activities of the Eugenics Society, who lobbied parliament to allow for selective breeding, in the early twentieth century, the Nazis' treatment of mentally handicapped or congenitally blind people and the treatment of the mentally handicapped in contemporary Britain.

Great Britain
1989, 42 monitor video wall
(with Mike Jones)

An examination of the historical relationships and elements that frame our perceptions of contemporary Britain. In a theatrical space, performers narrate a number of media and historical documents. A fragmented narrative and a complex collage of camerawork, music and the spoken word combine to reveal and unpack received notions of 'Britishness'.

From Generation To Generation
1989, installation, 2 monitors, 1 player, computer and printers

Video monitors are set within a wire cage within which encircling printers churn out information about Nazi eugenic experiments. Incorporating historical documentation with the theme of electronic surveillance, *From Generation To Generation* critiques systems of information and control brought to bear on those deemed 'mentally unfit'.

The Observatory

1993, installation, 2 video projectors,
2 players, 7 slide projectors

Glass and industrially-embossed perspex
screens, slide projections, computer
graphics, and sensor-activated video
projections are used to create an
environment which is changed by the
viewer as he or she moves around in the
gallery. Sensors pick up the movement
and cause the slide- and video-projected
images to change, while the glass and
perspex screens are reflective or transparent
according to whether or not light is playing
on them.

ABOVE:
GREAT BRITAIN

Biography

Born 1960, Mountain Ash, South Wales.
Studied Fine Art at Wolverhampton
Polytechnic 1980–83. MA Royal College of
Art, London 1986. Exhibitions of video
installations include: European Media Art
Festival, Osnabrück; Video Positive,
Liverpool; Photographers' Gallery, London;
Clermont Ferrand Festival; Chapter Arts
Centre, Cardiff; Wrexham Library Arts
Centre. Lecturer in Video and Computing,
Gwent College of Higher Education
1987–90; Lecturer in Fine Art, Southport
College 1992; Senior Lecturer in Electronic
Media, University of Salford 1994-.

George
Saxon

George Saxon's early work is durational and physical. There is a sense of venting anger and cruelty, whether he drips molten plastic onto a live audience in the video performance *Spectacular Anonymity (1 & 2)* (1978), or thuds his head against the wall in the film *Wall Support* (1977).

This raw theatrical confrontation and macabre humour resurface in *The House that Jack Built* (1985), where Jack (George) with blackened teeth, Dickensian, gnarled top hat, enters the house from the street like a touch of evil. The windows are lit with multiple images; Jack scurrying like a cockroach up the narrow stairway; Jack emerging in more than one image, shatters the (filmed) window pane. Coffins, dead flowers, baby-rocking and rhyme-singing give an edge to expanded cinema that few British film-makers possess.

Using a Super8 camera, and often just someone else to press the button, Saxon (alias Witkowski) condenses his multi-layered performance energies into the single screen. In *The Emperor's Mother* (1985), his long-time actor/collaborator D John Briscoe struts his stuff as a rag bag Emperor. In *Pig of Hearts* (1992), children's games mingle with images of war and the darker side of male conditioning. Time and wear and decay. Malone. Saxon's films are like things that go bump in the night. Religious references bleed through the browns and reds of heavy Polish interiors. Sounds that are eerie, self-constructed and half concrete, thread in and out like the strangled chords of a nursery rhyme turned upside down. A rancid pig's head ruptures the game. The young man is wrenched apart by an ominous gas-masked figure in a shock of violent flashbacks. Disconsolately, an amorous hetero couple peer through the wavering window; Mother and Father, distant and cold as icicles.

Anna Thew

Biography

Born London, 1955. Studied Film, Video and Performance, Royal College of Art, London 1977–79. Co-founder member of the Housewatch group (see separate entry); former Workshop Organiser at the London Film-makers' Co-op and consultant with London Video Access. Has taught at Byam Shaw School of Art, London and currently teaches at Winchester School of Art. Screenings include: European Media Art Festival, Osnabrück; Image Forum, Tokyo; Viper International Film and Video Festival, Lucerne; Exit Art, New York; San Francisco, Cinematheque.

The Jack Series
1985-88, 28min, colour, 16mm/video

A trilogy of films originally shown as a multi-screen site specific work. *The House That Jack Built* is a frenetic, blood-red, nightmarish film in which a string of characters comes to life in a darkly comic circus. Its humour belies "this Victorian England", and its inherent double standards. *House of Cards* brings together the characters of the court cards; the king, queen and knave or Jack – "a filthy top-hatted figure embodying the Dickensian nightmare of modern Britain [who] exhibits a theatrical swagger that draws as much on nursery rhyme violence and music hall as it does on the demon drink." Jack returns as the quasi-comical murderer of Wee Willie Winkie in *Jack's Dream*, which "evokes the sensations of fearful and uneasy fascination that a child feels when reading Struwelpeter for the first time."

Pig Of Hearts
1992, 15min, colour, 16mm

Inspired by the early life and poetry of Arthur Rimbaud, *Pig Of Hearts* is a semi-autobiographical account of violation and assault. The film explores a hallucinatory, childlike world of innocence and intoxication; a journey of visual delights and horrors in the guise of a children's game being played out. A walk in the country turns into a 'season in hell' as the protagonist is lead through a series of nightmarish tableaux and deceptions.

ABOVE:
THE HOUSE THAT JACK BUILT

Key works

Hole

1992, 18min, b&w, 16mm

Smith's first psychodrama, in black and white. A lone man lies in bed, dreaming of a young girl who walks along a passage calling to him. He cuts down a woman who is hanging from a tree and resuscitates her. His nose bleeds. He rows a boat round in circles, oblivious to the woman calling from the jetty. Throughout the film, he bores holes in his bedroom wall, eventually crawling through one of them to find himself face to face with the young girl from the beginning.

Up in the Clouds

1994, 10min, 16mm

A metropolitan couple drive to a flat, rocky, windswept moor. The man screws the ground, to the disgust of his companion, and eats leaves from a tree. The woman communes with a sheep and adds a slab to the top of a dry stone obelisk. Laconic, attenuated, 'smutty'.

Nick Gordon Smith's oeuvre reflects two connected tendencies in English artists' film. Firstly, the extension of artisanal practice to include laboratory procedures. This is an abiding feature at the London Film-makers' Co-op, which has always attracted a core of 'DIY' makers whose work involves manipulation of the image at the printing and processing stages. Secondly, the emergence through the late 1980s and early 1990s of narrative drama from people whose previous work came out of the structuralist tradition with which the Co-op is associated.

Smith's early films are typified by restricted cycles of shots which have been slowed down, looped and recoloured to the point where image content is largely subsumed by the material qualities of the medium: grain, colour, texture, light.

Bird Xerox (1983) and *Heaven of Animals* (1984) are animations, a medium traditionally associated with hand-made images. Yet in both films the imagery is generated mechanically. The resulting footage is then reprinted using colour filters.

Subsequently Smith has used live action as a starting point. In *Sermon* (1987), a static shot of a man's face is slowed down so that the only movement is the slow spluttering of enlarged grain. In *O* (1990), two or three live action loops of a Minnie Mouse figure are processed to the point where the colour in the image seems to ooze from areas of the face.

From *Hole* (1992) onwards, Smith has moved away from process work into absurdist psychodrama, but there is a definite continuity in the manic, rather sinister mood of his films.

Nicky Hamlyn

Biography

Born England, 1958. BA Fine Art, Chelsea School of Art 1977–81; studied sculpture but transferred to Film and Video. Workshop Organiser and Course Tutor at London Film-makers' Co-op 1986–89. Independent film-maker and freelance camera/lighting for film and television 1989-

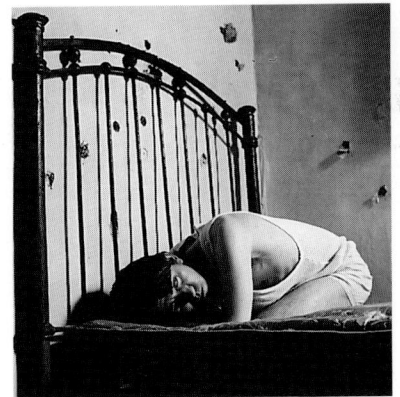

ABOVE:
HOLE

Guy
Sherwin

Guy Sherwin's early films were made within the structural film movement in the mid-1970s. Like his live-action performances of the time, they blend the investigative (mainly perceptual) with the poetic (mainly visual). *Musical Stairs* (1977) turns the horizontal lines of the London Film-makers' Co-op's iron stairs into direct 'serial music' by printing the image into the soundtrack area of the film.. You hear what you see. To reveal the everyday in a new imaginative light also characterises many of the titles in the *Short Film Series* (1976–9). Each film (there are over twenty to choose from) is three minutes long, ie, the length of a standard 16mm roll. They can be shown in any order. Some are studies of changing light, as in *Breathing*, where the rise and fall of a pregnant woman's belly is matched to a changing aperture which rhythmically focuses and then diffuses the light from a background window. *Clock and Candle* plays its two time-measures against a third (the time-lapse camera); a study in duration, its emblematic objects in fading light also imply the theme of mortality. The passage of time is often shadowed by loss and distance, as in *Chimney*, where a brief moment (a train leaving a city) is stretched by repeat-editing and fragmentation. This sense of visual ethics is raised to the compositional surface in such films as *Barn* and *Vermeer Frames*. Like the moving and gentle *Portrait with Parents*, they echo in theme and title the moral universe of Dutch painting.

Sherwin's major film of the 1980s was *Messages* (1981–84). Silent, like much of his work, this was an extended summation of his perceptual studies but on a wider scale. Its centre is the child's acquisition of language. Her vivid questions (which appear as hand-written text) punctuate the films's patient montage of 'visual language'. The camera plays over cuneiform tablets and Eastern calligraphy to seek analogies between languages natural and human, the curious 'signs' of speech. A stunningly fluent 'tree alphabet' is created by manipulating the tones of its latticed branches to form letter-shapes from A through Z. Within the broad time span of the film, these episodes evoke an underlying (or perhaps adjacent) social theme, as in the shots in which the child asks "Can there be women robbers?" and "Are there toys in prison for children?."

Biography

Born Ipswich, 1948. Diploma in Art and Design (Painting), Chelsea School of Art, London 1970. Workshop co-organiser, London Film-makers' Co-op 1975–77; Workshop organiser, Four Corners Film Workshop 1980–83. Currently Associate Senior Lecturer in Film and Video at the University of Wolverhampton. Screenings include: Hayward Gallery, London; National Film Theatre, London; Art Akademie, Trondheim, Norway; San Francisco Cinematheque; Tate Gallery, London. Films in the collections of: National Library of Australia, Canberra; Maison Jean Vilar, Avignon; Freunde der Deutschen Kinematek, Berlin.

Key works

Man with Mirror
1976, 10min, colour, Super8/performance

The film is projected onto a small hand-held screen, white one side and mirrored on the other. This screen is used by the performer to either 'catch' the projected image, or deflect it around the cinema space. The image on film is of the same activity taking place is a sunlit landscape. Visual echoes are set up between the live event and the recorded one. This performance can incorporate directional sound aimed at the screen, the movements of which bounce the sound around the space.

Short Film Series
1976–79, b&w, silent, 16mm

The various segments insist on being considered in the context of other segments, and not as discrete objects; those objects are then significantly altered as the immediate order/context is altered. Responsibility for the selection and order of these segments is conferred on the hirer, extending her/his determination of the viewing context. The selection can obviously be random (if the segments are totally unfamiliar) or can be constructively calculating; the overall impact is to shift greater responsibility onto the hirer/spectator as aesthetic-subject. A corresponding freedom from responsibility on the part of the film-maker as artistic-subject is exemplified in the way the film is conceived, executed, inflected...The result is in no sense a 'work-in-progress' as that term is currently understood; rather, it is a 'progressive work'. In contrast to recent efforts at feature-length and/or ambitious neo-narrative avant-garde films, the considered spontaneity and immediacy of

Sherwin issued few films for nearly a decade after this sometimes tentative but always perceptive work, although he stayed highly active as a teacher in experimental film. *Messages*, which verged on autobiography, was not followed by the 'next step' of sound film, dialogue and narrative, perhaps because he had already questioned the imaginary power of word over image, as well as the authority of the film-maker over the film. Whether this was so or not, Sherwin's welcome return to film-making in *Mile End Purgatorio* (1991) tellingly resolves the issue of speech and silence (public and private) by giving voice to writing, using a text by the poet Martin Doyle. His unerring pictorialist eye frames the shops and buildings of East London, using colour to illuminate space. The film's refreshing wit underlies a self-deflating reference to the "male mid-life crisis" in this vision-packed one-minute film, in which "Biblical and literary allusions reinforce the humour and sense of anxiety."

A L Rees

serial films offer a way forward which escapes both the rigidity of 'structural' constraints and the trap of attempting to produce a definitive and final 'masterpiece'.

Deke Dusinberre *Afterimage*

Messages
1981–84, 35min, b&w, silent, 16mm

Made over a three year period, when the film-maker's young daughter was first learning to talk and write. *Messages* is a film about childhood perception of the world, a response to his daughter's questions that challenge adult/established certainties of knowledge and communication.

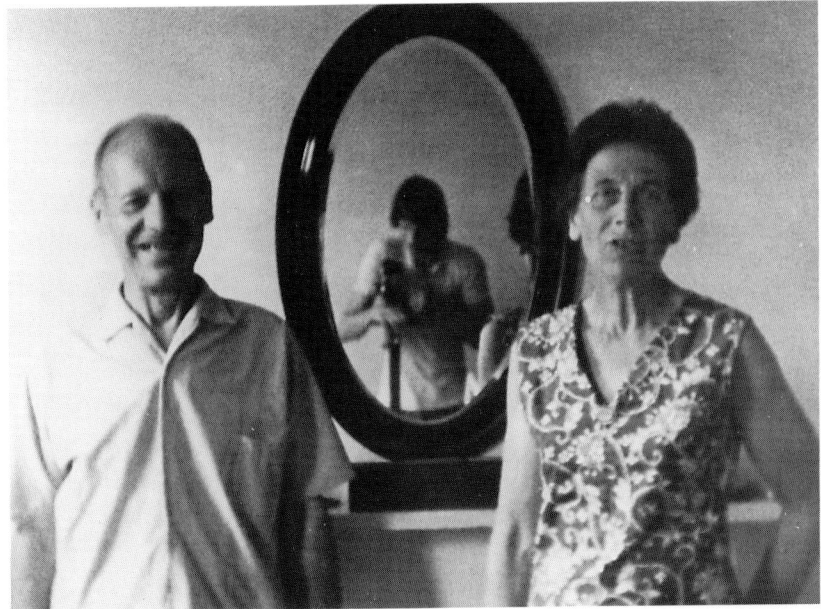

ABOVE:
**SHORT FILM SERIES:
PORTRAIT WITH
PARENTS**

171

Tony
Sinden

Film and light have always been central to Tony Sinden's practice but have never been the sole focus of his work. Early in his film making life Sinden became fascinated by the opportunities offered by what was known in the 1970s as expanded cinema. His influence on its early development was substantial. Since uncovering the possibilities of working with a projected image in a three dimensional space, the potential offered by the single screen has rarely been sufficient to sustain his practice.

Throughout the 1970s and early 1980s, Sinden worked on film based installations for gallery spaces. Although these were mostly solo projects Sinden was already beginning to collaborate, particularly with David Hall and with artists such as David Cunningham (a partnership which is still manifest some twenty years on).

In Sinden's solo installations sound, light and projected image have been combined with carefully selected objects to expand the architecture of the space in which he works. He creates a sense of an environment which is in constant flux. For the last twenty five years he has continued to uproot our understanding of an architectural space as fixed or permanent. As long ago as 1978, in his installation for the Acme Gallery *A Garden Site*, Sinden redefined the space using mirrors, projections, blinds and both artificial and natural light, creating an illusory space; an artwork to which the spectator could also contribute through shadow and movement. In his most recent solo projects that sense of reinvention of architectural space still operates, although the images are now more figurative and the use of sound and live video camera hint at more political uses of such technology in everyday life.

Since 1985 one of the most productive channels for Sinden's work with film has been with the group Housewatch, of which he is a founder member. Housewatch are best known for their marking of urban sites, using film, video, performance and installation. Their work will often re-present the history of a given location, sometimes conveying a new illusory experience of physical space, and – as in Sinden's earlier solo installations – the viewer can occasionally play a physical and visual part in the work. Sinden's individual contributions to the Housewatch portfolio in the form of film and videotapes projected onto multifarious surfaces have traced a route from initial, essentially formal investigation towards an evocation of 'emotional' response, underpinned by the same rigorous aesthetic structure apparent in his solo film work. The strength of Sinden's work in all these contexts rests with the way in which he manipulates seemingly straightforward imagery and in so doing undermines our expectations of the scene in which it is set.

Jeni Walwin

5 Films – View, This Surface, Actor, Edge, Between
1973, various lengths, colour, 16mm
(with David Hall)

These films are now history, although some of the ideas and concerns have, in retrospect, influenced each of us individually in the pursuit of new directions in films and other media since this collaboration. They represent..an important phase in our work in which we explored an area of film which would possibly locate a 'broader aesthetic' by relating avant-garde issues to the generally accepted framework of conventional film-making, and in some cases, specifically to narrative cinema.

TS/DH

A Garden Site
1978, installation, 8 x 16mm projectors, 1 monitor, video camera, mirrors

Since an earlier involvement with making environmental events, light-shows and Fluxus happenings during the mid 1960s..'location and site' and 'a sense of place' have been a consistent influence on the concerns and considerations of my installation pieces.
[...] My recent ideas begin to take their form only when they occupy a specific location, finding a structure the shape of which is descriptive in some way of aspects of the site's immediate surroundings; with projected looped-film, illusions and degradation of time, material, image etc, forming the essential 'evolving elements'.

TS

From Caligari to the Shadow of 1984

1983, installation, slide projectors, mirrors

This site-specific installation commissioned by the San Francisco Arts Commission Gallery was a meditation on war and nuclear holocaust. Suspended in the centre of the space was a black torpedo-shaped bomb, on either side two projected figures in red – as if dead or incinerated.

Ancestral Voices

1994, installation, 12 monitors, 3 players

Set in the medieval crypt of St Nicholas Church, Bristol, this installation used video and sound to create a slowly evolving relationship with the location which is situated next to the River Avon. In the absence of daylight the subterranean medieval architecture of the crypt became the focal point of the work, the video camera revealing momentarily isolated detail and texture of the surroundings. The interaction of the space, the technology and the lone spectator were vital parts of the encounter and transformation of the site.

Biography

Born Brighton. Began working with film, sound and expanded cinema in 1966. Screenings of single screen film and video include: National Film Theatre, London; Knokke-Heist, Belgium; Millennium, New York; Hayward Gallery, London (1979 Hayward Annual); Arsenal Kino, Berlin; Museum of Modern Art, New York. Exhibitions of site-specific installations include: Arnolfini Gallery, Bristol; International Kunstmesse, Vienna; Atholl McBean Gallery, San Francisco; Camerawork , London; St Nicholas Church, Bristol. Tony Sinden has been a member of Housewatch since the mid-1980s (see separate entry).

John
Smith

Key works

Structural film was at its peak in the mid-1970s when John Smith made his first films as part of the movement's 'second-wave'. This younger group of film-makers made striking new contributions to the movement, often (like Smith) while still students, but they already saw it with a more distant and critical eye. *Leading Light* (1975) and *Blue Bathroom* (1979) are classic explorations of light and space to reveal perceptual change. Other films develop Smith's most original hallmark, the use of oblique humour to imply narrative situations and then to question them.

In *The Girl Chewing Gum* (1976) a commanding voice-over appears to direct the action in a busy London street. As the instructions become more absurd and fantasised, we realise that the supposed director (not the shot) is fictional; he only describes – not prescribes – the events that take place before him. As the film progresses it suggests that he may be even further from the scene than we thought. Smith embraced the 'spectre of narrative' (suppressed by structural film), to play word against picture and chance against order. Sharp and direct, the film anticipates the more elaborate scenarios to come; witty, many-layered, punning, but also seriously and poetically haunted by drama's ineradicable ghost.

Smith continues to make short and pungent one-liners such as *Om* (1986) and *Gargantuan* (1992) in the spirit of his rebus-like *Associations* (1975), but *Shepherd's Delight* (1984) inaugurated an expanded narrative framework for increasingly complex 'language games', (here in a succession of shaggy-dog stories that scan the dark side of humour, invoking film's capacity to deceive even as it seems to get more confessional). The narrator of *The Black Tower* (1987) becomes obsessed with a mysterious building which he sees wherever he looks – an illusion created by tour-de-force editing, and the suggestive power of the spoken narrative. The brooding 'dark tower' of the British poets is here sited in the flow of daily life, while the changing face of street and skyline is charted by time-lapse. The final tilt (in a film made largely of still shots) evokes continuity even as a new narrating voice subtly disrupts it.

Biography

Born London, 1952. Diploma in Communication Design, North East London Polytechnic 1974; MA from the Royal College of Art Film School 1977. Associate Lecturer, University of East London since 1984; Visiting Lecturer, Central St Martins since 1989. Screenings include: Paris Biennale; Image Forum, Tokyo; International Experimental Film Congress, Toronto; Arsenal Kino, Berlin; New York International Film Festival; Experimenta '92, Melbourne; São Paulo Film Festival. Works broadcast on BBC2, Channel Four and Thames Television. One person presentations include tours of Poland and USA. Films in the collection of the National Library of Australia, Canberra.

Associations
1975, 7min, colour, 16mm

Images from magazines and colour supplements accompany a spoken text taken from *Word Associations and Linguistic Theory* by Herbert H. Clark. By using the ambiguities inherent in the English language, *Associations* sets language against itself. Image and word work together/against each other to destroy/create meaning.

JS

The Girl Chewing Gum
1976, 12min, b&w, 16mm

An authoritative voice-over pre-empts the events occurring in the image, seeming to order not only the people, cars and moving objects within the screen but also the actual camera movements operated on the street in view. In relinquishing the more subtle use of voice-over in television documentary, the film draws attention to the control and directional function of that practice. The most surprising effect is the ease with which representation and description turn into phantasm through the determining power of language.

Michael Maziere

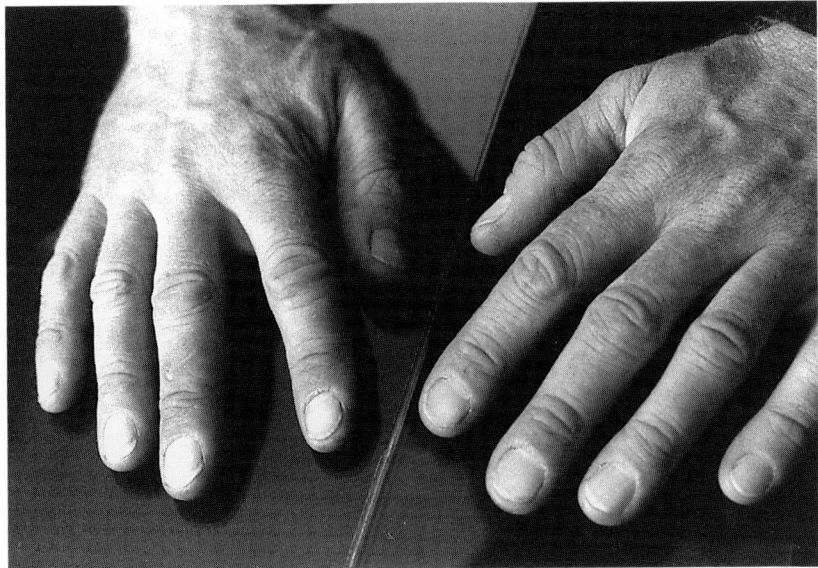

The Black Tower

1987, 24min, colour, 16mm

In *The Black Tower* we enter the world of a man haunted by a tower which he believes, is following him around London. While the character of the central protagonist is indicated only by a narrative voice-over which takes us from unease to breakdown to mysterious death, the images, meticulously controlled and articulated, deliver a series of colour coded puzzles, games, jokes and puns which pull the viewer into a mind-teasing engagement. Something more than a bleakly tragi-comic story, Smith's film is a stylish, entertaining and attractive composite of narrative, experimental concerns and low-key drama.

Nik Houghton

Slow Glass

1991, 40min, colour, 16mm

A nostalgic glazier shows off his knowledge and expounds his theories. Taking glassmaking processes and history as its central theme, *Slow Glass* explores ideas about memory, perception and change.

Smith refines rather than abandons the structuralist challenge to film's 'transparency' (ie, illusionism). The richly visual surface and engaging voice-over narration of *Slow Glass* (1991) extend the metaphor to link light, glass and lens, framed between an 'opening' shot (a smashed pane) and a 'closing' one (the window bricked up). The film slowly reveals its own artifice, as subtle gaps are opened in the film's apparent realism, invading the image ('wrong' reflections in a car mirror) and unsettling the authority of the word. In directly evoking the past (a gentle pastiche of a 1950s childhood) the film questions its supposedly authentic images of the present, down to a homely Thames-side pub. This immaculately crafted film scrutinises the very 'speculations' it incites.

These films offer the pleasures of camera-eye vision, often fooling the eye when distinct time-sequences are 'matted' to make up complex illusions within the frame (as in the changing seasons seen from a window in *The Black Tower*). They can be enjoyed as stories; films for everyone, especially in their humour. They comprise a personal topography of East London, blighted but alive. Echoes of British documentary in *Slow Glass* allude to (and perhaps mourn) the passage of time which all films encode. Viewers are enticed to interrogate the very illusions that films construct in front of their eyes – and behind their backs.

A L Rees

George
Snow

Perhaps the most immediately striking aspect of George Snow's work is its visual richness, vitality and sheer exuberance; whether it is a narrative piece such as *The Assignation* (1988), or a more abstract and visceral work such as *Motorway* (1992), his masterly use of colour, electronic enhancement, and virtuosity in manipulation of the image (both in shooting and post-production) result in a visually seductive experience.

Snow is inspired by classical architecture and literature, by the Gothic as represented by Poe and Escher, by science fiction (he cites writers such as Ray Bradbury as major influences), video games, new technologies and Futurism. His work reflects these eclectic interests, imaginatively juxtaposing the classical with the disposable, mixing time-lines, juggling the real with the synthetic, and combining live action with computer generated forms.

In this mix of image, sound, content and context, humour is a major element, emerging through his juxtaposition of the probable and improbable and manipulation of time and history. Snow expects his audience to revel in his virtuosity – laughter is permissible – his work is entertainment as well as art. This does not mean that the work lacks either complexity or depth; indeed his work enables us to look at the world with different eyes; but he insists that we should also enjoy the experience.

Snow is obsessed with history and architecture, with old cities and the connotations of place. While echoing the styles past and the passage of time, his works hint at improbable futures by highlighting the bizarre contrasts we already experience.

His work relies heavily upon narrative, but he treats it as potentially non-linear by playing with perceived time and space; offering up layers of possibilities whilst retaining an internal logic which makes compulsive viewing. This puts Snow at the forefront in the development of new forms of interactive storytelling. For his current project *APE*, he is developing 3D computer generated environments that can exist in real time and space. Snow has an original perspective on interactivity and Virtual Reality which is perhaps best illuminated by a quotation from Edgar Allan Poe's *The Assignation*:

"To dream has been the business of my life. I have therefore framed for myself, as you see, a bower of dreams...You behold around you, it is true, a medley of architectural embellishments, yet the effect is incongruous to the timid alone. Proprieties of place and especially of time are the bugbears which terrify mankind from the contemplation of the magnificent."

Jane Rigby

Muybridge Revisited
1986, 5min, colour, video

A tired man alone at night flips through a book of Muybridge stills, and through hallucination, their movement and the tape opens out and revels in computer animated Muybridge figures dancing spectacularly around a multi-layered ornamental backdrop.

The Assignation
1988, 12min, colour, video

Snow fuses the complex structure of Edgar Allan Poe's gothic story with the collage technique offered by modern technology. Pac-Man fish swim in the fluorescent canals of Venice; Snow's post-scratch approach underlining the comments of the voice-over, "The eye wandered from object to object and rested upon none."

Motorway
1992, installation, 4 video projectors, 4 players, surrounding screens

An ironic, amusing and clever tribute to motion, travel and the automobile... No attempt here to reproduce the motor-car experience, this is pure flight – no sensory sign of the engine but a deeply accelerated motion and the extreme psychedelic colouring and manipulation of the image. As you progress, low flying alien ships appear, space and colour are transformed, and the earthly motorway looks more like Kubrick than Kerouac.

Michael Maziere

Face to Space

1995, 4½min, colour, video

The argument for a centralised authority to administer London is made by the colossal steel framework of an unfinished building that evolves into a megalopolis. The giant structure sinks to its knees under the burden. The camera zooms into a room in Sir John Soane's Museum, where Ken Livingstone, clad in a toga, makes the case for co-ordinated town planning.

Biography

Born Hannover, Germany, 1948. Expelled from Hornsey College of Art 1970. Worked as a designer and illustrator for the underground press in the 1970s (*Oz, International Times*) as well as a press photographer in Northern Ireland for the left-wing press (*Morning Star, Socialist Worker, Black Dwarf*). In the 1980s, began computer programming and experimenting with video using the programmes he developed for IO Research's 'Pluto' computer. Commissioned by The Art of Noise, London Beat and The Stranglers to make music videos. Currently lecturer at the Danish Design School and the Media School, Royal Academy, Copenhagen. Screenings include: World Wide Video Festival, The Hague; São Paolo International Video Festival; ICA, London; Wroclaw, Poland; Montbeliard. One person retrospective at the Vigo Video Festival 1991.

Marty St James
Anne Wilson

Marty St James and Anne Wilson first received attention in the late 1970s and early 1980s as performance artists. Like other male/female double acts before them, they exploited gender roles as a basis for their art. Unlike others, whose work was often motivated by gender politics or by mystical allusion, St James and Wilson trawled the rich waters of pulp fiction and popular low-brow culture for imagery upon which to base their work. From Mills and Boon to the kitsch of the seaside guest house, from ballroom dancing to soap opera, they explored and exploited a language and culture that is anathema to the values of high art, and they did this in a way that was neither condescending nor provocatively 'alternative'. Had they been American instead of British, they might have occupied the niche that Jeff Koons later carved for himself in the art market.

Of the earlier video tapes, *Visual Art Songs for the '80s* (1984), a series of four short pieces, remains a landmark in its mixing of popular culture and performance art and its innovative use of video effects to create images with a paint-like quality. The series encapsulated many of the desires, memories, fears, aspirations and confusions of a generation born in the optimism of the 1950s, and who were still struggling to come to terms with the new realities of Britain in the mid-1980s.

The works of the early 1980s reach a logical conclusion in *Hotel* (1989) an ambitious installation at London's AIR Gallery, which also functioned as the launch pad for a made-for-television production of the same name. The gallery was transformed into a simulacrum of a hotel in which visitors could visit a cocktail bar or watch displays of ballroom dancing. Televisions in the bedrooms relayed endless soaps, while specially made video tapes in the lift and the shower 'populated' the hotel with ghostly entities.

Biography

St James born 1954, West Midlands; Wilson born 1955, West Midlands. Both studied at Cardiff College of Art and have worked together on performance, video and installation since 1982. Exhibitions of installations include: Rochdale Art Gallery; Aspex Gallery, Portsmouth; Arnolfini, Bristol; Air Gallery, London. Screenings of single screen tapes include: Montbeliard Festival; Institute of Contemporary Arts, Boston; Semana Internacional de Cine Espana. *Video Portraits* exhibited: European Media Art Festival, Osnabrück; Bonn Videonale; 101 Gallery Canada; National Portrait Gallery London; Artec Media Biennalle Nagoya Japan; Video Positive, Liverpool.

Key works

Hotel
1989, 22min, colour, video

A combination of fantasies and anecdotes investigating the conventions and structure of hotel life all over the world, *Hotel* features St James and Wilson as both guests and proprietors. Employing electronic imagery and layering, romantic parody and risqué stories, *Hotel* captures collective memories, expectations and aspirations. The single screen tape was originally shown as part of a larger installation exhibited at the Air Gallery, London in 1989.

The Smoking Man – Giuliano Pirani
1991, mounted cabinet containing 1 monitor, 1 player

Like the other video portraits for which St James and Wilson have become renowned, *The Smoking Man* is an individual portrait within a traditional ornate picture frame, but instead of the traditional static painting it features a moving video portrait of the subject, constructed to capture his particularly obsessive characteristics. Giuliano Pirani is placed in a Rembrandtian spotlight, his action of smoking performed, telescoped and repeated.

RIGHT:
**THE SMOKING MAN –
GIULIANO PIRANI**
FAR RIGHT:
**VIDEO PORTRAIT OF
NEIL BARTLETT**

Leaving aside the trappings of low culture, St James and Wilson next turned their attention to the opposite end of the spectrum and commenced a series of video works that took the form of the classical portrait. Their video portraits encompassed two variants: large, multi screen 'exploded' images, and single screen traditional portraits in ornate, often gilded, frames. The latter were the more successful, functioning best when their close conformity to the traditions of portraiture was subtly undermined by the management of time and change in the image. An apparently still face might suddenly speak, begin to cry, or turn its head to follow the viewer's movements through the museum. The portraits were often, and to best effect, exhibited in formal museum or gallery situations, including the National Portrait Gallery. True to the tradition of portraiture, many of the works were commissioned images of the famous or powerful, and the enthusiastic co-operation of the sitters clearly contributes to the success of the works. In 1993, St James and Wilson realised their ambition to create a 'civic' portrait – in this case a video of the mayor of Trondheim, whose electronic image commanded much attention during a three week exhibition at the city's gallery of contemporary art.

Jeremy Welsh

Andrew **Stones**

Renaissance and Enlightenment thinking is implicated in the formation of contemporary world views mediated by science and technology. Science has used techniques of representation, inherited from its common history with what have become the separate disciplines of art practice, in order to present its results, and to constitute itself as a cultural force. Conversely, it has returned to art practice new modes of representation apparently free of some of the problematics of value. Yet there is a politics associated with high rationalism which should not escape scrutiny because of a merely asserted neutrality. Ideas of value in many fields – science, medicine, race and gender politics, art – appear interrelated when their historical bases are traced and compared. The philosophical postures which sustain a creed such as Darwinism may also be identified with nationalism and racism; the gendered division and mastery of space established in Renaissance painting and architecture can be seen reflected in the 'extended reach' afforded by modern technological apparatus. No 'vision', it seems, can be neutral.

The videotapes and large-scale installations described below may be seen as symptomatic of a culture poised between an exaggerated sense of manipulative control, and the evidence of human frailty. They also allude to the often-repeated movement from Utopian to apocalyptic metaphor, where popular perceptions of the scientifically-mediated world are concerned.

The installation *Geiger* (1989) presents live action derived from the intricate placement of fuel rods in a nuclear reactor. The video sequence associated with this work shows a naked male figure in a sterile metal cell. Radioactivity as a cultural icon has undergone its own transition: from the Utopian, invisible wonder-ray of the early 1900s, to pernicious carcinogen. The figure in the cell is isolated either to make it safe in the light of this supremely penetrative threat, or to prevent its already contaminated nature from infecting others. The man is mercilessly framed by the boundary of the screen – as nature and the feminine were framed by the Renaissance perspective grid; his hands, held open, indicate the absence of a book, and his other actions are reduced to obsessive washing, and frozen gestures.

Key works

Common Knowledge
1989, 25min, colour, video

Common Knowledge uses the form of a journey undertaken by the camera/viewer through a series of territories: cornfield, marsh, garden, the pages of a dismembered encyclopaedia, woodland and conifer plantation. This framework provides a metaphor for a specific strand of history indicated in the sub-titles for each section of the tape: 'Finding – Europe 1934–38'; 'Gathering – USA 1933–39'; 'Fathering – USA 1942–45'; 'Japan 1945 – Angels Leaving'.

A History of Disaster with Marvels
1992, 12min, colour, video

An animated essay which presents several quotations from Francis Bacon (1561–1626) and graphic representations from early science and alchemy. A mythologised narrative which describes the progress of experimental science is interrupted by a series of apocalyptic 'marvels', which are presented as reports of real events given by telephone, radio, or word of mouth. These events are related within formalised, domestic interiors which repeatedly yield their solidity to reveal historical and elemental layers.

Class
1990, installation, video projector, desks, slide projectors, overhead projectors

An installation which reflects on how systems of social testing, exclusion/ inclusion – enshrined in law and culture – were diffused in the 19th century classroom, with an enduring legacy on European (and particularly British) notions of national identity and otherness. Visual elements range from images from 19th century natural history illustrations, a short video sequence which re-interprets the Queen's 1989 Christmas address to the nation and a split, projected postcard-image depicting a pageant in which children are dressed to signify different parts of the geography and culture of the United Kingdom.

Biography

Born Sheffield 1960. BA in Fine Art,
Sheffield City Polytechnic 1983. Resident
Artist: Newcastle Polytechnic 1986; Sheffield
Polytechnic and Mappin Gallery 1989.
Fine Art Research Fellow, Manchester
Metropolitan University 1994–6. Visiting
Lecturer, Royal Melbourne Institute of
Technology/Wollongong University,
Australia 1991. Part-time and Visiting
Lecturer and freelance video worker/editor
since 1984. Exhibitions include: Video en
Beeldende Kunst, Amsterdam 1987; Video
Positive, Tate Gallery, Liverpool 1983,
Bluecoat Gallery, Liverpool 1989; British
Artists of the 1990s Kunst-Werke, Berlin
1993. Manchester Metropolitan Galleries
1994. Screenings include: ICA Biennial:
'Arrows of Desire'; ICA Biennial: 'Between
Imagination and Reality'; World Wide
Video Festival, Den Haag; Muu Media
Festival, Helsinki; Australian International
Video Festival, Sydney. Work broadcast by
Ch4.

A similar scenario recurs in the installation *The Conditions* (1993) where a
rotating male torso, deprived (again via strict framing) of head, voice and
phallus, appears from a stream of milk. In response to the flash of a thorn-stem
down its spine, the figure displays a book of medicinal plants. The book is once
again employed as an iconic, cultural fetish, in this case a mask over the attack
from within the body. This figure from *The Conditions* occurs as part of a 15-
minute video/sound sequence constituted from three synchronised video
projector units. The placement of this panorama within an architecture suffused
by red light, analogous to the 'safe' light in a photographic darkroom, describes
certain managed conditions for seeing, for making visible. The work presents a
number of miraculous causalities which invert the canonical history of modern
science: denying gravity, milk transfers in a stream from one rotating bowl to
another, and a bouquet of bluebells burns and rots, to become a monumental
human arm.

The installation *Class* (1990) challenges a sense of cultural archaism still
present in Britain after the dissolution of the Empire. Latin maxims used in the
work are yardsticks whereby the right of residence in a given place may be
granted or rejected. *The Nature of Their Joy* (1994) also signals a critical view
regarding the end of Victorianism. Photographs of crowds celebrating both the
outbreak and the end of the Great War, are fragmented into individual faces,
mixed in fluid, and circulated in a transparent tube across the illuminated 'eyes'
of twelve portable microfiche readers. The work deliberately conflates the idea of
objective analysis via technological apparatus, with the cultural conundrum of
post-Victorian Britain.

Andrew Stones

Mike **Stubbs**

Mike Stubbs is an all-round time-based artist; his work encompasses film, video, performance and installation, and his contribution to each medium has been original, powerful and often humorous. His studies at the Environmental Media Department of the Royal College of Art in the early 1980s partly account for the broadness of his artistic outlook and practice. An early success, *Contortions* (1983), a 16mm film on the theme of youth and unemployment, confounded its audience with its dialectical use of narrative and visual styles, its questioning of class and intellect, and its critical irony.

Stubbs has been most prolific in video, and notable pieces have been *Greetings From The Cape of Good Hope?* (1986), a hard-edged and savage indictment of South African apartheid and the much acclaimed *Sweatlodge* (1991). *Sweatlodge* developed from a performance by the group Man Act, centres on the violent internal contradictions within 'masculinity' – competition, domination and submission. Its strength lies in its materials and form: raw black and white Super8 film transferred to video, shot in a subjective and engaged camera style; its resistance to the overtly lyrical and aestheticised 'dance video' genre.

Humour and adventurousness are also a feature of Stubbs' installation work. In *The Fragility of Things* (1987) which recalls his experience of a car crash, he suspended a saloon car over a human shape made of egg shells. In its directness, cheek and irony it encapsulates his irreverent style. As one of the film and video sector's polymaths, his work is at its most successful when – as in *Sweatlodge* – it juggles different practices to create a hybrid genre. His irreverent attitude to categories and genres gives his work its humanity and its ability to reveal the world.

Michael Maziere

Mike Stubbs was taught photography at the age of 12 by his Dad, a scientist. Cultural roots = TV, car racing and pop music. Later at art school he used Super8 and 16mm film. A tutor wanted a boy with technical competence to test out their new video gear. Mike did it. Early works – such as the 16mm experimental narrative *Contortions* and short video *Greetings from the Cape of Good Hope?* – produced for the anti-apartheid movement – were termed 'hard hitting' and 'political'. Success with performance companies such as Sweatlodge has meant getting grouped into the 'dance video' section of a few too many international festivals. Much of the work has enjoyed the use of humour and satire. This has often been necessary to offset the monumental aspect of video installation. A growing interest in performance and networked (computer-based) media art like *Truth Wars* promises a shift to a less physically substantial type of sculpture.

Mike Stubbs

Contortions

1983, 30min, colour, 16mm

Debunking cliché portrayals of the unemployed, *Contortions* depicts the life of Peter who is young and unemployed but capable of retaining a sense of humour about his situation. Incorporating narrative and a critical irony, the film ranges from the quasi-documentary to the surreal.

Sweatlodge

1991, 7min, b&w, 35mm/video

The ritual of the Sweatlodge illustrates the forms in which male relationships rigidly conform to patterns of competition and domination. Originally filmed on Super8 as documentation of a performance by Man Act of the same name, it is a powerful invocation of men, movement and violence.

Biography

Born 1958. BA in Fine Art, Cardiff College
of Art; MA in Environmental Media (Film
& Video), Royal College of Art, London.
Panel member at conference Technoculture:
Enriching the Artificial Environment,
Inverness 1990. Currently Artistic Co-
ordinator, Hull Time Based Arts. Screenings
include: Impakt Festival, Utrecht; European
Media Art Festival, Oberhausen; World
Wide Video Festival, Den Haag; Mediawave
Festival, Gyor, Hungary. *Sweatlodge*: ICA
Biennial: 'Arrows of Desire'; Golden
Artronic Award, Locarno Video Art Festival
1992. Film and video work broadcast on
Channel Four, S4C, HTV, Swedish and
French television.

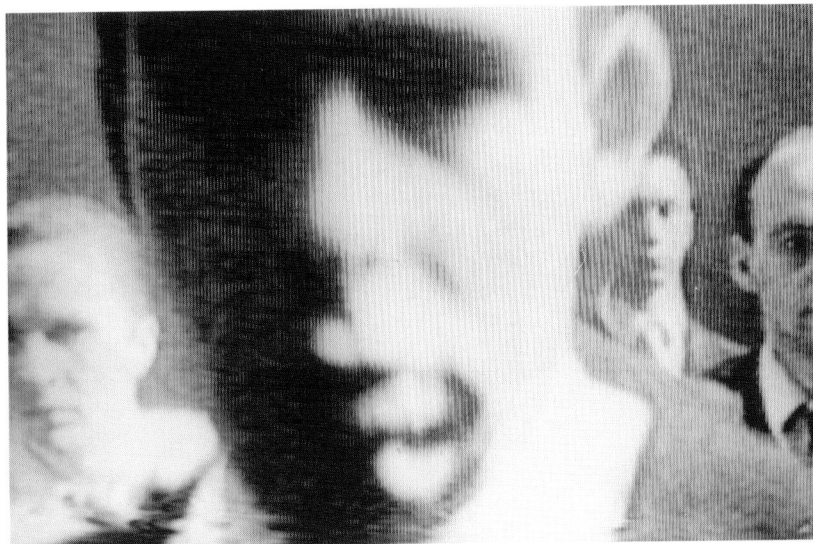

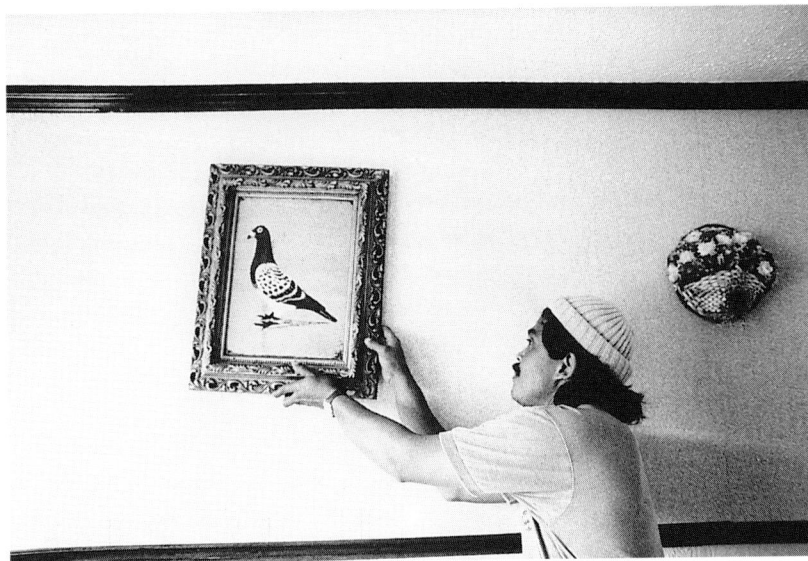

TOP:
SWEATLODGE
BOTTOM:
HOMING

Cordelia
Swann

Cordelia Swann was born and grew up in the United States, but has lived the greater part of her life in England, and the adeptness with which her films counterpoint personal history and myth with a forceful sense of social and political injustice sets them apart from work by British contemporaries. Her first film, *The Ten Commandments of Love* (1979), is a witty side-swipe at structural film, with a 1950s, photographed, kissing couple, frenetically coloured-by-numbers to the strains of a vocal refrain. *Phantoms* (1986) and *A Call to Arms* (1989), are dream-like celebrations of myth and memory, though *A Call to Arms*, now, seems resolutely of its time; a work of baroque Camp, it has Tilda Swinton in armour drag, the glinting ocean and billowing sheets, arrayed in a soft focus reclamation of a 19th century aesthetic, elaborated to create almost florid television.

The Citadel (1992), the one minute *Tall Buildings* (1992), *Out West* (1993), and *Desert Rose* (1995), are a significant departure from the style of the earlier work. An "air that kills" (A E Houseman *A Shropshire Lad*) – literally, in *Desert Rose* – breezes gently through these films, carrying with it a pervading sense of yearning and loss. Carefully composed images are ordered with precision, but their grace and calm beauty are betrayed by narrated recollections telling of conflict and violent disorder. These films are investigations: of authentic memories, real places and events. The camera moves headlong, surveying the terrain of past incident, sometimes pausing for thought, to recall or affirm. The world is viewed from a distance and at speed; the desert and Las Vegas are seen as drive-by, the Gulf War is a fly past and bill posters, while childhood is glimpsed from afar, by way of adult memory. The writing is suffused with the pain of displacement; the subject is our personal remove – from the world, from ourselves and from historic events which impact inexorably on our lives. The stories tell of the rational self thrust into chaos by the madness of circumstance, the emotional impact deriving from the tragedy of our never being able to return: "the land of lost content...where we cannot come again" (Houseman, ibid).

Swann has honed a modern aesthetic that provides visual references from our collective cultural history as the site and context for recollections of individual experience. *The Citadel*, in its surreal narrative, retains a reliance on the mythical which partly detracts from its central, political concerns. In *Tall Buildings* (where

Key works

The Citadel
1992, 13min, colour and b&w, Super8/video

Using a range of stunning imagery within an allegorical structure, *The Citadel* follows the imaginary journey of a woman through a city of beauty and desolation. Shot in a lyrical documentary tradition, akin to the work of Humphrey Jennings, the piece weaves together a subjective narrative with a visionary perception of London.

Michael Maziere

Out West
1993, 15min, colour, 16mm/video

The dazzling red of the Golden Gate Bridge set against a perfect blue sky opens *Out West* and immediately transports us to the rich imaginary of the artist's early years in America. Cordelia Swann brings together fragmented childhood memories with striking images, to capture a feeling of awe and a sense of timelessness. The silence of the landscape is broken only by a voice, whose reminiscences conjure up the child's clear yet disturbing vision of the world. The iconic value of the American landscape is strong...in a work which remains personal yet hauntingly powerful.

Michael Maziere

Tall Buildings
1992, 1½min, colour, 16mm/video

The brutal memories of childhood are combined with glimpses of the emotional landscape of Manhattan's skyscrapers.

Desert Rose
1995, 26min, b&w, 16mm/35mm/video

Moving from the cottonwoods and desert of southern Nevada we are taken from the innocence of early childhood in *Out West* to the nightmarish reality of both a contemporary and 1950s vision of casinos, hotels, wedding chapels and the neighbouring nuclear test site of Las Vegas where a seamy underside is revealed which is more sinister and tragic than mere glitter, vice or gambling.

Biography

RIGHT:
THE CITADEL

Born 1953, San Francisco. Studied at
the Pratt Institute, Brooklyn, New York
1970–72; De Vrije Akademie, The Hague
1972–74; North East London Polytechnic
1974–77. Screenings include: World Wide
Video Festival, The Hague; Berlin Video
Festival; Women In The Director's Chair,
Chicago; Video Brasil, São Paulo; Toronto
Film Festival; Videonale, Bonn; European
Media Art Festival, Osnabrück; London
Film Festival. *Out West*: American
Federation of the Arts/Museum of Modern
Art, New York: Touring Programme.
Broadcasts include: Channel Four, ZDF,
SBS Australia, Art TV Berlin. Curator:
Salons of 1983 and 1984 at the Institute
of Contemporary Arts, London; Cinema
Organiser, London Film-makers' Co-op
(1983–85); Programmer and Co-ordinator,
Film and Video Umbrella (1986);
Programmer, Art and Experiment section
of the London Film Festival (1992, 1993);
research and curation of Piper Heidseck/BFI
The Cinema of Humphrey Jennings project.
Lecturer, Central St Martins.

the camera submits to Manhattan) and *Out West*, images sometimes support,
and other times counter, the soundtracks' apparent narratives. A voice recounts
an abstracted memoir: fragments from a life, or lives. No one story is told, but a
singular reality is clearly understood. In *Desert Rose* there is no explicit recourse
to the autobiographical; witness accounts testify in Swann's most effective
protest yet against a nation's ill regard for its citizens.

The strange familiarity of many of the images employed – and hence the ease
with which the works allow us 'in' – derives from Swann's allusions to American
painting, photography and film. Her depiction of the Nevada Desert shows the
influence of Ansel Adams, Walker Evans, Georgia O'Keefe and Stan Brakhage,
while observational, documentary portraits and townscapes recall Paul Strand
and Gary Winogrand. It would be misleading to suggest that Swann deals in
homage and quotation; rather, it is a process of engagement. It is perhaps most
useful to reference John Ford, Terence Malick and Humphrey Jennings, with
whom she shares the rare ability to invest landscape and the city with a
metaphoric power and to convey the emotional impact of their terrible beauty.

Gary Thomas

Moira Sweeney

Moira Sweeney has made a firm distinction between her earlier short films and the more recent *Coming Home* (1994). But there is a common theme running through her work, that of 'home' and the search for roots. In the earlier films home is identified with specific places, but in *Coming Home* Sweeney looks for community not in place, but among people who, like her, have been displaced or dispossessed by political violence. Ultimately this requires coming to terms with rootlessness and embracing it.

In *Imaginary* (1989) an Irish coastal landscape is seen, mostly through the window of a house. Various domestic objects, surfaces and a log fire are intercut with the exterior views. As in all of Sweeney's work the imagery has been slowed down in an optical printer. Much of the film's characteristic lyricism comes from this treatment and from a fascination with surfaces and patinas. The window in *Imaginary* is both a framing device and a recurrent motif, functioning as an anchor for what might otherwise have been a disparate collection of shots. The frequent views through the window also suggest the beckoning of the world beyond and this leads to the global perspective of *Coming Home*.

Coming Home began as another 'experimental' work but during its preparation Sweeney's ambitions expanded. The securing of additional funding from Channel Four was prompted by a desire to make a more accessible and larger-scale work. Sweeney begins, in voice-over, by setting out her own position as a damaged escapee from sectarian violence in Enniskillen in Northern Ireland. After a brief spell as a half-hearted nationalist in London she travels to the Philippines, Africa, Brazil and Norway, meeting people whom she identifies as having been displaced, like herself, by political turmoil.

Key works

Looking for the Moon
1986, 7min, b&w, silent, 16mm

Evoking an iconography that stems from the work of Maya Deren, Sweeney uses both movement within the frame and editing as choreographic elements. The tension created is between the pull of an off-screen person's hands and the private world the woman sees through her window.

Emily Cronbach

Hide and Seek
1987, 16min, colour and b&w, 16mm

A metaphorical and lyrical journey of discovery through memory. Silent images of childhood memories contrast with room interiors and windows. The seemingly innocent nature of children at play is threatened by the haunting sounds of their voices over the interior spaces.

MS

Imaginary
1989, 17min, colour, silent, 16mm

Filmed in three sections, *Imaginary* was originally shot on standard and Super8, then reprinted on 16mm. Focusing on intimate moments experienced by the film-maker, the film is divided into three sections. 'From Today' recalls the experiences and perceptions of the deserted rural Ireland of Sweeney's childhood captured through slow rhythmic camera movements and the autumnal tones of the countryside and a house. 'Touched' tentatively traces a naked male body, in bluey black and white tones, offering an atmosphere of beauty, intimacy and gentleness. The final sequence shifts from the magical atmosphere of serenity into shots of a mysterious landscape, that echo the camerawork of the first sequence. They evoke the wonder that the discovery of a place can offer to the viewer.

Tim Highstead

Coming Home
1994, 40min, colour, 16mm

Coming Home is a journey meditating on the soul of life and power of nature across four continents. Contrasting with this is a deeply personal voice-over reflecting on the sometimes traumatic memories of growing up in Northern Ireland in the sixties and seventies. The images, celebrating survival, act as powerful backdrops while the film-maker in the voice-over slowly comes to terms with the effects of violence. Ultimately the film is not just about unacceptable levels of violence in Northern Ireland and the countries within the film. It is a tribute to the spirit and integrity of survival in the wake of psychic damage.

MS

Biography

Born 1962, Sheffield. BA in Fine Art (Media Studies), Newcastle Upon Tyne Polytechnic; MA Television Drama, Goldsmiths University of London 1995. Curator of An Eye for Ireland 1987; Cinema Programmer, London Film-makers' Co-op 1988–89; Film Curator, Film and Video Umbrella 1990–91; Curator, Innovation – Experimental Film Forum, Manchester 1993. Contributor to *Undercut*, *Variant* and *Independent Media* magazines. Screenings include: San Francisco Cinematheque; Millennium, New York; Toronto International Experimental Congress; Image Forum, Tokyo; Berlin Film Festival; Cork Film Festival; London Film Festival; Oberhausen; European Media Art Festival, Osnabrück; Feminale; Manila Film Festival. *Imaginary*: ICA Biennial: 'Between Imagination and Reality'; Honorary Award Retina Film Festival, Hungary 1989: Certificate of Merit Cork Film Festival 1990, screened by ZDF. *Coming Home* broadcast by Channel Four.

The work is composed of people and landscapes; forests and paddy fields, beaches, palm trees and the shadows they cast. Coastal drives, churches and aerial views of Rio de Janeiro. People are seen in various activities; gutting fish, mending nets, building fires and selling in markets, singing, dancing and playing. The material was shot hand-held on 16mm and, as before, much has been filmed in slow motion, or manipulated on an optical printer.

The film-maker narrates a diary of her movements, peppered with observations and thoughts on the different kinds of privation that the dispossessed experience. In the Philippines this is a by-product of separatist political struggles. In Brazil it stems from street crime and the fight for survival in Rio's shanty towns.

The film, though familiar in terms of subject matter, is very different in tone to that shot by visiting camera crews. The closeness of the film-maker to her subjects, for example in the scenes of an African fisherman mending his net, suggests a degree of familiarity that can only have been achieved by building up a relationship over a period of time. The voice-over, furthermore, gives a sense that Sweeney herself is "coming from here." It is clear that for Sweeney the process of making the film constitutes a therapeutic journey at the end of which she overcomes her negative feelings of homelessness. This is reinforced by the realisation that a return to Enniskillen could not be a return home.

Nicky Hamlyn

Alia
Syed

Of Alia Syed's six films, *Fatima's Letter* (1992) has received the most attention. The film revolves around the recollections and perceptions of a woman who has emigrated to London from Pakistan. While composing a letter to her friend Fatima on the underground, she becomes disoriented, and peoples the incident she is remembering with the strangers who surround her on the train. Whitechapel underground station becomes a confusing abstract landscape of shifting light and shadow; London elides with Pakistan as shadows take on form and become inhabited by memories. The film is deliberately obscure. We never see the woman who is writing the letter; we just hear a voice, reciting the letter in Urdu. Even the English subtitles – which follow the narration after long delays – do not necessarily connect up with either the image on screen or the voice-over; we are presented with white text, which is often quite difficult to read. The counterpoint between the two languages, and the failure of language to serve our needs, are the two main dynamics of the film. Notions of home and memory are revealed as necessary inventions – as fictions. The woman's story (and Syed's film) exists only in relation to other stories, and long-ago events are remembered so vividly that they eclipse the reality of the present day. Syed seems to be proposing that the happily remembered nostalgia conjured by the woman is a fiction as well. Life in London is not necessarily better or worse than living in Pakistan. It is just what it is: constantly variable, protean, slippery, spilling messily over fixed definitions and forms.

Syed freely borrows strategies from several schools of practice and theory. *Fatima's Letter* with its layering of imagery and meanings becomes at times a conceptual project, while the way in which it has been shot and edited to the rhythm of passing trains (evoking film passing through the projector) suggests a structural approach. *Swan* (1987), a short sensual film using repeated images of a swan preening itself, reveals her abilities as a formalist. The influence of race and feminist politics and theory and the issue-based work which those movements generated is apparent in *The Watershed* (1994).

Ian Iqbal Rashid

Fatima's Letter
1992, 21min, b&w, 16mm

The film has a vital mesmeric rhythm, rich texture and chiaroscuro lighting which vividly reveals a London physically resonant of Asia itself.

Michael O'Pray

The Watershed
1994, 8min, b&w, 16mm

Hands rub a woman's back, stroking and twisting her hair gently. The fingers are kind, there is no visible menace present, but eventually the touching begins to echo past violence and pain. Syed submits a memory of sexual abuse simply, effectively and with restraint, while delineating the effects of that abuse. In doing so, she denies the possibility of pleasure: to both survivors of sexual abuse in the power game of sexuality, and to the viewer who can find no remnant of comfort or sensuality in the images of a tender sexual encounter.

Ian Iqbal Rashid

Biography

Born in Swansea, educated in Glasgow and London. BA in Film, University of East London; MA in Film, Slade School of Fine Art. Screenings include: Collective For Living Cinema, New York; Viper Festival, Lucerne; Euclid Cinema, Toronto; Innovation – Manchester Film Forum, Cornerhouse, Manchester. *Fatima's Letter*: included in the touring exhibition Beyond Destination; ICA Biennial: 'Arrows of Desire'.

LEFT:
THE WATERSHED

I am concerned with relationships and conflicts that exist within the dichotomy of the interior and the exterior. More specifically, the places and bodies we inhabit that evoke both danger and safety, fear and desire, light and darkness, silence and sound.

Film is an organic medium, where ideas and images change and evolve through process. I deliberately have not used text or spoken language. I feel there is an essence of experience that is not expressed through language but through the body; in gesture, sound, movement and rhythm. If you record a conversation and rub away the edges around each word (so the word is no longer a word but a sound), then you can hear the emotion without the literal meaning of the word. I have worked with sound as a medium in its own right, using music, voice, *musique concrète* and experimental sound. I have worked on sound compositions and arrangements, for dance, performance and film.

Tanya Syed

Key works

Salamander
1994, 14min, colour, 16mm

A journey through desire, set in a fast food take-away in South London, and shot entirely at night. The excess of traffic, light, sound and movement creates a dynamic – a transient reality. Someone waits in the take-away, playing with a fruit machine. (Her hands play the keys incessantly). A lorry driver drives in the night; a woman plays cards with some friends in the backroom. The pacing of the film carries you forward, expectantly. Sometimes we cannot place things, or people; the images run over my eyes – fluid, like water.

TS

Delilah
1994, 11min, b&w, 16mm

Working with three women, through choreographed and improvised movements, this film explores lesbian expressions of power, desire and puissance. As the film progresses through ritualised gesture, moving between the stereotypical and archetypal, balancing action and reaction, the control shifts, relations evolve. "You moved like a warrior, but I could not hold you". The outside is within us.

TS

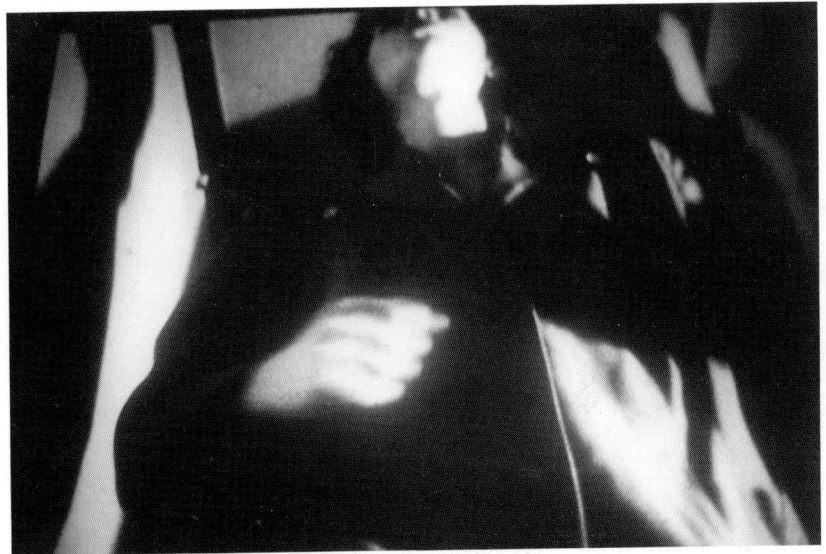

ABOVE:
DELILAH

Biography

Born 1967, Glasgow. BA in Fine Art, Goldsmiths College, London 1990. Education Organiser at the London Film-makers' Co-op 1991–1994. Currently Course Co-ordinator at Four Corners Film Workshop, London. Screenings include: Innovation – Manchester Film Forum, Cornerhouse, Manchester; IKON Gallery, Birmingham; Watershed, Bristol; Mutations de L'Image Festival, Paris 1994.

Margaret **Tait**

Margaret Tait studied at the Centro Sperimentale di Cinematographia in Rome between 1950 and 1952. The school was then at its high point, coinciding with the prominence of Neo-Realism (Rossellini, De Sica, Visconti), and a rapidly expanding production base aided by American capital.

A Portrait of Ga (1952), is characteristic of the work that was to follow her return to Scotland. Free camera movements frame a portrait of the film-maker's mother, while a monologue recalls her words. Its techniques revealed not just the physical appearance of the subject, but the terms under which the relationship between subject and film-maker (and between film and viewer) are established.

Several hand-painted films were to follow, always painted onto 35mm stock, alongside a printed sound track "in which the beat of the music could be seen, could be 'read' as it were", then reduced to 16mm. In addition to providing intimate contact with the film material, this technique had economic advantages, as it was costly only in terms of time, that commodity the under-funded film-maker has in abundance.

For the next twenty years, Tait had her registered office in Rose Street, Edinburgh, but also lived in Orkney and in Sutherland, and found her subjects in these places and amongst people she knew. *The Big Sheep* (1966) was filmed while she was living in East Sutherland, "where handed-down memories of the Highland Clearances still affect people"; *On the Mountain* (1974) – subtitled *The Changing Face of Rose Street* – is a portrait of part of the street as it was in 1956, and as it had become in 1973. Her intention was to earn a living by making films in her own environment, like the small Italian companies which produced documentaries and other shorts chronicling the shift from a largely agricultural economy to a modern industrial one. In Italy this was seen as an important contribution to the changing social and political conditions that fostered a new film industry. In Britain, the situation was different. There was no support or backing for film proposals without assured financial returns. As 35mm production entailed substantial capital investment, the film-maker or

Biography

Born 1918, raised in Orkney. Qualified in medicine at Edinburgh University 1941; studied film at Centro Sperimentale di Cinematographia, Rome 1950–52. Set up a base in Edinburgh and worked between there and Orkney; moved permanently to Orkney in the mid 1970s. Author of poems and stories. Screenings include: National Film Theatre, London; Berlin Film Festival; Centre For Contemporary Art, Warsaw; Arsenal Kino, Berlin; Pacific Film Archives, San Francisco; Knokke le Zoute; Delhi; Riga. Tait was accorded a retrospective at the 1970 Edinburgh Film Festival and has been the subject of profiles on BBC and Channel Four.

Key works

Where I Am Is Here
1964, 35min, b&w, 16mm

Starting with a six-line script which just noted down a kind of event to occur, and recur, my aim was to construct a film with its own logic, its own correspondences within itself, its own echoes and rhymes and comparisons, all through close exploration of the everyday, the commonplace, in the city, Edinburgh, where I stayed at the time. The music, *Hilltop Pibroch*, by Hector MacAndrew, is a setting of my poem of that name, and is played on the fiddle by MacAndrew himself, and sung by music-hall artiste Lilane, (Lilian Gunn) who accompanies herself on the piano accordion. The seven titles within the film are: *complex; here and now; interlude; crocodile; come and see this; out of this world; the bravest boat.*

MT

On the Mountain
1974, 32min, b&w and colour, 16mm

The film is about the life of the street. In the old days, children played 'peever' on the pavement and 'chainy tig' in the back lane, and sang skipping songs. Nowadays, shoppers can amble along in the middle of the street. The smoke has gone, but seemingly the same rubbish-cart collects the refuse, and the same window-cleaner is washing the very same window as 16 years before, although the shop has a different name. In 1973 there were still some great gap sites, towards Princes St and George St, with beavering bulldozers in their depths. I have tried to catch some of this turmoil, while the ghosts of the budding footballers of 1956 kick a ball around on the cobbles.

MT

Aerial

1974, 4min, colour, 16mm

Elemental images, air, water (and snow), earth and fire (and smoke) all come into it. The track consists of a drawn-out musical sound, single piano notes and some natural sounds. The picture is a colour print from an original which is partly in colour and partly in black and white.

MT

Land Makar

1981, 32min, colour, 16mm

Makar is the Scots word for poet. Margaret Tait observes the daily work of the crofter, her neighbour Mary Graham Sinclair, and describes her as a "poet of the land." The land is shaped by the crofter, ploughed and furrowed, year after year. Her life is intrinsically tied up with the land. Tait's camera, often hand-held, follows her through the seasons, through ploughing and haymaking, and catches the tiny details of an environment inside and out, like the swans nesting and the glowing fire indoors. Tait, in conversation with Mary Graham Sinclair, says, "I see you creating the beauty of the land" and Mary replies, somewhat wryly "some beauty." Tait's film is not a documentary. There is no commentary and no mediation, the Orcadian dialogue between Tait and crofter gives the film its absolute authenticity. Tait sees the film as a series of canvases. She describes certain scenes as paintings "with things moving in them."

Tamara Krikorian *The Elusive Sign*

TOP:
LAND MAKAR
BOTTOM:
BLUE BLACK PERMANENT

organisation seeking some kind of autonomy inevitably turned to 16mm, which was already becoming a recognised professional medium.

The assembling of *Hugh MacDiarmid – A Portrait* (1964) was similar to that of *A Portrait of Ga*. The camerawork clearly establishes the proximity/intimacy of the camera/operator to the subject, matter-of-fact scenes of the elderly poet in his Lanarkshire home, with his books and pictures, writing at a table, hearing the wireless 'news', contrasting with his rich verse. He reads his poem *Somersault* while – instructed by the film-maker – he balances precariously on a pavement's edge: "I lo'e the stishie o' earth in space / Breengin by at a haliket pace." This informal and humorous treatment certainly dissociates the poet and his work from conventional celebrations of genius and transcendence.

Colour Poems (1974) combines the evocation of distant causes with the "sturdy present" of contemporary Orkney. Optimistic images of freshly painted steamers, and the bustle of re-constructive activity in full colour contrast distinctly with the grainy black and white and greys of *The Drift Back* (1956). Shortly after completing this group of films, news came that the house which had been an integral part of Tait's life since the age of eight, was required by the local council for re-development.

Material for *Place of Work* (1976) and its coda *Tailpiece* was collected in the six months prior to moving, and assembled in the new home. *Place of Work* was shot entirely from within the perimeter wall of the detached three-storey house, moving freely from house to garden, and back again; looking out into the street and over the town to the bay of Kirkwall beyond. Human presences blend with the wildlife and the familiarity of a domestic space. The images are rich and comfortingly familiar, as they were to the film-maker, but the film's time-span is disconcerting. The sometimes hand-held camera moves sparingly, with changes in location figuring through cuts between shots, but such cuts act ambiguously. The careful viewer is likely to detect the repetitive seeding and blooming of the ubiquitous poppies, in an extremely short time-span. Both the sense of time passing and the accumulation of resonances are dependent on the absorption of camera and tape recorder in this space: this former place of work, a place we become familiar with through Tait's eyes and ears.

Mike Leggett *(from unpublished notes based on a correspondence with Margaret Tait)*

Blue Black Permanent
1992, 86min, colour, 35mm

Shot on location in Edinburgh, on the coast near Edinburgh and in the Orkney Islands, set in the present, the 1950s and the 1930s, this is the story of Barbara, whose mother Greta, a poet, died when she was only nine. Its theme echoes Yeats' line about "the pain of all the partings gone and the partings yet to be." "Using the available actuality ..comes right through from my association with the era of neo-realism. So that, in *Blue Black Permanent* as well as in my work up to then, I'm looking at what's there, seeing things as they are, and seeing the people playing the characters as they are, as well as how the characters are supposed to be. That was my intention, anyway. So that there's a kind of double-take for the audience to enjoy. The film is full of grief – grief which just doesn't go away however much you may 'get over it'. Sorrow continuing, happiness continuing, both together and forever."

MT

John
Tappenden

Key works

Dawn Chorus

1987, 4min, 35mm/16mm

Using a unique working method, John Tappenden literally engraves film with light to create a *tour de force* of colour and movement. Abstract figures are minutely choreographed to correspond to the mounting crescendo of a dawn chorus, gradually reaching a brilliant climax of vibrant colours and fluttering shapes. *Dawn Chorus*, through its intricate structure and composition, captures bird song on film in a fusion of sound and light.

Die Heilige Geist (The Holy Ghost)

1992, 4min, silent, 35mm/16mm

Using simple geometrical shapes, the film explores the fascination of Mercury's visual brilliance.

John Tappenden's work continues the tradition of near-abstraction exemplified by the musically inspired, highly-coloured films of Oscar Fischinger and Mary-Ellen Bute. There are also affinities with Vincent Grenier in the tantalising manner in which images refer back to the real world whence they were drawn.

Dawn Chorus (1987) comprises a number of simple colour shapes – discs, crescents and angular lines – that seem to derive from the sun and related phenomena. The soundtrack of birdsong reinforces this view. On a formal level, though, the work is abstract since it has clearly been constructed by superimposing the images in various combinations in a contact printer. The viewer gradually realises that the shapes have not been generated from natural objects, but from cut-out mattes. The opacity of the mattes helps to mask areas of the film from light during superimposing, so that the colour of some images is modified whilst those concealed by the mattes remain unaffected. In this way Tappenden builds up the work, which reaches a high peak of complexity before gradually returning to the initial image of a single disc.

Die Heilige Geist (1992) continues in a similar vein except here the orchestration of the imagery is more deliberate, recalling the highly controlled character of Viking Eggeling's *Diagonal Symphony* (1923–24). Tappenden embodies many of the virtues of the musician in that he is able to generate substantial works from a small amount of initial material. The delicacy and unpredictability of his films belies the manner in which they were created.

Nicky Hamlyn

Biography

Born Camberley, Surrey, 1953. Studied Cardiff College of Art 1973–76; Royal College of Art 1976–79. Worked as a lighting technician on commercial productions and for art colleges. Workshop Organiser, London Film-makers' Co-op 1989–92. As lighting designer he has collaborated with the sculptor Jim Whiting on shows in Basel, Zurich, Cologne, Hamburg, Glasgow and Aarhus. Screenings include: National Film Theatre, London; Edinburgh Film Festival; Kommunales Kino, Nuremberg, Germany.

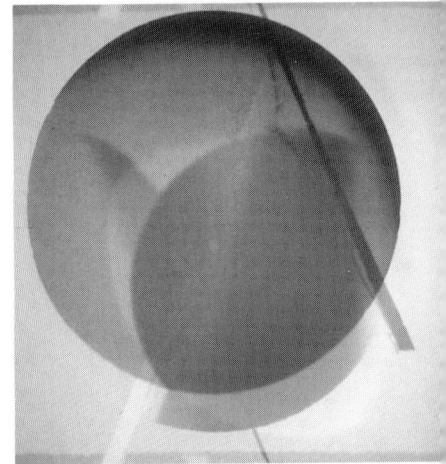

ABOVE:
DAWN CHORUS

Anna Thew

"**I** am taken up with language, word sound image, in discontinuity, as it actually is, to no purpose." Anna Thew

Anna Thew's films are concerned with the precise articulation of word, sound and image, colour, rhythm and music, an exacting ensemble which arrives at a particular vividness and vibrancy in *Cling Film* (1993).

Language is used as part of the filmic texture; quotations and voice-over in *Hilda was a Goodlooker* (1986), the dense collision of voices and texts in six different European languages in *Blurt Roll 2* (1987), bring language into focus as sign itself. This montage of intertextuality recalls Eliot's *The Waste Land*, the accumulation of "a head of broken images...these fragments I have shored against my ruins."

Narrative fragmentation contributes to this abundant intertextual play, a rich flow of verbal references is contained within an insistently visual framework. The fragments of overlapping voices and plangent piano in *Eros Erosion* (1990) and *Behind Closed Doors* (1988) are joined by glimpsed narratives and landscapes: the deposition of a naked body, pulled from the sea at night, the mourners and the moors, sunlit forests and golden sea.

Biography

Born Sheffield. Studied Italian and German at Manchester University; Painting at Chelsea School of Art, London. Began painting and art history research 1973, theatre and performance 1976, film-making 1979. Part-time lecturer in Film at St Martin's School of Art 1982-88. Currently Visiting Lecturer in Art History (Film) and Alternative Media. Panel member: *Innovation – Manchester Film Forum*, Manchester 1993; Media Minorities and World AIDS Day Conference, Meleg Film Festival, Budapest. Screenings include: Riga Film Festival; Cork Film Festival; Locarno Film Festival; Berlin Film Festival; Centre Georges Pompidou, Paris; Women's Film Festival, Minsk. Films have been included in touring programmes in Britain, USA and The Netherlands.

Hilda was a Goodlooker
1986, 60min, colour, 16mm

A selection of my mother's vivid recollections of childhood in Sheffield, from recordings made shortly before her unexpected death in 1983, are collaged on the soundtrack. Images relating to the narration and sound of her voice become changed and displaced through memory, and the process of making the film, to form an intricate web of associations. The substance of what is told becomes a quite separate event, a visual construction distinct from narrative, where images freewheel like snatched phrases dislocated in the listener's mind.

AT

Blurt Roll 2
1987, 10min, colour and b&w, 16mm

Black and white images of text and lettering are intercut with colour superimpositions of lipsticked mouths and flashes of a movie-maker mimicking sound sync speech, as a voice-over rapidly recites from untranslated literary text, Macchiavelli, Tzara, Brecht, Robbe-Grillet, Pirandello, Neruda etc., in a frenzied collage underlining the frustration and futility of language.

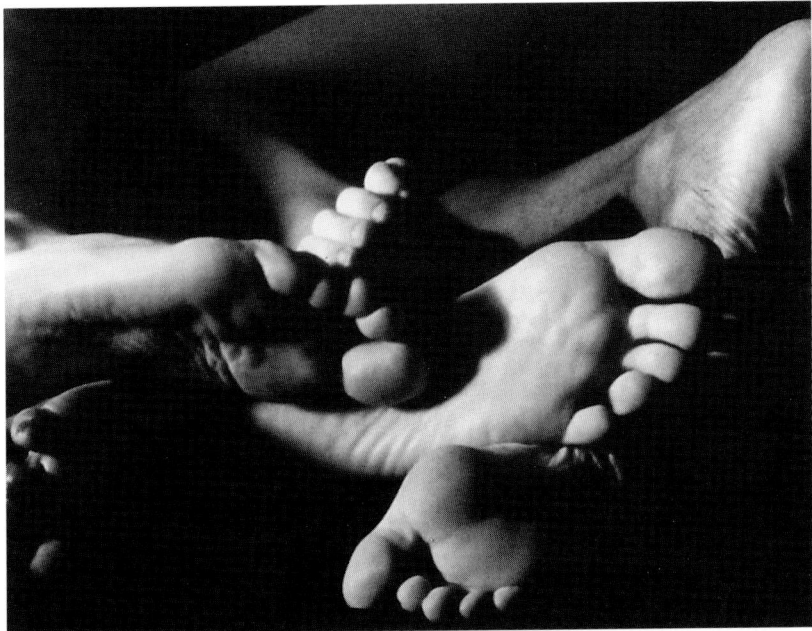

Eros Erosion

1990, 43min, colour, 16mm

An ancient elegy by Wei Wen Ti echoes the cold reality of hospital corridors. Through a flood of abstract and allegorical associations, the fugitive mind takes us, as in a fitful sleep, from scenes of northern landscape and industrial dereliction, to a distant, more mythical space; to the bad end of Naples and shuttered rooms. The murder in the dark alley mingles with giant ships and ropes and the open sea, as resonant sounds create an evocative undercurrent to the rich mosaic of images and spoken text. A film about desire and transience which shifts from personal experience to a wider perception of the fears and silences surrounding love, death, sexuality and AIDS.

AT

Cling Film

1993, 20min, colour, 16mm

A fast cut safe sex film which travels humorously and recklessly through a catalogue of sexual encounters and mishaps. Opening with sobering information from the World Health Organisation about the reality of heterosexual transmission of HIV and AIDS, the repressive, fear-mongering tactics of the media are shunned in favour of a direct attack on censorship and its bedmates, guilt and embarrassment. With clips of *Nosferatu* collapsing at the sight of a bit of rubber, and sections of the Indecent Displays Control Act graphically superimposed over the practical act of putting on a condom, Thew takes to the silent screen, making for some hilarious as well as confrontational episodes.

Cling Film offers the particular pleasure of finding formal precision in a work so 'rude'. There is an exactitude in the changing rhythms which shape its celebration of polymorphous sexuality. The film addresses persistent British sexual prurience and embarrassment – inhibitions in sexual relations which have become an actual threat to life in the age of AIDS. This subject invoked structures of censorship when the film was shown by Channel Four; but its redeeming public service message – inciting young people to practice safer sex, or say no – was probably the key factor which justified its transmission (with some more patently tumescent parts of the anatomy covered by black rectangles).

Rod Stoneman

Sarah
Turner

Sarah Turner's first film, *She Wanted Green Lawns* (1989), captures brilliantly the buoyancy of desire as it passes between two women, the mobile camera moving with the fluidity of a caress from the beloved's face to tall white lilies. Shot in sensuous black and white, the tonal quality of the film is carefully constructed to emphasise the beloved's glowing narcissism and the lover's darker hesitancy. The distracting nature of lust is conveyed by the fragmentary editing, offset with absurd irony by the seamless Carpenter's classic, *Close to You*. In one gloriously funny moment, the beloved looks to camera and blinks to the refrain, "golden starlight in your eyes of blue..." Set in a lesbian and gay bar, where looks and looking are exaggeratedly registered, desire is constructed as being so infectious that all the women line up to sashay to its rhythm with captivating joy.

In contrast, *One and the other time* (1990) is a complex account of claustrophobic, emotional merging. Shot in the dull blue tint of a bruise, a leafless branch shakes in the wind, while a row of kinetic silver balls knock each other back and forth, foreshadowing the violence between the narrator and her lover, told in a factual, deadpan tone. "We never went outside, it frightened both of us..." The effect of public restraint enforced by homophobia builds up with an insistent, drumming soundtrack until there is no space but the slow movement of reflected light on a white tiled ceiling. Beneath the sexual performance of the couple smoulders a social violence that is perceived as inadmissible. The branch moves more spasmodically and the balls hit each other more frantically as the narrator tells how she beat her lover. The disturbing power of the ending lies in its refusal to apologise or suggest a resolution.

Cherry Smyth

ABOVE:
**SHELLER SHARES
HER SECRET**

Biography

Born London, 1967. BA in Fine Art (Film and Video), St Martin's School of Art 1989; PG Dip, Slade School of Art 1991. Screenings include: Whitechapel Art Gallery, London; Feminale, Cologne; Hong Kong Lesbian and Gay Festival; European Media Art Festival, Osnabrück; Melbourne Lesbian and Gay Festival; New York Lesbian and Gay Festival; Innovation '93, Manchester. Member of Cinenova's Board of Directors 1987-91. Distribution Organiser, London Film-makers' Co-op 1991-93. Curator: LFMC/NFT monthly Avant-Garde Showcase, May 1992–August 1993; Co-curator with Ian Rashid, Hygiene and Hysteria: The Body Desired and the Body Debased, for LFMC. Visiting lecturer: Central St Martins, University of West of England.

A Tale Part Told
1991, 4min, colour, 16mm

A woman's voice-over narrates an elliptical story of personal loss, set to flickering shadows of a bicycle wheel's spokes and the distant, metallic whirr of the wheel's motion. A screen journey which is also a kinetic light sculpture, the film weaves a web of associations and fantasies.

Sheller Shares Her Secret
1994, 8min, b&w, 16mm

A woman's voice recounts a subversive tale, interweaving childhood defiance with suburban kitsch. A young girl's gaze interacts with the telling of the story, challenging the linearity of the interpretation of events. The film's axis is the tension between the abstract and the literal; an interrogation of the process of story telling.

Marion Urch's early work drew on feminist themes of representation and the effects of women's socialisation under patriarchy. Her *An Introduction to Womanhood in the Modern World* (1979) drew ironic parallels between the acquisition of acceptable feminine beauty and the consumption of a birthday cake in the shape of a young woman's face. Later works introduced themes of sexuality and its distortions throughout history – the burning of witches and the martyrdom and repression of women under Catholicism. Accessibility, lyricism and the evocative use of symbols have been a feature of Urch's work, most notably in here recent tapes exploring her Irish heritage.

The *Long Road* (1991) and the installation *Distant Drums* (1989) revolve around a series of journeys: remembered journeys from Ireland to England, and those of immigrants returning to their native shores. The Claddagh ring which was traditionally given to those leaving Ireland weaves in and out of personal testaments, an Irish dancer and a perpetually moving train. "Feelings of loss and exile" are evoked in this fusion of the personal and the political. We glimpse the conflicts of second generation immigrants who are searching for an identity, negotiating the opposing needs to integrate whilst simultaneously maintaining their cultural identity in a foreign land. Although Urch's work has always tackled political issues, she has rooted her political strategies in a strong visual tradition that allows moments of poetry and ambiguity to enrich her work. She continues to make videotapes and installations, but at the same time her energies have turned successfully addressing the wider audiences of radio broadcast.

Catherine Elwes

Out of the Ashes

1987, installation, 15min cycle, 5 monitors, 5 players

A row of monitors are arranged in a shop window. The symbolism of fire as it has evolved over the ages – in particular in relation to women's sexuality – is explored through images of the Sacred Heart, evocations of the burning of witches and references to the pagan goddess Vesta. Urch's installation conveys a sense of fire being symbolically stolen from women by men who have now associated it with destructive male ideals.

The Long Road

1991, 24min, colour, video

A young woman about to embark on a voyage to Ireland, reflects on the journey that brought her parents to England. As she speaks, a progressive layering of the sounds and images that circumscribe her Irish culture builds up and gradually enfolds her. Her reverie continues, shifting between the voices that shape her identity, and the links between her own experience and the historical and political roots of Irish emigration.

Born England, 1957; Irish citizen. BA in Fine Art, Brighton Polytechnic; MA in Environmental Media, Royal College of Art, London. Lecturer, Gwent College of Further Education 1985–87; Byam Shaw School of Art 1987–88; Distribution Manager, London Video Access 1987–89; Her fiction has appeared in the *Virago New Fiction Anthology*. *The Long Road* : LBC/GLA Radio Playwrights Festival Award in 1991. Her first novel *Dark Angels* will be published in 1995. Installations: Video Positive, Liverpool; Rochdale Art Gallery; Arts Council of Northern Ireland Gallery. Screenings include: Serpentine Gallery, London; "Women Live" National Film Theatre, London; Video Brasil, Rio de Janeiro 1986; Fukuaka Art Museum, Japan; MIMA, Melbourne, Australia 1990; Riga International Film Forum 1990; London Film Festival 1991.

ABOVE:
THE LONG ROAD

Chris
Welsby

Gradually [in the 19th century] a new scientific basis for observation of landscape was established, casting doubt on the old poetic and pastoral categories, challenging artists either to assimilate the new mode of observation or hold fast to their prodigious reveries [...]

It is in this tradition that Chris Welsby's landscape films must be placed. The invention of photography (near contemporary of meteorology and soon of course to become an essential instrument of it) and subsequently film, offered the artist new opportunities, new ways of integrating scientific observations with poetic impressions. It is worth remembering that 1878, the year in which Muybridge's famous photographs of Leland Stanford's horses were published in the *Scientific American*, was also the year in which Monet moved to Vétheuil, where he began to paint in series, mooring his boat on the Seine opposite the island of Saint-Martin to record the scene at every hour of the day and each season of the year. He had a slotted box made to hold a number of canvases, changing from one to the next throughout the day (seldom staying on one canvas for more than half an hour). Eventually he reached a point where he would have as many as one hundred canvases under way of a single subject. Muybridge's analytical photography provided a method of capturing the very sequence of instantaneities which came at the same time to obsess Monet.

It is significant that Muybridge's work was rediscovered by artists in the late 1960s, at the same time that 'land art' was developed. In Welsby's work we find Muybridge's analytic serialisation of time applied, through the mediation of meteorological investigation, to a revived non-painterly interest in landscape. Through control over the temporal sequence (time-lapse, shutter-speed) of

Biography

Born 1948, Exeter. BA in Fine Art, Chelsea School of Art, London 1973; HDip in Fine Art, Slade School of Art, London 1975. Co-founder and Lecturer in Fine Art Media Studies, Slade School of Art, London 1976–89. Assistant Professor of Film at the School for the Contemporary Arts, Simon Fraser University, Vancouver since 1989. Single person shows include: Pacific Cinematheque, Vancouver; Centre Georges Pompidou, Paris; Pacific Film Archives, Berkeley; Millennium, New York; Canyon Cinema, San Francisco; Pittsburgh Film-makers; Arsenal Kino, Berlin; Kommunales Kino, Frankfurt; Kommunales Kino, Stuttgart. Screenings include: Tate Gallery, London; National Film Theatre, London; Museum of Modern Art, Oxford; Centre of Contemporary Art, Warsaw; Stadtkino, Vienna. Films in the collections of: National Film and Television Archive; Tate Gallery, London; Centre Georges Pompidou, Paris; Archives du Film Experimental d'Avignon.

Seven Days
1974, 20min, colour, 16mm

The location for this film was by a small stream on the northern slopes of Mount Carningly in South West Wales. The seven days were shot consecutively and appear in that order. Each day starts at the time of local sunrise and ends at the time of local sunset. One frame was taken every ten seconds throughout the hours of daylight. The camera was mounted on an Equatorial Stand which is a piece of equipment used by astronomers to track the stars. In order to remain stationary in relation to the star field, the mounting is aligned with the Earth's axis and rotates about its own axis approximately once every 24 hours. Rotating at the same speed as the earth, the camera is always pointing at either its own shadow or at the sun...A rifle microphone was used to sample sound every two hours. These samples were later cut to correspond, both in space and time, to the image on the screen.

Stream Line
1976, 8min, colour, 16mm

Made on Mount Kinderscout in Derbyshire, the film is a continuous 'real time' tracking shot of a stream bed. The length of the track was ten yards. The camera was suspended in a motorised carriage running on steel cables three feet above the water surface. The sound of the water was recorded synchronously from the moving carriage.

RIGHT:
SKY LIGHT

Sky Light

1986, installation, 5 days, 6 x 16mm
projector installation, colour, silent

A gallery installation exploring the
perspective of a stormy sky, *Sky Light*
involves the introduction of a large element
of chance into the process of recording the
imagery. By frequently starting and stopping
the camera a large number of flash frames
were produced. The result is a six projector
film which not only represents a stormy
cloudscape but also represents the rotation
of the camera shutter and the process of
recording itself. The flash frames work in
opposition to the projected image of cloud
and blue sky illuminating the two
dimensional gallery wall in staccato rhythm
which varies continuously as the projectors
drift in and out of synch.

Sea Pictures

1992, 36min, colour, 16mm

A small child builds a sandcastle on a
deserted beach; in the background the
glass and steel towers of a city dominate
the horizon. A succession of landscape and
cityscape images weave dream-like patterns
on the screen. The reverie is broken by the
staccato bombardment of television images;
the child builds on, absorbed by the process
of creativity.

photography and the spatial orientation and movement of the camera and its
associated equipment (especially the mount and panning head), Welsby is able
to capture through the cinematographic process itself changes in the seasons,
the position of the sun, the force of the wind, the movement of the tides: a
whole range of natural and meteorological phenomena. Moreover, these
phenomena themselves are structured serially: we can envisage the sequence
of seasons, for instance, as being itself a sequence of temporal modules.

In addition, the techniques developed by Welsby made it possible for there
to be a direct ('indexical' in the semiotic terminology of Peirce) registration of
natural phenomena on film. Thus, camera movement could be determined by
wind-direction after a wind-vane was linked to the panning-head on the tripod.
Natural processes were no longer simply recorded from the outside, as object of
observation; they could be made to participate in the scheme of observation
itself. The point of observation was no longer the external 'Archimedean' point
of the artist's own consciousness. Furthermore, the automatic procedures of
science and technology, instead of being inflicted on nature in order to
dominate it, were directed by nature itself. The promise at the heart of Welsby's
work is that of a new type of relationship between science and nature and
between subject and object of observation.

Peter Wollen, *Chris Welsby Films/Photographs/Writings*

Jeremy
Welsh

Jeremy Welsh's long career spans and reflects many of the major trends in video art from the beginning of the 1980s to the present day. An awkward side-effect of this is the comparative difficulty one has in claiming any one piece (or style) of his work as 'representative' of the whole. Early tapes like *In Re Don Giovanni* (1982) reveal a penchant for Fluxus-inspired conceptualist conceits, often executed with the sort of exuberant flourish that mocked the stringent, serious-minded formalism of the first generation of British video art pioneers. Other pieces like *Reflecting* (1986) and *I.O.D* (1984) show a willingness to explore the emerging possibilities of video post-production, in which he patented a densely-layered (and, for the time, novel) form of electronic bricolage, that mirrored the enveloping, proliferating nature of the (post)modern mediascape. In contrast, works like *Echoes* (1988), while ranging across similar thematic terrain, hark back to Welsh's enduring interest in performance; often featuring a central to-camera monologue, or else deriving from an original live-art work.

These are multi-levelled, visually literate works whose sophisticated handling of complex, disparate material is hard to fault. Alongside them, however, exists a series of apparently minor-key pieces which sound a much more lyrical and reflective note. Tapes like *Factory* (1988), *Immemorial* (1989) and *Waterboy* (1990) turn on an elegant and lucid encapsulation of a potent, often poignant idea; their simplicity all the more affecting in its contrast to Welsh's high-powered yet occasionally over-elaborate 'major' works. This poetic sensibility similarly illuminates the installations *Forest Fires* (1983) and *Immemorial*, which are arguably Welsh's most resonant and satisfying works so far. Subtle, evocative and consummately-composed, they set the evanescent flicker of electronic images against the elemental pull of nature, memory and personal history, and with a rare clarity and force.

This pivotal relationship between the (fragile) natural environment and a rapidly encroaching media landscape continues in Welsh's recent Norwegian-

Biography

Born 1954, Gateshead. Studied at Trent Polytechnic and Goldsmiths College, London. Worked as Exhibitions Organiser for London Video Arts and as Video Curator for the Film and Video Umbrella. Lecturer at the Kunstakademiet, Trondheim, Norway since 1991. Recent screenings include: New Visions, Glasgow; Clermont Ferrand; Video Art Plastique, Herouville St Clair; Video Art Festival, Locarno; Oslo Film Festival. Exhibitions of video installations include: Museum of Modern Art, Oxford; Ikon Gallery, Birmingham; City Museum and Art Gallery, Stoke-On-Trent; Wolverhampton Art Gallery and Museum; National Museum of Contemporary Art, Oslo.

Key works

Echoes
1988, 25min, colour, video

Large sections of the tape offer up the artist – seated or standing – talking us through a series of interrelated stories, thoughts and personalised viewpoints, while various images – purposefully tacky computer graphics, the gleaming cityscape of New York, Welsh's child at play – illustrate and supplement the spoken word. Mixing footage from the live performance with other material, Welsh is once again exploring issues of memory, popular culture and experience. In returning to an often under used device – the performer telling stories or involved in simple actions – Welsh offers both spoken and visual examples to his own questions on such broad-ranging concerns as hyper reality, architecture and perception.

Nik Houghton, *Independent Media*

Immemorial
1989, installation, 3 monitors, 3 players

Immemorial is a 3 monitor installation, with each screen at the point of an equilateral triangle. Mirrored fronts to each monitor's plinth reflect partial images of the other two screens, and a crystal sphere in the centre of the triangle reflects complete, though miniature, images of all three screens. The images span the whole of the twentieth century, starting with the photographs and magic lantern slides from the artist's grandparents and ending with video images of the artist's young son.

Steven Bode

Talkbook

1988, performance with slide projection and
video

Talkbook is a live work combining
performance, video, slide projection and
sound. It is an exploration of the immediate
environment – developing ideas about the
transition from industrial to post-industrial
society. It might be said that if the
Industrial Revolution resulted in physical
damage to the environment through
pollution, then the Information Revolution
resulted in inflicting a kind of linguistic and
cultural damage through the ceaseless over-
production of signs and images.

JW

Forest Fires

1983, installation, 6-15 monitors, 1 player,
4 slide projectors, firewood, leaves

The present version of *Forest Fires* is
unambivalently concerned with the ever-
present threat of ecological disaster. The
installation uses two of the media that
deliver to us images of the ravaged natural
environment – video and photography –
and is concerned with the ambiguities
of the Media's position. While alerting us to
the dangers, it is nonetheless inescapably
implicated in the processes of destruction.
The work is not only concerned with 'the
forest' as a generalised concept, but with
those specific forests that are disappearing
or have already gone. Forests killed by
pollution in Eastern Europe or by human
expansion in the Amazon. And these
realities juxtaposed with an older view
of 'the forest' as a site of magical, mystical
or supernatural experience – an ancient
construction, buried deep in our collective
consciousness, but now almost burned away
by the searing heat of 'progress'.

produced work. If anything, the preoccupation is heightened – which may be
attributed to the proximity of breathtaking scenery and to Welsh's improved
access to an array of post-production technology. The twin poles of nature and
technology animate installations like *Flow II Flow* (1993) and the tape trilogy
Closing In (1991), *WTB* (1992) and *Pause* (1993). A common enough motif, but
here rendered with the assurance and élan that suggests that this particular video
art veteran still has ideas and energy to burn.

Steven Bode

ABOVE:
ECHOES

201

Pier
Wilkie

Pier Wilkie's films trace – as they unravel – the genre of the personal history project. In *Myths and Legends I & II* (1988 and 1989), she creates a 'past' by collecting fragments of stories and untrustworthy memories. The films oscillate between drawing on documentary traditions to tell these histories and blasting the notion of documentary as an arbiter of truth. In *How Wilkie Discovered England* (1993) she goes further, and dramatises moments of her father's migration from Barbados to England, using a trio of actors who step in and out of their enactment of her father's dreams and fantasies as a young man. Wilkie herself is an absent presence in the film: interviewing the actors in and out of character, as well as her real father. As a result, the film becomes both a construction and deconstruction of her take on his story. (Is she the Wilkie named in the title of the film?)

Wilkie's work is archaeological in essence. With affectionate humour, formal invention and thoughtfulness she constructs a testament to the resilience and achievements of many communities and generations of immigrants to Britain. Yet there is very little in the way of recorded history to provide her with help in telling her (father's) story. All she has to go on are bits and pieces, from parental cultural baggage, Hollywood films and television, photographs and music, all of which gain among the children of immigrants an iconic dimension. Throughout *How Wilkie Discovered England*, she invokes the spectre of Hollywood Westerns, imagining her father arriving in London to face a new frontier – the West – unknown to him except from what he has gleaned from popular cinema and his love of cricket. But in the end, the act of tracing, taking place in the present, is more important than the point of contact with any real or imagined past. With their allusions to memory and the construction of histories, Wilkie's films serve to make sense of living in Britain today.

Ian Iqbal Rashid

Key works

How Wilkie Discovered England
1993, 12min, colour, 16mm

We had just come back from seeing *Othello*. As we sat in 'double history', studying another episode in Europe's Empire-building across the globe, the teacher turned to us and told us that Olivier has given a brilliant performance in the film (despite leaving boot-black all over Maggie Smith's Desdemona on her death bed). Not because he had been compelling as a man consumed by jealousy, but because he had been able to play a black man. And that was a tremendously difficult feat. "isn't that so?" she asked, turning to me for confirmation. This begins the story of one man, among many men and women who were pioneers, conquering hostile territory. How the West (London) was won – without killing the natives.

PW

ABOVE:
**HOW WILKIE
DISCOVERED
ENGLAND**

Biography

Born London, 1964. BA in Film, 1985; Post-Graduate Diploma in Film and Television, University of Westminster 1989. Screenings include the London Film Festival; Feminale, Cologne; Frankfurt Filmmuseum; Tate Gallery, London; True Colours Festival, Euclid Cinema, Toronto; Commonwealth Games Film and Video Festival, Victoria, Canada. *How Wilkie Discovered England*: ICA Biennial: 'What You See is What You Get'. Worked as Distribution Organiser, London Film-makers' Co-op 1986-89; film tutor, Birkbeck College, London; theatre and radio director.

O riginally trained as a painter, Richard Wright is an electronic media artist who presents his work in the form of video animations and installations. *Corpus* (1992), which was produced over two summers Wright spent as a visiting artist at the School of Visual Arts, New York, explores the area between the organic and the inorganic, the sensual body and 'artificial life', the living computer and dead nature. Wright produces much of his own software and is familiar with the current state of research in computer graphics – a subject he teaches at various institutions. He also writes articles and essays about computer imagery in science and art for publications such as *Mediamatic* and exhibition catalogues for the ACM SIGGRAPH art shows. His latest project, *Heliocentrum* (1995), made collaboratively with Jason White, is a computer animation about Louis XIV and the technology of the imagination.

Richard Wright

Corpus

1992, 6min, colour, video

The word 'corpus' brings together ideas of the body and the corpse, and the animated un-life of computing machinery, born of a 'corpus' of knowledge. The body is animated in a subtly unnatural manner, relentlessly cycling through the same motions, like a dead frog twitching under electric shocks in an eighteenth century experiment. The animation is structured to seduce the viewer into studying the rich surfaces - to the point at which the digital image fragments into its constituent pixels, and so denies gratification of the desire to analyse and attain knowledge through vision.

RW

Heliocentrum

1995, 18min, colour, video
(made with Jason White)

Heliocentrum uses some aspects of the life and times of Louis XIV at his residence at Versailles to construct a fantastic narrative of power and narcissism using computer imaging. Evoking the operation of centralised power through technology, computer animation is used to reflect contemporary technologies such as virtual reality that purport to fulfil egocentric fantasies. The Sun King's Versailles is represented as a gigantic head, situated at the point of convergence of the roads and buildings in the landscape of the kingdom; once entered, its interior is represented as a galaxy of technologically enhanced marvels and distractions, expressed through a mixture of fantastic baroque decoration and protoplasmic video effects.

RW

Born Barnet, 1963. BA in Fine Art, Winchester School of Art 1986; MA in Computing In Design 1988. Research Fellow, IBM Scientific Centre 1986; part-time Lecturer in Computer Graphics, City of London Polytechnic 1991; Visiting Artist, School for Visual Arts, New York, summer 1991 and 1992; currently Lecturer in Computer Graphics, London Guildhall University. Writes much of his own software. Writer of articles for books and magazines, including *Mediamatic*. Screenings include: Berlin Videofest; SIGGRAPH '91 Art and Design Show, Las Vegas; Cardiff International Animation Festival. Installation exhibitions include: Kunstwerke, Berlin; Arnolfini Gallery, Bristol; Video Positive, Liverpool.

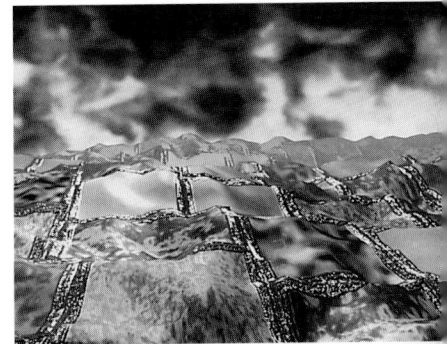

ABOVE:
HELIOCENTRUM

Stewart **Wilson**

Observations of daily life are often my starting point. The passage of people in public places, children at a museum, a plume of smoke from a factory chimney. Isolated incidents evidencing transition between place, present and past, material state. Film and video allow the direct use of these observations, changing the emphasis of what we often consider as background or unconscious habit to a position of focus.

Shadows pass, light and colour ignite in darkness – recordings of actual events. Momentary truths abstracted, compiled, re-presented. Mood dictated by architectural constraints. Emotion influenced by environmental cues. I am interested in how we position ourselves in society and physically experience the world through contradictions. Distance and proximity, gentleness and violence, growth and decay.

Senses, memory, information technologies compete and meld. Hierarchies form and disband, fleeting connections are made. The singular image/sound is given an instant of independence and clarity before being subsumed within the mass; co-opted by metaphor and meaning.

Stewart Wilson

Biography

Born 1961, Bonnybridge, Scotland. Engineering apprenticeship 1977–81; BA in Sculpture, Wimbledon School of Art 1988; MA in Sculpture, Royal College of Art, London 1990. Exhibitions of installations include: London Film Festival in conjunction with Camden Arts & Entertainment; Riverside Studios Gallery, London; Peacock Artspace, Aberdeen; Cambridge Darkroom; Harris Museum and Art Gallery, Preston; Colchester Institute.

Key works

Census

1990, installation, 15min cycle, colour, 9 monitors, 9 players

Nine domestic video monitors, varying in size, are placed within the space at specific heights and distances; one suspended at ceiling height, others obscured from certain viewpoints. A discrete fifteen minute video sequence of a gridded pavement skylight, as seen from an underground location, has been compiled for each monitor. The screen images consist of views of an empty grid or silhouetted figures being monitored from below as they pass across the grid, alone or in groups. The monitor speakers are used as a spatial nine-track mixer – moving sound around the space in a directional manner, drawing attention to, or undermining visual screen crossings. Footsteps, breathing, isolated industrial noise, water and an audible counting mechanism are used singly or in subtle combinations.

"Stand still or pass on, enter or stay outside. Have or have not. This exposed and displayed machine-play is not 1984 but 1990s London, Britain. There is a metaphor at work here, another language, another set of questions. These TVs – so often watched – are the watchers now, looking back, putting us under surveillance. Cameras have made a census, and now this juxtaposition does likewise"

Nigel Rolfe

Burner

1993, installation, 26min cycle, colour,
silent, 42 monitors, 42 players

Mesmeric, elusive images of smoke and
burning flicker across the screens. Sporadic
chain reactions suggest themselves through
illusions of growth and decay, building to
a unified upward rush of billowing smoke,
purposeful, controlled, yet seemingly
exploding the confines of the structure
itself. Confounding our desire for narrative
closure, the sequence concludes in disunity,
with powder spiralling downwards through
the screens, casting a stillness which
envelopes the entire structure in emptiness.
Imagining a context in which to view
the abstract form, a natural history film,
a culture dish, organic matter, fireworks;
audiences come to 'see' relationships
between images.

Anna Douglas

Stewart Wilson's use of domestic audio-
visual equipment implies 'living room'
technology on a huge scale. Forty-two
families watching, flicking from channel
to channel; smoke sequences to ashes.
But here, the remote control is out of
our control as we are guided through five
distinct yet unfamiliar burning sequences;
smoulder, tear, smoke, column, ash...
It is the firelessness of *Burner* which is so
intriguing. The lack of flame, but the
presence of fire's other embodiments, that
of smoke and ashes, contradicts popular
notions of fire and burning.

Lesley Hynes

Joanna
Woodward

I made my first film, *The Grid* (1980), while at art school, and combined in it sculptural ideas and live action. After I left art school my paintings began to be shown in London, and in 1983 I was invited to create a series of works for a touring exhibition which re-examined the myth of Pandora – the beautiful goddess who brought evil into the world when she opened her box. However, I was frustrated because my images didn't move and I was determined to make another film, so I made *The Poet of Half Past Three* (1984) by scratching directly onto the film. I was pleased with this because it was painterly and explored movement. I then started making films using a cheap Super8 camera. Looking back, I feel that being involved with the music and fashion of the late 1970s has influenced my work. During that period creativity was very healthy, and was more about energy and ideas and not expensive production values, and I am still keen to keep a rawness in my work.

My first narrative film, *The Hump Back Angel* (1985), was also my first film on the theme of female sexuality – an ongoing interest in my work. *The Brooch Pin and the Sinful Clasp* (1989) explores misconceptions about female sexuality from an imaginary male point of view, which makes for a wry sense of humour, especially because the film is made by a woman. *The Weatherhouse* (1991), a collaboration with the I.O.U Theatre Company commissioned by BBC Bristol, explores the consequences of a relationship that is fixed into a set pattern. The response of the weatherhouse to rain and sun is used symbolically; live

Biography

Born Taplow, 1958. Studied Film at the National Film and Television School 1985–88. Screenings include: Tate Gallery, London; Zagreb Animation Festival; ICA, London; Kettle's Yard, Cambridge; London Film Festival. *The Brooch Pin and the Sinful Clasp*: ICA Biennial: 'Between Imagination and Reality'. Films have been broadcast on Channel Four and the BBC; retrospectives at Leeds and Stuttgart film festivals (1991–92). Paintings have been included in many open exhibitions in Britain and models for the films were the subject of a solo exhibition at the City Gallery, Leicester.

The Hump Back Angel
1985, 13min, colour, 16mm

A story about a king who gets a woman pregnant and then eats the baby. At first glance *The Hump Back Angel* appears to be a conventional animated film of a traditional fairy tale; until one realises that the story has made two or three unexpected leaps and that the animation itself often flies into different perspectives and drawing styles. Even the happy ending is pleasantly rearranged. Originally shot on Super8 and then blown up to 16mm, this film must have been very laborious to make (especially as Super8 cameras are not designed for accurate animation), it's an astonishing technical feat.

Cordelia Swann

The Brooch Pin and the Sinful Clasp
1989, 18min, colour, 35mm

An early morning pedestrian sees a ballerina dancing at the top of a tower block. He is convinced she is trying to attract his attention, so he sets out to become acquainted with her. His obsessive journey to find her takes him into a vivid world in the tower block, where the loneliness of the inhabitants is masked by their frivolity, and an overwhelming desire for intimacy. He ends up in a lurid restaurant at the top of the tower where he finds out the ballerina was not the beauty he had imagined, but bait used by the cook so that she can include him in her elaborate recipe.

The Weatherhouse

1991, 10min, colour, 16mm

Joanna Woodward's drama tells the story of a couple in a weatherhouse torn between love and duty. Representing rain, the man is a melancholy figure with a Max Wall hairstyle, forever carrying his brolly. Sunshine is represented by a doll-like woman in a yellow dress with big red spots. As the weather changes, one must be ready to leave the other to stand watch outside. It is not the best recipe for domestic harmony. Woodward opens up the situation by sending the man across a lake on a special mission to get a wedding ring, leaving the woman to sit and knit. The staging which mixes puppets with real actors, is ingenious and the outcome unexpected.

The Times

Sawdust for Brains and the Key of Wisdom

1993, 11min, colour, 16mm

Imagine you are being twitched by some god-like character from elsewhere, in a world where you have no control over your destiny. The conveyer belts of time carry you into a meaningless landscape of pre-ordained events. You are prey to your fears and desires which never remain consistent, you are constantly changing, and are never the same person for long.

JW

A colourful yet sinister mix of painting, puppets and real people.

Gill Edwards

action events inside the house alternate with a fantasy world outside, portrayed in animation.

I was commissioned by Channel Four to make *Sawdust for Brains and the Key of Wisdom* (1993), which features the extraordinary actress Moya Brady and mixes animation and live action. One of the things the film deals with is the idea that we may have a destiny that has been marked out for us, and there may be no way to escape the events that await us in our lives. This coincides with my increasing fascination with the remarkable work of clairvoyants. I am concentrating on my writing as I want to produce more substantial works, and am currently working on an opera, *The Snow Queen* and a feature film, *The Kiss of Life*.

Joanna Woodward

ABOVE:
SAWDUST FOR BRAINS

List of
Works

Works are colour/sound except where stated, main sources of funding are in brackets.

MINEO AAYAMAGUCHI

Video:

There-Then 1982, 30min, b/w
Landscape 1983, 15min (Air Gallery/LVA)
Pictura 1983, 8min
Feet 1983, 10min
Inner Colour 1984, 15min (AC)
Outer Colour 1985, 10min
Beyond Colour 1986, 14min
Kaleidoscope 1988, 10min
(AC/GLA/ICA/LVA)
Primary Contrasting Elements 1993, 1min
(AC/BBC)

Installation:

Landscape 1983, silent, 2 monitors, 2 video
cameras (Air Gallery/LVA)
Beyond Colour 1986, 30min, 9 monitors,
2 players (Air Gallery/LVA)
Light/Water 1986, 14min, 10 monitors,
2 players (with Jeremy Welsh)
Kaleidoscope 1988, 10min, 25 monitors,
3 players, ICA London (AC/GLAA/ICA/LVA)
Phosphor 1989, 4min, 4 monitors, 1 player
(NRLA)
Obelisk 1992, 8min, silent, 4 monitors,
1 player (AC/Artangel Trust/LVA)
Foot 1992, 10min, 2 monitors, 1 player
Distribution: LEA

JOHN ADAMS

Video:

Stories 1981, 13min (NA)
Bob & Jill Part 2 1982, 9min (AC)
Sensible Shoes 1983, 11min (NA)
Intellectual Properties 1985, 60min,
(NA/Arts & Humanities Council
Massachusettts)
**It Seems Strange But It's Almost
Dinner Time, Margaret** 1986, 1min (NA)
We Are the Country, This Is the Man
1987, 5min (Arts & Humanities Council
Massachusettts)
Jamaica Plain 1991, 75min (Arts &
Humanities Council Massachusettts)
Goldfish Memoirs 1993, 26min (NA)
Railway Lines 1995, CD-Rom

Installation:

Reflections 1978, b/w, 2 monitors, 2 players,
ARP Synthesiser, tinted plexiglass
Kick in the Eye 1979, 3 monitors (1 modified
to collapse the image to a line), 2 players, video
switcher, Biddock Farm Tyne & Wear

Goldfish Memoirs & the Think Tank 1993,
2 monitors, 2 players, plexiglass tank, 1000
litres oil, air pump (NA)
Railway Lines 1995, video projector,
computer, railway station
Distribution: LEA

JOHN AKOMFRAH

Film and video:

Handsworth Songs 1986, 58min, 16mm
Testament 1988, 80min, 16mm (Ch4)
A Touch of the Tar Brush 1991, 40min,
video (BBC)
Who Needs a Heart 1991, 80min, 16mm
(Ch4/ZDF)
Seven Songs for Malcolm X 1993, 52min,
16mm (Ch4)
Lush Life 1995, 40min, 16mm (Granada)
Distribution: BFI, Black Audio Film Collective

DAVID ANDERSON

Film:

Dreamland Express 1982, 14min, 35mm
(NFTS)
Dreamless Sleep 1986, 9min, b/w, 35mm
(Ch4)
Deadsy 1989, 5min, 35mm (Ch4)
Door 1990, 5min, 35mm (Ch4)
In the Time of Angels 1994, 15min, 35mm
(Ch4)

Key Advertising Works:

Royal Bank: Business Animal 1987
Royal Bank: Portcullis 1987
MotorFair 1988
Purdeys 1991
McEwans 1991
Access: Knobs 1993
Access: Cinema 1993
Distribution: BFI

REECE AUGUISTE

Film:

Twilight City 1989, 52min, 16mm (Ch4)
Mysteries of July 1991, 52min, 16mm (Ch4)
Distribution: Black Audio Film Collective,
Jane Balfour Films

GEORGE BARBER

Film and video:

The Truth About John and Greenwich
1980, 20min, S8mm
Divorce 1981, 20min, S8mm (AC)
The Fruits of Holiday 1982, 16min, video
Bob Sewell's Story 1983, 5min, video

Desert Airport 1984, 20min, video
Scratch Free State 1984, 5min, video
Tilt 1984, 5min, video
Groove Jumping 1984, 4min, video
Um Um Um Branson Um 1984, 4min, video
(BBC)
Yes Frank No Smoke 1985, 5min, video
Absence of Satan 1985, 5min, video
Taxi Driver II 1987, 9min, video (BFI/Ch4)
The Venetian Ghost 1989, 12min, video
(BFI/Ch4)
Desperately Seeking Dave 1990, 15min,
video (AC)
Viking 1990, 5min, video (BBC)
1001 Colours Andy Never Thought Of
1991, 5min, video
Search for Dave Goes On 1991, 3min,
video
Jazzland 1992, 4min, video
Curtain Trip 1993, 4min, video
Passing Ship 1994, 6min, video
Burt Circus 1994, loop, video
Distribution: LEA

BREDA BEBAN & HRVOJE HORVATIC

Film and video:

Plan 1985, 7min, video (Film Val Zagreb)
Meta 1986, 16min, video (Film Val Zagreb)
She, Four Things 1986, 20min, video
(TV Beograd)
Bless My Hands 1986, 11min, video
(Film Val Zagreb)
**All Our Secrets Are Contained in an
Image** 1987, 10min, video (TV Skopje)
Cherishing the Heart 1987, 8min, b/w
(TV Sarajevo)
Taking on a Name 1987, 25min, video
(TV Skopje)
Terirem 1988, 13min, video (Film Val Zagreb)
**For You in Me and Me in Them To Be
One** 1988, 30min, video (Huzjan Film &
Video/TV Beograd)
Geography 1989, 9min, video (TV Skopje)
For Tara 1991, 4min, video (Studio 5
Zagreb/Momentum London))
The Lifeline Letter 1992, 1min, video
(AC/BBC)
The Left Hand Should Know 1992, 43min,
video (AC/Ch4/Ontario AC/Banff Centre)
Absence 1994, 15min, video (AC/Ontario
AC)
Irina Is Not Herself Anymore 1995,
4½min, 35mm (Carlton/LAB/LPF)

Installation:

House 1989, 2 monitors, 2 players, lighting, Galerija PM Zagreb (Film Val Zagreb)

Geography 1990, 1 projector, 1 player, Galerija Karas Zagreb (Zagrebacki Salon)

Geography 2, Life Is Very Precious Even Right Now 1991, 3 monitors, 3 players, Tate Gallery Liverpool (Video Positive)

The Shape of Pain 1992, 1 projector, 1 player, Art Gallery of New South Wales Sydney (Global Video)

Before the Kiss 1993, 3 projectors, 1 player, 2 cameras, 3 large translucent screens, Prema Arts Centre Uley Gloucestershire (AC)
Distribution: FVU, LEA

SIMON BIGGS

Video:

Ten Computer Pieces 1981, 60min, silent

Three Computer Pieces 1982, 20min, silent

Le Desir (Prisoners) 1987, 8min (Video Nu Video Centrum Stockholm)

A New Life 1989, 4min

The Wheel 1989, 1½min, silent

The Temptation of St Anthony 1990, 4½min

The Rosenberg Variations 1991, 2min

Pandaemonium 1992, 4½min

Voices 1993, 5½min

Book of Shadows 1995, CD-Rom

Installation:

The Reproductive System 1983, multi media, silent, Adelaide Festival of Arts (South Australian Dept. for the Arts)

Recombinant Figure 1984, computer, video, multi-media, silent, Avago Gallery Sydney

Torso 1985, multi-media, video, 5 channel computer, silent, Roslyn Oxley Gallery Sydney

Recombinant Figure Extended 1986, video, multi-media, silent, Adelaide Festival of Arts

Golem 1988, multi-media, 12 channel sound European Media Art Festival Osnabrück

Alchemy 1990, 2 channel interactive laser-disc, silent, Rijksmuseum Twenthe Enschede The Netherlands

On Sight 1991, interactive video projection installation, silent, Academy Minerva Groningen The Netherlands (Academic Hospital Groningen)

Solitary 1992, interactive video projection, b/w, silent, Gallery Otsu Helsinki

Heaven 1992, interactive video projection, silent, European Media Art Festival Osnabrück

Portrait of a Young Man 1993, interactive video projection, silent, Brick Lane Studio London

Shadows 1993, interactive video projection, b/w, silent, Centre for Contemporary Art Warsaw

Book of Shadows 1993, interactive multi-media, b/w, multi-channel sound

The Soft Room 1994, interactive video projection, multi-channel sound, performance with 'Acting Up', Stoke Newington Hall London (AC)

The Living Room 1994, interactive video projection, multi-channel sound, Brick Lane Studio London (AC)
Distribution: LEA

IAN BOURN

Film and video:

Lenny's Documentary 1978, 45min, b/w, video

Wedding Speech 1978, 10min, b/w, video

Mayday 1979, 30min, video

From the Junkyard 1979, 25min, b/w, video

B.29 (Three Nights In) 1979, 20min, b/w, video

Making Yourself at Home 1981, 30min, S8mm

The End of the World 1982, 10min, video (AC/Sheffield City Poly)

The Last Lark 1983, 8min, b/w, S8mm

Interference/Heatwave 1983, 30min, 16mm (AC/Sheffield City Poly)

Tips for Travelling Salesmen 1987, 30min, video (AC)

What Is He Doing Now 1988, 10min, 16mm

Sick as a Dog 1989, 30min, video (AC/Ch4)

Out of It 1991, 1min, video (AC/BBC)

Breathing Days 1992, 14min, video (GLAA)
Distribution: LEA
see also: Housewatch

IAN BREAKWELL

Film:

Sheet 1970, 21min, b/w, 16mm (with Mike Leggett)

Nine Jokes 1971, 12min, b/w, 16mm

Growth 1972, 9min, b/w, 16mm

Repertory 1973, 10min, 16mm (AC)

The Journey 1975, 30min, 16mm (AC)

The Institution 1978, 50min, 16mm (AC)

The News 1980, 11min, video (Carlisle Museum/Aidavision)

In the Home 1980, 10min, video (Carlisle Museum/Aidavision)

The Sermon 1983, 15min, video

Auditorium 1993, 32min, video (with Ron Geesin) (AC)

As writer/presenter/co-editor:

The Continuous Diary 1977, 13min, (dir Alan Yentob) (BBC)

Ian Breakwell's Continuous Diary 1984, 118min (21 programmes of 3–11min) (Ch4)

Ian Breakwell's Xmas Diary 1984, 65min (8 programmes of 3–11min) (Ch4)

Public Face, Private Eye 1988, 57min (5 programmes of 3–11min) (Ch4)

Seeing in the Dark 1990, 20min, (dir Vanessa Engel) (BBC)

Mask to Mask 1994, 40min (dir Phil Lewis) (HTV)
Distribution: Annalogue, Auditorium, LEA, LFMC, Ian Breakwell, 121 Albion Rd, London N16 9PL

PAUL BUSH

Film and video:

The Cow's Drama 1984, 38min, b/w, 16mm

O Quanta Qualia (So Many, So Magnificent) 1987, 45min, 16mm

Forgetting 1990, 33min, 16mm

Lost Images 1990, 1min, video (2 versions) (AC/BBC)

Lake of Dreams 1991, 13min, 16mm (GLA)

His Comedy 1994, 8min, 35mm (AC/Ch4)

Still Life with Small Cup 1995, 3min, 35mm (Carlton/LAB/LPF)

The Rumour of Truth 1995, 30min, 16mm (AC/Ch4)
Distribution: BFI, LEA, LFMC

JOHN BUTLER

Video:

World Peace Thru Free Trade 1989, 4min

Leisure Society 1990, 5min

Lovesigns 1991, 4min

First World Boutique 1992, 3min

The City Is No Longer Safe 1994, 2min

Wave of Rage 1994, 4min

Installation:

Dream of Freedom 1994, interactive (with Paul Butler), Tramway Glasgow; Bluecoat Liverpool; Camerawork London. (Tramway)

Karneval 1996, interactive (Tramway)
Distribution: LEA

NICK COLLINS

Film and video:

Horden Beach 1977, 4min, b/w, silent, 16mm

After the Music by François Couperin: Les Baricades Mystérieuses 1979, 7min, b/w, 16mm

Cornish Winter Reeds and Skies 1980, 7min, b/w, silent, 16mm (AC)

Journeys 1982, 5min, b/w, 16mm

Self-portrait 1983, 4min, silent, 16mm

Passage 1983, 13min, b/w, 16mm (AC)

Time at Night 1984, 6min, 16mm

Deptford Creek 1985, 13min, silent, 16mm (AC)

Looking In and Out (A Winter Diary) 1986, 9min, b/w, 16mm (AC)

Valletta 1986, 2½min, silent, 16mm

Greenwich Park 1986, 2½min, silent, 16mm

Sanday 1988, 16min, 16mm (AC)

Romney Marsh 1989, 1min, b/w, silent, 16mm

Views From a City 1992, 19min, 16mm (AC/Ch4)

Bureau de Change 1992, 11min, 16mm (with Rose Finn-Kelcey) (AC)

Steam Installation 1993, 4min, video (with Rose Finn-Kelcey)
Distribution: LFMC

SUSAN COLLINS

Video:

Would You Like To Be Mother? 1987, 3min

Going for Goldfish 1990, 2min (with Julie Myers) (AC/FVU/Cornerhouse Manchester)

Coming Attractions 1991, 2min

Installation:

Camouflage 1992, 3 x 16mm loop projectors, back projection (Illinois Art Gallery, Chicago).

Introductory Exchanges 1993, 2 video projectors, 2 players, 8 personal stereos, speakers, infra-red sensors, 'River Crossings Festival' Woolwich Foot Tunnel London(Camerawork)

Handle With Care 1993, 3 slide projectors, 1 video projector, laserdisc player, robot with torch, 6 personal stereos, speakers (Museum of Science & Industry Manchester)

Litter 1994, video projector, computer, infra-red sensor, speakers, Bluecoat Gallery Liverpool (AC)

Pedestrian Gestures 1994, 3 computers, 3 video projectors, speakers, infra-red sensors, Paragon Station Hull (AC/HTBA)

AudioZone 1994, 3 computers, 3 video projectors, 3 infra-red sensors, 5 CD players, 8 infra-red transmitter/headphones, 'V-topia Tramway' Glasgow (FVU/Moviola/Tramway)
Distribution: Moviola, HTBA

LEI COX

Video:

The Breakfast Trilogy (57 Varieties, Eat or Be, Fulcrum) 1986, 9min

Lighthead 1987, 4½min

Torso 1988, 3min

Fish Observation 1988, 3min

The Parallel 1988, 3min

Lei Can Fly 1988, 1min

Fusion and the Electrical Prowess 1989, 4½min

Three Unanswered Questions 1990, 8min

The Leaning 1992, 2min

The Moaning 1992, 1min

Insect 1993, 1½min

Installation:

The Size of Things 1988, 20min, 7 monitors, 7 players, stereo, Sheffield Media Show

The Untitled the Observed 1988, 3min cycle, 3 monitors, 3 players, Third Eye Centre, Glasgow

Fusion and the Electrical Prowess 1989, 9min cycle, stereo mix, 7 monitors, 7 players, AVE, Arnheim

Giant 1990, 60min, 36 monitors, 6 players, with live musicians, stage set for dancers, Tramway, Glasgow (19:4:90)

Magnification Maximus 1991, 6min cycle, 4–16 monitors, 4 players, surround sound, Tate Liverpool (Video Positive/AC/SAC)

The Sufferance 1993, 3min cycle, 7 monitors, 7 players, Bluecoat Liverpool (Video Positive/AC/SAC)

Flower Field 1995, 3 video projectors, 3 players, 6 electronic flowers, 2 computers (Video Positive/AC/SAC)
Distribution: LEA, Moviola

MICHAEL CURRAN

Video:

The Small Boy's Dream 1991, 2½min, b/w

Double 1993, 2½min

Disclaimer 1993, 5min

Echo 1993, 7min

Mutter 1993, 5min

Translation 1993

Larynx 1993, 5½min

L'Heure Autosexuelle 1994, 6min

Amami Se Vuoi 1994, 4min

Agalma 1994, 5min

Les Souffrance du Dubbing 1994, 6½min

Portfolio 1994, 8min

All My Little Ducks 1994, 7min b/w

Installation:

Panopticon 1991, 4 monitors

Untitled (skipping) 1994, 1 monitor
Distribution: FVU, LEA

NINA DANINO

Film:

First Memory 1980, 30min, two screen, tape-slide, S8mm

First Memory 1981, 20min, 16mm

Close to Home 1985, 28min, b/w, 16mm (AC)

Stabat Mater 1990, 8min, 16mm (AC)

"Now I am yours" 1993, 30min, 16mm (AC/Ch4)

Temenos 1995, 30min, 16mm (LPF/LFVDA)
Distribution: LEA, LFMC

TACITA DEAN

Film:

Eternal Womanly 1987, 7min, silent, 16mm

Goat and Me 1988, 8min, silent, S8mm

The Story of Beard 1992, 8min, 16mm

The Martyrdom of St Agatha (in several parts) 1994, 14min, 16mm (AC)

Girl Stowaway 1994, 8min, 16mm (LAB)

A Bag of Air 1995, 3min, b/w, 16mm
Distribution: Frith Street Gallery London

ALNOOR DEWSHI

Film:

The Airwave Spectrum Has Some Defections 1989, 4min, b/w, 16mm (SWA)

Latifah and Himli's Nomadic Uncle 1992, 15min, b/w, 16mm (AC/SWA)

Anton and Minty 1994, 28min, 16mm (BFI/Ch4)
Distribution: LFMC

VIVIENNE DICK

Film and video:

Guerillère Talks 1978, 30min, S8mm

She Had Her Gun All Ready 1978, 30min, S8mm

Beauty Becomes the Beast 1979, 45min, S8mm

Liberty's Booty 1980, 50min, S8mm

Visibility: Moderate 1981, 45min, S8mm

Trailer 1982, 10min, S8mm
Like Dawn to Dust 1983, 7min, S8mm
Rothach 1986, 7min, 16mm (AC)
Pobal – the Artist 1988, 28min, 16mm
London Suite 1989, 28min, 16mm (AC/Ch4)
Let Me Tell You a Story 1990, 10min, S8mm
Two Pigeons 1990, 4min, video
3am 1990, 1min, video (AC/BBC)
New York Conversations 1991, 20min, video (AC)
A Skinny Little Man Attacked Daddy 1994, 23min, video (AC)
Distribution: LEA, LFMC

WILLIE DOHERTY

Installation:
The Only Good One is a Dead One 1993, 30min cycle, 2 video projectors, 2 players, 2 speakers, personal stereo (Matt's Gallery)
At the End of the Day 1994, 30min cycle, 1 video projector, 1 player, 2 speakers, The British School Rome
No Smoke Without Fire 1994, 30min cycle, 1 video projector, 1 player, 2 speakers, 'The Raw and The Cooked' Reina Sofia Madrid
Reconstruction 1995, 30min cycle, 1 monitor, 1 player, wall bracket, sited in a space (hallway, corridor, staircase) adjacent to variable number of cibachromes, Kerlin Gallery Dublin
Distribution: Matt's Gallery, 42–44 Copperfield Road, London E3 4RR

MIKE DUNFORD

Film and video:
Part-Time Virgin 1972, 35min, 16mm
Tree 1972, 9min, b/w, silent, 16mm
True Love 1972, 9min, b/w, silent, 16mm
Silver Surfer 1972, 15min, b/w, silent, 16mm
Deep Space 1973, 10min, b/w, silent, 16mm
Synch Sound 1973, 10min, 16mm
Lens Tissue 1973, 5min, silent, 16mm
Tautology 1973, b/w, silent, 16mm
Route 66 1973, 30min, silent, 16mm
Still Life with Pear 1974, 12min, b/w, 16mm
Arbitrary Limits 1974, 30min, 16mm (AC)
In the Dark 1975, 25min, b/w, 16mm
Still Image 1976, 60min, 16mm (BFI)
Culture of Domination 1983, 50min, video
Order 1985, 40min, video
Very Funny 1985, 5min, video
Nohi Abassi 1989, 15min, video
Windless Closure 1993, 25min, video(AC)
Distribution: LEA, LFMC

STEVEN DWOSKIN

Film and video:
Asleep 1961, 4min, b/w, 16mm
American Dream 1961, 3min, silent, 16mm
Alone 1964, 13min, b/w, 16mm
Naissant 1964, 14min, b/w, 16mm
Chinese Checkers 1964, 13min, b/w, 16mm
Soliloquy 1964, 8min, b/w, 16mm
Dirty 1965–67, 10min, b/w, 16mm
Me, Myself and I 1967, 18min, b/w, 16mm
Moment 1968, 12min, 16mm
Take Me 1968, 30min, b/w, 16mm
Trixi 1969, 30min, 16mm
C-Film 1970, 30min, 16mm
To Tea 1970, 30min, 16mm
Times For 1971, 80min, 16mm
Dyn Amo 1972, 120min, 16mm
Jesus Blood 1972, 32min, 16mm
Tod und Teufel (Death and the Devil) 1973, 94min, 16mm
Behindert (Hindered) 1974, 96min, 16mm (ZDF)
Girl 1975, 30min, silent, 16mm
Just Waiting 1975, 10min, 16mm
Laboured Party 1975, 20min, b/w, 16mm
Central Bazaar 1976, 156min, 16mm (BFI)
Kleiner Vogel 1976, 40min, 16mm
Silent Cry (Stiller Schrei) 1977, 96min, 16mm (ZDF/INA)
Outside In (Das Innere Bloss) 1981, 105min, 16mm (ZDF)
Shadows From Light 1983, 60min, b/w, 16mm (AC)
Ballet Black 1986, 86min, 16mm (AC)
Further and Particular (La Solution Imaginaire) 1988, 112min, 16mm (Ch4)
L'Esprit de Brendan Behan (The Spirit of Brendan Behan) 1990, 30min, 16mm (La Sept/ARTE)
Face Anthea 1990, 60min, video (La Sept)
Face of Our Face 1992, 52min, 16mm (Ch4)
Trying to Kiss the Moon 1994, 95min, 16mm (AC/Ch4)
Distribution: ACE, Stephen Dwoskin, (0181 671 5241)

CATHERINE ELWES

Video:
Kensington Gore 1981, 15min
The Critic's Informed Viewing 1982, 26min
Nostalgia 1982/83, 15min
There Is a Myth 1984, 10min
Sleep 1984, 8min
With Child 1984, 18min (AC)

The Gunfighters 1985, 6min
Post Card 1986, 4min
Play 1986, 4min
Winter 1987, 15min (Ch4)
Spring 1988, 8min (Ch4)
Grown Up 1990, 2½min (Ch4)
Autumn 1991, 18min (Ch4)
Introduction to Summer 1992, 2min
The Liaison Officer 1995, 20min (SA)

Installation:
Myth 1983, 1 monitor, 1 player, 2 small speakers, 'Cross Currents' (RCA)
First House 1986, 2 monitors, 2 players, edit controller, Festival of Women Sculptors (Canterbury Festival)
(Wishing) Well 1991, 1 monitor, 1 player, 'Video Positive' Bluecoat Gallery Liverpool (HTBA)
Le Refus de la Honte 1995, 2 video projectors, 3 monitors, 5 players (SA)
Distribution: LEA

STEVE FARRER

Film and video:
Silk Screen Films 1974, 15min, 16mm
Mirror Films 1974, 13min, 16mm
Ten Drawings 1976, 20min, b/w, 16mm
Lensless and Gateless Films 1977–79, 30min, two screen, 16mm
Sound Painting 1979, 45min, 16mm
Blue Erection 1979, 3min, three screen, 16mm
Train of Thought 1979, 5min, two screen, 16mm
Muscle Lens 1980, 3min, S8mm
Salon of '83 1983, 10min, 8mm
Ocean Wave 1983, 10min, S8mm
My First Gay Film! 1984, 13min, S8mm
Dead Sea Fragments 1985, 30min, 8mm
Real as a Dream 1985, 22min, S8mm
Past Possessed 1985, 12min, two screen, S8mm
Big Parade 1985, 10min, S8mm
Atilio Sketches 1985, 12min, S8mm
Crimson Joy 1986, 15min, S8mm
(Construction and Exhibition of) The Machine 1978–88, 20min, video (documentation)
Kiss 25 Goodbye 1992, 3min, 35mm, 10min, video

Installation:
Subliminal Machine 1980, 16mm, Berlin Film Festival
Salon of '84 1984, S8mm, ICA London
Mobile 1986, 16mm, four screen performance 'Daylight Club' Diorama London

Machine Tests 1978–88 35mm, 'Against the Steady Stare' Diorama London, MOMA Oxford(AC)
Ghost Train 1989, 35mm, (for The Machine) 'Camera Natura' Middleburg Netherlands installation (AC)
Kiss 25 Goodbye 1991, 35mm, loop, 'Pitch' 114 Leyton Road Kentish Town
Distribution: LFMC

DAVID FINCH

Film and video:
The Fall of the House of Usher 1981, 28min, b/w, 16mm (AC)
Troilus & Cressida 1982, 11min, S8mm
The Fog 1982, 13min, video
1983 1983, 18min, b/w, 16mm (AC)
Heart of Gold 1985, 3min, b/w, video
The Rest Is Lost 1985, 4min, b/w, video
Forgotten Fictions 1986, 19min, video (AC)
The Flying Trunk 1987, 15min, video (AC)
Man of Stones 1989, 32min, video (AC)
Stone Steps 1992, 21min, 16mm (AC)
Postcard from Mam Tor 1992, 3min, 16mm
Clee Hill 1994, 3min, 16mm
On the Water 1994, 3min, 16mm
Berlin 1994, 3min, 16mm
Fire Festival 1994, 10min, 16mm (LPF/LFVDA)
Coney's Island 1994, 3min, 16mm
Distribution: LEA, LFMC

ROSE FINN-KELCEY

Film and video:
Variable, Light to Moderate 1971, 10min, S8mm
Cut-Out 1982, 15min, video (FRIGO)
Glory 1983, 20min, video (with Steve Hawley & Harry Walton) (AC)
Bureau de Change 1992, 11min, 16mm (with Nick Collins) (AC)
Steam Installation 1993, 4min, video (with Nick Collins/Illuminations) (AC)

Installation:
Blazon 1986, 9 monitors, 3 players, The Window Box Show (LVA/Air Gallery)
Bureau de Change 1988, live camera, 1 monitor, currency, security guard, false floor, viewing platform, Laing Gallery Newcastle, Cartwright Hall Bradford, Cornerhouse Manchester, (Projects UK) revised for Matts Gallery London
When Your Ship Comes In 1989, 1 miniature monitor, 1 player, 3 'floating' trunks, The Suitcase Show (FVU)
Distribution: Cinenova, LEA

TERRY FLAXTON

Video:
Opening Up 1976, 16min
The Executives 1977, 7min
Gong 1977, 35min
Git Govind 1977, 45min
The Fashion Show 1979, 5min
Talking Heads 1979, 20min
Presentiments 1979, 16min
Documentary Rape 1980, 5min
Towards Intuition: An American Landscape 1981, 50min (GLAA)
Eisenstein: Programme of Attractions 1982, 35min (GLAA)
Making News 1982, 32min
Eurythmics 1983, 26min
Money Talks 1983, 30min
The Gap 1983, 10min
Circumstantial Evidence 1984, 20min (GLAA)
Prisoners 1985, 16min
On Video 1 1988, 60min (Ch4)
On Video 2 1988, 60min (Ch4)
On Video 3 1988, 80min (Ch4)
On Video 4 1988, 60min (Ch4)
On Video 5 1988, 60min (Ch4)
The World Within Us 1988, 16min (Ch4)
The Byker Wall 1988, 10min (BBC)
The Cold War Game, the Soviet Union 1988, 60min (Ch4)
D10 Boots Building 1989, 10min (BBC)
The Lloyds Building 1989, 10min (BBC)
In the Belly of the Beast 1989, 10min (Granada)
Zagorsk 1991, 5min
The Colour Myths:
  The Inevitability of Colour 1990, 16min (AC/Ch4)
  Echo's Revenge 1991, 5min
  The Object of Desire 1991, 6min
  Unreal Timepiece 1992, 1min
  Echo's Compassion 1993, 5min
  The Eye Projects the World 1994, 1min
  The Mystery of Colour 1995, 7min
Distribution: LEA

FORKBEARD PRODUCTIONS

Film and video:
Could a Whale Fly? 1980, 7min, b/w, silent, 16mm (Tim Britton, animation)
The Bonehunter 1984, 23min, 16mm (SA)
Worm 1985, 13min, 16mm
The Birdwatcher 1985, 8min, video (Ch4)
The End 1986, 10min, 16mm
The Red Strimmer 1987, 5min, S8mm

Boxmanship 1988, 5min, 16mm (Tim Britton, animation)
Chablis at Celluloid Divide 1991, 7min, 16mm (TSW)

Performance:
The Clone Show 1979, 60min, 16mm
Ghosts 1984, 60min, S8mm
Who Shot the Cameraman? 1986, 25min, 16mm (AC)
Roller Blind 1986, 2min, b/w, S8mm
A Serious Leak 1989, 80min, 16mm & S8mm (AC)
Experiment in Contraprojection 1990, 35min, 16mm (AC)
Bidet 1990, 3min, S8mm (Chris Britton, animation)
Invasion of the Bloopies 1991, 80min, 16mm (AC)
The India Rubber Zoom Lens 1993, 80min, 16mm (AC)
Distribution: Forkbeard Productions, Moor Cottage, Huntsham, Tiverton, Devon EX16 7NF

SERA FURNEAUX

Video:
Portrait 1982, 8min, silent (AC)
14 minutes 1982, 14min, silent (AC)
Portrayal 1984, 18min, silent
Lessness – Parts I, II and III 1986, 42min (LVA)
Canvas 1987, 11min (AC/Ch4)
A Garden... 1989, 4min
Cow Song 1990, 3min
Ginevra Sketches 1991, 4min
Anxiety, Rest 1991, 12min
Smoked Salmon 1995 (AC)

Installation:
Travelling Boxes 1992, model railway, travelling trunk, miniature video monitor, 1 player, City Racing Gallery London
Distribution: LEA

CHARLES GARRAD

Film:
MOMI Avant-Garde Film 1988, 20min, 16mm (BFI)
Engaged 1988, 3min, 35mm
Time Passing Series: 1992, 16mm, 10min each (BBC)
  One Year
  Wedding Day
  Nine O'Clock
  The Tide

Eight Minutes
The Past
Inside Out 1993, 1min, 16mm (AC/BBC)

Installation:
Cinema 1983, S8mm projector, screen, mirror, architectual/sculptural environment, 'Summer Show' Serpentine Gallery London (GLAA)
Monsoon 1986, 1 monitor, 1 player, architectural/sculptural environment (Ikon Birmingham)
T.V.Times 1991, 25 monitors, 8 players (with David Watson & Denise Corrigan) (MCA Sydney)
Distribution: LEA

ROB GAWTHROP

Film and video:
Littlehamptons 1974–80, 30min, 16mm
Preservation 1976–82, 24min, 16mm
Musical 1979, 24min, 16mm
Distancing 1979, 15min, silent, 16mm (AC/RCA)
Project I and II 1981, 12min, two screen, 16mm
Married Print 1982, 6min, 16mm
Coastal Calls 1982, 12min, 16mm (AC)
The Miller and the Sweep 1984, 6min, b/w, silent, 16mm (with Joanna Millett) (AC)
Projections for Percussion and Improvisation 1985–90, b/w, various formats, mostly 16mm (AC)
Budget Sound Tapes 1988, 2min, two screen, video (AC)
Observation 1992, 10min, 16mm (AC)
What the Eye Doesn't See, Post Industrial Studies 1 – Coal and Transport 1993, 12min, b/w, 16mm (with Mike Stubbs) (Camerawork)
Now You See It Now You Don't, Post-Industrial Studies 3 1995, 8min, 16mm (University of Humberside)

Installation/Music/Sound Performance with Film:
Improvisations for . . . Percussion and Projection 1985, 4–8 16mm projectors, 2 tape recorders, amplifier, speakers, Aberystwyth Arts Centre
Improvisations for . . . Shawm, Tape-Treatment & Projection 1985, 2 16mm projectors, 2 tape recorders, 2 mics/stands, amplifier, speakers, London Film Makers Co-op
Field Cymbal Phase 1988, 4 monitors, 4 players, Ferens Gallery, Hull (AC)

Projections for . . . Improvisation, Percussion, Balloons, Toys and Other Stuff 1988–90, 2–8 16mm projectors, speakers, plus site specific equipment, Ferens Gallery Hull (AC)
What the Eye Doesn't See 1993, 6 16mm projectors, PA, lighting, steam locomotive, coal (with Mike Stubbs) 'River Crossings' Old Railway Museum, North Woolwich Station London (Camerawork London)
The University of Humberside Band 1994 an eight to twenty piece experimental music/performance ensemble New Adelphi Club, Hull.
Distribution: HTBA, LFMC

CONSTANTINE GIANNARIS

Film and video:
Framed Youth 1984, 40min, video (GLAA)
Jean Genet Is Dead 1987, 40min, 16mm (AC)
Disco's Revenge 1988, 25min, video
A Matter of Life and Death 1989, 20min, b/w, video
Trojans 1989, 35min, b/w, 16mm (AC)
A Short Film About Greek Homosexuality 1991, 20min, video (Ch4)
A Desperate Vitality 1991, 20min, video (BBC)
Silences 1991, 10min, b/w, 16mm (GLAA)
North of Vortex 1991, 58min, b/w, 16mm (AC/Ch4)
Caught Looking 1991, 35min, 16mm (Ch4)
A Place in the Sun 1994, 50min, 16mm (AC/Ch4)
Three Steps to Heaven 1995, 88min, 35mm (BFI/Ch4)
Distribution: MayaVision

PETER GIDAL

16mm Film:
Room (Double Take) 1967, 10min, b/w
Key 1968, 10min
Loop 1968, 10min, b/w,
Still Andy 1968, 5min
Clouds 1969, 10min, b/w
Heads 1969, 35min, b/w, silent
Subject/Object Portrait 1970, 10min, b/w, silent
8mm Film Notes on 16mm 1971, 40min, silent
Bedroom 1971, 30min
Movie No 1 1972, 5min
Upside Down Feature 1972, 76min
Movie No 2 1972, 5min
Room Film 1973 1973, 55min, silent

Photo/Graph/Film 1973, 5min, b/w, silent
Film Print 1974, 40min, silent (AC)
C/O/N/S/T/R/U/C/T 1974, 26min, silent
Condition of Illusion 1975, 30min, silent (AC)
Kopenhagen/1930 1977, 40min, b/w, silent
Silent Partner 1977, 35min (BFI)
Fourth Wall 1978, 45min, silent
Epilogue 1978, 7min, silent (NEA USA)
Untitled 1978, 7min, silent (NEA USA)
Action at a Distance 1980, 35min
Close Up 1983, 70min (AC)
Denials 1985, 25min, silent (AC)
Guilt 1988, 40min, silent (AC)
Flare Out 1992, 20min (AC)
Distribution: LFMC

CLIVE GILLMAN

Video:
W.A.R 1983, 17min
Meltdown 1983, 8min
Electrical Development 1986, 10min
Timezones 1986, 12min (with St.John Walker)
Sad But New 1987, 10min
Solid State Remains 1987, 10min
Saboten Boi 1988, 46min (with St.John Walker) (EMAB)
The Attack of the Deadly Alien Graces 1989, 13min
NLV1 (Strange Attractor) 1989, 4min
NLV6 (Sublime) 1990, 2min
NLV7 1990, 4min
Losing 1991, 10min
Advent 1995, CD-Rom (NWA)

Installation:
MIRA 1984, 8 monitors, 2 players, 'Ch5 Video Festival' TV Rental Shopwindows (LVA)
The Date 1987, 3 monitors, 2 players, stereo, LFF LFMC
Timezones 1988, 12 monitors, 2 players, stereo, (with St.John Walker) LFF LFMC
Something in the Air 1988, 3 monitors, 1 player, painted wooden objects, circular glazed maps, Changing Room Gallery London
Virus 1990, 13 monitors, 4 players, various museum cabinets and other objects, Leicester Museum (with St.John Walker) (Leicester International Film Festival)
Losing 1991, 11 monitors, 1 video projector, 4 players, 1 computer, 1 slide projector, 1 goal, artificial turf, Open Eye Gallery Liverpool (Video Positive)

The Picture That Ate My Soul 1992,
1 computer, 1 monitor, 1 arcade computer
console, 1 mirror ball, various painted objects,
site specific interactive computer, Bluecoat
Gallery Liverpool, Prema Gallery Gloucester
Pirates Lament 1992, 2 slide projectors
(850 watts), dissolve unit, outdoor projected
computer images; Root 92 Festival, Hull; River
Crossings, London; Visionfest, Liverpool
(Camerawork/HTBA/Moviola)
When Freedom Comes 1993, 1 computer,
1 monitor, 1 satellite dish, various objects
including, wooden aircraft, pebbles, earth, blue
light bulbs, rope (Holden Gallery Manchester)
To Be This Good . . . Rock of Ages 1994,
interactive, 8 computers, 1 LCD projector,
1 slide projector, 8 Appletalk network connec-
tors, V-Topia Tramway Glasgow & Bluecoat
Liverpool (FVU/Moviola/Tramway)
Distribution: LEA, Moviola

JUDITH GODDARD

Video:
Time Spent 1982, 12min
Go into Your Fridge (Stilted Life) 1982,
14min
Under the Rose 1983, 12min
You May Break . . . 1983, 5min
Who Knows the Secret? 1984, 8min (AC)
Lyrical Doubt 1984, 16min
Celestial Light and Monstrous Races
1985, 4min (Space X Exeter/Plymouth Art
Centre)
Luminous Portrait 1990, 1min (AC/BBC)
Glasgow – a Bluish-Green 1990, 7min
(BBC)
The Garden of Earthly Delights, 1991,
9min (Complete Video/Video Positive)

Installation:
Celestial Light and Monstrous Races
1985, 4min, 8 monitors, 1 player (Space X
Exeter/Plymouth Art Centre)
Television Circle/Electron 1987, 4½min,
7 monitors, 1 player, outdoor site-specific
Dartmoor (TSW)
Urban Turner/First Light 1989, 7min,
42 monitors (videowall), 1 player, Tate Gallery
Liverpool (Video Positive/Samcom)
The Garden of Earthly Delights 1991,
9min cycle, 3 monitors, 3 players, Bluecoat
Gallery Liverpool (Complete Video/Video
Positive)
Descry 1992, 5min cycle, 8 monitors,
8 players (AC/Kettle's Yard Cambridge)

Reservoir 1993, 1 video projector, 3 monitors,
4 players, 1 surveillance camera, electrical spark
(Wimshurst machine), dripping water (strobe
lit and sound amplified), John Hansard
Gallery Southampton (AC)
Helen's Room 1995, 1 monitor, 1 surveillance
camera with computer controlled motorised
pan and tilt, Kettle's Yard Cambridge (Henry
Moore Foundation)
Distribution: Fields and Frames, LEA, Moviola

PETER GREENAWAY

Film and video:
Train 1966, 5min, 16mm
Tree 1966, 16min, 16mm
Revolution 1967, 8min, 16mm
5 Postcards from Capital Cities 1967,
35mm, 16mm
Intervals 1969, 7min, b/w, 16mm
Erosion 1971, 27min, 16mm
H is for House 1973, 10min, 16mm
Windows 1975 4min, 16mm
Water 1975, 5min, 16mm
Water Wrackets 1975, 12min, 16mm
Goole by Numbers 1976, 40min, 16mm
Dear Phone 1977, 17min, 16mm
1–100 1978, 4min, 16mm
Vertical Features Remake 1978, 45min,
16mm (AC)
A Walk Through H 1978, 41min, 16mm
(BFI)
Zandra Rhodes 1979, 15min, video
The Falls 1980, 185min, 16mm (BFI)
Act of God 1981, 25min, video
The Draughtsman's Contract 1982,
108min, 35mm (BFI/Ch4)
Four American Composers
(documentaries on **John Cage, Robert
Ashley, Philip Glass, Meredith Monk**)
1983, 4 x 55min, video (Ch4)
Making a Splash 1984, 25min, video
Inside Rooms – 26 Bathroooms 1985,
25min, video
A Zed and Two Noughts 1986, 115min,
35mm (BFI/Ch4)
Belly of an Architect 1987, 105min, 35mm
(Ch4)
Drowning by Numbers 1988, 118min, 35mm
(Ch4/VPRO Holland)
Fear of Drowning 1988, 26min, video
Death in the Seine 1988, 44min, video
A TV Dante (Cantos I-VIII) 1989,
8 x 10min, video (with Tom Phillips) (Ch4)
Hubert Bals Handshake 1989, 5min, video
**The Cook, The Thief, His Wife and Her
Lover** 1989, 125min, 35mm (Erato Films/
Films Inc)

Prospero's Books 1991, 120min, 35mm
(Canal+/NHK)
M is for Man, Music and Mozart 1991,
29min, video (BBC)
Rosa 1992, 15min, video
Darwin 1992, 52min, video
(Ch4/Antenne2/RA12)
The Baby of Macon 1993, 120min, 35mm
(La Sept/Ch4/Canal+)
The Stairs, Geneva 1994, 100min
(TV Suisse Romande)
Distribution: BFI

DAVID HALL

Film and video:
Motion Parallax 1968, 15min, b/w,
two screen, 16mm
Vertical 1970, 17min, 16mm (AC)
Timecheck 1971, 45min, 16mm (BFI)
7 TV Pieces 1971, 24min, b/w, video
(SAC/STV)
View 1973, 9min, 16mm (with Tony Sinden)
(AC)
Actor 1973, 11min, 16mm (with Tony Sinden)
(AC)
This Surface 1973, 12min, 16mm (with Tony
Sinden) (AC)
Edge 1973, 10min, 16mm (with Tony Sinden)
(AC)
Between 1973, 17min, 16mm (with Tony
Sinden) (AC)
Phased Time² 1974, 16min, 16mm
This is a Video Monitor 1974, 12min, b/w,
video
Relative Surfaces 1974, 10min, b/w, video
Vidicon Inscriptions 1974, 12min, b/w,
video
This is a Television Receiver 1976, 8min,
video (BBC)
TV Fighter (Cam Era Plane) 1977, 11min,
b/w, video
Ghost Story 1978, 10min, video
La Belle Niçoise 1979, 12min, b/w, video
Stooky Bill TV 1990, 4min, video (Ch4)
ecstaseeTV 1993, 1½min, video (MTV)
contexTV 1993, 1min, video (MTV)
exiTV 1993, 1min, video (MTV)
withouTV 1993, 1min, video (MTV)
interacTV 1993, 1min, video (MTV)
reacTV 1993, 1min, video (MTV)

Installation:
60 TV Sets 1972, 60 old TV sets, scaffolding,
two 'technicians' in white coats (with Tony
Sinden) (Gallery House London)

Progressive Recession 1974, 9 monitors, 9 cameras, plinths and corridor enclosure, 'Video Show' Serpentine Gallery London (AC)
101 TV Sets 1975, 101 old TV sets, scaffolding (with Tony Sinden) 'Video Show' Serpentine Gallery London (AC)
Vidicon Inscriptions (the Installation) 1975, 1 monitor, 1 camera, lighting, plinth, corridor enclosure, Tate gallery London & Third Eye Centre Galsgow (SAC/Tate)
Waterwork (Narcissus) 1976, 1 monitor, 1 camera, metal and glass fluid container
The Situation Envisaged 1978, 8 identical television sets, 1 monitor, 1 player, plinth, Video '78 Hebert Gallery Coventry (AC/Lanchester Poly)
The Situation Envisaged II 1979, 8 identical TV sets, 1 monitor, 1 player, plinth, Air Gallery London
A Situation Envisaged: The Rite 1980, 16 identical TV sets, 1 monitor, 1 player, electric turntable, plinth (South Hill Park Arts Centre Bracknell)
A Situation Envisaged: The Rite II (Cultural Eclipse) 1988, 15 monitor video wall, 5 players synchronised, plinth, 'Video Positive' Tate Gallery Liverpool (BC/MOMA/Moviola)
Distribution: Annalogue, BFI, Fields and Frames, LEA

NICKY HAMLYN

Film:
Rhythm 1 1973, 3min, b/w, 8mm
Rhythm 2 1973, 3min, b/w, silent, 8mm
Silver Street 1974, 4min, 16mm
Window 1975, 3min, three screen, 16mm
Window Lapse 1975, 3min, silent, two screen, 16mm
Cloister 1976, 6min, b/w, three screen, 16mm
Second Look 1976, 5min, b/w, silent, 16mm
Sundial 1976, 6min, silent, two screen, 16mm
Inside Out 1978, 38min, 16mm (AC)
Guesswork 1979, 11min, 16mm (AC)
Not to See Again 1980, 13min, 16mm (AC)
Synch-Sound Sketches 1980-84, 12 x 4min, S8mm
Anagram 1982, 40min, 16mm (AC)
Ghost Stories 1983, 30min, b/w, 16mm (AC)
Confessional Fragments 1983, 20min, tape/slide
That Has Been 1984, 40min, 16mm (AC)
Uncertainty 1987, 22min, 16mm (AC)
Minutiae 1989, 1min, 16mm (AC/BBC)
There Again 1991, 16min, 16mm (AC)
Only at First 1991, 22min, 16mm (AC)
Hole 1992, 2min, 16mm

Performance:
4 X Loops 1974, 5–10min, b/w, silent, 16mm (live event with 4 moving projectors) 'Festival of Expanded Cinema' ICA
Distribution: LFMC

MONA HATOUM

Video:
So Much I Want to Say 1983, 5min, b/w (Western Front Video Vancouver)
Changing Parts 1984, 24min, b/w (Western Front Video Vancouver)
Measures of Distance 1988, 15min (AC/Western Front Video Vancouver)

Installation:
Hidden from Prying Eyes 1987, 5 monitors, player, slide projector, corrugated metal sheets, gravel, light, Air Gallery London
Corps Étranger 1994, 10min cycle, video projector, player, amplifier, 4 speakers, wooden cylinder structure, Pompidou Centre collection Paris (Pompidou)
Distribution: LEA

STEVE HAWLEY

Film and video:
Those Flashes of Insight Which 1981, 14min, video
Bad Reasons 1982, 20min, video
We Have Fun Drawing Conclusions 1982, 8min, video
Drawing Conclusions – The Science Mix 1983, 5min, video (with Tony Steyger)
The Dictionary 1983, 25min, video (AC/North East London Poly)
On and Off the Maps 1984, 26min, two screen, video (with Jane Wells)
Another Look at Geography 1986, 10min, S8mm
One Shot Jack 1987, 5min, video (with Tony Steyger)
Trout Descending a Staircase 1987, 5min, video
The Chemistry Set 1987, 11min, video (with Tony Steyger)(AC/Ch4)
Trout Descending a Staircase 1990, 1min, video (AC/BBC)
A Proposition is a Picture 1992, 22min, video
Human and Natural History 1992, 5min, video
Language Lessons 1994, 40min, video (with Tony Steyger)(AC/Ch4)
The Man from Porlock 1995, 30min, video (Sheffield Hallam University)
Distribution: LEA

TONY HILL

Film:
Steps 1969, 1min, silent, S8mm
Heads 1971, 5min, 16mm
Doors 1973, 10min, S8mm loop
Heartburn 1973, 2min, S8mm
Expanded Movie 1 1973, 8min, S8mm
Ceiling Film 1973, 3min, silent, S8mm
Point Source 1973, 8min, shadow projection performance
Toeknee Chestnut 1973, 3min, silent, four screen, S8mm
Train Eye 1973, 3min, S8mm
Handscape 1973, 2min, silent, S8mm
To See 1 1976, 4min, two screen, S8mm
Radiation 1976, 6min, S8mm loop
Orientation 1977, 8min, 16mm
To See 1982, 15min, two screen, 16mm (AC/YAA)
Downside Up 1985, 17min, 16mm (AC/LHA)
Water Work 1987, 11min, 16mm (AC/Ch4)
Striking Images 1990, 1min, 16mm (AC/BBC)
Expanded Movie 1990, 13min, 16mm (AC)
A Short History of the Wheel 1992, 1min, 16mm (AC/BBC)
Holding the Viewer 1993, 1min, 16mm (AC/BBC)

Installation:
1st Floor Film 1971, 7min, silent, S8mm, Festival of Independent Avant-garde Film ICA London 1973
2nd Floor Film 1972, 8min, silent, S8mm, Festival of Independent Avant-garde Film ICA London 1973
Floor Film 1975, 30min, 16mm, Festival of Independent British Cinema Watershed Bristol (AC)
Distribution: LEA, Tony Hill (01538 304 355)

SUSAN HILLER

Video:
Belshazzar's Feast 1984, 20min (AC)

Installation:
Pray (Prayer) 1969, 3 hour, b/w, interactive video event for 10 participants
Enquiries 1973, slide projection, 2 cycles of 100 slides (Gallery House London)
Inquiries 1975, slide projection, 2 cycles of 100 slides (Serpentine Gallery London)
Belshazzar's Feast/The Writing on Your Wall 1984, original video installation, Tate Gallery collection London (site-specific variations created for other exhibitions)

Magic Lantern 1987, 11min, 3 projector tape/slide, stereo (Whitechapel Gallery London)

An Entertainment 1990, 20min cycle, 4 video projectors, 4 players (synchronised), quadraphonic sound, (Matt's Gallery London/Mappin Gallery Sheffield/Third Eye Centre Glasgow)

At the Freud Museum 1992–4, 24 boxes individually titled containing artefacts, texts etc, one includes **Bright Shadow** (Bookworks London)

Bright Shadow 1994, 7min cycle, silent 1 monitor (miniature l.c.d or large screen), 1 player
Distribution: LEA

STUART HILTON

Film:
Terrain 1988, 2min, b/w, 16mm
Starting 1988, 3min, 16mm
Dog End 1988, 1min, b/w, silent, 16mm
Machine Word 1988, 1min, b/w, 16mm
Wrong 1991, 4min, 16mm
Pendulum 1991, 2min, 16mm
Dyers Hall Road 1991, 1min, b/w, 16mm
Procession 1991, 1min, b/w, 16mm
Argument in a Superstore 1992, 6min, 16mm (AC)
Save Me 1994, 6min, 35mm (AC/Ch4)
Distribution: BFI

HOUSEWATCH

Installation:
Up, Down, Dancing Dogs 1985, Tony Sinden, Claremont Road E11

Cinematic Architecture for Pedestrians 1985, Claremont Road E11.
Works included:
Compendium of Games Ian Bourn
Red Tape Lulu Quinn
The House That Jack Built George Saxon
Improvising on an Architectural Concept Tony Sinden
Unfathomed Chris White
Red Room Alison Winckle

Cinematic Architecture for Pedestrians 1986, Great Russell Street, Bloomsbury; Stadium Street, Chelsea; Princelet Street, Spitalfields.
Works included:
Good Value Cafe Ian Bourn
Ancestors Lulu Quinn
The House That Jack Built George Saxon

Pedestrian Colours Tony Sinden
Full Fathom Chris White
Yellow Room Alison Winckle

Night Assembly 1987, The Assembly Rooms, George Street, Edinburgh.
Works included:
Devotions (Haringay to Powderhall) Ian Bourn
Feast of Stone Lulu Quinn
Jack's Dream George Saxon
Pedestrian Colours – An Architectural Lament Tony Sinden
Red Room Alison Winckle

7 Pelham Square/Housewatch in Bath (Brighton and Bath Festivals) 1988.
Works included:
Under the Hammer, Compendium of Games Ian Bourn
Feast of Stone Lulu Quinn
The House That Jack Built, Jack's Dream George Saxon
Pedestrian Colours (versions 3 and 4), Pedestrian Voices Tony Sinden
Red Room, Housebound Alison Winckle

Wounded Knee 1990, Claremont Road, London E11.
Works included:
Sunken Love Ian Bourn (music performed live by Mosquitoes), 8 Claremont Road
Home Beat Lulu Quinn, 12 Claremont Road
Deceleration/Desire Tony Sinden, Volvo car
Tunnel Vision George Saxon and Alison Winckle, Metro car, corrugated fencing, 9 Claremont Road

Contraflow 1992, 5 day duration event. Film, video and performance, 18 Morris Minor vehicles at Broadgate Centre, Liverpool Street, London. A collaborative HOUSEWATCH project with performance by John Carson and Lucy Bagley

Little Big Horn 1992, Southbank, London. Various motor vehicles in the undercroft beneath the Queen Elizabeth Hall.
Works included:
Isle of Capri Ian Bourn
Fatal Instincts Lulu Quinn
Car Moment George Saxon
Deceleration/Desire, Acceleration/Arrest Tony Sinden
Universal Power Drive Stan Steele
Sweet Nothing Alison Winckle

Imaginary Opera 1992, Kyoto Museum building, Sanjo Street, Kyoto, Japan. Projection and performance with orchestra (music "Crossing the Border" by Steve Martland)

Paperhouse 1992. Purpose-built house (wood, rice paper) touring three sites (Kobe, Kyoto, Mito) in Japan. twelve screen projection.
Works included:
Moving House Ian Bourn
One for the Pot Lulu Quinn
Goldfish Drowning in Mummy, Daddy's Dream Home George Saxon
Turbulent Water Tony Sinden
Fuel Stan Steele
The Hot House Alison Winckle
Distribution: Housewatch,c/o 313 Grove Green Road, Leytonstone, London E11 4EB

DEREK JARMAN

Film and video:
Studio Bankside 1970, 6min, S8mm
Miss Gaby 1971, 5min, S8mm
A Journey to Avebury 1971, 5min, S8mm
Garden of Luxor (aka **Burning the Pyramids**) 1972, 6min, S8mm
Andrew Logan Kisses the Glitterati 1972, 8min, S8mm
Tarot (aka **The Magician**) 1972, 10min, S8mm
The Art of Mirrors (aka **Sulphur**) 1973, 10min, S8mm
The Devils at the Elgin (aka **Reworking the Devils**) 1974, 15min, b/w, S8mm
Ula's Fete (aka **Ula's Chandelier**) 1974, 10min, S8mm
Fire Island 1974, 5min, S8mm
Duggie Fields 1974, 5min, S8mm
Picnic at Ray's 1975, 10min, S8mm
Sebastiane Wrap (aka **Home Movies reel 1**) 1975, 10min, 16mm
Gerald's Film 1976, 12min, S8mm
Sloane Square, A Room of One's Own (aka **Removal Party** and part of **Home Movies reel 2**) 1976, 12min, 16mm (AC)
Houston Texas 1976, 10min, S8mm
Sebastiane 1976, 86min, 35mm (AC)
Jordan's Dance 1977, 1min, S8mm
Every Woman for Herself and All for Art (part of **Home Movies reel 2**) 1977, 1min, b/w, 16mm
Jubilee 1978, 104min, 35mm
The Pantheon 1978, 3min, S8mm
The Tempest 1979, 85min, 35mm (Don Boyd)

Broken English 1979, 12min, 16mm
(Island Records)
In the Shadow of the Sun 1980, 60min,
16mm (Freunde der Deutschen Kinemathek)
TG Psychic Rally in Heaven 1981, 8min,
16mm (AC)
Pirate Tape/Film 1982, 17min, video
Pontormo and Punks at Santa Croce
1982, 10min, S8mm
Ken's First Film 1982, 5min, S8mm
Waiting for Waiting for Godot 1983,
18min, S8mm/video
B2 Tape/Film 1983, 30min, video
Dream Machine 1984, 35min, 16mm
(with Michael Kostiff, Cerith Wyn Evans,
John Maybury) (AC/BFI)
Catalan 1984, 7min, 16mm
Imagining October 1984, 27min, 16mm
The Angelic Conversation 1985, 78min,
35mm (BFI)
Caravaggio 1986, 93min, 35mm (BFI/Ch4)
The Queen is Dead 1986, 13min, 35mm
(Rough Trade)
Depuis Le Jour, segment of **Aria** (Don
Boyd) 1987, 5min, 35mm
The Last of England 1987, 87min, 35mm
(Ch4/ZDF/British Screen)
L'Ispirazioni 1988, 2min, 35mm (Florence
Opera House)
War Requiem 1989, 82min, 35mm
(BBC/Polygram)
The Garden 1990, 92min, 35mm
(Ch4/British Screen/ZDF/Uplink)
Edward II 1991, 90min, 35mm (BBC/Uplink)
Wittgenstein 1993, 75min, 35mm (BFI/Ch4)
Blue 1993, 75min, video
(AC/BBC/BC/Ch4/Uplink)
Glitterbug 1994, 60min, 35mm (BBC)
Distribution: Basilisk, BFI

ISAAC JULIEN

Film and video:
Who Killed Colin Roach? 1983, 38min,
16mm
Territories 1984, 30min, 16mm (AC)
The Passion of Remembrance 1986,
85min, 16mm (Ch4/GLC)
This Is Not an AIDS Ad 1987, 14min, video
Looking for Langston 1989, 45min, b/w,
16mm (Ch4)
Young Soul Rebels 1991, 105min, 35mm
(Ch4/Sankofa/La Sept/Kinowelt/
Iberoamericana)
The Attendant 1992, 8min, 35mm (BFI/Ch4)
Black and White in Colour 1992, part 1
50min, part 2 58min, video (BFI/BBC)

The Darker Side of Black 1994, 59min,
16mm (AC/BBC)
Distribution: ACE, Albany Video, BFI, LEA

TINA KEANE

Film and video:
The Swing 1978, 12min, b/w, video
Playpen 1979, 20min, b/w, video
Shadow of a Journey 1980, 20min, 16mm
(AC)
Clapping Songs 1981, 8min, b/w, video
Bedtime Story 1982, 20min, video
Hey Mack 1982, 15min, 16mm
Demolition/Escape 1983, 15min, video
In Our Hands, Greenham 1984, 40min,
video
Media Snake 1985, 8min, video
Hopscotsch 1986, 12min, video
Faded Wallpaper 1988, 18min, 16mm (AC)
Olympic Diver 1990, 5min, video
(AC/Cornerhouse Manchester/FVU)
Neon Diver 1991, 16min, 16mm (AC/Ch4)
Frankfurter 1994, 4min, b/w, 16mm
Caution X Ray 1994, 4min, video
Deviant Beauty 1995, 15min, 16mm
(LPF/LFVDA)

Installation:
Alice in Wonderland 1977, 1 monitor,
1 player, effects machine projecting storm
clouds, AIR Gallery London
The Swing/Alice Through Reflection
1978, interactive installation, 3 swings one
with surveillance camera attached to seat,
3 monitors, 'Summer Show' Serpentine Gallery,
London
The Swing 1978/9 interactive, 1 swing with
2 surveillance cameras attached, video mixer,
2 monitors, Galleria del Cavallino, Venice
See-Saw 1980, 2 monitors, 2 players,
2 mirrors, wooden see-saw, red neon sign,
'About Time' ICA London (ICA)
Demolition/Escape 1983, 7 monitors
(stacked with every other one upside down),
1 player, blue neon numbers 1 to 9, train set,
AIR Gallery London (AC)
A Bouquet 1984, 12 monitors, in 3 semi-
circles suspended from ceiling, 2 players, 'Cross
Currents' RCA London (RCA)
In Our Hands 1984, 12 monitors, 2 players,
scaffolding, A Space Toronto (BC)
Media Snake 1985, 20 monitors, 2 players,
(ICA)
Hopscotsch 1985, 1 monitor embedded in
floor face up, 1 player, blue neon numbers
1 to 9 arranged in a spiral (Interim Art
London)

Hopscotsch (version 2) 1985, 9 monitors
embedded in floor face up, 2 players, blue
neon numbers 1 to 9 arranged in a spiral
(Art Ware Hamburg)
Faded Wallpaper 1986, 11 monitors,
2 players, Serpentine Gallery London (AC)
The Diver 1987/8, 30 monitors face up,
3 players, Neon Diver sculpture (City Museum
and Art Gallery Stoke-on-Trent)
Escalator 1988, 22 monitors, 2 players,
6 light boxes, scaffolding, lighting, (Riverside
Studios London)
Circus Troupe 1990, 3 monitors, 3 players,
red neon hoop, 2 neon trapeze artist
sculptures, steel tight-rope, (AC/Nottingham
Media Centre)
Circus 1991, 10 monitors, 5 players, red neon
hoop, 2 neon trapeze artist sculptures, steel
tight-rope, 8 red fluorescent lights
(BC/Nottingham Media Centre/Studiogalerie
Museum Morsbroitch Leverkusen Germany)
Shattered Neon 1991, 1 monitor in steel
case, 1 player, 25 light boxes suspended face
down from ceiling above 'stream' of broken
glass, flashing neon sign (Central Space Gallery
London/GLAA)
Under the Surface 1991, two works in
sub-way, 'Topographie II' (Vienna Festival)
  Under Foot 6 monitors (videowall) face up
  beneath grid in ground, 6 players, infra-red
  signal for sound interaction
  End of Line video projection (onto steps),
  1 monitor (out of its casing), neon sign
Circus Rehearsal Space 1992, 3 monitors,
3 players, neon hoop, LFF LFMC
Caution X Ray 1992, 2 monitors, 2 video
projectors, 4 players, neon sign, 'Sanart '92'
Ankara Turkey (BC/Sanart)
Caution: Thin Ice 1993, 1 monitor, 1 player,
neon sign & sculpture, broken glass
(Kunstlerhaus Graz Austria)
Acrobat 1993, 1 monitor, 1 player, neon hoop,
'Pushing the Boundaries' Letherby Gallery
London (Nottingham Media Centre)
Caution: Thin Ice (version 2) 1994,
1 monitor, 1 player, glass table top, neon sign
(London Institute Gallery)
Urban Breast 1994, 1 miniature monitor,
1 player, model train set, red spotlight,
'Pushing the Boundaries' (Letherby Gallery
London)
Distribution: Cinenova, LEA, LFMC

JEFF KEEN

Film and video:

Wail 1960, 5min, b/w, silent, 8mm
Like the Time Is Now 1961, 6min, b/w, silent, 8mm
The Autumn Feast 1961, 14min, silent, 8mm
Breakout 1962, 10min, b/w, silent, 8mm
House of Secrets 1964-5, 15min, silent, 8mm
The Pink Auto 1964-5, 15min, silent, 8mm
The Games & Diversions of Doctor Gaz 1965, 8min, silent, 8mm
Mr Soft Eliminator 1966, 8min, silent, 8mm
Marvo Movie 1967, 5min, 16mm (BFI)
White Lite 1967, 3min, b/w, 16mm (BFI)
Cine Blatz 1968, 2½min, 16mm (BFI)
Meatdaze 1968, 8min, 16mm (BFI)
Monstra 1968, 8min, silent, 8mm
Mothman 1968, 30min, silent, 8mm
The Mutt'n Jeff Ice Cream Sundae 1969, 30min, silent, 8mm
Day of the Arcane Light 1969, 12min, silent, 8mm
Raydayfilm 1969, 18min, 16mm
Good Earth Film 1971, 30min, silent, 8mm
Stolen Moments 1972, 30min, silent, 8mm
White Dust 1972, 35min, 16mm
The Lost World of Doctor Gaz 1973, 30min, silent, 8mm
Lone Star 1974–75, 30min, silent, 8mm
24 Films 1975, 18min, silent, 16mm
Dr Gaz Against the Art of the Cinema 1976, 3min, 16mm (AC)
Godzilla Last of the Creatures 1976, 30min, silent, 8mm
The Return of Doctor Gaz 1978, 30min, silent, 8mm
Mad Love 1978, 48min, 16mm (SEA)
The Cartoon Theatre of Dr Gaz 1979, 12min, 16mm (AC)
Dr Gaz in Search of the Picturesque 1982, 5min, silent, 8mm
Gazwrx 1986, 10min, silent, S8mm
Blatzom 1986, 12½min, 16mm (AC)
Transfigured Blatz 1989, 30min, silent, video
Ray-Day-O 1989, 30min, silent, video
B-B-B-Bom + Lifestorm 1990, 5min, video (AC)
Omozap 3 + Platzmatic Blatz 1991, 10min, video (AC)
Graficoblatz 1991, 2½min, video (AC)
Auto Blatzo 1991, 8min, video (AC)
Omozap 1 & 2 1991, 2min, 16mm
Artwar 1993, 12min, silent, S8mm
Artwar Fallout 1993, 10min, silent, S8mm
Artwar 1993, 4½min, video (AC/Ch4)

Artwar – The Last Frontier 1993, 20min, video
Distribution: BFI, LFMC

PATRICK KEILLER

Film:

Stonebridge Park 1981, 21min, b/w, 16mm
Norwood 1983, 26min, b/w, 16mm (AC)
The End 1986, 18min, b/w, 16mm (AC)
Valtos 1987, 11min, b/w, 16mm (AC/Ch4)
The Clouds 1989, 20min, b/w, 16mm (BFI)
London 1994, 85min, 35mm (BFI)
Distribution: BFI, LFMC

ANDREW KÖTTING

Film and video:

Cement the Land 1982, 4min, b/w, S8mm
Dead Relatives 1983, 5min, b/w, S8mm, (with h. van der Ploeug)
Don't Shout 1983, 4min, b/w, S8mm (with h. van der Ploeug)
Skinned Alive 1983, 4min, b/w, S8mm (with Leila McMillan)
Forgive Me 1983, 8min, b/w, S8mm (with D. Burnand)
Klipperty Klopp 1984, 12min, b/w, 16mm
Anvil Head the Hun 1986, 35mm, b/w, S8mm
Self Heal 1987, 30min, 16mm
Erik and Ingrid 1988, 20min, video (with Leila McMillan)
Jäckofalltradesmasterofnôneinalandof maneàtingtrees 1988, 15min, video
Hub Bub in the Baöbabs 1989, 35min, b/w, 16mm
Hoi Polloi 1990, 1min, video (AC/BBC)
Hoi Polloi 1990, 10min, S8mm
Acumen 1991, 20min, 16mm (AC/Ch4)
Diddyköy 1992, 6min, video, (with Nick Gordon-Smith)
H.B. 1829 (His Badblood) 1992, 6min, S8mm
Fleshfilm 1992, 6min, S8mm
Smart Alek 1993, 18min, 16mm (BFI/Ch4)
Festival of Brent 1993, 20min, video (with Nick Gordon-Smith)
Gallivant 1994, 8min, video
Là Bas (down there) 1994, 19min, b/w, S16mm (BBC/BFI)
Jaunt 1995, 5min, S8mm (Carlton/LAB/LPF)
Distribution: BFI, LEA, LFMC, Tall Stories, (0171 703 2529)

JULIE KUZMINSKA

Video:

Archaos I 1990, 11min
Archaos II 1991, 11min
Chaos 1992, 3min
Siren 1993, 5min
The Winds Begin to Sing 1994, 7min (AC)
Distribution: LEA

RICHARD KWIETNIOWSKI

Film and video:

Alfalfa 1987, 9min, 16mm (SWA)
Ballad of Reading Gaol 1988, 12min, 16mm (AC/Ch4)
Flames of Passion 1989, 18min, b/w, 16mm (BFI/Ch4)
Proust's Favourite Fantasy 1991, 1min, b/w, 16mm (with Roger Clark) (AC/BBC)
The Cost of Love 1991, 2min, b/w, 16mm
Pigs' Trotters at the Palace 1991, 30min, video (BBC Wales)
Actions Speak Louder 1992, 22min, video (Ch4)
Poems on the Box 1993, 12 x 1min, video (BBC Bristol)
A Night with Derek 1994, 22min, video (Ch4)
Distribution: BFI

SANDRA LAHIRE

16mm Film:

Arrows 1984, 15min
Terminals 1986, 18min
Edge 1986, 8min
Plutonium Blonde 1987, 15min (AC)
Uranium Hex 1988, 11min (AC/Ch4/Illuminations)
Serpent River 1989, 30min (AC/Ch4)
Lady Lazarus 1991, 25min (BFI)
Eerie 1992, 1min, b/w (AC/BBC)
Night Dances 1995, 15min (AC)
Johnny Panic 1995, 35min (BFI)
Distribution: BFI, Cinenova, LEA, LFMC

RICHARD LAND

Video:

Flux 1990, 7min (with Paul Lamb) (FVU)
Flight 1991, 8min (with Paul Lamb) (FVU)
Fuse 1992, 6min (with Paul Lamb) (FVU)

Installation:

The Tunnel 1988, 1 video projector, 1 computer, audio (with Richard Brown and Andrew Bailey) (International Film and Video Festival, Osnabrück Germany)

The Mirror 1989, 1 monitor, 1 camera, 1 computer (with Richard Brown) (Air Gallery London)
Image and Object 1990, 60min, 12 monitors, 3 players (with Richard Brown) (Pompidou Centre Paris)
Mirror Images (video link) 1993, 2 monitors, 2 cameras, 2 computers, at two remote sites linked by modem (with Paul Lamb) Festival of Photography Derby; European Media Art Festival Osnabrück (FVU)
Mirror Images (single installation) 1994, 1 monitor, 1 camera, 1 computer (with Paul Lamb) V-Topia, Tramshed Glasgow, Bluecoat Liverpool (FVU)

Performance:
Negative Image 1989, 20 monitors, sound triggered computer (with Richard Brown) 'Negative Image' Royal Academy of Arts London
Flight 1990, 1 video projector, 1 monitor, 1 camera, 3 MIDI-based instruments, 3 computers (with Paul Lamb) Interactive Seminar ICA London (FVU/ICA)
Distribution: FVU

DAVID LARCHER

Film and video:
Mare's Tail 1969, 150min, 16mm (Alan Power)
Monkey's Birthday 1975, 360min, 16mm (Alan Power)
EETC 1986, 69min, video (Ch4)
Granny's Is (version 1) 1989, 47min, 16mm (BFI)
Granny's Is (version 2) 1990, 78min, video (Ch4)
videØvoid – The Trailer 1993, 33min, video (AC/Ch4)
videØvoid – Text 1995, 30min, video (part of planned cycle of 7 x 30 min tapes)

Installation:
Ich Tank Dur . . . 1983, Berlin
Zenozone 1992, 12 monitors, 1 player
Distribution: LEA, LFMC, David Larcher (0171 370 0662)

WILLIAM LATHAM

Film and video:
Tid-Tug 1981, 3min, 16mm
The Empire of Form 1984, 3min, 16mm
The Conquest of Form 1988, 5min, video (IBM)

A Sequence of the Evolution of Form 1989, 2½min, 35mm & video (IBM)
The Process of Evolution 1990, 2½min, video (IBM/Natural History Museum London)
Mutations 1991, 4min, video (IBM)
The Garden of Unearthly Delights 1993, CD-Rom (IBM)
Biogenesis 1993, 5min, video (AC/Ch4/IBM)
Organic Television 1993, 30min, video (AC/IBM/Manchester City Art Gallery)

Installation:
Organic Television 1993, 32 monitors, 6 players 'Organic TV' Royal Festival Hall London (AC/Manchester City Art Gallery)
The Second Listening Room 1995, 7 monitors, 2 players, walk-thru inflatable pink pumpkin, 'Art & Electronics '95' Hong Kong Arts Centre (BC)
Distribution: Computer Art Works Ltd (0171 439 1001)

MALCOLM LE GRICE

Film and video:
China Tea 1965, 10min, silent, 16mm
Castle 1 1966, 22min, b/w, 16mm
Little Dog for Roger 1967, 12min, b/w, 16mm
Yes No Maybe Not 1967, 7min, b/w, 16mm
Talla 1967, 20min, b/w, silent, 16mm
Blind White Duration 1967, 10min, b/w, silent, 16mm
Castle 2 1968, 32min, b/w, two screen, 16mm
Spot the Microdot 1969, 10min, 16mm
Your Lips 1 1970, 3min, silent, 16mm
Lucky Pigs 1970, 4min, b/w, 3 screen, 16mm
Reign of the Vampire 1970, 16min, b/w, single and two screen versions, 16mm
Berlin Horse 1970, 9min, single and two screen version, 16mm
Love Story 2 1971, 10min, two screen, 16mm
1919 1971, 12min, three screen, 16mm
Your Lips 3 1971, 3min, 16mm
Newport 1972, 15min, b/w, silent, 16mm
Whitchurch Down 1972, 15min, b/w, silent, 16mm (AC)
Threshold 1972, 17min, single and four screen versions, 16mm (AC)
Blue Field Duration 1972, 8min, two screen, 16mm
White Field Duration 1973, 12min, two screen, 16mm
After Leonardo 1973, 22min, six screen, 16mm
Don't Say 1973, 10min, two screen, 16mm

After Lumière – L'arroseur arrosé 1974, 12min, 16mm
After Manet, After Giorgione, Le Déjeuner sur l'herbe, or Fête Champêtre 1975, 60min, four screen, 16mm (AC)
Academic Still Life 1976, 6min, 16mm
Time and Motion Study 1976, 12min, 16mm
Blackbird Descending – Tense Alignment 1977, 120min, 16mm (AC)
Emily – Third Party Speculation 1979, 60min, 16mm (AC)
Finnegan's Chin – Temporal Economy 1981, 80min, 16mm (BFI)
Sketches for a Sensual Philosophy 1988, 60min, video (Ch4)
Chronos Fragmented 1995, 55min, video (AC/Ch4)

Installation/Performance:
Grass 1968, 10min, tape-slide
Wharf 1968, 30min, film, tape-slide
Drama in a Wide Media Environment 1968, 2 weeks, Drury Lane Arts Lab
Typodrama 1970, computer generated text for performers, Computer Arts Society's 'Event One' RCA
Love Story 1 1971, 8min, film-shadow performance
Horror Film 1 1971, 14min, film-shadow performance
Love Story 3 1972, 10min, film performance
Horror Film 2 1972, 25min, 3D shadow performance (red and green spectacles)
Pre-production 1973, 15min, slide performance
Matrix 1973, 18min, six projector performance
Four Wall Duration 1973, film-loop installation, continuous
Gross Fog 1973, film-loop installation
Joseph's Coat 1973, film-loop installation or performance
Principles of Cinematography 1973, 15min, performance
Screen Entrance Exit 1974, 10min, film performance
Videobscura 1974, CCTV and polaroid performance, Exeter
After Leonardo 1974, CCTV video installation, Exeter
Improvised and Computer Music 1989, London Film-makers Co-op (with Keith Row)
Distribution: BFI, LFMC

219

DAVID LEISTER

Select Filmography 16mm film:
Magic Act 1985, 8min, b/w
Wind-Up 1985, 12min, b/w
Smoke 1985, 8min, b/w
Notes on a Line 1987, 14min, b/w (AC)
Pointillist Dance 1988, 14min, b/w
Interlude 1989, 12min, b/w
Timepiece 1989, 5min, b/w
Faith Triumphant 1989, 5min, b/w
Nature Boy 1990, 12min, b/w
Waves and Graves 1985/91, 14min, b/w
Headgear 1992, 8min, b/w
Driving the Loop 1992, 7min, b/w
Lacing Film 1993, 14min, b/w (AC)
Distribution: LFMC

STEVE LITTMAN

Video:
Mirror 1979, 5min, b/w
Please Turn Over Over Over . . . To 1979, 5min
Have I Seen You Before 1979, 12min, b/w
The Turn 1979, 5min, b/w
You Make Me Shout 1980, 3min
Crisps 1980, 4min
Bicycle-Road, Movement Turning 1980, 12min
Swimmer 1980, 8min
Water, Noise, Shape & Pattern 1980, 8min
The Column No.1 1981, 10min
The Venezuelan Sequence 1982, 8min, (with Impact Theatre Co-operative)
Still Life No.1 1982, 11min, (with Zoe Redman)
The Smoker Tapes 1983, 28min
Mother – Son 1983, 10min
I Really 1984, 7min,
The Long Search for the Necessary Tool 1984, 75min, (with Jeremy Peyton-Jones/Regular Music)
Surfing on Short Waves 1985, 30min
The Winner 1986, 16min
In the Name of the Gun 1987, 4min
Big Time – The House 1990, 4min

Installation/Performance:
Sound and Rhythm 1979, 8min, 4 monitors, 4 players
The Line 1980, 10min, 2 monitors, 2 players
The Wait 1980, 10min, 2 monitors, 1 player
Still Life No.1 1982, 7min, 3 monitors, 3 players
Picture Memoirs 1982, 14min, 3 monitors, 3 players

I Want 1983, 30min, 4 monitors, 5 players
Mother – Son 1983, 10min, 2 monitors, 2 players
Smiling 1984, 20min, 3 monitors, 4 players
The Long Search for the Necessary Tool 1984, 80min 30 monitors, 2 players, (with Jeremy Peyton-Jones & Regular Music)
Surfing on Short Waves 1985, 60min, 2 monitors, 2 players (original performance work with tapes, made with Peter Anderson, Tim Buckley, Steve Hawley, Phil Herbert, Blue Jean Tyranny.)
Overseen – Overheard – Overlooked 1986, 60min, 60 monitors, 12 players (performance and installation)
Hidden Grin "The Suburbs of Hell" 1986, 90min, 12 monitors, 4 players
Smile 2 1987, 20min, 6 monitors, 5 players
Streetlife . . . Something of the Present 1987, 7min, 5 monitors, 5 players
Overseen – Overheard – Overlooked 1987, 60min, 30 monitors, 8 players
On a Clear Day You Can See Forever 1989, 8min, 3 video walls, 3 players
Kiss (version 1) 1991, 10min, 4 monitors, 4 players
Ritual Kiss 1992, 10min, video wall, 2 players
The Enlightenment 1993, 60min, 4–20 monitors/players
Distribution: Annalogue, LEA

LOOPHOLE CINEMA

Film Installation/Performance:
Event 1989, 14 S8mm, 1 16mm, LFMC and Third Eye Centre Glasgow
Effects of Darkened Rooms 1990, shadow wall performance, cacophany room, shadow maze, S8mm and 16mm, live sound, National Review of Live Art Glasgow
Shadow Engine 1991, shadow wall performance, cacophony room, shadow maze, S8mm and 16mm, live sound, noise and shadow constructions, LFMC
Propaganda Beacons 1991, constructed light and sound mechanisms, LFMC (LFF)
Vacant Possession 1992, 16mm, multiple sound environment, wall demolition with sledgehammers, drill, 4 x 1000w lights, derelict tower block, Birmingham (Fine Rats International)
Light-chain 1993, film, video, computer probability text generator, kinetic mechanisms, ICA London
Levitating a Body 1993, shadow performance, sound samples, levitation, Red Rose Club London

Shadow Eating 1993, shadow performance, film manipulation, expanded projection, improvised music, Reading Film Festival
The Fire Cabinets 1993, 9 metal cabinets with film, strobe, extractor fan, fire, distress signals, Brockwell Lido London
Circus of the Senses 1993, film, video, slide projectors, moving screen, gantry crane, sound mapping, fire, European Media Arts Festival Osnabrück
Night of the Fire Cabinets 1993, projection, strobes, sound samples, hanging lights and objects, 4 metal fire cabinets, distress flares, The Tannery London
Prism Engine 1994, three sided translucent container, sound light and kinetics, 'Quick Festival' South Bank London
Down There 1994, film, video, sampled sound, prepared Dansettes, 'London Underground Festival' Bridewell Theatre
Guy Fawkes Stalks Belgium 1994, film, fire-works, fire-crackers and distress flares, live music (prepared saxophone and voice), sampled sound, 'Kino Flash Flood Experience' Deux Achren Belgium
Distribution: c/o Greg Pope, 2 Flaxman Road, London SE5 9DH

TIM MACMILLAN

Time-Slice Works:
Water I 1983, loop, silent, 16mm
Water II 1983, loop, silent, 16mm
Jump 1983, loop, silent, 16mm
Spilt Milk 1984, 3min, 16mm
Pinhole Films Compilation 1989, 10min, silent, video, works in sequence :
Geisha and Pigeons 1988 (AC)
Cat and Tuna Head 1988 (AC)
Jump 1983
Geisha and Umbrellas 1988 (AC)
Water I 1983
Two Men Jump 1988 (AC)
Spilt Milk (one take) 1984
Confetti 1988 (AC)
Multiple Exposure 1988 (AC)
Nude Double Exposure 1988 (AC)
Water II 1983
A Journey at the Speed of Light 1993, 4min (showreel), video, works in sequence :
Carmen and Water I 1993 (AC)
Carmen Jumps Through Fire 1993 (AC)
Carmen and Water II 1993 (AC)
Carmen and Grapefruit and Sparkler 1993 (AC)
Geisha and Umbrellas 1988 (AC)
Dog 1993 (AC)

Time-Lines Compilation 1993, 10min, silent, video, works in sequence :
   Dream Jump I 1993 (AC/Derby City Council/EMA/Metro Photography)
   Dream Jump II 1993 (AC/Derby City Council/EMA/Metro Photography)
   Dream Jump III 1993 (AC/Derby City Council/EMA/Metro Photography)
   Carmen Jumps Through Fire 1993 (AC)
   Carmen and Grapefruit and Sparkler 1993 (AC)
   Dream Cereal I 1993 (AC/Derby City Council/EMA/Metro Photography)
   Carmen and Water I 1993 (AC)
   Dog 1993 (AC)
   Water (Right to Left) 1993 (AC)
   Dream Circles of Fire 1993 (AC/Derby City Council/EMA/Metro Photography)
   Dream Cereal II 1993 (AC/Derby City Council/EMA/Metro Photography)
   Dream Cereal III 1993 (AC/Derby City Council/EMA/Metro Photography)
Homage to Edgerton 1994, 4min, silent, video
Distribution: Montage Gallery, 35–36 Queen's Street, Derby, DE1 3DS (01332 295858)

STUART MARSHALL

Film and video:
Go Through the Motions 1975, 6min, b/w, video
Just a Glimpse 1975, 8min, b/w, video
Screen 1976, 10min, b/w, video
Mouth Room 1976, 8min, b/w, video (AC)
Still Life Animation 1976, 12min, b/w, video
Sound Cuts 1977, 14min, b/w, video
Distinct 1979, 38min, b/w, video (AC)
The Streets of . . 1979, 26min, video (AC)
A Question of Three Sets of Characteristics 1980, 55min, video (AC)
The Love Show (part 1) 1980, 55min, video (AC)
The Love Show (part 2) 1980, 11min, video (AC)
The Love Show (part 3) 1980, 12min, video (AC)
Kaposi's Sarcoma 1983, 29min, video
Bright Eyes 1984, 80min, video
Pedagogue 1988, 10min, video
Desire 1989, 50min, b/w, 16mm (Ch4)
Comrades in Arms 1990, 50min, 16mm (Ch4)
Over Our Dead Bodies 1991, 50min, 16mm (Ch4)
Robert Marshall 1991, 10min, video
Blue Boys 1992, 25min, video (Ch4)

Video Installation:
Privileged View 1976
Orientation Studies 1976
Orientation Studies 2 1977
Fiery Romance 1978
Excesses 1978
Memory Space 1978
For Queen Eleanor of England, Duchess of Aquitaine, Her Daughter Countess Marie of Champagne and Her Chaplain Andreas 1982
A Journal of the Plague Year '84 1984 (RCA/AC)
Distribution: LEA, Maya Vision

JOHN MAYBURY

Film and video:
Modern is as Modern Does 1978, 15min, S8mm
Cosmetic Angels Under Pressure 1978–80, 20min, S8mm
Sunbathing for Idols 1978–80, 25min, S8mm
So This is Now 1978–80, 30min, S8mm (also installation)
Continuous Beauty Brainwash 1979–81, 30min, S8mm
A Courtesan and Her Reflection 1980–81, 16min, S8mm
Is Like a Melody 1980–81, 9min, S8mm
The Technology of Souls 1980–81, 10min, S8mm
Solitude 1981, 10min, S8mm
A Fall of Angels 1981, 40min, three screens, S8mm
Exiled from the Image Repertoire 1981, 10min, two screens, S8mm
Shallow Terrorists 1981, 24min, two screens, S8mm (also 40min with spoken text)
Court of Miracles (Moments Before Desire) 1982, 41min, S8mm
Tortures That Laugh aka **The Cultural Impotence of Stupid Boys** 1983, 27min, 16mm (18min, S8mm)
Baby Monkey's Bad Trip 1983, 15min, S8mm
Pantomime Incubus 1983, 10min, S8mm
The Bird Sings with its Fingers 1983, 10min, S8mm
Pagan Idolatry 1984, 10min, 16mm.
sequence for **The Dream Machine** (Derek Jarman, Michael Kostiff, Cerith Wyn Evans) (AC)
Circus Logic I – IV 1984, 4 x 30min, video
Big Love 1984, 30min, video
The Union Jacking Up 1985, 25min, 16mm
Ecce Homo Promo 1986, 10min, video

L'Inspirazioni 1988, 2min, 35mm (with Derek Jarman) (Florence Opera House)
War Requiem (Derek Jarman) 1988, (sequence) 16mm (BBC)
Absurd 1990, 5min and 40min, video (LWT/South Bank Show)
Tunnel of Love 1990, 7min, video (BBC)
Man to Man 1992, 73min, 16mm (BBC)
Remembrance of Things Fast 1993, 60min, video/16mm (AC/Ch4)
Premonition of Absurd Perversion in Sexual Personae – Part 1 1993, 60min, video
Distribution: BFI, LEA

MICHAEL MAZIERE

Film:
Sketch for Films 1977, 3min, S8mm
A Sentimental Journey 1978, 7min, 16mm
Clear Cut 1979, 18min, 16mm
Untitled 1980, 18min, 16mm
Colour Work 1981, 15min, silent, 16mm
Silent Film 1982, 15min, silent, 16mm (AC)
Skylight 1983, 3min, silent, 16mm
Image Moment 1984/5, 25min, two screen, b/w, silent, 16mm
Space Painting 1986, 6min, two screen, silent, 16mm
The Bathers Series:
   Les Baigneurs 1986, 6min, 16mm (AC)
   Swimmer 1987, 7min, 16mm (AC)
Unspoken 1987, 12min, 16mm (AC)
Message from Budapest 1987, 15min, 16mm (with Moira Sweeney) (AC/BC)
Cezanne's Eye I 1988, 20min, silent, 16mm (AC)
Cezanne's Eye II 1991, 20min, 16mm
The Red Sea 1992, 20min, 16mm (AC)
Distribution: LFMC

JULIET MCKOEN

16mm Film:
A Day in the Night 1988, 25min
Blood Sisters 1991, 17min (GLAA)
Song of the Sands 1993, 12min, (with Peter Croskery) (NAB/BFI)
Rites of In/Fertility 1994, 18min, (NAB)
Stories from the Sands 1994, 40min, (with Peter Croskery) (BFI)
Distribution: Phoenix Films (0171 247 7221)

CHRIS MEIGH-ANDREWS

Video:

Continuum 1977, 3min, b/w, two screen (with Gabrielle Brown)
The Viewer's Receptive Capacity 1978, 20min, b/w (with Gabrielle Brown)
3:4 1978–79, 30min, b/w, (with Gabrielle Brown)
Horizontal and Vertical 1979, 15min
Scanning 1979, 10min
Clockwise and Counter Clockwise 1979, 15min
The Distracted Driver 1980, 18min
The Chance Meeting 1981, 14min
The Room with a View 1982, 12min
Time Travelling/A True Story 1982, 8min (GLAA)
Interlude (Homage to Bugs Bunny) 1983, 4min
5 Minutes 1984, 5min
Still Life with Monitor 1984, 7min
On Being 1985, 2½min (GLAA)
Other Spaces 1986, 5min
An Imaginary Landscape 1986, 6min (GLAA)
The Stream 1987, 12min (GLAA)
Domestic Landscapes 1992, 18min
Domestic Landscapes 1994, CD-Rom (Oxford Brookes University/Oxford Photography/SA)
A Sense of Myself 1994, CD-Rom (Oxford Brookes University/Oxford Photography/SA)

Installation:

Field Study 1979, 3 monitors, 3 players, The Basement Newcastle
Light, Time, Memory . . . 1981, 1 slide projector, 1 b/w monitor, CCTV, Woodlands Gallery Greenwich
Inspiration 1984, 1 monitor, CCTV, 'Annual Living Room Festival' Odder Denmark (Danish Film Institute)
An Imaginary Fountain 1989, 9 monitors, 3 players, Canada House London
Eau d'artifice 1990, 35 monitors, 4 players, Harris Museum Preston (AC/Samuelsons)
Streamline 1991, 9 monitors, 9 players, Mercury Court Liverpool (AC/Bluecoat Gallery)
Heaven and Earth 1992, monitor, projector, 2 players, London Film-Makers Co-op
Cross-Currents 1993, 8 laser prints, monitor, projector, CCTV, Cafe Gallery London (AC/Camerwork)
Zoetrope 1993, 8 monitors, CCTV, (University of Central Lancashire)

Perpetual Motion 1994, 1 monitor, 2 computers, wind turbine, Saw Gallery Ottawa (NWA/Oxford Brookes University/Oxford Photography/SA)
Fire & Ice 1995, 1 projector, 1 computer
Distribution: FVU, LEA

KATHARINE MEYNELL

Film and video:

Housework 1980, 20min, b/w, video
She Talks to Herself Often 1981, 6min, 16mm
RCA Women's Group 1982, 10min, video
Momento 1983, 5min, video
Belly 1983, 2min, video
The Sister's Story 1984, 17min, video (AC)
Untitled – Ectopic Pregnancy 1985, 11min, video
Hannah's Song 1987, 8min, video (AC)
Blackstock Estate Tapes 1987, 30min, video (GLAA/Islington Council)
Medusa 1988, 20min, video (BFI)
As she opened her eyes she looked over her shoulder and saw someone passing the other side of the doorway with a strange smile 1990, 10min, video (BBC Scotland)

Installation:

Belly 1983, 1 monitor, in ceiling of tissue paper tent, 1 player, RCA London
A Book for a Performance 1986, 2 monitors, 2 players, Air Gallery London (AC/LVA)
Hannah's Song 1986, 5 monitors, 2 players, drawing, false wall, 'Women Sculptors Today' Canterbury Festival
Group Portrait 1987, 3 monitors, 3 players, Blackstock Community Centre Islington (GLAA/Islington Council)
Her Gaze 1988, 2/6 monitors, 2 players, 'Bookworks' Victoria & Albert Museum London
Moonrise 1988, video wall in 3 groups, or 4 small monitors and 1 large monitor, 3 players, Tate Gallery Liverpool (Video Positive)
Ants and Balls 1990, 2 monitors, facing each other in doorway, 2 players, Sheffield Media Show
Eat 1992, 1 projector, 5 monitors, 6 players, Kettle's Yard Cambridge (AC)
Vampire S Eat 1992, 1 LCD screen in chair, 1 player, Kettle's Yard Cambridge (AC)
Poznan Installation 1993, 2 monitors (1 unconnected), 1 player, box, salt drawings, International Artists' Centre Poznan Poland (BC)

Dis-enchantment Re-enchantment 1993/4, 2 monitors (colour, b/w), LCD screen, 3 players, 3 wooden boxes, 2 sound sources, 2 light boxes, Quicksilver Gallery (Middlesex University)
Lost and Found 1994, 4 monitors, 1 projector, 5 players, Quicksilver Gallery (Middlesex University)
Distribution: LEA

PHIL MULLOY

Film:

Allow Me 1972, 3min, b/w, 16mm (RCA)
Still 1974, 10min, b/w, 16mm (RCA)
A History and the City 1977, 25min, b/w, 16mm (AC)
In the Forest 1979, 90min, b/w, 16mm (BFI)
Gertler 1981, 60min, 16mm (AC)
Give Us This Day 1983, 60min, 16mm (AC)
Through an Unknown Land 1986, 60min, 16mm (Ch4)
The Return 1988, 90min, 16mm (Ch4)
The Eye of the Storm 1988, 18min, 16mm
Tinfish 1989, 1min, 16mm (AC/BBC)
Possession 1991, 18min, b/w, 16mm (AC)
Cowboys 1991, 6 x 3min, 35mm (AC/Ch4)
  Outrage
  That's Nothing
  The Conformist
  Slim Pickin's
  Murder!
  High Noon
Ding Dong Bell 1992, 1min, 16mm (AC/BBC)
The Cowboy Collection of Adverts 1992, 6min, 16mm
The Sound of Music 1993, 11min, 35mm (Ch4)
The Ten Commandments: 35mm
  No.5 Thou Shalt Not Kill 1993, 3min,
  No.6 Thou Shalt Not Commit Adultery 1994, 5min
  No.7 Thou Shalt Not Steal 1994, 4½min
  No.1 Thou Shalt Not Adore False Gods 1995, 4min
  No.4 Honour Thy Father and Thy Mother 1995, 4min
The History of the World 35mm (LPF/LFVDA)
  Episode 65 – The Age of Reason Begins 1993, 3min
  Episode 10 – The Discovery of Language 1994, 3min
  Episode 16 – The Invention of Writing and its Destruction 1994, 4min

Laughing Moon Films 1994, 7 x ½min, 35mm (MTV)
Distribution: BFI, Spectre Films
(01267 241 740)

LAURA MULVEY and PETER WOLLEN

Work by Mulvey and Wollen:
Penthesilea 1974, 90min, 16mm
Riddles of the Sphinx 1977, 99min, 16mm (BFI)
AMY! 1980, 30min, 16mm (SA)
Crystal Gazing 1981, 90min, 16mm (Ch4)
Frida Kahlo and Tina Modotti 1982, 30min, 16mm (AC)
The Bad Sister 1983, 90min, video (Ch4)

Work by Mulvey:
Disgraced Monuments 1992, 50min, video (with Mark Lewis) (Ch4)

Installation:
New Horizons 1987, 2½min, 36 monitor videowall, 'The Lunatic of One Idea' Shopping Mall Toronto, Tate Gallery Liverpool (Public Access Toronto)

Work by Wollen:
Reading the U.S. Press 1985, 30min, video (with Manuel De Landa) (Paper Tiger Television)
Friendship's Death 1987, 78min, 35mm (BFI)
Images of Atlantis 1992, 45min, video (Ch4)
Full Cycle 1992, 45min, video (Ch4)

Installation:
Welcome Aboard Soyuz 1985, videowall (Palladium Club New York)
Some Uncertain Signs 1986, animated pixelboard (Electromedia Toronto)
Distribution: BFI

JULIE MYERS

Video:
Going for Goldfish 1990, 2min (with Susan Collins) (AC/FVU/Cornerhouse Manchester)
Trim to Fit 1993, 3min (AC)
Shooting the Breeze 1995, CD-Rom ('Toybox' compilation) (AC)

Installation:
Blowing the Whistle 1991, ½min cycle, football stadium lightboard, (with Anna Douglas) (AC/Moviola)
Screen Deep 1992, 20min cycle, National Portrait Gallery London
Distribution: LEA, Moviola

VERA NEUBAUER

Film:
Genetics 1970, 1min, 16mm
Animation-Allegation 1970, 20min, 16mm
Cannon Fodder 1970, 1min, 16mm
Pip and Bessie 1973–75, 6 x 6min, 16mm (Bayerischer Rundfunk TV)
Fate 1976, 1min, 16mm
Animation for Live Action 1978, 25min, 16mm (BFI)
The Decision 1981, 33min, 35mm (BFI)
The World of Children 1984, 15min, 16mm (Ch4)
Mid Air 1986, 16min, 16mm (Ch4)
The Mummy's Curse 1987, 30min, 16mm (AC)
Passing On 1988, 30min, 16mm (Ch4)
Don't Be Afraid 1990, 28min, b/w, 16mm (Ch4)
Live TV 1993, 1min, 16mm (AC/BBC)
The Lady of the Lake 1995, 20min, b/w, 16mm (AC)
Distribution: BFI, Cinenova

CHRIS NEWBY

Film:
Black Nectar, 1980, 16mm
Elegy 1981, 16mm
Feast 1983, 16mm
Hoy 1984, b/w, 15min, 16mm (RCA/AC)
Stromboli 1990, 16mm (AC)
The Old Man of the Sea 1990, 20min, b/w, 35mm (AC/Ch4)
Kiss 1991, 5min, 16mm (Ch4)
Relax 1991, 25min, 16mm (BFI)
Anchoress 1993, 108min, b/w, 35mm (BFI/Ch4)
Madagascar Skin 1995, 96min, 35mm (BFI/Ch4)
Distribution: BFI

JAYNE PARKER

Film and video:
Free Show 1979, 16min, b/w, 16mm
I Cat 1980, 10min, 16mm
RX Recipe 1980, 12min, 16mm
I Dish 1982, 16min, b/w, 16mm
Snig 1982, 6min, silent, 16mm
Almost Out 1984, 105min, video (AC)
En Route 1986, 15min, video (AC)
The Cat and the Woman 1987, 2½min, 16mm
K. 1989, 13min, b/w, 16mm (AC)
The Pool 1991, 10min, b/w, 16mm (AC/Ch4)
Cold Jazz 1993, 17min, b/w, 16mm (BFI/Ch4)

Crystal Aquarium 1995, 35min, b/w, 16mm (AC/Ch4)
Distribution: LEA, LFMC

KAYLA PARKER

Film and video:
Adult Day Return 1986, 2min, 16mm
The Internal Voice 1988, 5min, 16mm
Lighter Hands 1989, 3min, video
Looks Familiar 1989, 3min, 16mm
Nuclear Family 1990, 5min, 16mm (TSW/SWA)
Fanny and Johnny on Acid 1990, 10min, video (with Stuart Moore)
Unknown Woman 1991, 9min, 16mm (AC/SWA)
Puirt-a-beul 1992, 2min, 16mm (STV)
Canntaireachd 1992, 1min, 16mm (STV)
Cage of Flame 1992, 10min, 16mm (AC/Ch4)
Night Sounding 1993, 1min, 16mm (AC/BBC)
As Yet Unseen 1994, 2min, 16mm (BFI)
Elemental 1994, 10min, S8mm (with Stuart Moore) (Plymouth City Museum and Art Gallery)
Walking Out 1995, 15min, 16mm (SWA)

Installation:
As Yet Unseen 1994, living room set with fireplace, photographs, TV set and player, 'Frame by Frame' Plymouth Art Centre
Distribution: BFI, LEA, LFMC

PRATIBHA PARMAR

Film and video
Emergence 1986, 20min, video
Reframing AIDS 1987, 35min, video
Sari Red 1988, 11min, video (AC)
Memory Pictures 1989, 26min, video (AC)
Bhangra Jig 1990, 4min, video (Ch4)
Flesh & Paper 1990, 24min, 16mm (Ch4)
Khush 1991, 24min, 16mm (Ch4)
A Place of Rage 1991, 54min, 16mm (Ch4)
Double the Trouble Twice the Fun 1992, 24min, video (Ch4)
Taboo 1993, 24min, video (Ch4)
Warrior Marks 1993, 54min, 16mm, (with Alice Walker) (Ch4)
The Colour of Britain 1994, 50min, 16mm (AC/Ch4)
Memsahib Rita 1994, 20min, 16mm (BBC/BFI)
Distribution: Cinenova

STEPHEN PARTRIDGE

Video:

Easy Piece 1974, 6min, b/w
Scrutiny 1974, 10min, b/w
Grey Scale 1974, 5min, b/w
Overload 1974, 15min, b/w
Monitor 1975, 10min, b/w
Interlace 1975, 15min, b/w
Episodes-Interposed 1979, 29min (AC)
Black Skirt 1979, 7min
Interplay 1980, 9min (AC)
Soundtapes 1982, 6min,
(with David Cunnigham)
Dialogue for Two Players 1984, 18min
(Ch4)
One Thousand and One Boys' Games
1984, 10min, (with John Yeadon)
Two Reelers 1985, 32min, (written by
Tom McGrath for cablevision) (SAC)
Vide Voce (The Three's in the Four)
1986, 10min, (with David Cunnigham and
Mary Phillips) (SAC)
Sentences 1988–93, various works 1–2min,
(with David Cunnigham) (De Arte del Video)
The Sounds of These Words 1990, 4min
(Ch4)
Monitor (version 2) 1993, 5min, b/w
Nonsense, No-sense, Sentences 1994,
CD-Rom

Installation:

Triad 1976, 3 projector slide installation, ICA
London
Installation No.1 1976, 6 monitors,
4 cameras, Third Eye Centre Glasgow (SAC)
8 X 8 X 8 1976, 8 monitors, 8 cameras, auto
switcher, Tate Gallery London
**A Spatial Drawing: A Condition of
Space** 1976, 8 slide projectors, Butlers Wharf
London
Delineations 1977, 2 100 foot audio tape
loops, Ayton Basement Newcastle-upon-Tyne
A Coincidence of Space 1977,
10 monitors, 2 players, Paris Biennalle (BC)
Dialogue for Four Players 1978,
4 monitors, 4 players, Air Gallery London
Sketch for a Square 1978, 4 monitors,
Herbert Gallery Coventry
Study in Blue 1979, 4 monitors, 2 players,
The Kitchen New York
Display-displaced 1981, 12 monitors, Ikon
Gallery Birmingham (AC)
Scape 1985, 6 monitors, 2 players (Duncan of
Jordanstone College Dundee)
Interrun 1986, 16 monitors, 3 players,
Transmission Gallery Glasgow (SAC)

Interrun 1989, 34 monitor videowall,
3 players, Tate Gallery Liverpool (Moviola)
Video Miniatures
1992–95, series of wall mounted or table top
miniature video sculptures
Distribution: Annalogue, Fields and Frames

JO PEARSON

Film and video:

All in Your Head, 1991, 6min, b/w, video
(Westminster City Council)
Missing Pieces 1992, 3min, video
(Ray Finnis Trust)
Do What You Like 1992, 1min, video
Un-fit 1992, 1min, video (AC/BBC)
Closed Circuit 1992, 3min, b/w, video
Armour 1992, 3min, b/w, video
Edge 1992, 2min, video
Extract 1993, 7min, b/w, 16mm (AC/Ch4)
Distribution: Cinenova, LEA

PICTORIAL HEROES (DOUG AUBREY AND ALAN ROBERTSON)

Video:

Passage '85 (Between Two States) 1985,
5min, b/w
Faction>Tottenham Version 1985, 7min
The Cover Up 1986, 10min
The Last Man in Europe 1986, 1min, b/w
Arrests 1987, 7min
Sniper 1987, 22min (SAC)
Sniper (version 2) 1988, 15min
Reflections on the Art of the State
1988, 12min
George Squared (1919–1990) 1990,
4min (Ch4)
Work, Rest and Play
  **Episode 1 – Light Sound Motion and a
  Guy Called Frank** 1991, 24min
  **Episode 2 – Good Times, Bad Times,
  Propaganda and a Swiss Army Knife**
  1992, 23min
  **Episode 3 – Love, Lead and Pre-cast
  Concrete** 1993, 22min
  **Episode 4 – Iron, Steel and Paper,
  Blood, Sweat and Lager** 1995, 22min
  **Episode 5 – Dreams, Light and the
  Darkness at the Edge of Town** 1995,
  20min
Work, Rest and Play 'Special Edition'
1995, 90min

Installation:

Factions>Fragments>Divisions 1986,
28 monitors, 6 players, Transmission Gallery
Glasgow

Faction>The Thin Blue Line 1986,
10 monitors, 4 players, McLellan Gallery
Glasgow
Faction>All the King's Forces 1986,
24 monitors, 6 players, Royal Scottish
Academy Edinburgh
The Great Divide 1987, 13 monitors,
4 players, Seagate Gallery Dundee
Search 1987, 15 monitors, 6 players, Royal
Scottish Academy Edinburgh
The Great Divide: Southern Version
1987, 5 monitors, 5 players, Riverside Studios
London
The Great Divide: End of the Line 1987,
22 monitors, 6 players, Glyn Vivian Gallery
Swansea
State of the Art 1988, 5 monitors, 3 players,
Angela Bradshaw Gallery Dundee
Distribution: LEA

KEITH PIPER

Video:

Mandela Video 1988, 1min
(ICA/TSI/Nelson Mandela 60th Birthday
Celebrations London)
The Nation's Finest 1990, 7min
(AC/Cornerhouse Manchester/FVU)
Go West Young Man 1995, 7min (AC/Ch4)

Installation:

Step into the Arena 1991, computer
animation, 4 monitors, 2 players,
(AC/Rochdale Art Gallery)
Surveillances/Tagging the Other 1991,
computer animation, 4 monitors, 4 players,
'PhotoVideo' (AC/Impressions Gallery York)
The Fire Next Time 1991, computer
animation, 3 monitors, 3 players, 'A Ship called
Jesus' Camden Arts Centre London
(AC/Camden Council/Ikon Birmingham)
Trade Winds 1992, computer animation,
12 monitors encased in wooden crates,
4 players, Merseyside Maritime Museum
Liverpool (Moviola/AC)
Another Step into the Arena 1992,
computer animation, 4 monitors, 1 projector,
3 players, 'Front' Het Kijkhuis, Den Haag
Holland (World Wide Video Centre)
Cargo Cultures 1992, computer animation,
8 monitors, 4 players, 'Front' Het Kijkhuis,
Den Haag Holland (World Wide Video
Centre)
Mapping the Face 1992, computer
animation, 3 monitors, 1 projector, 3 players,
'Front' Het Kijkhuis, Den Haag Holland
(World Wide Video Centre)

Exotic Signs 1993, 2 video projectors, 2 players, 8 slide projectors, muslin screens, 'Sonsbeek 93' (Gallery Theesalon Arnham Holland)
The Exploded City 1994, 4 monitors, 4 players, Centre 181 Gallery London (LAB)
Final Frontiers 1994, 3 light boxes, 1 monitor mounted in replica telescope, The Royal Observatory London (Greenwich Festival)
The Unmapped Body 1994, 3 monitors, video projector, 4 players, 'The Raw and the Cooked' (Reina Sofia Madrid)
Distribution: LEA

STEVEN PIPPIN

Film and video:
Beach-Bath 1983, 2min, S8mm
Photo-Booth 1984/87, 9min, S8mm
Photo-Booth #2 1985, 5min, S8mm
Follys of an Amateur Photographer 1986, 10min, b/w, S8mm
Photo-Booth #3 1986, 30min, video
Follys of an Amateur Photographer #2 1987, 10min, 16mm
Laundramatic 1988, 12min, video
Launderama 1989, 9min, b/w, silent, 16mm (GLAA)
Never Mind the Bolex 1990, 2min, video
Laundromat Pictures 1991, 15min, video
The Continued Saga of an Amateur Photographer 1993, 22min, video
Distribution: Steven Pippin

SALLY POTTER

Film and video:
Jerk (In Three Parts) 1969, 4min, b/w, 8mm
The Building 1970, 7min, two screen, 8mm
Play 1971, 15min, two screen, 16mm
Hors D'Oeuvres 1971, 10min, 16mm
Combines 1972, 35min, three screen, 16mm
Thriller 1979, 35min, b/w, 16mm (AC)
The Gold Diggers 1983, 90min, b/w, 35mm (BFI/Ch4)
The London Story 1986, 15min, 35mm (BFI)
Tears, Laughter, Fears and Rage 1986, 4 x 30min, video (Ch4)
I Am an Ox, I Am a Horse, I Am a Man, I Am a Woman 1988, 60min, video (Ch4)
Orlando 1992, 93min, 35mm (British Screen/Lenfilm/Rio/European Co-production Fund)
Distribution: BFI, Electric Pictures, Metro Pictures

SARAH PUCILL

16mm Film:
You Be Mother 1990, 8min (Hull Time Based Arts/AC)
Milk and Glass 1993, 10min (AC)
Back Comb 1995, 3min (Carlton/LAB/LPF)
Measured Level 1995, 10min, b/w (AC)
Distribution: BFI, Cinenova, LFMC

SIMON PUMMELL

Film and video:
Surface Tension 1986, 26min, b/w, 16mm
Secret Joy of Falling Angels 1991, 12min, 35mm (Ch4)
Stain 1992, 1min, video (AC/BBC)
The Temptation of Sainthood 1993, 14min, video (AC/Ch4)
Rose Red 1994, 19min, 35mm (BFI)
Butcher's Hook 1995, 5min, video (Ch4)
Distribution: BFI, LEA

QUAY BROTHERS

Film:
Nocturna Artificiala, Those Who Desire Without End 1979, 21min, 16mm (BFI)
Ein Brudermord 1981, 5min, 16mm (BFI)
Igor – The Paris Years Chez Pleyel 1982, 26min, 16mm (Ch4)
Leoš Janáček: Intimate Excursions 1983, 26min, 16mm (AC/Ch4)
The Cabinet of Jan Švankmajer 1984, 14min, 16mm (Ch4)
This Un-nameable Little Broom 1985, 11min, 16mm (BFI)
Street of Crocodiles 1986, 21min, 35mm (BFI)
Rehearsals for Extinct Anatomies 1987, 14min, b/w, 35mm (BFI)
Stille Nacht I 1988, 11/2min, b/w, 35mm
Ex-Voto 1989, 1min, 35mm
The Comb 1990, 18min, 35mm
De Artificiali Perspectiva´– Anamorphosis 1990, 14min, 35mm (Metropolitan Museum NY)
The Calligrapher (Parts I,II,III) 1991, 1min, 35mm (BBC)
Stille Nacht II (Are We Still Married) 1991, 3min, b/w, 35mm
Look What the Cat Drug In 1992, 4min, 35mm
Stille Nacht III (Tales from Vienna Woods) 1992, 3½min, 35mm
Stille Nacht IV (Can't Go Wrong With You) 1993, 3½min, 35mm

Institute Benjamenta 1995, 105min, b/w, 35mm (Ch4)
Distribution: BFI

WILLIAM RABAN

Film and video:
Basement Window 1970, 10min, S8mm
Skyfilm 1970, 5min, silent, four screen, S8mm
View 1970, 5min, 16mm
River Yar 1972, 35min, two screen, 16mm, (with Chris Welsby)
Colours of This Time 1972, 3min, 16mm
Broadwalk 1972, 14min, 16mm (AC)
2'45" 1972, 3min, b/w, 16mm film event
Diagonal 1973, 5min, three screen, 16mm
Soft Edge 1973, 6min, b/w, 16mm
Angles of Incidence 1973, 10min, silent, two screen, 16mm (AC)
Take Measure 1973, 16mm film event
Breath 1974, 16min, 16mm
Time Stepping 1974, 20min, 16mm (AC)
At One 1974, 20min, 16mm
Sunset Strips 1975, 8min, silent, 16mm
After Eight 1975, 35min, 16mm (BFI)
Moonshine 1975, 8min, two screen, 16mm
Canal Incident 1975, 12min, two screen, 16mm
Surface Tension 1976, 18min, two screen, 16mm
Thames Barrier 1977, 8min, silent, three screen, 16mm
Autumn Scenes 1979, 20min, silent, 16mm
Black and Silver 1981, 75min, 16mm, (with Marilyn Halford) (BFI)
Waterfall 1983, 8min, b/w, 16mm
Thames Film 1986, 66min, 16mm (AC)
From 60 Degrees North 1991, 52min, 16mm, (with Begonia Tamarit) (Ch4)
Sundial 1992, 1min, video (AC/BBC)
A 13 1994, 12min, video (available on 16mm) (AC)
Island Race 1995, 26min, video (AC/Ch4)

Installation:
Pink Trousers 1977, 16mm (with Marilyn Halford), Acme Gallery London
Illusionists 1977, 10min, silent, 16mm, performance (with Marilyn Halford)
Wave Formations 1978, five screen, 16mm, LFMC (AC)
Distribution: BFI, LEA, LFMC

ANNE REES-MOGG

16mm Film:

Nothing is Something 1966, 10min, silent
Relations 1966, 16min
One 1969, 20min
A Length of Time 1970, 32min, b/w
Real Time 1974, 32min
Muybridge Film 1975, 5min, b/w, silent
Sentimental Journey 1977, 30min (AC)
Living Memory 1980, 39min
Transmogrification 1980, 7min
Grandfather's Footsteps 1983, 33min, b/w
(AC)
**Macbeth (A Tragedy) and
Welcome/Adieu** (2 films on one reel), 1983,
3½min and 3min
Distribution: LFMC

DANIEL REEVES

Video:

Thousands Watch 1979, 7min,
(with Jon Milton)
Body Count 1980, 9min, (with Jon Milton)
Smothering Dreams 1981, 23min
Hey Joe 1982, 5min
Arches 1982, 5min
Children's Thoughts About Nuclear War
1983, 7min
Amida 1983, 9min
Sabda 1984, 15min
A Mosaic for the Kali Yuga 1986, 5min
Ganapati/A Spirit in the Bush 1986,
45min
Sombra A Sombra 1988, 17min (New
Television/WGBH/WNET/Ch4)
Try To Live To See This 1990, 3 player,
90min
Obsessive Becoming 1995, 60min
(AC/Ch4/NEA/NYC State Council on the
Arts/Rockerfeller Foundation)

Installation:

Another Man's Floor 1974, Living-room
set, Ford pick-up, dead TV. 1333 Danvy Rd,
Ithaca, NY.
The White TV 1975, Gutted TV with objects.
The Barn, Ithaca NY.
The Well of Patience 1988, 3 players,
12 video projectors on carousel, panoramic 32ft
screen, 1,500 rat traps, 343 wine glasses/work-
men's hammers/Amida Buddha figures.
Tate Gallery Liverool (Video Positive 89)
Angels/Anvils 1989, 10 players, 10 video
projectors, 7 monitors, 3 screens, 7 wardrobes,
1,500 whiskey tumblers. Third Eye, Glasgow
(National Review of Live Art)

Eingang (The Way In) 1990, 3 players,
7 large and 7 small monitors, sections of Rocky
Mountain fir trees, water-filled/rice and
saffron-filled glass bowls, stones.
High Museum of Art, Atlanta, Georgia.
Jizo Garden 1992, 60min cycle, 3 players,
14 monitors, 21 crystal globes, 7 Jizo figures,
beach stones. Centre for Contemporary Arts,
Glasgow. (SAC)
The Sleepers 1993, 3 monitors and players,
7 architectural fragments, 3 crystal spheres.
An Lanntair Gallery, Stornaway
Distribution: LEA, Shakti (01880 820084)

LIS RHODES

Film and video:

Dresden Dynamo 1971, 10min, 16mm
Amenuensis 1973, 8min, b/w, 16mm
Print Slip 1975, 10min, b/w, 16mm
Rip It Up 1975, 8min, b/w, 16mm
Light Music 1975, 25min, b/w, two screen,
16mm
Untitled 1975, 14min, b/w, video
Notes from Light Music 1976, 25min,
16mm
Notes from Light Music 1976, 15min, b/w,
two screen, 16mm
Light Reading 1978, 20min, b/w, 16mm
Pictures on Pink Paper 1982, 35min, 16mm
(BFI)
Hang on a Minute 1985, 13 x 1min, 16mm
(with Jo Davis and Rose English) (Ch4)
  Tiger Lily
  Swing Song
  White Words
  Windscale
  Ironing To Greenham
  Washing Up
  Goose and Common
  Pornography
  Words and Wealth
  Pink Patterns
  No.8 Bus
  Much Madness
  Petal for a Paragraph
A Cold Draft 1988, 28min, 16mm (AC)
Deadline 1991, 28min, video (AC)
Just About Now 1993, 22min, video (AC)

Performance:

Rumour Shock for the Lab.R. 1974,
(9–10 hours), b/w, two screen, 16mm
(with Ian Kerr)
Cut A X 1975, (18–20 hours), b/w, two screen,
16mm (with Ian Kerr)
Light Music 1975, 25min, b/w, two screen,
16mm

Bwlhaictke 1976, (18–20 hours), b/w,
two screen, 16mm (with Ian Kerr)
Distribution: Cinenova, LFMC

SIMON ROBERTSHAW

Video:

Shot Dead in Armagh 1984, 4min
Some Months 1985, 24min (AC)
This Is Henry Champ 1985, 5min
The Engagement 1985, 25min, (with
Clifford House Video)
**One of Those Things You See All the
Time** 1986, 7min
Biometrika 1987, 11min (AC)
Faster Manchester (Seoul II Salford)
1990, 2min, (with Mike Jones)
(FVU/Cornerhouse)
Video Diaries 1991, 27 x 2min diaries (with
various artists on Merseyside) (Video Positive)
Great Britain 1991, 7min, (with Mike Jones)
(Video Positive)

Installation:

The Rise of Public Man 1987,
(with Mike Jones)
Great Britain 1989, 42 monitor video wall
(with Mike Jones) (Video Positive)
From Generation to Generation 1989,
2 monitors, 1 player, 1 computer with printers,
constructions (AC)
S.T.R.E.S.S. 1990, (with Residents from
Southgate Housing Estate, Runcorn) (Moviola)
Bio Optic 1990, 1 video projector, 1 player,
constructions (FVU/Impressions Gallery York)
Video Diaries 1991, 'Video Positive'
Liverpool (Moviola)
My Idea of Paradise 1991, (with Ashworth
North Hospital) 'Video Positive' Liverpool
(Moviola)
The Observatory 1993, 2 video projectors,
2 players, 7 slide projectors, constructions
(Moviola/Oriel 31 Wales)
The Self 1993, (with Ashworth North
Hospital) (Moviola)
The Errors of Art and Nature 1994,
4 video projectors, 4 players, Boddingtons Art
Festival Manchester (Moviola/Boddingtons)
Distribution: FVU, LEA, Moviola

KATHLEEN ROGERS

Video:

The Art of Losing Memory 1991, 10min,
b/w
The Still Room 1992, virtual reality
Hopscotch 1992, virtual reality
Flatland 1994, virtual reality

Installation:
The Glass House 1985, 25min, silent
Cathy Come Home 1986, 60min, silent
(with Nuala Cashman)
Conversazione 1990, 45min, b/w
The Still Room 1992, 60min, b/w
(AC/SWA)
Al-Kymia 1993, 22min, b/w
Distribution: LEA

GEORGE SAXON

Film and video:
On White/Off White 1976, 3min, b/w, silent,
two screen
Child Rising 1976, 3min, b/w, silent,
two screen
Whispering Lights 1976, 3min, b/w, silent
Spectacular Anonymity 1977, 10min, b/w
Wall Support 1977, 10min, b/w
Spectacular Anonymity (1 & 2) 1978,
25min, b/w
Chance/Arranged Meeting 1978, 20min,
b/w
Soul with Symbols of Life and Breath
1979, 15min, b/w
Another Window (Variations) 1983, 20min
**The Emperor's Mother and Other
Songs** 1985, 25min
Heads for the Talebearer 1985, 10min
The Jack Series:
  The House That Jack Built 1985, 7min
  (AC)
  House of Cards 1987, 17min (AC)
  Jack's Dream 1988, 4min
Pig of Hearts 1992, 15min (AC)

Installation:
Light Support 1977, 10min, a cinematic
performance, 'Projections' Paris
God of Iron and Steel 1990, 15min, four
screen work for interior of railway depot,
'Test Dept.' The Second Coming, Glasgow.
Distribution: LEA, LFMC
See also: Housewatch

GUY SHERWIN

Film:
Newsprint 1972, 5min, b/w, 16mm
Silent Film 1974, 8min, b/w, silent, 16mm
At the Academy 5min, b/w, 16mm
Interval 1974, 6min, b/w, two screen, two
soundtracks, 16mm
Short Film Series 1976–79, 3min each;
selection on 15min reel; full programme
70min, b/w, silent, 16mm (AC)

Coming into Kew 1976, 6min, b/w, silent
16mm (AC)
Riding Ring 1976, 4min, 16mm (AC)
Sound Track 1977, 8min, b/w, 16mm (AC)
Railings 1977, 10min, b/w, 16mm (AC)
Musical Stairs 1977, 10min, b/w, 16mm
(AC)
Jug 1977, 12min, b/w, 16mm (AC)
Platform 1979, 8min, 16mm (AC)
Bath 1979, 30min, 16mm (AC)
Night Train 1980, 4min, b/w, 16mm (AC)
Notes 1981, 3min, S8mm
Connemara 1981, 33min, 16mm (AC)
Messages 1981–84, 35min, b/w, silent, 16mm
(AC)
Extracts from a Diary 1983–85, 30min, b/w,
16mm (AC)
Salt Water 1986, 18min, S8mm
In Camera 1986–87, series of 3min films,
silent, S8mm
Views from Home 1987, 20min, silent,
S8mm
Mile End Purgatorio 1991, 1min, 16mm
(with Martin Doyle) (AC/BBC)

Installation/Performance:
Paper Landscape 1975, 10min, silent,
S8mm, performance with special screen
Self-Portrait 1975, 10min, b/w, two screen
performance, 16mm
Man with Mirror 1976, 10min, S8mm, silent
or sound, performance with special screen
Cross Section 1977, film installation,
two screen, two soundtracks, 16mm
Still Life with Video Loop 1978, video
Wolverhampton Polytechnic
Firescreen 1985, film/slide performance at
night, 16mm
Distribution: LFMC

TONY SINDEN

Film and video:
Da da da 1967, 8min, 8mm
Arcade 1969, 15min, 16mm (BFI)
Size M 1969, 11min, 16mm (BFI)
Ababa 1972, 15min, 16mm
View 1973, 9min, 16mm (with David
Hall) (AC)
This Surface 1973, 12min, 16mm
(with David Hall) (AC)
Edge 1973, 10min, 16mm (with David Hall)
(AC)
Between 1973, 17min, 16mm (with David
Hall) (AC)
Actor 1973, 11min, 16mm (with David Hall)
(AC)

Kino-Sketches 1974, 10min, silent, two
screen, 16mm
Intermittent Intervals 1974, 10min, b/w,
16mm
Time and Motion 1976, 15min, b/w, 16mm
(BFI)
Can Can 1976, 10min, 16mm, single and
two screen (BFI)
Wipers and Whippersnappers 1976,
15min, 16mm (BFI)
Reversal Rotation 1976, 10min, 16mm
(BFI)
Functional Action 1976, 10min, 16mm (BFI)
Mechanical Moments 1976, 15min, 16mm
(BFI)
Light Sensitive 1976, 10min, b/w, video
Functional Action 1,2 & 3 1977, 20min,
b/w, video (with David Cunningham)
Aspects of . . . 1978, 15min, video
Beginning in the First Instance 1978,
18min, 16mm, single and two screen (AC/SEA)
Space Between/Space Beyond 1981,
10min, video (documentation of two
installations shown in the UK and the USA)
Installation Tape 1988, 20min, video
(documentation of installations 1972–88)
Time-Based-Work 1994, 20min, video
(documentation of installations 1988–94)

Installation:
Plastic Motorcycle Event 1969, expanded
cinema, slide projectors, mixed media, motorcycle, performance, empty shop front (with
Jeff Keen and Jim Duke) Brighton Fringe
60 TV Sets 1972, 60 old TV sets, scaffolding,
two 'technicians' in white coats (with David
Hall) (Gallery House London)
Video Self Portraits 1975, multi monitors,
2 players, Serpentine Gallery London (AC)
101 TV Sets 1975, 101 old TV sets,
scaffolding (with David Hall) 'Video Show'
Serpentine Gallery London (AC)
Cinema of Projection 1975, 10 16mm
projectors with loops; ICA London (AC)
Behold/Vertical Devices 1976, b/w,
9 monitors, 1 player, plastic chair, plank;
Third Eye Gallery Glasgow (SEA)
Gallery Walls 1976, 6 16mm projectors with
loops; Arnolfini Bristol (SWA)
Time/Upstairs 1977, b/w, 9 monitors,
1 player, staircase; South Hill Park Bracknell
Desert/Oasis 1977, 8 16mm projectors with
loops, 4 slide projectors, 4 large mirrors and
screens, chairs, water tank, palm tree; Arnolfini
Bristol (AC/SWA)
Vacant Possession 1977, 4 16mm
projectors with loops; SAC Gallery Edinburgh
(SAC)

Black/Surface Motion 1978, 4 16mm projectors with loops and black screens, Kunstmesse Vienna (BC)

A Garden Site 1978, 8 16mm projectors with loops, 4 standing mirrors and screens, 1 monitor, 1 video camera, sculptural mixed media, Acme Gallery London (AC)

Chairs 1978, 4 slide projectors and chairs; Acme Gallery London

The Space Surrounding, the Interior Design and the Garden Beyond 1979, 4 16mm projectors with loops, photography, mirrors, chairs, screens, South Hill Park Bracknell (SA)

Another Aspect/Another Time 1979, 8 16mm projectors with loops, 4 slide projectors, 8 sculptural lecterns, 4 chairs, mixed media; Hayward Gallery London (AC)

Beginning in the First Instance 1979, 4 16mm projectors, sculptural mixed media, colour photography; Serpentine Gallery London (AC)

Whose Afraid of Black and White 1980, light, mirror, canvas, colour photography; Lewis Johnstone Gallery London

San Francisco/London 1980, sculptural mixed media; Lewis Johnstone Gallery London

Museum Cabinet 1980, 16mm projector with loop, mixed media; Funchal Opera House Madeira (BC)

Space Between/Space Beyond 1981, 2 16mm projectors with loops, 4 slide projectors, large scale photography, mixed media; Acme Gallery London, Atholl McBean Gallery San Francisco (AC/SFA)

Chair, Mop and Bucket 1982, slide projector, chairs, mixed media; San Francisco Art Institute

Paint Job 1982, 2 16mm projectors with loops, slide projector, mixed media; Cinemateque San Francisco (SFA)

American Chairs 1982, mixed media, photography; Pacific Film Archive California

Plus/Minus 1983, slide projection, video, mixed media; Langton Street Gallery San Francisco (NEA)

From Caligari to the Shadow of 1984 1983, slide projection, mirrors, mixed media, bomb casing; San Francisco Arts Commission Gallery (NEA)

Roman Fence 1985, light, photography, mixed media; Camerawork London (AC)

Pedestrian Colours II 1988

Chair Wired for Light/Hat Goes in a Spin 1989, light, sculptural mixed media, Guildhall Gallery London

Video: Roman Portraits 1989, 20min, 3 monitors, 3 players

Nobodies: About Face 1993, 16 monitors, 3 players, mixed media, St. Peter's Church Site Bristol (AC/SWA)

Ancestral Voices 1994, 12 monitors, 3 players, St. Nicholas Church Bristol (AC/SWA)

Fallow Field 1994, 16 monitors, 2 players, sculptural mixed media, large barn structure (with Lulu Quinn and Stan Steele) Royal Festival Hall London (AC/Southbank/Paul Hamlyn)

Distribution: Tony Sinden
See also: Housewatch

JOHN SMITH

Film and video:

Triangles 1972, 3min, 16mm

Someone Moving 1972, 5min, 16mm

The Hut 1973, 5min, 16mm

Words 1973, 5min, 16mm (with Lis Rhodes)

William and the Cows 1974, 6min, silent, 16mm

Faces 1 1974, 11min, b/w, silent, 16mm

Faces 2 1974, 3min, b/w, silent, 16mm

Associations 1975, 7min, 16mm

Leading Light 1975, 11min, 16mm (AC)

Nine Short Stories 1975, 3min, b/w, silent, 16mm

Subjective Tick-Tocks 1975, 11min, b/w, 16mm

The Girl Chewing Gum 1976, 12min, b/w, 16mm

Summer Diary 1977, 30min, 16mm

Hackney Marshes – November 4th 1977 1977, 15min, silent, 16mm (AC)

Gardner 1977, 6min, video

Hackney Marshes (TV version) 1978, 30min, video (Thames TV)

7P 1978, 7min, 16mm (AC)

Blue Bathroom 1979, 14min, 16mm (AC)

Celestial Navigation 1980, 10min, 16mm (AC)

Spring Tree 1980, 3min, silent, 16mm

Shine So Hard 1981, 32min, 16mm

Light Sleep 1981, 6min, 16mm (AC)

Shepherd's Delight 1984, 35min, 16mm (AC)

Om 1986, 4min, 16mm

The Black Tower 1987, 24min, 16mm (AC)

Dungeness (3 films for theatre production), 1987, silent, 16mm

Slow Glass 1991, 40min, 16mm (AC/Ch4)

Gargantuan 1992, 1min, 16mm (AC/BBC)

Home Suite 1994, 96min, video

Blight 1995, 10min, 16mm (AC)
Distribution: LFMC, John Smith
(0181 556 4363)

NICK GORDON SMITH

Film and video:

Bird Xerox 1983, 7min, b/w, 16mm

Heaven of Animals 1984, 8min, 16mm (AC)

Sermon 1987, 15min, 16mm (AC)

O 1990, 10min, 16mm (AC)

Hole 1992, 18min, b/w, 16mm

Diddyköy 1992, 6min, video (with Andrew Kotting)

Farmer's Son 1992, 3min, b/w, video

Up in the Clouds 1994, 10min, 16mm (AC/Ch4)
Distribution: LFMC, Tall Stories
(0171 703 2529)

GEORGE SNOW

Video:

Dogs 1984, 7½min

Love Video 1985, 9min

Shuttle Disaster 1985, 6min

Muybridge Revisited 1986, 5min (BFI)

The Man of the Crowd 1987, 11min (AC/Illuminations/Ch4)

The Assignation 1988, 12min (Illuminations/Ch4)

Face to Space 1995, 4½min (Carlton/LAB/LPF)

Installation:

Motorway 1992, 4 video projectors, 4 players, custom built screen, 1992 World Wide Video Festival Den Haag; 1993 Melk Veg Amsterdam; 1994 Video Brasil São Paolo.
Distribution: LEA

MARTY ST JAMES & ANNE WILSON

Video:

A Video Tape By . . . 1982, 14min

An American Romance 1983, 6min

Visual Art Songs for the '80s 1984, includes

  True Life Romance 6min
  Beatnik 5min

Iron Heart 1986, 8min

Timecode 1987, 7min (Ch4)

Comment 1987, 3min (Ch4)

Hotel 1989, 22min (AC/Ch4)

Portraits:

Laughing Portrait, Cynthia Odogwu 1990

Portrait of Neil Bartlett 1990

Crying Portrait, Homage to Picasso's Weeping Woman Sitter, Geraldine Pilgrim 1990
The Twins, Barrie and Donovan, Black and White Twins 1990
Running Woman, Paula Dunn British 100 metres Champion 1990
The Actress, Julie Walters 1990 (National Portrait Gallery)
Portrait of Sally Burgess Opera Singer 1990 (National Portrait Gallery)
Portrait of Shobana Jeyasingh 1990, 14 monitors, (London Borough of Camden)
The Swimmer, Duncan Goodhew 1990, 11 monitors, (National Portrait Gallery)
Washdeh, Eyah Dakota Sioux Indian 1991, Ottawa Canada
The Smoking Man – Giuliano Pirani 1991, Ottawa Canada
Triptych of Doreen Stevens Algonquin Native Canadian Indian 1991, 3 monitors, Ottawa Canada
Ordfurher, the Mayor of Trondheim 1993, Norway
Dream Soul 1993, self portrait, Norway
Hospaderia 1994, video portrait story english/spanish
The Sea 1994
Cuckoo 1994, self portrait, London
Animal Portraits 1994–95
The Sky 1994–95
Distribution: LEA

ANDREW STONES

Video:
The Animals on the Island 1987, 25min (AC/Newcastle-upon-Tyne Poly/Sheffield Independent Film Ltd)
Common Knowledge 1989, 25min (AC/Sheffield City Poly/Mappin Art Gallery)
A History of Disaster with Marvels 1992, 12min (AC/Ch4)

Installation:
Salmon Song 1986, 5 monitors, 5 players, 4 channel sound (AC/NA/Newcastle-upon-Tyne Poly/Projects UK)
Harvest Festival 1989, 10 monitors, 10 players, slide projection, constructions and lighting, Bluecoat Gallery Liverpool (Video Positive)
Geiger 1989, 1 projector, constructions, live action (AC/Mappin Art Gallery /Sheffield City Poly)

The Tide 1990, 1 video projector, 1 player, slide projection, constructions, lighting, Posterngate Gallery Hull (HTBA)
Flare/Cataract 1992, 1 projector, 1 LCD monitor, 2 players, lens mounted in scope construction, 3 channel sound, lighting, SIF Sheffield (Sheffield Cultural Festival/Sheffield Independent Film Ltd)
Class 1993, 1 projector, 6 school desks, illuminated image/text plates, slide & OHP projection, stereo sound, lighting, City Gallery Leicester, Kunst-Werke Berlin (Harris Gallery Preston/Leicester International Video Festival)
The Conditions 1993, 3 projectors, 3 players, lighting, constructions, stereo sound, Tate Gallery Liverpool (Video Positive)
The Nature of Their Joy 1994, Manchester Metropolitan Gallery (AC)
Those Days are Gone 1994, Manchester Metropolitan Gallery (AC)
Distribution: Andrew Stones (0114 255 4750)

MIKE STUBBS

Film and video:
Naval Death 1978, 18min, video
Flapping My Cheeks 1978, 60min, video
Cooking with Katie 1979, 35min, video
Self Accusation 1980, 60min, video (based on the text by Peter Handke)
Snot Face 1981, 20min, 16mm
Z.G. Presents 1982, 40min, video (with Attalia Shaw)(ZG Magazine)
Waiter There's a Fly on My Wall 1982, 20min, b/w, video
Contortions 1983, 30min, 16mm (WAC)
Pigeons 1985, 10min, 16mm (with Claire Pollack)(S4C)
Man Act 1986, 14min, b/w, video
Greetings from The Cape of Good Hope? 1986, 4min, video (Chapter Video Workshop Cardiff)
God 1986, 1min, video (with John Hessey)
John 1987, 1min, video
Who Can Eat the Hottest Curry? 1987, 1min, video
The Fragility of Things 1987, 6min, video
Things I've Seen 1989, 8min, video
Animal Magic 1990, 4min, video
Life Water II 1990, 5min, video
Soapless 1990, 55min, 16mm (WAC)
Sweatlodge 1991, 7min, b/w, 35mm & video
Pants Make Spam 1992, 13min, video (Arnolfini Bristol)
Lake of the Eyes 1993, 11min, video (with Sanchari) (Sanchari Productions)

What the Eye Doesn't See, Post Industrial Studies 1 – Coal & Transport 1993, 12min, b/w, 16mm (with Rob Gawthrop) (Camerawork London)
Homing 1994, 11min, 35mm (with Roland Denning) (BFI/YHA)
Lifelines 1995, 5min, video (AC/BBC)

Film and Video Performance:
False Pretence 1981, ICA, London; Basement, Newcastle
Hero of the Hour 1981 (with The Starless Cast) (Chapter Cardiff)
Punishment by Roses 1982 (with the New Arts Consort) Edinburgh Fringe Festival (WCA)
The Fragility of Things 1987, Usher Gallery Lincoln
Things I've Seen 1989, Humberside University
Prontawipe 1992, (with Nina Edge) 'Quick Festival' Royal Festival Hall London (Projects UK)
What the Eye Doesn't See 1993, 6 16mm projectors, PA, lighting, steam locomotive, coal (with Rob Gawthrop) 'River Crossings' Old Railway Museum, North Woolwich Station London (Camerawork London)
Ice Cream 1993 (with Bisarkha Sarker) (AC/Leicester Museum & Art Gallery)

Installation:
Funhouse 1984, infra red light, b/w monitor, camera, (Chapter Cardiff/Mickery Amsterdam)
The Fragility of Things 1987, S8mm projection, (Ferens Gallery Hull/LHA)
Myths of Speed 1989, 3 x 16mm projectors, 1 monitor, 1 player (Usher gallery Lincoln)
Desert Island Dread 1989, 2 monitors, 2 players, 3 mono record players, Video Positive Liverpool (Moviola)
Theme Shopping Time Bomb Park 1990, 3 surveillance cameras, 3 b/w surveillance monitors, 1 monitor, 1 player, (with Dick Powell) 'North Face' Bluecoat Gallery Liverpool (Moviola)
Bedtime Stories: Highlights from the Gulf War 1991, 2 surveillance cameras, 2 surveillance monitors, 1 video projector, 1 monitor, 1 player (Manchester City Art Gallery)
Here Comes Another Jelly Rabbit 1992, 4 surveillance cameras, 4 surveillance monitors, 1 monitor, 1 player, (with Dick Powell) Ferens Gallery Hull
Distribution: BFI, HTBA, LEA

CORDELIA SWANN

Film and video:
The Ten Commandements of Love 1979, 3½min, 16mm
The Olympia File 1979, 13min, b/w, tape/slide
The Mysteries of Berlin 1980, 24min, tape/slide, two screen
Kiev Code 1980, 6min, tape/slide
Der Engel 1981, 3½min, tape/slide
Passion Tryptych 1982, 3min, three screen, S8mm
Red 1982, 3min, two screen, S8mm
Greek and Turkish Life 1982, 3min, S8mm
Rosemarie 1983, 7min, tape/slide
Lust for Life 1983, 16min, video
Winter Journey in the Hartz Mountains 1983, 8min, three screen, video
Again 1983, 3min, S8mm
All Kinds of Torture 1984, 12min, tape/slide (AC)
Phantoms 1986, 18min, video (AC)
A Call to Arms 1989, 26min, video (AC/Ch4)
The Citadel 1992, 13min, video (AC)
Tall Buildings 1992, 1½min, video
Out West 1993, 15min, video (AC)
Desert Rose 1995, 26min, b/w, 35mm (AC)
Distribution: LEA

MOIRA SWEENEY

16mm Film:
Within a Move 1983, 15min
One Day 1984, 15min
Ain't Got No 1985, 15min
She Continues 1985, 15min
Looking for the Moon 1986, 7min, b/w, silent
Hide and Seek 1987, 16min
Message from Budapest 1988, 15min (with Michael Maziere) (AC/BC)
Imaginary 1989, 17min, silent (AC/BC)
Coming Home 1994, 40min (AC/BC/Ch4)
The Gift 1995, 15min (Fuji)
Distribution: LFMC

ALIA SYED

16mm Film:
Durga (A Ritual) 1986, 23min, b/w
Swan 1987, 4min, b/w, silent
Un-folding 1987, 14min, b/w
Three Paces 1989, 12min, b/w
Fatima's Letter 1992, 21min, b/w
The Watershed 1994, 8min, b/w (AC)
Distribution: LFMC

TANYA SYED

16mm Film:
Chameleon 1990, 4min, b/w
Salamander 1994, 14min (AC/Ikon Birmingham)
Delilah 1994, 11min, b/w (AC)
Distribution: LFMC

MARGARET TAIT

Film:
Three Portrait Sketches 1951, 10min, b/w, 16mm
One is One 1951, 35min, b/w, 16mm
The Lion, the Griffin and the Kangaroo 1952, 18min, b/w, 16mm (with Peter Hollander) (Ente per Turismo/University per Strameri/USIS)
A Portrait of Ga 1952, 4min, 16mm
Happy Bees 1955, 20min, 16mm
Orquil Burn 1955, 35min, 16mm
The Leaden Echo and the Golden Echo 1955, 7min, 16mm
Calypso 1955, 4min, 16mm
Rose Street 1956, 10min, b/w, 16mm
The Drift Back 1956, 10min, b/w, 16mm (Orkney FE Dept)
Hugh MacDiarmid – A Portait 1964, 9min, b/w, 16mm
Palindrome 1964, 3min, b/w, 16mm
Where I Am is Here 1964, 35min, b/w, 16mm
The Big Sheep 1966, 40min, b/w, 16mm
Splashing 1966, 6min, b/w, 16mm
A Pleasant Place 1969, 21min, b/w, 16mm
He's Back (The Return) 1970, 20min, b/w, 16mm
Painted Eightsome 1970, 7min, 16mm
John MacFadyen (The Stripes in the Tartan) 1970, 3min, 16mm
On the Mountain 1974, 32min, 16mm
Aerial 1974, 4min, 16mm
These Walls 1974, 4min, 16mm
Colour Poems 1974, 12min, 16mm (SAC)
Place of Work 1976, 30min, 16mm
Tailpiece 1976, 10min, b/w, 16mm
Shape of a Town (Aspects of Kirkwall 2) 1977, 10min, 16mm
Occasions (Aspects of Kirkwall 3) 1977, 10min, 16mm
The Ba, Over the Years (Aspects of Kirkwall 4) 1981, 65min, 16mm
The Look of the Place (Aspects of Kirkwall 5/1) 1968–81, 18min, b/w, 16mm
Some Changes (Aspects of Kirkwall 6) 1981, 22min, 16mm

Land Makar 1981, 32min, 16mm (SAC)
Blue Black Permanent 1992, 86min, 35mm (BFI/Ch4)
Distribution: BFI, LFMC

JOHN TAPPENDEN

Film and video:
Fall 1976, 10min, silent, 16mm
Return 1976, 20min, b/w, silent, video
Silver Jubilee 1977, 3min, silent, 16mm
Storm 1981, 11min, b/w, 16mm (AC)
Rotor 1981, 7min, b/w, silent, 16mm
Colour Experiments 1983, 4min, silent, 35mm
Dawn Chorus 1987, 4min, 35mm/16mm (AC)
Die Heilige Geist (The Holy Ghost) 1992, 4min, silent, 35mm/16mm (AC)
Distribution: LFMC

ANNA THEW

Film:
From Face to Face 1979, 18min, S8mm
Lost for Words 1980, 27min, 16mm
Berlin Meine Augen 1982, 23min, two screen, S8mm
Wordpaintings 1983, 5min, 16mm
Garden Film 1983, 15min, S8mm
Shadow Film 1984, 5min, b/w S8mm
Rome Movie 1984, 24min, two screen, S8mm
Sailor Trailer and the Tinkling Laughter of Little Girls 1984, 7min, three screen, S8mm (AC)
Mourning Garden Blackbird 1984, 8min, two screen, 16mm
Citta Spelata 1984, 3min, S8mm
Sicilia Cantar/ Train to Siracusa 1985, 20min, S8mm
Kummer 1986, 3min, three screen, 16mm
Hilda was a Goodlooker 1986, 60min, 16mm (AC)
Ramblas Ramblas 1987, 3min, S8mm
Blurt Roll 2 1987, 10min, 16mm
Behind Closed Doors 1988, 14min, 16mm (AC/Ch4)
Machine Parts and Portraits 1988, 5min, b/w, S8mm
Eros Erosion 1990, 43min, 16mm (BFI/Ch4)
Dominica Diary 1991, 15min, 16mm
Snow Frames 1992, 1min, S8mm
Cling Film 1993, 20min, 16mm (AC/Ch4)
Bartok in Budapest 1994, 5min, S8mm
Minsk Girl (Zhensheenaminkaya) 1994, 5min, 35mm

Performance/Installation:
What I Meant to Say Was 1977,
performance, slide/light, recordings of
audience participation; Artists for Democracy
London
On Leonardo 1977, 30min, burning screens,
tape/slide, earth, air, fire and water
Split City Rushes 1982, 30min, multi-screen
S8mm, live song and performance; Centre
Charles Peguy London
Blurt 1983, 30min, 2 film loops, video, mobile
S8mm, performance; London Musicians
Collective
Pressed Dance Dream 1983, 20min,
S8mm, involving the film-maker, polythene,
live music, (with performance by David
Medalla) Air Gallery London
**Representing Reproduction or Badly
Reproduced Babies** 1983, 25min, S8mm,
snapshots, live performance; Wapping Studios
London
Distribution: BFI, LEA, Exile Films
(0171 222 0457)

SARAH TURNER

16mm Film:
She Wanted Green Lawns 1989, 5min,
b/w
One and the other time 1990, 4min
A Tale Part Told 1991, 4min
Sheller Shares Her Secret 1994, 8min,
b/w (AC)
Distribution: Cinenova LFMC

MARION URCH

Video:
**An Introduction to Womanhood in the
Modern World** 1979, 19min
The Fascinating Art of the Ritual Feast
1980, 19min
Speak English Cathleen 1982, 30min,
tape/slide
The Venus Tape 1984, 36min (AC)
To the Dancer Belongs the Universe
1985, 8min
From Russia with Love 1986, 4min
Out of the Ashes 1986, 10min (AC)
The Long Road 1991, 24min (AC)

Installation:
Out of the Ashes 1987, 15min, 5 monitors,
5 players, Festival of Women Sculptors
Cambridge
Distant Drums 1989, 10min, 10 monitors,
2 players (Video Positive)
Distribution: LEA

CHRIS WELSBY

16mm Film:
Wind Vane 1972, 8min, two screen,
River Yar 1972, 35min, two screen, (with
William Raban)
Winter and Summer 1973, 5min, silent
(AC)
Park Film 1973, 7min, silent (AC)
Windmill 1973, 8min (AC)
Running Film 1973, 4min
Forest Bay II 1973, 4min, silent
Windmill III 1974, 10min, silent
Tree 1974, 5min, silent
Anemometer 1974, 10min, silent (AC)
Seven Days 1974, 20min (AC)
Colour Separation 1975, 2½min, silent
Wind Vane II 1975, 26min (BFI)
Stream Line 1976, 8min (AC)
Cloud Fragments 1978, 12min, silent
Wind Vane III 1978, 20min, three screen
Sea/Shore 1979, 6min, silent
Estuary 1980, 55min (AC)
Sky Light 1988, 26min (AC)
Sea Pictures 1992, 36min (AC/NFB
Canada)
Drift 1994, 17min (AC/NFB Canada)

Installation:
Shore Line 1977, six screen, silent,
Acme Gallery London (AC)
Shore Line II 1979, six screen, silent,
Tate Gallery London
Rainfall 1983, one horizontal screen,
Slow Dancer Studios London
Sky Light 1986, six screen, silent, Serpentine
Gallery London (AC)
Rainfall (revised version) 1990, one horizontal
screen, MOMA Oxford (BC/MOMA)
Distribution: LFMC

JEREMY WELSH

Film and video:
Illuminations 1977, 12min, 16mm
Red Film 1977, 6min, silent, S8mm
Walking Film 1978, 10min, silent, S8mm
B 1980, 10min, video (with Keith James)
Insomnia 1981, 14min, video
**These Days Everybody's a
Conceptualist** 1982, 9min, video
In Re Don Giovanni 1982, 2½min, video
(with Michael Nyman)
Tense 1983, 7min, video(with Marty St James
and Anne Wilson) (GLAA)
Shout 1983, 6min, video
The Jugo Beat 1983, 6min, video
(TV Lubljana Slovenia)

Elevator 1984, 3min, silent, S8mm
I.O.D 1984, 9min, video
Red Raw Steel Drum 1985, 15min, video
(with Fast Forward and Yves Musard)
Reflecting 1986, 28min, video
Labyrinths 1986, 14min, video
Democracy 1987, 5min, video (music by
The Picassos)
Labyrinths II 1987, 4min, video (music by
The Picassos)(AC)
Echoes 1988, 25min, video (AC/Projects UK)
Factory 1988, 9min, video (Midlands
Performance Consortium)
Immemorial 1989, 15min, video
Day 1989, 18min, video
Waterboy 1990, 7min, video
Sondag, 1990, 8min, video
Closing In 1991, 7½min, video
WTB 1992, 11min, video
Pause 1993, 7min, video
Grey 1994, 11min, b/w, video
Winter Sun 1995, 10min, video

Installation:
The Theoretical Demise of Mr. X 1981,
slide projection, lighting, mixed media
That Elusive Quality of Romance
1982, video for shop window
Forest Fires 1983, 6–15 monitors, 1 player,
4 slide projectors, stereo sound, firewood,
leaves
Elementary 1985, 4 players, 16 or more TV
rental store TVs
Light/Water 1986, 10 monitors, 2 players
(with Mineo Aayamaguchi)
Immemorial 1989, 3 monitors, 3 players,
Bluecoat Gallery Liverpool (Video Positive)
ABC: Baby Sees 1989, for Spectacolor sign,
Piccadilly Circus. (Artangel)
Shadow and Traces 1991, 4 slide projectors,
lighting
39 Steps 1992, slide projector, auto-timer
Flow II Flow 1993, video back projection,
2 monitors, 3 players, Trondheim Arts Centre
(Norwegian AC/Norwegian Dept.of
Culture/Trondheim City Culture Dept)
Encapsulated 1993, 5 monitors, 5 players,
computer prints
Security 1993, for a bank vault, 2 monitors,
2 players, Media Gallery Turku Finland
Passing Through 1993, 2 monitors, 1 player,
wood and glass
Natural History 1994, 2 video projectors,
7 monitors, 5 players, 2 amplifiers, 4 speakers,
polystyrene beads, wood, mirrors, lighting,
National Museum of Contemporary Art Oslo

Grey 1994, 2 video projectors, 1 monitor
2 players, 2 slide projectors, stereo, Trondheim
City Museum & Art Gallery
Dis-Placed 1994, 1 monitor, 2 video
projectors, 3 players, 3 slide projectors

Performance:

Installation/Action series 1976–79, site-
specific
Alienation 1980, performance with
installation
Fractured 1981, video, pre-recorded sound,
improvised music
Elephant Rhythms 1982, performance with
pre-recorded video and drumming toy rabbit
Echoes 1987, performance with text, sound,
slide projection and video (Projects UK)
Talkbook 1988, performance with wooden
objects, slides, sound, computer, video,
lighting, text, Lighthouse Media Centre
Wolverhampton (Midlands Performance
Consortium)
Virtual Archeology 1991, performance with
text, video projector, player and sound
Mnemosyne 1992, performance with sound,
lighting, text, live music, video projector and
player
Breaks in Transmission 1993, performance
with text, video projector and player
Distribution: LEA

PIER WILKIE

Film:

The Rest Was Just for Pleasure 1985,
23min, 16mm
**Please, Lets Not Mention Any Hot
Countries** 1986, 1min, S8mm
Party Dress 1987, 3min, silent, 16mm
Myths and Legends 1988, 7min, 16mm
Myths and Legends II 1989, 3min, 16mm
A Postcard 1990, 12min, 16mm
How Wilkie Discovered England 1993,
12min, 16mm (AC)
The Emigrants 1995, 15min, 16mm (AC)
Unfinished Gestures 1995, 15min, 16mm
(LPF/LFVDA)
Distribution: LEA, LFMC

STEWART WILSON

Film and video:
Untitled 1989, 8min, silent, video
Museum 1989, 10min, video
Factory 1990, 15min, b/w, 16mm (SAC)

Installation:
Census 1990, 15min cycle, 9 monitors,
9 players (Camden Arts)

Burner 1993, 26min cycle, silent, 42 monitors,
42 players (AC/Cambridge Darkroom/Harris
Museum Preston)
Distribution: Stewart Wilson (0181 778 7902)

JOANNA WOODWARD

Film:

The Grid 1980, 30min, S8mm (with Peter
Murphy)
The Poet of Half Past Three 1984, 9min,
16mm
The Hump Back Angel 1985, 13min, 16mm
**Two Children Threatened by a
Nightingale** 1986, 18min, 35mm (NFTS)
The Brooch Pin and the Sinful Clasp
1989, 18min, 35mm (with Rose English)
(NFTS)
The Weatherhouse 1991, 10min, 16mm
(with I.O.U. Theatre) (BBC/YA)
**Sawdust for Brains and the Key of
Wisdom** 1993, 11min, 16mm (with Moya
Brady) (Ch4)
Distribution: BFI, LFMC

RICHARD WRIGHT

Video:
Cells 1986, 2min
Studies in Rhythm 1987, 2min
Superanimism 1991, 4min (with Jason
White)
Corpus 1992, 6min
Heliocentrum 1995, 18min (with Jason
White) (AC/Ch4)

Installation:
Corpus 1993, 4 monitors, 4 players, movable
trolleys (AC/Video Positive)
Distribution: LEA

The distributor listed for a particular artist
may not be the only source for their work but
is a primary contact.

Abbreviations:

AC	Arts Council
BBC	British Broadcasting Corporation
BC	British Council
BFI	British Film Institute
Carlton	Carlton Television
Ch4	Channel Four Television
EMA	East Midlands Arts Board
FVU	Film and Video Umbrella
GLA	Greater London Arts
GLC	Greater London Council
HTBA	Hull Time Based Arts
ICA	Institute of Contemporary Arts, London
INA	Institut National de l'Audiovisuel, France
LAB	London Arts Board
LEA	London Electronic Arts
LFF	London Film Festival
LFMC	London Film-makers Co-op
LFVDA	London Film and Video Development Agency
LHA	Lincoln and Humberside Arts
LPF	London Production Fund
LVA	London Video Access
NA	Northern Arts Board
NEA	National Endowment for the Arts (USA)
NFTS	National Film and Television School
NRLA	National Review of Live Art
NWA	North West Arts Board
RCA	Royal College of Art
SA	Southern Arts Board
SAC	Scottish Arts Council
SEA	South East Arts Board
STV	Scottish Television
SWA	South West Arts Board
TSW	Television South West
WAC	Welsh Arts Council
YA	Yorkshire Arts
YHA	Yorkshire and Humberside Arts Board

DISTRIBUTORS:

Albany Video
Battersea Studios
Television Centre
Thackeray Road
London SW8 3TW
Telephone: 0171 498 6811
Fax: 0171 498 1494

Annalogue
20 Starfield Road
London W12
Telephone: 0181 743 3630

Basilisk
31 Percy Street
London W1P 9FG
Telephone: 0171 580 7222
Fax: 0171 631 0572

BFI
Distribution
21 Stephen Street
London W1P 1PL
Telephone: 0171 255 1444
Fax: 0171 436 7950

Black Audio Film Collective
7–12 Greenland Street
London NW1 0ND
Telephone: 0171 267 0846
Fax: 0171 267 0845

Cinenova
113 Roman Road
London E2 0HU
Telephone: 0181 981 6828
Fax: 0181 983 4441

Fields and Frames
Corshellach
Bridgend
Dunning
Perthshire
PH2 0RS
Telephone: 01764 684 200
Fax: 01764 684 200

Film and Video Umbrella
2 Rugby Street
London WC1N 3QZ
Telephone: 0171 831 7753
Fax: 0171 831 7746

Hull Time Based Arts
8 Posterngate
Hull HU1 2JN
Telephone: 01482 216 446
Fax: 01482 218 103

Jane Balfour Films
Burghley House
35 Fortess Road
London NW5 1AD
Telephone: 0171 267 5392
Fax: 0171 267 4241

London Electronic Arts
3rd Floor
5–7 Buck Street
London NW1 8NJ
Telephone: 0171 284 4323
Fax: 0171 267 6078

London Film-makers' Co-op
42 Gloucester Avenue
London NW1 8JD
Telephone: 0171 586 4806
Fax: 0171 483 0068

MayaVision
43 New Oxford Street
London WC1A 1BH
Telephone: 0171 836 1113
Fax: 0171 836 5169

Moviola
45–46 Bluecoat Chambers
School Lane
Liverpool L1 3BX
Telephone: 0151 709 2663
Fax: 0151 707 2150

OTHER ORGANISATIONS:

The Arts Council of England
Film, Video and Broadcasting Department
14 Great Peter Street
London SW1P 3NQ
Telephone: 0171 333 0100
Fax: 0171 973 6581

The British Council
Films, Television and Video Department
11 Portland Place
London W1N 4EJ
Telephone: 0171 930 8466

British Film Institute
21 Stephen Street
London W1P 1PL
Telephone: 0171 255 1444
Fax: 0171 436 7950

London Film and Video Development Agency
Telephone: 0171 383 7755

Eastern Arts
Telephone: 01223 215 355

East Midlands Arts
Telephone: 01509 218 292

London Arts
Telephone: 0171 240 1313

Northern Arts
Telephone: 0191 281 6334

Northern Ireland Film Council
Telephone: 01232 232 444

North West Arts
Telephone: 0161 228 3062

Scottish Film Council
Telephone: 0141 334 4445

South East Arts
Telephone: 01892 515 210

Southern Arts
Telephone: 01962 855 099

South West Arts
Telephone: 01392 218 188

Wales Film Council
Telephone: 01222 578 633

West Midlands Arts
Telephone: 0121 631 3121

Yorkshire and Humberside Arts
Telephone: 01924 455 555

Bibliography

BOOKS

Sean Cubitt *Timeshift* (Routledge 1991)
Sean Cubitt *Videography: Video Media as Art and Culture* (MacMillan 1993)
David Curtis *Experimental Cinema: A Fifty Year Evolution* (London: Studio Vista and New York: Delta 1971)
Steven Dwoskin *Film Is...* (Peter Owen 1975)
Philip Hayward (ed) *Culture, Technology and Creativity* (AC/John Libbey 1990)
Julia Knight (ed) *Diverse Practices: British Experimental Video* (AC/John Libbey 1996)
Malcolm Le Grice *Abstract Film and Beyond* (Studio Vista 1977; MIT Press 1977)
Michael O'Pray (ed) *British Avant-garde Film* (AC/John Libbey 1996)
John A Walker *Arts TV: A History of Arts Television in Britain* (AC/John Libbey 1993)
Jeremy Welsh *The Shiny Toys of Thatcher's Children: British Video in the '80s* (Helsinki: Video Taida Media 1993)

ARTICLES AND ESSAYS

David Curtis "A Tale of Two Co-ops" *To Free the Cinema* (ed David James Princeton University Press 1992)
Peter de Kay Dusinberre "St George in the Forest: the English Avant-garde" *Undercut 6* 1976
Peter de Kay Dusinberre "English Avant-garde Cinema 1966-1974" *MPhil Thesis* (unpublished) (University College 1977)
David Hall "British Video: Towards an Autonomous Practice" *Studio International* May/June 1976
Mick Hartney "The Early Chronology of Video Art (1959-1976)" *London Video Arts Catalogue* 1984
Tamara Krikorian "Video installations in Britain" *London Video Arts Catalogue* 1984
Michael O'Pray "Shows, Schisms and Modernisms" (article tracing the evolution of British Video Art) *Monthly Film Bulletin* February 1988
Jeremy Welsh "Creating a Context for Video" *Undercut 7/8* Spring 1983
"Black Film British Cinema" *ICA Documents 7* 1988
"The Avant-garde in England and Europe" *Studio International* (see especially in vol.190 No.978 Nov/Dec 1975)

EXHIBITION AND FESTIVAL CATALOGUES

19:4:90 Television Interventions (Third Eye Gallery Glasgow 1990)
Cross Currents, Ten Years of Mixed Media, an RCA Perspective (ed. Chrissie Iles) (RCA Oct 1984)
The Elusive Sign – British Avant-garde Film and Video 1977–1987 (ed. David Curtis Arts Council/British Council touring exhibition catalogue 1988)
Festival of Expanded Cinema (ed. Deke Dusinberre, ICA London 1976)
Film as Film: Formal Experiment in Film, 1910–1975 (ed. Philip Drummond) (Hayward Gallery London 1979)
ICA Biennial of Independent Film and Video 1990: Between Imagination and Reality (selected by Tilda Swinton, introduced by Peter Wollen)
The Second ICA Biennial of Independent Film and Video: Arrows of Desire 1992 (selected and introduced by Peter Wollen)
The Third ICA Biennial of Independent Film and Video: What You See Is What You Get 1995 (selected and introduced by John Wyver)
A Perspective on English Avant-garde Film (Arts Council/British Council touring exhibition catalogue 1976)
Perspectives on British Avant-garde Film (Hayward Gallery exhibition catalogue, Arts Council 1977)
Signs of the Times (exhibition catalogue Museum of Modern Art Oxford 1990)
Video Positive catalogues (Moviola 1989 1991 1993 1995)

DISTRIBUTOR'S CATALOGUES

Cinenova (1994)
London Film-makers Co-op (1993)
London Video Arts (1978)
London Video Arts (1984)
London Video Access (1991)
BFI Avant-garde Film Catalogue (1994)

Mineo Aayamaguchi

Mineo Aayamaguchi (catalogue) (ICA London 1988)

John Akomfrah

Reece Auguiste, Paul Gilroy, Jim Pines "Handsworth Songs: Some background notes - Audiences/Aesthetics/Independence" *Framework 35* 1988
L Jackson, J Rasenberger "Young, British and Black" *Cineaste 16/4* 1988
"Black/White" interview with Pervaiz Khan *Sight and Sound 2/14* 1988

David Anderson

Jill McGreal "Dreamland Express" (review) *Sight and Sound* Sept 1992

Reece Auguiste

Reece Auguiste, Paul Gilroy, Jim Pines "Handsworth Songs: Some background notes - Audiences/Aesthetics/Independence" *Framework 35* 1988
Reece Auguiste "Artists from the Hell Screen: Reports, Observations and Other Disturbing Things" *Border/Lines 29/30*
Reece Auguiste "Antillean Cinema in the Absence of Ruins: The Case of Felix de Rooy" *CineAction 32* Autumn 1993
Daniel Marks "Twilight City" *International Documentary* Fall 1989
Reece Auguiste (introduction) Martina Attille, Reece Auguiste, Peter Gidal, Isaac Julien, Mandy Merck (discussion) "Aesthetics and Politics: Working on Two Fronts" *Undercut 17* Spring 1988

George Barber

Julian Petley "Cooking for Terrorists" *New Statesman* June 1988
Michael O'Pray "Scratching Deeper" *Flash Art* 1986
George Barber "Scratch and After: Edit Suite Technology and the Determination of Style in Video Art" *Culture, Technology and Creativity* (ed. Philip Hayward) (AC/John Libbey 1990)
Steven Bode "The Venetian Ghost" *Independent Media 77* May 1988

Breda Beban and Hrvoje Horvatic

Michael O'Pray "Taking on a Name: Breda Beban and Hrvoje Horvatic, Videotapes 1986-1994" *Whitechapel Gallery* London 1994
Steven Bode "Mosaics of Light The Videotapes of Breda Beban and Hrvoje Horvatic" *Mediamatic 6/1* 1991

Chris Darke "Everything is Connected" *Sight and Sound* February 1995
Breda Beban and Hrvoje Horvatic "Photo-piece" *Undercut* 18 Autumn 1989

Simon Biggs
Sean Cubitt "False Perspective in Virtual Space" *Variant* 11 Spring 1992
"The Sorcerer's Apprentice: Simon Biggs, A Profile" *Computer Images*, July/August 1988
Simon Biggs "Byzantine (E) Valuations" *Mediamatic* 2/1 1987
Simon Biggs "World Wide Video Festival 3: Review" *Mediamatic* 3/2 1988

Ian Bourn
Stuart Morgan (review) *Art Forum* November 1979
John Roberts (review) *Artscribe* April 1980

Ian Breakwell
Ian Breakwell's Diary 1964-1985 (Pluto Press 1986)
"Ian Breakwell: recorded live (in conversation with Chris Garrat and Mick Kidd)" *Journal of Art and Education* 10 1986.
Majorie Allthorpe-Guyton "Virile Games" (catalogue) (Anthony Reynolds Gallery London 1989)

Nick Collins
Michael O'Pray "Nick Collins" *Perspektief* 1982
Barbara Meter (article) *Undercut* 19 1990
Nick Collins "Documentation in Sand" *Undercut* 2

Susan Collins
Carrie Blackford "Without Walls" *Design Week* October 1994
Susan Collins "Redressing the Myth" *Independent Media* May 1994
"The Exploding Gallery" *Creative Camera* February 1993
"River Crossings" (review) *Hybrid* June 1993
Jim Mclellan "V-topia" (review) *Observer Magazine* August 14 1994

Lei Cox
(review) *Hybrid* 3 June/July 1993

Nina Danino
Nina Danino "The Mother's Garden" (photo-piece) *Undercut* 19 1990
Jean Mathee "On Wounds, Artificial Flowers, Orifices and the Infinite: a Response to the Films of Nina Danino" *Undercut* 20 1990

Nina Danino "The Object of Attention" *Reading the Glass* (eds. Charles Barber, Sharon Kivland, Conrad Leyser) (Bookworks 1991)

Tacita Dean
"Girl Stowaway" and "The Martyrdom of St Agatha (in several parts)" *Mise-en-Scène* (catalogue) (ICA 1994)
David Bate "Uncanny Tales" *Mise-en-Scène* (catalogue) (ICA 1994)

Vivienne Dick
Scott MacDonald "Vivienne Dick" *A Critical Cinema: Interviews with Independent Film-makers Volume 1* (University of California Press 1988)
Scott MacDonald "Interview with Vivienne Dick" *October 20* 1982
Jim Hoberman "A Context for Vivienne Dick" *October 20* 1982
Jim Hoberman "The Avant-garde Now" *Film Comment* May–June 1981

Willie Doherty
Iwona Blazwick "Interview with Willie Doherty" *Art Monthly* December/January 1993/94
Linda Jablonsky "Willie Doherty" *Art Forum* December 1994
Jeffrey Kastner "The Only Good One is a Dead One" (review) *Freize* 1994
Willie Doherty "They're All The Same" (project) *Frieze* 2 1991

Mike Dunford
Mike Dunford "Four Statements" *Structural Film Anthology* (ed. Peter Gidal) (BFI 1976)
Mike Dunford "Experimental/ Avant-garde/Revolutionary Film Practice" *Undercut* 6 1976

Stephen Dwoskin
Stephen Dwoskin *Film Is* (Peter Owen Ltd 1975)
Stephen Dwoskin *Ha! Ha!* (*La Solution Imaginaire*) (The Smith New York 1993)
Paul Willemen "Voyeurism, The Look and Dwoskin" *AfterImage* Summer 1976
"Directing the Avant-garde: Stephen Dwoskin interviewed by Raymond Durgnat" *Films* May 1984
Laura Mulvey "Trying to Kiss the Moon" (Arts Council of England 1995)

Catherine Elwes
Catherine Elwes "Floating Femininity: a look at Performance Art by Women" and "Lighting a Candle" *Women's Images of Men* (Writers and Readers 1985)
Illppo Pohjola "Winter Break" *Independent Media* 77 1988.
Catherine Elwes "A Language of the Personal in Video Art – One Mother's View" *Mothers* (exhibition catalogue Ikon Gallery Birmingham 1990)
Catherine Elwes "Notes from a Video Performance" *Undercut* 1 1981

Steve Farrer
Rod Stoneman "360 Degrees" *ArtScribe* Summer 1989
Julia Knight "Video Versus Experimental Cinema" *American Book Review* 2/2 May/June 1989
Deke Dusinberre "See Real Images – On Lis Rhodes, Steve Farrer, Guy Sherwin" *Undercut* 8/9 1981

David Finch
Nicky Hamlyn "From Structuralism to Imagism" *Undercut* 19 1990
Michael Maziere "The Good Father" *Independent Media* 90 June 1989
Nicky Hamlyn "The Films of David Finch" *Independent Media* 74 February 1988
David Finch "A Third Something: Montage, Film and Poetry" *Undercut* 18 Autumn 1989

Rose Finn-Kelcey
Rose Finn-Kelcey (catalogue) (Chisenhale Gallery London; Ikon Gallery Birmingham, 1994)
Jennifer Walwin "Rose Finn-Kelcey" (essay) *The British Show Catalogue* (Australian Touring Show 1985)

Sera Furneaux
Paul Wallace "Media Production in Higher Education: The Problem of Theory and Practice" *Undercut* 16 1986
Tamara Krikorian "Lessness Parts 1, 2 and 3" *The Elusive Sign: British Avant-garde Film and Video 1977-1987* (ed. David Curtis)(Arts Council and British Council Touring Exhibition 1988)
"Anxiety/Rest" *Arrows of Desire* (ICA Biennial catalogue London 1992)

Charles Garrad
Waldemar Januszcak *Monsoon* (catalogue)
(Ikon Gallery Birmingham 1986)

Constantine Giannaris
(Review) *Sight and Sound 2/5* September 1992

Peter Gidal
Books by Gidal:
Structural Film Anthology (BFI 1978)
Materialist Film (Routledge 1990)
Andy Warhol, Films & Paintings (Studio Vista
1971)
Understanding Beckett (Macmillan 1986)
Essays/Articles by Gidal:
"Technology and Ideology in Avant-garde
Film: an Instance" *The Cinematic Apparatus*
(eds. Stephen Heath, Teresa de Lauretis)
(Macmillan 1986)
"Theory and Definition of
Structural/Materialist Film" *Studio
International* November 1975
"The Anti-narrative" *Screen* Summer 1979
"On Malcolm Le Grice's Feature" *Undercut 5*
1985
"Against Sexual Representation in Film" *Screen*
November 1984

Clive Gillman
Nik Houghton "Monster Crash and the
Culture War" *Independent Media* March 1988
Nik Hougton "Solid State Remains: Clive
Gillman" *Independent Media* November 1987
Nik Houghton "Metronine and the Media
Mix Up" *Independent Media* May 1987
Clive Gillman "Stepping Down From the
Screen: Interactivity and the Art Game
Algorithm" *Undercut 19* Autumn 1990

Peter Greenaway
Books by Greenaway:
A Zed and Two Noughts (Faber 1986)
Drowning By Numbers (Faber 1988)
The Belly of an Architect (Faber 1988)
The Cook, The Thief, His Wife and Her Lover
(Editions Dis Voir 1989)
Papers: Peter Greenaway (Editions Dis Voir
1990)
*Prospero's Books: A Film of Shakespeare's The
Tempest* (Chatto and Windus 1991)
The Physical Self (Museum Buymans-Van
Beumingen, Rotterdam 1992)
The Falls (Editions Dis Voir 1993)
The Baby of Macon (Editions Dis Voir 1994)
Books on Greenaway:
Laura Denham *The Films of Peter Greenaway*
(Minerva Press 1993)

Jonathan Hacker and David Price *Take Ten:
Contemporary British Film Directors* (Clarendon
Press 1991)
Liz Reddish (ed) *The Early Films of Peter
Greenaway* (BFI 1992)
Articles:
Film Quarterly 45/2 Winter 1991/2
Film Comment 26/3 March 1990
Film Comment 18/1 January/February 1982
Sight and Sound Summer 1987
Sight and Sound May 1991

David Hall
David Hall "The Video Show" *Art and Artists*,
May 1975
David Hall "Structures, Paraphenalia and
Television: Some Notes" *Signs of the Times*
(catalogue) Museum of Modern Art, Oxford,
1990
David Hall "British Video: Towards an
Autonomous Practice" *Studio International*
November 1975
David Hall "Video Art Education: 20 Years
On" *The Luminous Image* (catalogue) Stediljk
Museum, Amsterdam 1984
Mick Hartney "The Early Chronology of
Video Art: 1959–1976" *London Video Arts
catalogue* 1984
Michael O'Pray "David Hall" *Variant 11* 1992
Michael O'Pray "TV Fighter (Cam Era Plane)"
(review) *Monthly Film Bulletin* February 1988
Sean Cubitt *Videography: Video Media as Art
and Culture* (Macmillan 1993)

Nicky Hamlyn
Michael O'Pray "Guesswork" (review) *Monthly
Film Bulletin* October 1983
Michael O'Pray "Ghost Stories" (review)
Monthly Film Bulletin October 1984
Nicky Hamlyn "Dora – A Suitable Case for
Treatment" *Undercut 3/4* Winter/Spring
1981/82
Nicky Hamlyn "Photo-Piece" *Undercut 12*
Summer 1984
Nicky Hamlyn "Frameless Film" *Undercut 13*
Winter 1984/85

Mona Hatoum
Desa Philippi "Mona Hatoum: The Witness
Beside Herself" *Parachute* (Montreal) April
1990
Renee Beart "Desiring Daughters" *Screen 34/2*,
Summer 1993
Laura U Marks "Sexual Hybrids: From
Oriental Exotic to Postcolonial Grotesque"
Parachute (Montreal) April/May/June 1993

Guy Brett "Mona Hatoum at the Showroom"
Art in America November 1989
Caryn Faure Walker "Mona Hatoum" *Art
Monthly 164* March 1993

Steve Hawley
Nik Houghton "From Wittgenstein to Jack:
Steve Hawley, International Video and
Monomedia Star" *Independent Media*
December 1987

Susan Hiller
Books:
Susan Hiller *Dreams: Visions of the Night*
(Thames and Hudson 1989)
Susan Hiller *The Myth of Primitivism*
(Routledge 1992)
David Coxhead *Thinking About Art:
Conversation with Susan Hiller* (Manchester
University Press 1995)
Catalogues:
Jean Fisher *Susan Hiller* (Matt's Gallery
London 1990)
Lucy Lippard "Out of Bounds" *Susan Hiller*
(ICA London 1986)
Susan Hiller: The Revenants of Time (Matts
Gallery London; Mappin Art Gallery,
Sheffield; Third Eye Centre Glasgow 1990)
Articles:
Barbara Einzig "Within and Against: Susan
Hiller's Nonobjective Reality" *Arts* October 1991
Marina Warner "Penis Plenty or Phallic Lack:
Exit Mr. Punch" *Parkett 33* September 1992
Guy Brett "Wicked, Wicked, Wicked: Susan
Hiller's An Entertainment" *Performance 64*
Summer 1991
Guy Brett "Susan Hiller's Shadowland" *Art in
America* April 1991

Housewatch
Ian Bourn "Housewatch" *Performance 37*
October/November 1985
Naseem Khan "Work in Progress: Window
Pain" *New Statesman* September 1986
Brian Hatton "Housewatch at Spitalfields"
Artscribe November/December 1986

Derek Jarman
Books by Jarman:
Dancing Ledge (Quartet Books 1984)
Last of England (Constable 1987)
Queer Edward II (BFI 1991)
Modern Nature (Century 1991)
At Your Own Risk: A Saint's Testament (Century
1992)

Blue (Channel Four/BBC Radio Three 1993)
Chroma: A Meditation on the Nature of Colour (Random House 1994)
A Finger in the Fishes Mouth (1972)
Caravaggio (Thames and Hudson 1986)
AfterImage 12 October 1985, Special Issue including:
Simon Field and Michael O'Pray "Imagining October, Dr Dee and Other Matters"
Mark Nash "Innocence and Experience"
Michael O'Pray "Derek Jarman's Cinema; Eros and Thanatos"

Isaac Julien
"The Passion of Remembrance" (interview) *Cineaste 16/4* 1988
Isaac Julien and Colin MacCabe *Diary of a Young Soul Rebel* with the screenplay by Paul Hallam and Derek Saldaan McClintock (BFI 1991)
Isaac Julien and Kobena Mercer (eds) "The Last Special Issue on Race?" *Screen* 1988
Isaac Julien and Jon Savage (eds) *Critically Queer* (Critical Quarterly May 1994
Isaac Julien and Kobena Mercer (eds) *Male Order* (Lawrence & Wishart 1989)
Black and White in Colour (conference monograph) (BFI 1993)

Tina Keane
Rosika Parker and Griselda Pollock *Framing Feminism* (1987)
Peter Wollen *Undercut 2* 1981
Tamara Krikorian *Art Monthly* February 1983
Jean Fisher *Art Forum* May 1983
Michael O'Pray *Art Monthly* November 1984

Jeff Keen
Tony Rayns "Born to Kill: Mr Soft Eliminator" *AfterImage* Summer 1976
Jeff Keen "Gazapo Kalypse" *Undercut 13* Winter 1984/85

Patrick Keiller
Patrick Keiller "Atmosphere, Palimpsest and other interpretation of Landscape" *Undercut 7/8* 1983
Patrick Keiller "The Poetic Experience of Landscape and Townscape, and Some Ways of Depicting it" *Undercut 3/4* 1982
Nina Danino "On Patrick Keiller's 'Stonebridge Park'" *Undercut 2* 1981
William Raban "'London' – The Background" *Vertigo 4* 1995
John Mepham, Mark Fisher, Bambi Ballard, Mike Phillips and Adam Kossof "Five Views" *Vertigo 4* 1995

Andrew Kötting
Moira Sweeney "Signs of the Times" *Between Imagination and Reality* (ICA Biennial catalogue London 1990)

Richard Kwietniowski
Richard Dyer "Alfalfa" (review) *Monthly Film Bulletin* January 1988

Sandra Lahire
Pam Cook "Serpent River" (review) *Monthly Film Bulletin* August 1990

David Larcher
Steve Dwoskin "Mares Tail" *Undercut 2* 1970
Raymond Bellour "La Double Hélice" *Passages de l'Image* (catalogue) (Centre Georges Pompidou 1990)
David Larcher *David Larcher* (Centre Internationale de Creation Video France 1992)

William Latham
Stephen Todd and William Latham *Evolutionary Arts and Computers* (Academic Press 1992)
The Empire of Form: Computer Graphics by William Latham (exhibition catalogue) (O Art Museum Tokyo November 1991)
The Conquest of Form: Computer Art by William Latham (exhibition catalogue) (Arnolfini Gallery Bristol December 1988)
Colin Sanderson "William Latham on the Computer" *Modern Painters 1/4* 1988
Sean Cubitt Videography: *Video Media as Art and Culture* (Macmillan 1993)

Malcolm Le Grice
Malcolm Le Grice *Abstract Film and Beyond* (Studio Vista 1977; MIT (2nd edition) 1981)
Malcolm Le Grice "Thoughts on Recent Underground Film" *AfterImage 4* 1972
Malcolm Le Grice "Towards Temporal Economy" *Screen 20/3 & 4* 1986
Malcolm LeGrice and P Adams Sitney "Narrative Illusion Versus Structural Realism" *Millenium Film Journal 16/17/18* Fall/Winter 1986/7
Malcolm Le Grice "Problematising the Spectator Placement in Film" *Undercut 1* 1981

David Leister/Kino Club
David McGillvray "On and Off the Wall" *What's On* December 19 1990
Jonathan Romney "Split Screen Performance" *New Statesman and Society* April 1993

Tim MacMillan
The Photographic Journal October 1993

John Maybury
Patricia Dobson (profile) *Screen International, London Film Festival Supplement* November 12 1993
Mark C O'Flaherty "No More Taboos" *The Pink Paper* December 10 1993

Michael Maziere
Anne Barclay Morgan "Interview with Michael Maziere" *Art Papers (USA) Art and Public Education 17/6* November/December 1993
Nicky Hamlyn "From Structuralism to Imagism: Peter Gidal and His Influence in the 1980s" *Undercut 19* 1990
Michael Maziere "Mother Desire" (photopiece) *Undercut 19* 1990

Juliet McKoen
Michael O'Pray "Blood Sisters" *Arrows of Desire:* (ICA Biennial catalogue London 1992)

Chris Meigh-Andrews
"Eau d'Artifice" (1990) *Artscribe International* April/May 1991
Catherine Elwes "On 'Eau d'Artifice'" (review) *Performance* Spring 1992
Sean Cubitt *Videography: Video Media as Art and Culture* (Macmillan 1993)
Chris Meigh-Andrews "Video Sculpture and Installation" *Visions & Transmissions catalogue* (Harris Museum Preston)

Katharine Meynell
Katharine Meynell *A Book for a Performance* (Bookworks 1986)
Abina Manning "Snakes and Giros" *Independent Media* April 1989
Keith Ball, Almuth Hargreaves, Peter Kennard, Katharine Meynell, Helen Underwood, Stephen Williams (catalogue) (International Artists Centre Poznan Poland 1993)
Abstract, Still life, Portrait (catalogue) (Kettles Yard Cambridge, 1992)

Laura Mulvey and **Peter Wollen**
Books by Mulvey/Wollen:
Laura Mulvey Visual and Other Pleasures (Macmillan 1989)
Douglas Sirk Laura Mulvey and Jon Halliday (eds) (Edinburgh Film Festival 1972)
Laura Mulvey *Citizen Kane* (BFI 1992)
Laura Mulvey *Peeping Tom* (spoken commentary on laser disc edition, Voyager Company New York 1994)

Laura Mulvey *Fetishism and Curiosity*
(BFI 1995)
Peter Wollen *Signs and Meanings in the Cinema*
(Secker and Warburg 1969)
Peter Wollen *Readings and Writings: Semiotic
Counter-Strategies* (Verso 1982)
Peter Wollen *Raiding the Icebox: Reflections on
Twentieth Century Culture* (Verso 1993)
Peter Wollen *Singin' In The Rain* (BFI 1993)
Claire Johnstone and Paul Willemen
"Penthesilea: Queen of the Amazons: Interview
with Peter Wollen and Laura Mulvey"
Screen 15/3 1974
Simon Field "Two Weeks on Another Planet"
(interview with Peter Wollen about
Friendship's Death) *Monthly Film Bulletin*
November 1987
F Oppe and D Ranvaud "Crystal Gazing"
(interview with Mulvey and Wollen) *Framework
19* 1982
Scott MacDonald "Riddles of the Sphinx:
Laura Mulvey and Peter Wollen" *Avant-garde
Film: Motion Studies* (Cambridge University
Press 1993)
Kaja Silverman *The Acoustic Mirror (Riddles of
the Sphinx)* (Indiana University Press 1988)
E Ann Kaplan *Women and Film (Riddles of the
Sphinx and AMY!)* (Methuen 1983)
Lucy Fisher "The Bad Sister" *Shot Counter
Shot* (Princeton University Press 1989)

Julie Myers
Clive Caldwell "My, how you've changed" *The
Times* April 16 1992
"A Portrait of the Artist: Julie Myers" *Amiga
Format* April 1992

Vera Neubauer
Annette Kuhn and Susannah Radstone "Vera
Neubauer" *The Women's Companion to
International Film*
Claire Barwell "Interview with Vera Neubauer"
Undercut 6 1982/83
C Taylor "The World of Children by Vera
Neubauer" *Undercut 13* 1984/85
Leslie Felperin Sharman *Women in Animation;
A Compendium* (ed. Jayne Pilling BFI 1992)

Jayne Parker
A L Rees "Almost Out" (review) *Monthly Film
Bulletin 649* Feb 1988
Catherine Lacey *The Elusive Sign: British Film
and Video 1977-1987* (catalogue)
(Arts Council/British Council 1988)

Kayla Parker
Women in Animation; A Compendium
(ed. Jayne Pilling BFI 1992)
Michael O'Pray "Unknown Woman"
(catalogue entry) *Arrows of Desire* (ICA
Biennial catalogue London 1992)

Pratibha Parmar
Pratibha Parmar, Martha Gever, John Greyson
(eds) *Queer Looks: An Anthology of Writings
about Lesbian and Gay Media* (Routledge 1993)
"Other Kinds of Dreams: An interview with
June Jordan" *Feminist Review* 1988
Pratibha Parmar "Many Voices, One Chant:
Black Feminist Perspectives"
Feminist Review 1982
Pratibha Parmar and Alice Walker
*Warrior Marks: Female Genital Mutilation and
the Sexual Blinding of Women*
(Jonathan Cape 1993)

Stephen Partridge
Hugh Stoddart *Stephen Partridge* (catalogue)
(Ikon Gallery Birmingham 1981)

Pictorial Heroes
Colin McArthur "On the Trail of Two Scottish
Road Movies: Bypassing Hollywood on the
Clyde" *Scottish Film and Visual Arts* Summer
1993

Keith Piper
Keith Piper "Separate Spaces: A Personal
Perspective on Black Art and the New
Technologies" *Variant 14* Summer 1993
"Keith Piper" (interview)
Art and Design 8/7 & 8 1993
Keith Piper "Forty Acres and a
Microprocessor" *Place, Position, Presentation,
Public* (Jan Van Eyck Akademie 1992)
"Step into the Arena – Black Art and
Questions of Gender" *Art & Design 31 World
Wide Video Issue* 1993

Steven Pippin
Stuart Morgan "The Waiting Game" *The
Rigmarole of Photography: Stephen Pippin*
(ICA 1993)
Craigie Horsefield "The Continuing Story of
An Amateur Photographer" *Frieze 20*
January/February 1995
Alison Sarah Jacques (interview) *Flash Art
26/171* Summer 1993
Anthony Gormley "On Steven Pippin's Video"
The Guardian August 15 1995

Sally Potter
Annette Kuhn *Women's Pictures: Feminism and
Cinema* (Verso 1993; Routledge and Kegan Paul
1982)
Sally Potter *Orlando* (Faber and Faber 1994)
Penny Florence "A Conversation with Sally
Potter" *Screen 34/3* Autumn 1993
Walter Donohue "Immortal Longing: on
'Orlando'" *Sight and Sound* March 1993
Pam Cook "The Gold Diggers: Interview with
Sally Potter" *Framework 24* Spring 1984
Gillian Swanson and Lucy Moy Thomas "An
Interview with Sally Potter" *Undercut 1* Spring
1981

Sarah Pucill
"You be Mother" *Variant* Autumn 1991

Quay Brothers
Jonathan Romney "The Same Dark Drift"
Sight and Sound 1/11 March 1992
Paul Hammond "In Quay Animation"
AfterImage 13 Autumn 1987
Tony Rayns "Street of Crocodiles" (review)
Monthly Film Bulletin June 1986
Peter Greenaway "Street of Crocodiles" *Sight
and Sound* Summer 1986
Philip Strick "Leoš Janáček: Intimate
Excursions" (review) *Monthly Film Bulletin*
June 1986

William Raban
Peter Gidal (ed) "William Raban" *Structural
Film Anthology* (BFI 1976)
Malcolm Le Grice "Abstract Film and Beyond"
(Studio Vista 1977; MIT (2nd edition) 1981)
Michael O'Pray "William and Marilyn Raban's
'Black and Silver'" *Undercut 5* 1982
Michael O'Pray "Landscape Films" (review)
Undercut 7/8 1983

Daniel Reeves
Marita Sturken "What is Grace in all this
Madness: The Videotapes of Dan Reeves"
AfterImage (USA) Summer 1985
Jizo Garden: Daniel Reeves (catalogue) (Scottish
Arts Council, June 1992)
Linda Dubler "Eingang (The Way In)" *Art at
the Edge.* (High Museum of Art Atlanta
Georgia 1990)
"Obsessive Becoming" *Scraping the Surface*
(catalogue) (Scottish Arts Council 1994)

Lis Rhodes

Sandra Lahire "A Cold Draft" *Undercut 19* Autumn 1990
Lis Rhodes "Whose History?" *Film as Film* (touring exhibition catalogue 1979)
Peter Gidal "Lis Rhodes' 'Light Reading'" *Materialist Film* (Routledge 1989)
Susan Stein "On 'Pictures on Pink Paper'" *Undercut 14/15* Summer 1985
Lis Rhodes "Light Reading: The Script" *Heresies 16* 1983

Simon Robertshaw

The Observatory (catalogue) (Moviola; Oriel 3 Powys; Wrexham Arts Centre Clwyd 1993)

Kathleen Rogers

Kathleen Rogers "The Labyrinth of Lace" *Women's Art* November 1991
Kathleen Rogers "Virtual Real Estate" *Variant* 1992
Kathleen Rogers *Sleepless Dreaming* 1993

Marty St James and Anne Wilson

Jeremy Welsh "A Holiday Romance" *Mediamatic* 1989
Video Portraits by Marty St James and Anne Wilson (catalogue) (National Portrait Gallery London, 1990)

George Saxon

George Saxon "Another Window – Cues and Clues" *Undercut 12* 1984
George Saxon "The House that Jack Built (This Victorian England)" *Undercut 16* 1986
Malcolm Le Grice "Wolves" (review) *Studio International 1* 1977

Guy Sherwin

Deke Dusinberre "See Real Images" *AfterImage 8/9* 1981
Deke Dusinberre "Short Film Series" (review) *Monthly Film Bulletin* October 1983
Peter Gidal "British Avant-garde Film" *Millenium Film Journal 13* 1984
Gillian Swanson "'Messages' A Film by Guy Sherwin" *Undercut 12* 1984
A L Rees "Messages" *Monthly Film Bulletin* October 1984

John Smith

"Leading Light (1975)" *A Perspective on English Avant-garde Film* (catalogue) (Arts Council/British Council 1978)
Michael Maziere "John Smith's Films: Reading the Visible" *Undercut 10/11* 1983/84

George Snow

Steven Bode "Dal Ponte dei Sospiri to Eco Beach" *Mediamatic 3/1* September 1988

Andrew Stones

Andrew Stones "Geiger and Common Knowledge" (catalogue) (Sheffield Arts Department 1989)

Moira Sweeney

Michael O'Pray "Hide and Seek" *Independent Media* January 1988
Nicky Hamlyn "Imaginary" *Art Monthly* February 1989
Moira Sweeney "Signs of the Times" *Between Imagination and Reality* (ICA Biennial catalogue London 1990)
Moira Sweeney "She Continues..." (photopiece) *Undercut 19* Autumn 1990

Margaret Tait

Robert Yates "Blue Black Permanent" (review) *Sight and Sound* April 1993
Jan Moir "First Person Highly Singular" *The Guardian* March 31 1993
Tamara Krikorian "Townscape and Landscape in Margaret Tait" *Undercut 7/8* Spring 1983

Anna Thew

"Hilda was a Goodlooker" (review) *Monthly Film Bulletin 53* November 1986
Paul Wallace "Media Production in Higher Education" *Undercut 16* 1986

Marion Urch

"London Video" *Artweek USA 14/3* 1983
"Third Generation" *Performance* November 1986
Marion Urch *History Angel* (Hodder Headline 1996)
Short Circuits (anthology of new writers) (Virago 1996)

Chris Welsby

"Chris Welsby: Films, Photographs, Writings" (introduction by Peter Wollen) (Arts Council 1980)

Jeremy Welsh

Catherine Elwes "Profile" (interview) *Independent Media* May/June 1989
Jeremy Welsh "Power, Access and Ingenuity: Electronic Imaging Technologies and Contemporary Art" *Culture, Technology and Creativity* (ed. Philip Hayward) (AC/John Libbey 1990)
Jeremy Welsh "Resigning Not Resigned" *Undercut 19* Autumn 1990

Stewart Wilson

Bob Last "Burner" (review) *Variant* January 1994

Joanna Woodward

Nik Houghton "Tales from the Riverside" *Artists' Newsletter* April 1990
Nik Houghton "Knick-Knacks and Nightmares" *Independent Media* January 1990
Beyond Walt Disney: An Exhibition from Animation Film by Joanna Woodward (catalogue) (Leicester City Council 1990)
Jonathan Romney "The Brooch Pin and the Sinful Clasp" (review) *Sight and Sound* 1990

Richard Wright

Richard Wright "The Image in Art and Computer Art" *Computer Art in Context SIGGRAPH '89* Boston USA
Richard Wright "Soft Future" (catalogue) *Video Positive* Liverpool 1993